The Making of Mod

D0106264

Volume 1 The Nineteenth Century

A.E. Afigbo B.A., Ph.D.
Professor of History, University of Nigeria at Nsukka

E.A. Ayandele B.A., Ph.D.
Formerly Professor of History, University of Ibadan

R.J. Gavin M.A., Ph.D.
Professor of History, University of Ulster

J.D. Omer-Cooper M.A.
Professor of History, University of Otago, Dunedin

This edition revised in collaboration with
Robin Palmer B.A., Ph.D.
Professor of History, University of Malawi

George Newton

Longman

Longman Group UK Limited,
Longman House, Burnt Mill, Harlow,
Essex CM20 2JE, England
and Associated Companies throughout the world

First published 1968
New Edition 1986
Second impression 1986

Set in 10/12 pt Plantin (monophoto)

Produced by Longman Group (FE) Ltd
Printed in Hong Kong

ISBN 0-582-58508-2

Contents

Part two
Northern Africa E.A. Ayandele

7 The Maghreb and European intervention 176

Part three
Southern and Central Africa J.D. Omer-Cooper

8 Southern and Central Africa at the beginning of the nineteenth century 211

11 The consolidation of white rule in Southern Africa   281

Part four
Middle Africa R.J. Gavin

12 States and societies in Middle Africa in the nineteenth century   306

13 Crisis, revolution and colonial conquest in Middle Africa, 1840–1900   317

Conclusion R.J. Gavin

14 The European conquest of Africa   340

Index   364

List of maps

Acknowledgements

The publishers are grateful to the following for permission to reproduce photographs:

BBC Hulton Picture Library for pages 52, 66 and 296; British Museum, London for page 322; Historical Picture Service, Chicago for pages 286 and 289; Illustrated London News for page 270; Mansell Collection for pages 159, 173, 302 and 335; National Archives of Zimbabwe for page 246; Popperfoto for page 135; Public Record Office for pages 122, 123, 124, 303 and 304; Robert Harding Picture Library for page 212; Royal Commonwealth Society for pages 47 and 50; the Slide Centre for page 247; Werner Forman Archive for pages 9, 18, 20, 22 and 27.

The publishers regret that they have been unable to trace the copyright owners of artwork and photographs not credited in the above acknowledgements and would welcome any information enabling them to do so at the first opportunity.

The cover illustration shows the defeat of the Italians at the Battle of Adowa in 1896 and was provided by the Mary Evans Picture Library.

Introduction

The geography of Africa

In size the African continent with its 30 233 100 square kilometres may be compared with Asia (27 593 900 square kilometres), and the USSR (22 401 000 square kilometres). This vast land mass straddles the equator, facing the Mediterranean Sea in the north and the Antarctic in the south. Its wide variety of climates and natural conditions has greatly influenced the development of its inhabitants.

One characteristic of Africa is the striking regularity of its coastline, which has relatively few bays and inlets or peninsulas reaching out to sea. This has meant that the African peoples have not had the same opportunities and incentives for the development of navigation on the sea, whether for long- or short-range trade, as have the peoples of Europe and Asia. Thus, except for the countries bordering the Mediterranean, they have not until comparatively recent times been brought into close and frequent contact with other continents. Until the nineteenth century African development was relatively self-contained, though this does not mean that there were no contacts with other nations, nor that such contacts were unimportant.

The northern part of the continent lies along the Mediterranean Sea and enjoys a climate similar to, though warmer and drier than, that of southern Europe. This Mediterranean area is a narrow coastal strip varying in width according to geographical circumstances. It is widest in the north-west corner of the continent, known as the Maghreb (the Arabic word for west), where the modern states of Morocco, Algeria and Tunisia are situated. There the Atlas mountains cause winds from the Mediterranean and the Atlantic to deposit their moisture and the soil has been noted for its fertility from ancient times.

Behind this narrow strip of fertile country with its Mediterranean climate lies the vast desert of the Sahara, greater in extent than the whole of Europe and by far the largest desert in the world. This huge area – which is now almost entirely uninhabited outside the occasional oases which provide welcome islands of green in the almost endless wastes of barren rock and burning sands – was once very different. In remote prehistoric times it enjoyed a reasonable rainfall and supported a considerable population. Gradually, for reasons which are still not well understood, it dried up and its peoples congregated around the oases or moved further afield. By the times of the ancient Greeks and Romans it was in

Africa at the beginning of the nineteenth century

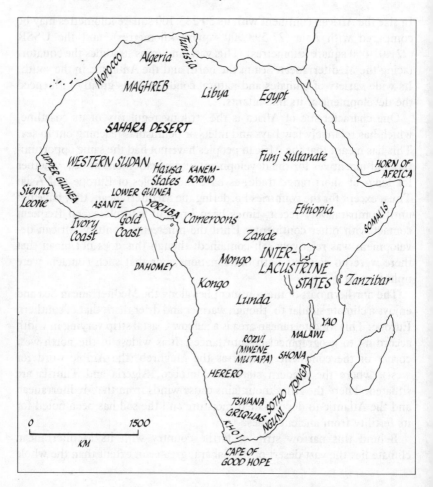

much the same condition as today. But though the Sahara is such a vast and formidable desert it must not be thought that it separated the northern part of the continent from all contact with the centre and south.

On the eastern side of the continent the river Nile, starting from two sources, one in the highlands of Ethiopia (the Blue Nile) and the other in the Lake region of East Africa (the White Nile) threads it way across the desert to reach the sea through the many mouths of its delta in Egypt. Every year the rains in Ethiopia and East Africa cause the river to overflow its banks, and as the water subsides it leaves behind a layer of fertile mud which it has brought from the Ethiopian highlands. Along the banks of the Nile there is a narrow cultivable strip containing some of the richest agricultural land in the world. Though it is often no more than a few kilometres wide it can support a dense population and it gave rise to one of the world's most ancient and elaborate civilizations. Navigation is possible along great stretches of the river, and the winding thread of water and the vivid strip of green beside it form one of the strongest links binding the history of the peoples north and south of the Sahara.

In the central and western parts of the Sahara the mountains of Tibesti, Aïr and the Hoggar capture sufficient rain to make agriculture possible. In other places underground water provides wells and springs to nourish oases. These provide natural staging posts on the caravan routes which from ancient times have criss-crossed the desert, bringing the peoples of West Africa and the Maghreb into contact with each other.

To the south of the Sahara in the west, desert conditions gradually give way to increasing vegetation nourished by the rains brought by warm equatorial winds from the Atlantic. A great belt of savanna which is called the Sudanic belt stretches across the continent. South of the Sudanic belt, along the coast of much of West Africa, stretching inland to varying distances, lies the great West African rain forest which, with a few gaps, meets the dense forests of Zaire (formerly the Belgian Congo) to form one of the largest tropical forests in the world.

Thus the pattern of West African geography consists of a fairly regular succession of belts of vegetation, from the Sahara desert, across the grasslands of the savanna belt to the lush forests of the coastal strip. But this pattern is broken by major rivers which have had a significant influence on history, such as the complex Niger-Benue river system which might be described as the Nile of West Africa. Rising in the mountains of the Futa Jallon range in modern Guinea, the river Niger makes a great northward loop almost into the Sahara before turning south into modern Nigeria where it links up with the Benue, another mighty river which rises in the mountains of Cameroon. The combined waters finally find their way to the sea through the maze of creeks and rivers of the Niger delta. In its northward path the Niger runs for part of its course over level ground where it overflows its banks every year when the rains in the Futa Jallon bring down the flood waters to form what is often called the inland delta of the Niger. A relatively dense population can be supported there and it is not surprising that the valley of the Niger should have been the centre of some of West Africa's most ancient and powerful kingdoms. Further east, Lake Chad, lying on the fringes of the Sahara and fed by rivers rising in the Cameroon mountains, also modifies the climate and provides agricultural opportunities.

On the eastern side of the continent the highlands of Ethiopia, lying within the triangular projection known as the Horn of Africa, constitute a special environment of their own. They consist largely of volcanic material which breaks down to give a rich soil of almost unlimited depth. It is this soil which washes down the Nile to provide the fertility of Egypt. Abundant rains fall every year and the climate of the cool uplands has been described as the closest to paradise on earth. No wonder the ancient Greeks regarded Ethiopia as the favourite earthly residence of the gods. Between this fertile highland area – a natural centre of civilization – and the sea, is the plain of Somalia largely dry and torrid and therefore for the most part suitable only for nomadic herdsmen and incapable of sustaining a large settled population.

Further south again, the African continent consists of a vast plateau rising to its highest point in the Ruwenzori mountains, sometimes described as the spine of Africa. To the west of the Ruwenzori lies the great basin of the Zaire and Kasai rivers system, much of it covered by forest which towards the south gives way to savanna and the Benguella and Shaba (formerly Katanga) plateaux where the Zambezi river has its source. East of the Ruwenzori is the region of the Great Lakes: Victoria, Tanganyika, Malawi and many others that are smaller but still large and important. In spite of the presence of the Great Lakes much of this East and Central African plateau is hot and rather dry, covered with a poor tree scrub. There are important exceptions, however. The cool and fertile Kenyan highlands provide excellent farming country. The area between Lakes Victoria, Kyoga and Kivu, the so-called inter-lacustrine region which forms the heart of modern Uganda, benefits from abundant rains which make it a green and fertile land. Here was another natural centre for the development of African civilizations. The slopes of Mount Kilimanjaro and the Shire highlands of modern Malawi are other examples.

The southernmost part of the continent constitutes a prolongation of the great African plateau, surrounded by a coastal strip of varying width, the result of age-old erosion of the plateau edge. Like most of the African plateau this is generally rather dry, open savanna country with grass or bush or thorn scrub. Its climate is strongly affected by its southerly latitude and the winter months of June and July can be bitterly cold. On the other hand the southern part of the continent is free from malaria and the tsetse fly which are plagues north of the equator. It is ideal country for cattle-keepers and mixed farmers but cannot support a dense agricultural population.

The peoples of Africa north of the Sahara

The peoples of this vast continent and the story of their development are as varied as the geography. The northern part of the continent, facing the Mediterranean Sea, and including the lower reaches and delta of the Nile, was the home of the ancient Egyptians and the Berbers in the Maghreb. They were basically similar in appearance and physique to the people of southern Europe and the structure of their languages suggests a link with Mesopotamia and Arabia also. Men of a similar stock probably formed the basic population of the Ethiopian highlands, though there and in the upper Nile valley they intermarried with blacks and hence came to be known by the name of 'Ethiopians', which means 'burnt face'.

In the Nile valley, where the conditions for human settlement were particularly favourable, a dense population grew up in very ancient times and one of the most important civilizations of the ancient world developed. It was a civilization strongly influenced by the natural conditions of the Nile valley and the dependence of man on the river and its floods. For the large population to support itself it was essential to make the best use of every drop of the flood waters and of the rich mud which they spread over the land. This could only be done successfully if irrigation and land-use up and down the valley were carefully controlled. Thus, from about 3000 BC, a very powerful state system grew up which exercised close control over the use of water and land and the crops derived from them. As these were the matters of fundamental importance to the Egyptian peasants the state virtually controlled all the most important aspects of their lives. One of the world's earliest known systems of writing, the hieroglyphic script, was developed, and an elaborate civil service of scribes grew to perform the complex tasks of administration. The king, or pharaoh, was, at least in theory, all-powerful and the owner of all the land in Egypt. It was believed that he was divine and that he and his ancestors in the spirit world influenced the fertility of the land. He was thus a central figure in an elaborate religious system with a complicated order of gods served by powerful priests. Though the standard of living of the ordinary peasant was always low, the king, the civil servants and the priests were able to live in great luxury and splendour. The mighty pyramids which have fascinated all subsequent generations were built as tombs for some of the kings, while others were buried in vast chambers cut out of the rock of mountain sides and decorated with paintings of rich and almost unbelievable beauty. Palaces too were built and splendid temples of great size. Arts and crafts of many different kinds were developed to a high pitch of perfection.

The Egyptian kingdom was not self-contained but traded widely with the outside world, using the enormous surpluses of wheat grown on the rich valley soil to profit from high prices resulting from famine in various parts of the Mediterranean world. Relations with the neighbouring and in some ways similar civilization of Mesopotamia were always close, though often hostile. Syria and Palestine suffered much in biblical times from the competition of the two world powers of the day. For long Egypt exercised imperial authority over Syria but gradually its power declined and it was itself conquered, first by the Assyrians (663 BC) and then for a longer term by the Persians (525–332 BC). Thereafter Egypt was conquered by the Greeks (332 BC) and later by the Romans (30 BC). It formed one of the richest provinces of the Roman Empire and was converted, like most of the Empire, to Christianity. It was there that the idea of religious men withdrawing from the world to found monasteries for prayer and meditation was first developed and subsequently spread to Europe.

In AD 640 Egypt was conquered by the Arabs, who brought with them Islam, a religion and a way of life which has formed the basic framework of the life of the majority of Egyptians ever since. Egypt after the Arab conquest knew a variety of different rulers, including a long period from AD 1259–1517 under dynasties of foreign soldiers who were originally recruited as slaves (*mamluks*) and were consequently known as the Mamluks. In the sixteenth century the Mamluks were conquered by the Ottoman Turks and Egypt became part of the Ottoman empire. But under the Turkish administration the Mamluks were allowed to rise again and by the end of the eighteenth century they were virtually independent of the Turkish sultan who was their nominal ruler.

In spite of all these changes, certain factors have remained constant in Egyptian life from the time of the pharaohs to the present day: the absolute dependence on the Nile and the irrigation system, and rising from this, the high degree of dependence of the people on the administrative system; the powerful position of rulers and civil servants; and the large role played by the state in all development. These are not so much the results of particular ideologies and beliefs as of the inescapable facts of Egyptian life.

A Mamluk

Though Egypt traded widely with Mediterranean lands and competed with the Mesopotamian civilizations for control of the Middle East, it was no less interested in its African neighbours higher up the Nile in the northern parts of the modern Sudan. This part of Africa was inhabited from very early times by black peoples and Egypt was always a multi-racial state, or rather a state in which peoples of different race lived together without attaching much importance to racial differences. There are, it is true, pictures of pharaohs conquering the black peoples of the upper Nile and capturing them as slaves, but statues of important officers show that blacks could rise to high positions in the state. As a result of Egyptian influence in the upper Nile valley, a civilization grew up there based largely on the Egyptian pattern though modified by local traditions. Its rulers became very powerful and about 730 BC the great Nubian warrior Piankhy conquered Egypt and established a new dynasty generally known as the Ethiopian dynasty, on the throne of the pharaohs. After being defeated by an Assyrian attack, in 663 BC, however, the Nubians severed their connection with Egypt and established an independent state on the upper Nile known as the kingdom of Kush. The first capital of the kingdom was at Napata. Later it was moved further up the Nile from Napata to Meroe and there the kings and queens of Kush continued to keep alive a form of the Egyptian civilization – even building small-scale pyramids – long after the old religion and way of life had died out in Egypt itself. Gradually the state was weakened, probably by the decline of agriculture caused by soil exhaustion, and by trade competition from the rising kingdom of Axum in Ethiopia. About AD 350 King Ezana of Axum stormed the capital and the kingdom came to an end.

This did not mean the end of civilization and independent development for the upper Nile valley. Missionaries from Egypt, then under the Eastern Roman, or Byzantine empire, introduced Christianity into Nubia and a number of Christian kingdoms grew up where beautifully decorated churches and monasteries were built. These kingdoms too fell into decline and Muslim merchants and missionaries from Egypt converted many of the people to Islam. Then in the sixteenth century a brilliant leader, Amara Dunkas, in alliance with the Abdullab, the most important of the Arab sheikhs who had penetrated the upper Nile valley, conquered the whole area of the previously Christian kingdoms and united them in a Muslim sultanate known as the Funj kingdom with its capital at Sennar on the Blue Nile. This kingdom survived until the nineteenth century, though it was by then in the last stages of decline.

The history of Ethiopia is closely linked with that of the upper Nile valley on one side and of South Arabia, across the narrow straits of the Bab-el-Mandeb, on the other. Movements of population have probably taken place in both directions. Certainly, when powerful kingdoms grew up on the mountain plateau of modern Yemen it was only natural that they should take an interest in the fertile highlands, so similar to their own country, across the narrow seas. A series of South Arabian city-state colonies grew up in Ethiopia, taking with them the pagan religion of ancient Sabaea and the ancient South Arabian language and script. Eventually these separate cities were brought under the control of Axum, which laid the foundations of the Ethiopian empire. In Axum a form of the South Arabian language was used, modified by local influences, to form a national language known as Geez. The holy books of Ethiopia are written in this language which is also used in Church services. Amharic, the modern official language, is related to it in the sense that both probably have a common root, rather than – as was once believed – Amharic having developed out of Geez.

As Axum extended its authority over the city-states of Ethiopia it became rich and powerful. Mighty temples were erected to the gods and colossal monuments were erected in their honour. Axum also became a naval power with a strong interest in the Red Sea trade, and at times it extended its authority over parts of South Arabia whence much of its culture originally came. These developments brought Ethiopia into con-

Royal burial monument at Axum (c. AD 400)

tact with the outside world and made it one of the recognized world powers. Greek traders from the eastern parts of the Roman empire thronged its court and Greek became a second official language in which some of the royal inscriptions were written.

Through these contacts Ethiopia was brought in touch with the religious changes taking place in the world. Many were converted to Judaism, which was spreading actively in South Arabia, and a Judaic community sprang up which still survives. In the reign of the same King Ezana who destroyed the kingdom of Kush about AD 350, the kingdom as a whole was converted to Christianity, which remained the state religion until the overthrow of Haile Selassie in 1974. With the rise of Islam and the Arab conquest of Egypt the kingdom was isolated from the rest of the Christian world. It also suffered from internal upheavals; the old dynasty which claimed descent from Solomon and the Queen of Sheba went into eclipse for a time and the kingdom lost control of trade routes to ports on the vital coastlands occupied by the nomadic Somalis who adopted Islam as their religion. After this dark period the empire revived. The Solomonic dynasty was restored and by the beginning of the sixteenth century it was once more a powerful state engaged in attempting to reassert its control over the Muslim states along the coast. Just when it seemed at the high tide of prosperity, however, a brilliant Somali leader, Mohammed Gran, relying on the religious fervour of his supporters and a troop of Turkish musketeers, turned the tide and came near to conquering the whole of Ethiopia. In despair the Ethiopian king turned to the Portuguese, who had already established contact with the kingdom, for help against his Muslim enemies. With their aid Mohammed Gran was killed and the Somalis defeated, but disagreements on religious matters between the Roman Catholics and the national Church of Ethiopia led to a number of upheavals and much bitterness. Ultimately the Catholics were expelled and the traditional Church re-established, but the monarchy had been weakened and it was faced with a new threat in the form of the slow but steady infiltration of the nomadic and warlike Oromo (Galla) from the south-east. Princes and local chiefs struggled over succession to the throne and the empire almost ceased to exist as an effective state. But the long tradition of past history and the strength of the national Church kept the feeling of unity alive and made it possible for a series of powerful rulers in the nineteenth century to revive the kingdom, expand its empire and make it a state to be reckoned with in world affairs.

The Maghreb has from very ancient times been the home of many different Berber peoples. Their way of life depended largely on geographical circumstances. Some who lived on the rich lands near the coast or in well-watered parts of the mountains were settled agriculturalists; others on the desert fringes or in the Sahara itself lived the life of nomadic pastoralists. The basic pattern was only slightly modified when traders from Phoenicia on the Syrian coast established the city of Carthage in about 750 BC. An empire was gradually built up along the coastal strip and more intensive methods of agriculture were introduced. Carthage had imperial interests in southern Spain and in Sicily, where it engaged in a long struggle with the Greek city-states. This ultimately brought it into conflict with the rising power of Rome, and after the failure of Hannibal's heroic but futile invasion of Italy (218–203 BC) the power of Carthage was destroyed, most of the Maghreb being taken into the Roman empire. A long period of peace and prosperity followed. Agriculture was greatly improved, irrigation works established and desert land brought into cultivation. The Berber peoples increasingly took to settled life and many new cities were founded. To this day the ruins of mighty theatres and other monuments standing in what is now virtually desert land testify to the prosperity of the Roman period. The wealth of the Maghreb cities was not due only to their agriculture, for even at that time caravans were crossing the Sahara to West Africa and bringing back precious cargoes of gold and ivory.

Under the Roman empire Christianity spread to the Maghreb, which produced one of the most revered of Christian scholars, St Augustine of Hippo. But by this time the Roman empire was already in the last stages of decay and excessive taxation and resulting over-farming were wreaking havoc on the Maghreb's agricultural system. As the Roman empire in the west collapsed the Maghreb was overrun in AD 429 by Germanic warriors known as the Vandals. Their kingdom in turn was destroyed in AD 534 by the forces of the Byzantine empire, which under Justinian was attempting to recapture the lost western provinces. The Byzantine empire, faced with mounting burdens of military expenditure, was oppressive and inefficient. It failed to keep the loyalty of the Berber peoples or to establish itself firmly in the country. In about AD 670 Uqba ibn Nafi began the long series of campaigns which culminated in the Arab conquest of the country. The decadent Byzantine administration offered little resistance but the Berbers held out desperately until AD 709. Thereafter they joined with their conquerors and participated in the Muslim conquests of Spain and Sicily.

The Arab conquest brought with it a major revolution through the introduction of Islam, which entirely replaced Christianity. Under the new religion the Maghreb went through a long series of political changes. Successive attempts were made to bring the whole area under unified political control together with Muslim Spain, and repeatedly they broke down, giving rise to kingdoms roughly corresponding to the present division into Morocco, Algeria and Tunisia. The city life of the Roman period continued to flourish and the Maghreb enjoyed a high level of cultural development in the early Muslim period.

The most important development between the Arab conquest and the nineteenth century, however, was the migration into the area of nomadic Beduin Arab peoples generally known as the Banu Hilal and the Banu Sulaym. Their invasion began in the second half of the eleventh century. They infiltrated on to the cultivated land like a swarm of locusts and gradually spread westward from Tunisia to Morocco. The rulers often ignored or even encouraged this invasion for they saw in the newcomers valuable irregular troops who would be pleased to fight under any banner in return for land on which to settle. As the nomads spread out, their demands and the over-grazing of their animals tended to drive the settled cultivators off the land. Much agricultural land reverted to desert conditions. Towns diminished or were abandoned altogether and power shifted nearer to the coast where trade with the outside world still provided a measure of prosperity. All over the fertile lands of the Maghreb agriculture decayed and the intensive techniques of the past gave way to mixed farming of a very poor type. At the same time the coming of the Beduin peoples brought considerable numbers of true Arabs into the Maghreb where previously they had been a tiny minority. Through intermarriage a high proportion of the Berbers were assimilated to the Arabs and the Arabic language became the normal everyday tongue for most of the population, except in mountainous areas such as the Atlas range in Morocco and the Kabylie mountains of Algeria, where the Berbers maintained their old language and culture together with a fierce spirit of independence.

As Muslim Spain receded before the progress of the Christian reconquest, the weakened Maghreb states suffered from repeated invasions from across the Straits of Gibraltar. In the fifteenth century Portuguese and Spanish strongholds were established on the coast though there was little attempt at outright conquest of the whole country. This Christian invasion in turn fired the spirit of national and religious resistance. As the states proved ineffective in fighting the infidels, religious organizations known as the sufi brotherhoods took over leadership of resistance. In Algeria and Tunisia the Turks were invited to come to the aid of their fellow Muslims and in the sixteenth century seized control of these countries, which became incorporated in the Ottoman empire.

In Morocco a new and vital dynasty, the Saadian, came to power and the Portuguese were drastically defeated at the Battle of the Three Kings in 1578. The Moroccan ruler died of natural causes at the beginning of the battle and his brother succeeded to the throne and the glory with the title of El Mansur ('the victorious'). He ruled from 1578 to 1603. He restored the power of the state in Morocco and then in 1591, hoping to increase his revenues in order to meet the expenses of his large army, he sent an expedition on a fantastic march across the Sahara to seize the empire of Songhai, whence caravans brought gold to Morocco. The expedition succeeded in destroying the greatest of the black kingdoms of West Africa but it could not establish an effective administration to succeed it. El Mansur was temporarily enriched by the gold looted from Songhai cities but in the long term the trade of his kingdom was damaged. After El Mansur's death, his sons fought for the crown and Morocco fell into chaos again until after 1660 when a new dynasty, the Alawite, established itself.

Under the energetic ruler Mawlay Ismail (1672–1727), who based his power on a large army of black slaves from the Niger area, the kingdom once more knew unity and strong government, but after his death it split up ·again and, although the dynasty survived, by the beginning of the nineteenth century it effectively controlled only a part of the country.

In the rest of the Maghreb, Turkish administration declined, as it did in the whole Ottoman empire. In Algeria the finances and prosperity of the state were heavily dependent on the profits of war at sea against the shipping of Christian powers. This not only led to a lack of attention to the administration and development of the hinterland, parts of which, like the Kabylie mountain area, were never brought under effective control, but also excited the hostile attention of European powers and the United States. By the nineteenth century all the Maghreb states were in a weak position for they had not been able to keep pace with the progress of western European countries. But where religion formed the basis of life, community of religion between the rulers and the people, even when the rulers were foreigners, assured them of a considerable measure of loyalty in the face of any infidel power.

The peoples of Africa south of the Sahara

The black peoples of Negro physical type who now occupy practically the whole of Africa south of the Sahara were once confined to a relatively small part of it. Their early place of origin and the course of their migrations have been much debated but no definite conclusions have been drawn. Nevertheless, it seems fairly certain that at one time they were settled along the Sudanic belt to the south of the Sahara and for a considerable way into the Sahara itself at a time when it was more suitable for human habitation. South of this the whole of the rest of the continent was occupied by other peoples who are now known mainly by discoveries of their stone implements, cave paintings, and occasional skeletons. Throughout most of East, Central and Southern Africa the early inhabitants probably belonged to a people related to the San (or Bushmen) who still survive in parts of Southern Africa. They lived by hunting and gathering wild fruits and tubers. In part of East Africa skeletons and other remains suggest at one time the people there may have been similar to those of North Africa and the lower Nile valley, and in Zaire and parts of the West African forestlands the earliest inhabitants may have been related to the pygmies who still live in the forests of Zaire.

In course of time the peoples of Negro physical type living in the eastern part of the Sudanic belt around the upper Nile valley tended to diverge culturally from the West African group. Their languages developed a very different pattern and their way of life became nomadic and pastoral, based on cattle. They probably also mixed to a considerable extent with the peoples of the Nile valley. The blacks of West Africa, where higher rainfall and the fertile lands of the inland delta of the Niger encouraged a sedentary way of life, became mainly agriculturalists, though there is a major exception in the case of the Fulani, who probably mixed extensively with Berber-speaking groups such as the nomadic Tuareg of the desert. The two main sections of the Negro peoples were never entirely separate; migrations took place in both directions and some of the peoples around Lake Chad, for example, are thought to have come from further east.

The agricultural Negroes of West Africa were naturally able to develop much larger and more dense populations than those who relied exclusively on cattle-keeping. It is probable that they domesticated crops of their own from wild plants, and they also began to grow crops domesticated elsewhere. Then at a period in the remote past which is still unknown, they began to expand very rapidly. This may have been the result of the introduction of techniques for producing and using iron which made it possible to clear the bush more easily, and perhaps also of the introduction of new crops from Asia. Not only did they colonize the great forest areas of West Africa itself but one branch of them spread out of West Africa altogether and gradually spread over almost the whole of the continent south of the Sahara, giving rise to the great family of Bantu-speaking peoples.

These peoples have developed many different ways of life and hundreds of different languages, but they are called by a single name because, although the speakers of one language cannot understand the others, a study of the languages shows that they are related to one another and must have developed from a common origin. Recent research has shown that these Bantu languages are related to the main language group of West Africa and probably developed out of one of its languages.

As the Bantu-speaking peoples advanced they gradually absorbed or expelled the previous inhabitants. In East Africa they came in contact with the cattle-keeping peoples known as the Nilotes and Southern Nilotes. The two groups, Bantu and Nilotes, have commonly been hostile to one another but they have also influenced each other. It may be that it was from contact with the Nilotes that some Bantu-speaking groups acquired the habit of cattle-keeping which they carried with them on their migrations to the south. The expansion of the Bantu-speakers over more than half the surface of Africa was a slow and gradual process taking hundreds of years. Though they began to enter Central Africa in the first few centuries AD, Bantu colonization of Southern Africa was not complete by the nineteenth century. The southern tip of the subcontinent and the area now known as Namibia still provided a home for the earlier peoples who elsewhere had disappeared. Indeed the San and their relatives, the Khoi (or Hottentots), still form a significant element in the population of modern Botswana and Namibia, and it is only comparatively recently that Bantu-speakers began to settle in significant numbers in the neighbourhood of Cape Town.

For thousands of years the Bantu-speaking peoples have been engaged in a tremendous enterprise which even to this day is not fully complete. They have had the task of opening up most of sub-Saharan Africa to settled agriculture. They are the true pioneers of Africa. When in addition it is remembered that millions of Africans, including Bantu-speakers, were carried across the sea to the Americas and now form the vast majority of the population of the West Indies as well as a significant part of the population of both the American continents, the scale of their expansion can be realized. Inevitably this colossal colonizing effort absorbed much of their energies.

The development of a complex material civilization depends on the growth of large towns and the development of specialization and division of labour. These in turn require a relatively dense population with a well-established agricultural system. Over much of Africa these conditions were lacking. Nature had still to be tamed or natural conditions precluded dense settlement. Furthermore, for geographical reasons, much of the continent was isolated from the contact with other peoples and cultures which is always the greatest stimulus to the development of new ideas and techniques. Thus over much of the continent the life of the average man has remained that of the simple peasant, tilling the land with the simplest of tools, living in a humble hut built of mud and thatched with grass or leaves, and recognizing a political order no wider than that of his clan. But this is not the whole story. Wherever conditions were favourable Africans abundantly proved their ability for constructing complex political systems and mastering sophisticated techniques.

The upper Nile valley was one of these areas, where as we have seen (p. 19) the kingdom of Kush, in spite of its isolation, preserved and modified the heritage of Egyptian civilization for hundreds of years before being replaced by the Christian kingdoms of Nubia and later by the Funj sultanate. Meroe, as the huge heaps of slag found around the site of the ancient city show, was a great centre of iron-working and may have been the main centre from which knowledge of the technique spread to other African peoples.

The Sudanic belt of West Africa was particularly favourable to the development of complex civilization. The fertility of the upper Niger area and modern northern Nigeria encouraged the growth of a relatively dense agricultural population, well placed to trade local products and those of the forest belt for those of North Africa, using the caravan routes across the desert. In particular the presence of gold deposits in the western parts of the savanna and the adjacent forest was a powerful stimulus to trade. The powerful empire of Ghana, essentially a trading state, with its capital on the fringe of the Sahara, flourished from the eighth century AD until at least the latter half of the eleventh, and was still a force to be reckoned with in the twelfth century. In the eleventh century Ghana came into contact with the Almoravids, a movement of religious reform in Islam among the Tuareg of the western Sahara under the inspiration of a holy man who settled on the Senegal river. In addition to their contact with Ghana – which has often been interpreted as a conquest of that state – the Almoravids conquered most of the Maghreb and Spain. The interpretation which sees Ghana as having been attacked and destroyed by the Almoravids in 1076 needs, however, to be treated with caution, and not only because of the clear evidence of Ghana's importance in the twelfth century. Positive evidence of an Almoravid conquest is scanty and, indeed, what evidence there is suggests co-operation between the Almoravids and Ghana as much as conflict.

By the beginning of the thirteenth century Ghana had virtually disappeared, perhaps as much because of environmental degradation of its always marginal desert-side lands as because of military defeat. The vacuum left was filled by the rise of a new empire, the kingdom of Mali, based on the agriculture of the upper Niger valley but also actively engaged in the trans-Saharan trade. This kingdom became officially Muslim under the rule of its best-known king, Mansa Musa (1312–37) who made a pilgrimage to Mecca in 1324 and created a sensation in Cairo by his immense wealth and lavish gifts of gold. Under the Mali empire West African towns like Timbuktu and Jenne became important centres of Islamic learning and scholarship and missionary activity. Internal disputes gradually weakened the Mali empire and nomadic Tuareg from the desert and hostile neighbours from the south began to raid its provinces. When it finally crumbled in the fifteenth century its place was taken by the Songhai empire, which had its base in what had once been the easternmost province of Mali. Songhai was the largest of the West African Sudanic empires. It was a great Islamic centre and exercised a wide influence, particularly on the Hausa towns of modern northern Nigeria which were growing into important centres of trade and civilization. It was destroyed in the sixteenth century by the Spanish mercenaries of El Mansur, the king of Morocco, who sent his forces across the desert to capture the sources of the rich gold trade. The Moroccan army broke up the Songhai empire but failed to provide a stable alternative government. New kingdoms like the Bambara states of Segu and Kaarta arose, but the collapse of the old order was a blow for the cause of Islam in West Africa. The religion did not die out and a community of learned men still survived who kept alive the tradition of scholarship and contact with the holy places of Arabia, but they often found themselves living under rulers who practised traditional religion or were only partly Islamized, who did not respect Islamic law but feared the political power of the Muslim holy men.

To the east of Songhai and the Hausa city states, a powerful kingdom developed in Kanem, north-east of Lake Chad, which traded in slaves and ivory with Tripoli in modern Libya. The precise data of the kingdom's foundation is not known but it was possibly between AD 700 and 800. The conversion of one of the early rulers to Islam provoked a split in the ruling family, and prolonged hostilities between the two sections led the royal family to flee south into Borno (Bornu) in 1384. The Kanem-Borno kingdom, thanks to the energy of some of its rulers, for example Mai Idris Alooma (1571–1603), was able to conquer many of the earlier inhabitants of the Borno area and incorporate them permanently into itself. At its high point it controlled the Fezzan, now a province of Libya, and in spite of the attacks of many enemies it was still powerful in the nineteenth century and survives as an important element in northern Nigeria today. Further east still the states of Bagirmi, Wadai and Darfur stretched out to meet the Funj sultanate of the Nile valley.

Though the Sudanic belt was particularly favourable for the development of complex societies it did not have a monopoly. The forest and its fringes in West Africa also saw the rise of powerful kingdoms. Amongst the most remarkable of these was the civilization of the Yoruba peoples in what is now western Nigeria. Its ancient centre was the town of Ife, with its magnificent artistic tradition of bronze casting and modelling in terra cotta, its stone carvings and monoliths and the potsherd floors of its tightly packed mud houses. Under its cultural influence a whole series of city-states grew up, some in the heart of the forest, others well to the north of it, each ruled by a king, who possessed some of the attributes of divinity, and a complex hierarchy of chiefs.

During the fourteenth century one of these city-states, Oyo, near the northern limits of Yoruba settlement, became an important military power and built up a supremacy over other towns which extended outside the limits of modern Nigeria to what is now the modern state of Benin (formerly Dahomey). One of the cities which experienced the influence of Ife was Benin amongst the Edo people. It in turn became a powerful empire with a highly developed bronze casting tradition based on that of Ife, and exercised influence over a wide area. It was already a powerful state when Portuguese travellers arrived there in 1485 and is today a Nigerian state capital.

Another kingdom whose history is closely bound up with that of the Yoruba is Dahomey. It emerged as a powerful state centred on Abomey in the eighteenth century when Agaja Trudo conquered the small city-states of the Aja people and brought them under unified control (1724–30). Dahomey developed a highly complex administrative system including a method of maintaining an accurate population census. It was dominated by Oyo throughout most of the eighteenth century, but strengthened itself through the slave trade with Europeans. In the nineteenth century it was able to assert its dependence and engaged in a series of ferocious wars against the Yoruba.

Further west the powerful kingdom of Asante was founded in the late seventeenth century by Osei Tutu, who bound a number of small Akan states together in a federation under the paramountcy of the Asantehene. The association was given permanence by the religious reverence attached to the Golden Stool, the symbol of Asante unity, and by the nature of the military system. Originally created as a measure of self-defence, the Asante empire soon became the dominant power in the area of modern Ghana. It was at its height in the early years of the nineteenth century.

In addition to these particularly powerful states there were many others which though less extensive showed a high degree of administrative complexity and sophistication: the Fante states of the coast of modern Ghana, the city-states of the Niger delta area, the rich commercial cities of Hausaland, the mysterious kingdom of the Kwararafa on the Benue, which suddenly expanded vigorously in the seventeenth century and then rapidly declined; and the kingdom of the Nupe with its complicated political system and its tradition of handicrafts.

Though the peoples with large-scale political structures have naturally tended to receive the greatest attention from the historians it should not be thought that the culture and skills of those whose political life was organized around clan villages was necessarily inferior. Peoples like the Igbo (Ibo) of modern Nigeria may not have built large kingdoms, but they produced bronzeworks of great beauty such as those found at Igbo Ukwu.

Bronze from Igbo Ukwu in the form of a shell surmounted by a leopard, possibly a ritual drinking vessel

Further south, down the western coast of Africa, the land around the southern banks of the Zaire river, where the forest gives way to savanna, was the centre of a complex and powerful kingdom which attracted the attention of the early Portuguese travellers. The Portuguese, who made contact with the kingdom in 1483, hoped to convert the king and people to Christianity and to build up the Kongo kingdom as a powerful Christian ally. Nzinga Nkuwu, who took the name Afonso I, the most famous of the Kongo kings (1506–40), gave himself wholeheartedly to the project but the Portuguese expected to be reimbursed for their expenses in slaves, the only commodity the Kongo had to sell which could command a large market. Gradually the slave trade corrupted the fabric of the kingdom and the Portuguese connection became a curse rather than a blessing. By the eighteenth century the kingdom had almost ceased to exist as an effective political system, though its memory persists amongst the Bakongo people of modern Zaire, Congo and Angola. Further into the interior of Zaire, the Luba people developed a powerful state, possibly as early as AD 1500, which had a far-reaching influence and stimulated the development of other political systems. Amongst these was the powerful kingdom of the Lunda of Katanga under their king, the Mwata Yamvo. This state benefited from trade with the Portuguese. It was at its height in the eighteenth century when one of its armies under a general called Kazembe established a Lunda kingdom on the Luapula river in modern Zambia. Also in the Zaire area was the Kuba kingdom with its tradition of beautiful wood carving.

The East African coastline was visited by ships trading in the Indian Ocean from very remote times. An account written in the first century AD mentions that there was a large port, possibly on the Tanzanian coast, called Rhapta, where Arab merchants settled and intermarried with the African population. Later, Persian and Arab refugees from political persecution settled on the East African coast and a chain of towns grew up stretching from Mogadishu in modern Somalia to Sofala in Mozambique. The population of these towns was a mixture of Arabs and Bantu-speakers. There the Swahili language was developed, a basically Bantu tongue with strong Arabic influences which now forms a common language in much of East Africa and is widely spoken in Zaire also. The East African coastal cities lived largely by trading in ivory and other African commodities. Sofala also exported considerable quantities of gold and iron which was considered to be of the highest quality for making sword blades. These goods were taken to India and China by Arab ships which in return imported Chinese porcelain and Indian and Chinese cloths. The Chinese themselves made two voyages to the East African coast, but the direct trade contact was not maintained. Diplomatic relations survived,

19

however, and early in the fifteenth century the ruler of Malindi sent a giraffe as a present to the Chinese emperor. In the towns the richer citizens enjoyed a high standard of living and were dressed in the most expensive cloths of the East. Kilwa boasted neat streets of stone houses and a large mosque. Some towns minted their own coins and Islamic scholarship was eagerly pursued. The arrival of the Portuguese in the fifteenth century brought the golden age of the East African cities to an end. The Portuguese, inspired by a mixture of greed and religious enthusiasm, brutally pillaged the cities and largely destroyed their trade. Thereafter they mouldered on, a shadow of their former glory, until the

Part of the Great Mosque at Kilwa, built in the fourteenth and fifteenth centuries

nineteenth century when the coming of the Omani ruler, Sayyid Said, to Zanzibar infused new life into the old trading system.

In the interior, the fertile area of the inter-lacustrine region was a natural centre of African civilization. Legends speak of a mysterious people called the Bachwezi and an ancient kingdom of Kitwara. Whatever the truth of those legends may be, the discovery of ancient earthworks shows that powerful states existed there in remote times. In more recent periods the area saw the rise of a series of related kingdoms, Bunyoro, Nkore, Buganda, Toro, and Busoga.

Bunyoro, one of the oldest, was for long the most powerful, but during the eighteenth century the newer state of Buganda with its highly centralized administrative system and efficient military force began to get the upper hand. Further south in the mountainous areas around Lake Kivu there were the two powerful kingdoms of Rwanda and Burundi, each ruled by an aristocracy of cattle keepers, probably of Nilotic descent.

The area south of Lake Tanganyika and north of the Zambezi river (now occupied by the republics of Zambia, Malawi and Mozambique) is one of the great crossroads in African history.

The first Bantu-speakers probably arrived there soon after the beginning of the Christian era and thereafter successive groups of immigrants came into the country, steadily driving out or absorbing the earlier population of 'bushmen' and pygmies. These first waves of Bantu settlement seem to have come from the north and the early Bantu-speaking settlers brought with them the art of cattle-keeping which they took on their further migrations across the Zambezi into what are now Zimbabwe and South Africa.

Long after these immigrants from the north another chain of migrants began to move into the area, this time from the west. The centre of this movement seems to have been the area occupied by the Luba and Lunda peoples on the Shaba plateau of Zaire, and its cause may have been the political upheavals in those two kingdoms which have been mentioned earlier. Some of the earliest of these immigrants from the west were the Yao and Makua and the Chewa and other related peoples who are known as the Malawi or Maravi. The present Republic of Malawi is named after them. They established a network of interrelated kingdoms in modern Malawi and the eastern part of modern Zambia. These kingdoms were in contact with the Portuguese from the sixteenth century. In the late seventeenth and eighteenth centuries still further migrations from the Luba–Lunda area took place. These included the Bisa and the Bemba who built up a powerful kingdom around Lake Bangweulu. The establishment of the Lunda kingdom of Kazembe on the Luapula river by one of the generals of the Lunda king, Mwata Yamvo, in the eighteenth century was

Great Zimbabwe: the solid drystone 'conical tower' built within the 'elliptical building'

one of the latest of these migrations. It is also probable that a migratory group from the Luba–Lunda area was responsible for building up the powerful kingdom of Lozi on the flood plain of the upper Zambezi.

These migratory groups from the west brought with them their custom of matrilineal descent and a predominantly agricultural culture. They largely overlaid the previous migrations from the north, though some peoples who belonged to the earlier group survived and maintained their cultural identity. It is because of the west to east migrations that there has come to be a great belt of matrilineal agricultural peoples known as the Central Bantu separating the patrilineal cattle-keeping peoples of East Africa from the patrilineal cattle-keepers of South Africa who probably originated from them.

South of the Zambezi in what is now the Republic of Zimbabwe there arose one of the most extensive and interesting African kingdoms. This was the empire of Mwene Mutapa, whose rulers built elaborate stone buildings at Zimbabwe and many other sites. Its origin is lost in obscurity but it was certainly flourishing by AD 950 when the Arab traveller, al Masudi, visited East Africa. Its prosperity was based on the export of gold and other minerals from innumerable small diggings which were sold to Arab traders at Sofala. When the Portuguese seized Sofala from the Arabs they made contact with the empire and established markets at Sena and Tete on the Zambezi as well as at other points in the kingdom. Portuguese traders took advantage of quarrels in the ruling family to gain concessions of land for themselves and to bring the king under their control. The kingdom was weakened to the verge of collapse, but in the late seventeenth and early eighteenth centuries a new group, which had once been tributary to the Mwene Mutapa, made its appearance. This was the Rozvi under a dynasty of rulers called Changamire. The Rozvi defeated the Portuguese and though they did not expel them altogether they confined their occupation to Sena and Tete and a few points on the coast. Under the Rozvi the old stone-building culture flourished again and in the eighteenth century the buildings at Zimbabwe were enlarged to the impressive size of the ruins which now survive. At the beginning of the nineteenth century Mwene Mutapa under its new rulers appeared as strong as ever.

External influences on Africa before 1800: Islam and the Arabs

The most important external influence on Africa before the nineteenth century was that of the Arabs and Islam, and it may be worth pausing for a moment to examine some of the most striking characteristics of a cultural system which has vitally influenced the life of a very large part of the continent.

The Holy Prophet Muhammad was born in about AD 570 and brought up in Mecca, a trading city on an important caravan route through Arabia. He had visions in which he believed that he received direct messages from God (Allah) through the Angel Gabriel. These divine messages were written down without modification and make up the Quran (Koran). This holy book is therefore for all Muslims the direct word of God, recorded in the original Arabic words used in the Revelation. It contains injunctions to believe in the unity of God and the duty of prayer, but also many commands of a moral or even legal nature. As Muhammad became well known and began to gather a body of disciples around him he became unpopular in his native city where it was believed that his attacks on idol-worship would damage the trade derived from pilgrims who visited the pagan shrines of the city. In AD 662 he and his followers fled on what is called the Hijra ('exodus') to the neighbouring city of Medina and a separate religious community was constituted under the authority of the Prophet. In this community there was naturally no distinction between the faith and society, or between civil and religious laws. The whole society was a religious body, its ruler was the Prophet of God, and its whole life was dedicated to God. In 630 Muhammad and his followers conquered Mecca and under his successors the Islamic community engaged in a spectacular career of conquest and expansion. But because of its early history the Muslim community has always regarded itself in theory as a single religious body in which religious belief and conformity to religious law is the qualification for membership. Other religious bodies which believed in a single God and had written scriptures were recognized be the Prophet. He laid down that they should be well treated, protected and left free to practise their religion, but they could never become part of the Islamic community itself. They were not supposed to participate in military service in Islamic countries or to take part in affairs of state, but they paid a special tax, the *jizya*, in return for protection.

Within the Muslim community itself there was no distinction in theory between religious and civil affairs. The words of the Quran, the practice of the Prophet and the way of life of the early community as handed down by tradition constituted a basic law, the *sharia*, which every Muslim, whether ruler or commoner, was bound to respect. This law was administered by learned men known as *qadis*. The Prophet himself and the caliphs or deputies who succeeded him were both political and religious heads of the community they governed, and they led the people in prayer. There was never a formal hierarchy of priests similar to that of the Roman Catholics; any good Muslim could lead prayer in the mosques. In practice, however, this duty was generally the prerogative of learned men known as *imams* who, together with the *qadis*, made up the class of *ulema* or men of learning, one of the most influential bodies in any Islamic society. As the Arab conquests gave them control of Persia, most of the lands of the eastern Roman empire, Egypt and North Africa, they became heirs to the greatest civilization in the world of the time. For centuries they were far in advance of western Europe and preserved and expanded the wisdom they inherited from others. Philosophy, poetry, mathematics, medicine, architecture and many other arts were cultivated while education was developed to a high level in the *madrasas*, as Muslim universities were called, with their magnificent libraries. For centuries scholars laboured on codifying the *sharia* law and eventually four great schools, Hanbalite, Malikite, Shafiite, and Hanafite emerged. They differ slightly in interpretation but recognize one another as valid.

In spite of the vast area covered by the Arab conquests the Islamic community has never ceased to feel itself a single body, and this has been reinforced by the spread of Arabic as the universal language of learning and often of everyday speech throughout the Muslim world, by the custom of facing towards Mecca during prayers, and by the duty which every good Muslim feels of making a pilgrimage *(hajj)* to the Holy Places if he can possibly afford it. Every year this brings Muslims from the most remote parts to Mecca and Medina, and powerfully emphasizes the unity of the religious community.

At first in practice, and always in theory, the whole Islamic community had one head, the caliph or deputy of the Prophet, but early in the history of Islam disagreement occurred about the qualifications for rulership. Ali, the son-in-law of the Prophet, became the fourth caliph in 656, but he was challenged by Muawiya, who used the strength of the army in Syria to secure his overthrow and founded the Umayyad dynasty of caliphs in 661. This led to a split between those who believed that the only person entitled to lead the Islamic community must be a member of the family of the Prophet and the direct descendant of Ali and Fatima, the Prophet's daughter (they are called Shi'ites), and those who felt that the choice of a leader depended on the will of the community (these are the Sunni). As the direct line of descendants from Ali was broken, some Shi'ites developed the theory that the last true caliph had disappeared and would come back to earth in the fullness of time as the saviour or Mahdi. The Mahdi would head the whole Muslim body and restore the faith to perfection, a variant of belief in a Mahdi which differs from its recurrent appearance among Sunni Muslims. Generally the Sunni group were politically more successful than the Shi'ites, but Shi'ite dynasties arose from time to time in Africa as well as elsewhere. Shi'ism is still dominant in Iran and in other parts of the world there are powerful Shi'ite groups such as the Ismailis, who have many adherents in East Africa.

Although all Muslims believed that there ought to be one head of the whole community, political unity did not survive after AD 750. Quarrels over who should be the true caliph led to the rise of separate caliphates. The most important caliphs, those in Baghdad, fell under the control of the commanders of their Turkish bodyguards who took the title of sultan, reducing the caliphs to mere figureheads.

The slave soldiery who ruled Egypt under the name of Mamluks from 1259 to 1517, maintained a nominal caliph in Cairo, but when Egypt fell to the forces of the Ottoman Turks in 1517 the authority of the caliph was taken over by the Turkish sultan. Nevertheless the belief in unity continued, and is inseparable from the religious beliefs of Islam. What is more, throughout the Muslim world a fairly uniform pattern of government emerged. Every community was governed by a single head who might be called caliph if he believed that he was entitled to be the supreme head of all Muslims, otherwise sultan if he was very powerful, or alternatively *amir* (emir). *Amir* simply means commander and one of the titles of the caliph is *amir al-muminin* (Commander of the Faithful). Under the head there was always a chief minister known as *wazir*, and judges called *qadis* who administered the *sharia*. All rulers in theory recognized this as the highest law, but in practice they also applied a good deal of executive law, administered through the *wazirs* rather than the *qadis*, concerning matters not covered by the *sharia*. Revolutions have been common in the Islamic world, but until very recent times they never took the form of trying to replace this type of government by some other system such as representative democracy, but simply of attempts to purify the system or to place someone who was believed to be the rightful ruler on the throne. Claims to descent from the Prophet have also often formed the basis of claims of political authority. (Such people are called *sharifs* or *sayyids*.) From time to time also people have appeared in various parts of the Islamic world claiming to be the Mahdi and therefore rightful rulers of the whole Muslim world.

One of the most important forms of organization in the Islamic world is that of the sufi brotherhoods. Islam is very much a written religion with hard and fast doctrines and set duties. Some people found the mere conformity to the religious commands of their faith too cold and formal. They formed associations dedicated to the contemplation of God and the attempt to enter into a mystic sense of unity with him. Though they conformed to the requirements of prayer and other duties they laid more emphasis on the emotional side of religion, the love of God rather than formal obedience to his commands and correctness of belief. These brotherhoods appealed particularly to the less educated who could not read for themselves, and the brotherhoods became the most powerful missionary organization in Islam. Their number is very large. Some run right through the Muslim world; others are local. Most of them have a strong sense of community and often revere their founders as saints. Inevitably the brotherhoods have often wielded political power and because of the closeness within their ranks they are often jealous or even hostile to one another and to all powers outside themselves. It sometimes happened that when people belonging to different societies became converted to Islam they joined different brotherhoods and kept up their feuds.

The influence of Islam in Africa has been, and is, enormous. After the Arab conquest of Egypt in AD 640 that country became overwhelmingly Muslim, though a substantial Coptic Christian community survives. Arabic became the language of daily life as well as of learning, and Islamic law set the pattern of existence. From Egypt Islam travelled up the Nile and became the religion of the Funj sultanate in the northern part of the

The Great Mosque at Jenne in Mali

27

present Sudan. In the Maghreb also Islam became dominant after the Arab conquest, and from there it was carried along the caravan routes across the Sahara to establish itself in the states of the Sudanic belt. From there in turn it has been and still is being carried south into the forest lands. Today it is estimated that roughly 45 per cent of the population of Nigeria, which has far more people than any other West African state, is Muslim. In East Africa also Islam was brought by Arab traders and refugees to the coastal city-states. It established itself firmly there and spread inland along the caravan routes. In the nineteenth century Muslim communities had begun to arise as far inland as the inter-lacustrine region.

External influences on Africa before 1800: Europeans

In comparison with the effects of the Arab invasions and the coming of Islam, European contacts were much less significant. Only at the southern end of the continent could they be said to have had results for the life of African peoples in any way like those of Islam.

Apart from the northern coastline of Africa, which was always in contact with European states across the Mediterranean, European contact with Africa began with the voyages of the Portuguese in the fifteenth century. They were inspired by a mixture of economic, military and religious motives. The Portuguese wanted first to discover a route of their own to the gold of West Africa which did not pass through the hands of their traditional enemies, the Muslims of the Maghreb. Later they sought a direct sea route to India and its rich trade. They also hoped to find in Africa the legendary Christian king known as Prester John who they felt would prove an invaluable ally and enable them to attack the Muslims from the rear. They also sought to convert Africans to Christianity and to develop alliances with African kingdoms which would give them trade advantages and possibly military assistance. Their voyages brought them first to West Africa in 1482 when they established a fort on the coast of modern Ghana called São Jorge da Mina (now known as Elmina castle). There they traded for gold and succeeded in diverting part of the supplies from the northern route. They also made contact with the empire of Benin and colonized the islands of São Tomé and Principe. Their attempts at evangelization were far from successful, and increasingly they turned their attention to the slave trade.

Their policy of building up Christian allies in Africa was centred on the Kongo kingdom but as we have seen the plan was compromised by dependence on the slave trade and ended in collapse. In neighbouring Angola the Portuguese established a more permanent settlement after

1576. This was essentially a colony of slave traders who used local agents to maintain the supply of human beings to be loaded on the ships for transport across the sea to Brazil. Though the capital of the settlement, Luanda, was rich enough to be described in the eighteenth century as Lisbon in Africa, its prosperity rested on a very slender basis and the settlement had little direct effect on development inland apart from encouraging wars and supplying arms which ambitious rulers could use to strengthen and expand their kingdoms.

When they rounded the Cape of Good Hope and reached the East African coast the Portuguese found the flourishing Muslim trading cities. The Portuguese intrusion, however, had disastrous results on their prosperity and threw the old trading system into a long period of decline and decay. Only in Mozambique did the Portuguese acquire a permanent foothold. They were attracted by the gold trade of the Mwene Mutapa empire and succeeded in establishing trading posts within the heart of the kingdom. By adapting themselves to African conditions the local Portuguese acquired a great deal of influence in the empire and virtually brought the king of Mwene Mutapa under their control. But their numbers were always very small indeed and their behaviour was often such as to make them very unpopular. With the rise of the Rozvi in the late seventeenth century their wide influence and landholdings disappeared and by the beginning of the nineteenth century Portuguese influence in Mozambique hardly extended beyond gunshot range from their forts.

In addition to establishing two small white communities in Angola and Mozambique the Portuguese contributed in two ways to African development. In the first place they were responsible for introducing a whole range of new crops which had their natural home in South America. These included cassava (manioc), maize, groundnuts and tobacco. Some of these, particularly cassava and maize, have been of tremendous importance as they have come to form the staple diet of large sections of the African population, partially replacing the indigenous millets and yams. The effect which this has had on the development of Africa can only be guessed at, but it must be enormous. The second way in which the Portuguese influenced Africa was through the introduction of the Atlantic slave trade.

There had always been a slave trade with the Arabs in parts of Africa, and in North Africa European slaves were bought and sold, but the trade across the Atlantic was to eclipse in scale anything of the kind that had happened before. At first the Portuguese were mainly interested in the gold trade but they always wanted slaves to sell in Portugal where there was a great shortage of labour. In time the African slaves formed about 5 per cent of the population of Portugal. But the slave trade only became really massive with the development of sugar planting on São Tomé and its later transference to Brazil and the West Indies. This created an almost unlimited demand for labour. The Portuguese, the Dutch, the Danes, the French and the British transported millions of Africans across the Atlantic. The Portuguese mainly traded from Angola though in the eighteenth century they revived their West African trade from the coast of modern Benin. The other nations traded mainly from West Africa and there the British succeeded in controlling the major portion.

The trans-Atlantic slave trade is one of the greatest crimes in all human history whether we think of the personal sufferings of the captives, their treatment on board ship, the degradation and humiliation of the life to which they were doomed or the misery, loss of life and brutalization which it brought to the African communities from which the slaves were taken. Undoubtedly the colossal business in human beings had terrible and widespread effects on the development of African societies, making warfare profitable, supplying the firearms which made it more deadly, encouraging militarism and a callous attitude to the value and dignity of human life.

Nevertheless it should not be imagined that the slave trade completely dominated the development of African societies. On the contrary, the period of the slave trade was one in which some of the most important and impressive African kingdoms developed or reached their high point and a study of their history shows that the slave trade in many cases played a relatively minor part in their lives. Throughout most of Africa south of the Sahara, therefore, pre-nineteenth-century European contacts were relatively superficial. The Europeans were confined to a few forts along the coast; the indirect effects of the slave trade may have been great but the direct impact of European culture was minimal.

An exception to this is found in modern South Africa where the Dutch East India Company established a small colony at the Cape of Good Hope to provide fresh vegetables for its ships travelling to India. In the healthy climate this tiny white community began to expand vigorously. As it did so it took away the land of the aboriginal San and Khoi, fighting and largely destroying the San and turning the Khoi into labourers on white farms. By the nineteenth century this community, still growing rapidly, was in contact with the advance guard of the Bantu-speakers who were pushing steadily southward.

The changed situation in the nineteenth century

Up to the nineteenth century the main direct outside influence on African societies was that of Islam, and over the greater part of the continent

African peoples continued to evolve their own cultural systems without much interference or stimulus from outside the continent. During the nineteenth century, however, Africa underwent a dramatic period of revolutionary change which is still continuing. Part of this process was due to external factors. The Industrial Revolution was already under way in Britain, and Europe would soon be looking to Africa as a source of raw materials and as a market for the goods produced by the new factories. Europe was also acquiring technical means which would make it relatively easy to break down the physical barriers to penetration into Africa and an overwhelming military power sufficient to annihilate resistance. At the same time the social changes brought about by the Industrial Revolution aroused stirrings of conscience. A more vital attitude to religion sprang up, a hostility to the slave trade, and a desire to convert the heathen which went well with a situation in which it seemed more profitable to trade with Africans in Africa than to export them elsewhere, and in which Christian conversion seemed necessarily to imply the adoption of European tastes and a demand for European goods. Thus through traders and dedicated missionaries Europe began to exert an influence by actually changing African societies in the light of Christian ideas. This inevitably brought with it political consequences. European political authority gradually extended itself until under the influence of almost hysterical competition between the European powers it culminated in the Scramble for Africa which brought the vast preponderance of the continent under the control of European states.

It must not be thought, however, that the revolutionary changes in African history were all the result of external influence. By the beginning of the nineteenth century internal stresses within the continent were preparing the way for two massive movements. In West Africa the inevitable tensions occurred between Muslims and rulers who practised traditional religions. These resulted from the situation caused by the fall of Songhai and were coming to a head, preparing the way for a whole series of religious movements known as the West African jihads. In modern South Africa population pressure in Zululand had already set in motion a process which was to culminate in the dramatic rise of the Zulu as a military power and a vast series of wars and migrations which vitally affected the whole history of Southern and Central Africa.

Contents and division of the two volumes

The partition of Africa between European powers forms a natural division in the history of Africa since the beginning of the nineteenth century.

Subsequent developments took place within the new borders imposed by colonialism which often bore little logical relationship to older divisions between peoples. From this point on the story is of the struggle of African peoples to master the techniques of their white rulers, of their regaining their independence and the developments which have followed and created the picture of Africa as it is today.

It is with this revolutionary period in African history that this book is concerned. The first volume will deal with the changes leading up to partition, and the second with developments from then till the present. Our purpose is to describe the development of the African peoples themselves and to deal with external influences from the point of view of their effects on Africa rather than as a subject in their own right. For this purpose it is necessary to look closely at the histories of particular peoples rather than just at continent-wide developments, and we have found it necessary to study the continent region by region. The development of the continent will throughout be treated in accordance with these regions, except for the case of the process of partition itself (discussed in the Conclusion to this volume) which is most easily looked at from a continental point of view. The regions have been chosen on historical grounds. Africa north of the Sahara forms a natural unit of study and with this is connected the history of the Nile valley and neighbouring Ethiopia. West Africa, again, is a convenient unit from the geographical and historical points of view. In talking of the great block of Africa from Zaire to East Africa as another division we had in mind the effects of Arab penetration from the East African coast to the Zaire river in the nineteenth century. Finally Southern and Central Africa, including South Africa, Zimbabwe, Zambia, Malawi and Mozambique, have links which make it convenient to group them together. It should not be thought, however, that these regions are absolute, or that they have any other purpose than as a convenience to avoid the difficulty of trying to talk about everything at once. There are no sharp divisions between the peoples of the continent and the history of every African people is connected with that of its neighbours in a great network which covers the continent without a break. It would be perfectly possible to use different divisions from those we have chosen; any such divisions are arbitrary and useful only as an aid to explanation.

1 West Africa to 1800

Introduction

If history is not to be mistaken for antiquarianism, it must be written with the eyes firmly focused on those events, factors and persons which help to explain the present look of things, or how the present evolved from the past. Thus while it is true that in 1800, West Africa was colourful and richly varied geographically, ethnically, economically and politically, it is not this rich variety which by itself explains the transformation which the region underwent in the one and a half centuries or so that followed. Rather that change can be accounted for mainly in terms of two factors. The first was international trade and the attempt to ensure the conditions considered appropriate for carrying on with it. The second was religion. This chapter is therefore concerned to give a brief analysis of the origins of these two factors in West African history and of their state of development by 1800. This will help to highlight the factors of change and continuity in West African history.

Each of the above two factors divides into two. For West Africa around 1800, international trade was made up of the trans-Saharan caravan trade and the trans-Atlantic trade. The factor of religion was made up of Islam and Christianity. Both Islam and Christianity were alike in that each is exclusivist, that is intolerant of the idea of any other religion co-existing with it. Each centred around a belief in the unquestionable authority of a book – the Quran for Islam, and the Bible for Christianity. Each laid emphasis on literacy. The spread of either, but more so of Islam, was closely associated with the growth of trade and of centralized authority able to maintain law and order over a wide area. But while Islam was not prepared to make any distinction between religion and politics, Christianity had conceded control over the state to secular politicians on condition that its claim to a monopoly over the spiritual welfare of peoples was not contested by the state. These elements of similarity and difference are important for an understanding of the fortunes and roles of the two religions in the period under study.

From what follows it will be seen that the habit of dividing history into neat periods, though a convenient and widespread practice amongst historians, is justly condemned as artificial and misleading. The factors which transformed West African history after 1800 were already present in her society in one form or the other before that date.

Trans-Saharan trade routes

For well over sixteen centuries after Christ, the dominant factor in West African history was the trans-Saharan caravan trade, in which the initiative lay outside West Africa, or, to be more exact, in the Maghreb and North Africa. Recent evidence from archaeology and geology has established beyond reasonable doubt that in the very distant past the region of the present Sahara desert, which now looks like a formidable divide between West Africa and North Africa, carried a richer vegetation and enjoyed a better supply of rivers and rain. It was therefore more thickly populated by mixed groups of Caucasoid and Negroid physical type, some of whom lived from seasonal agriculture and others of whom grazed large herds of cattle. As the Sahara began to dry up, the Caucasians retreated northwards and the Negroes southwards. Continued contact was possible, however, because here and there in the Sahara there survived green patches, known as oases, carrying enough water and vegetation to support human existence. Contact in the forms of trade and war led to established routes from one oasis to the other, and thus linked the fertile belts which lay to the north and south of the Sahara.

Until the fifteenth century these routes across the Sahara remained West Africa's most sure and certain link with the outside world, while until even later the trade and ideas which penetrated the region through them constituted the most dynamic forces in its history. Because of its location and peculiar characteristics, the Sudan of West Africa benefited more from this link than the Guinea lands and so assumed historical leadership of West Africa. The Sudan, with its vegetation of grass and orchard bush, is a more open country than Guinea, with its vegetation of thick evergreen bush; thus travel was easier. This advantage of the Sudan over Guinea was emphasized through the use by the Sudanese of beasts of burden, especially with the introduction of the horse as a riding animal. This ease of travel favoured conquerors and traders, as well as the rise of empires and of commercial centres enjoying international renown.

The Sudan also had the advantage of being able to support a wider variety of occupations than Guinea; it was able to combine occupations borrowed from the desert to the north of it, and the tropical rain forest to the south. Along the main river banks the Sudanese practised artificial irrigation agriculture, as did the Negroes of the Saharan oases and of the Sahel. With this, in certain areas, they combined rainy season agriculture supplemented by husbandry, which was more characteristic of the forest zone. Certain classes of Sudanese peoples, especially the cattle Fulani, practised nomadic pastoralism, and in addition there was long-distance trade. From this rich variety of occupations the Sudan was able to support a sizeable population and maintain the soldiers and politicians required for large-scale political organization.

Because of its location, the Sudan was able to play a key role in the international trade that went to North Africa. This trade was between the products of the Mediterranean and Europe on the one hand, and of the forest zone of West Africa – gold, kola nuts, ivory and slaves – on the other. The Sudan had a few gold-bearing areas, in the valleys of the Senegal and the Niger, and produced animal skins, but the actual role of the Sudanese in the trade was to collect the products of their forest neighbours to the south for exchange with the dates, salt and manufactured articles brought from the desert, North Africa and Europe by the North African caravans. In a sense, therefore, the historical pre-eminence of the Sudanese in West Africa was for centuries rooted in their economic exploitation of their neighbours to the south. The impression which the outside world had of Sudanese wealth was so exaggerated that, even up to the nineteenth century, European travellers expected to find Timbuktu a fabulously wealthy city and were disappointed to find it a decaying town with only drab mud huts and mosques. But, however exaggerated the wealth of the Sudan was in European and Asiatic imagination, there is no doubt that the trade made the Sudan, until about the eighteenth century, a much richer land than Guinea.

Islam

International trade brought the Sudan in particular, and West Africa in general, face to face for the first time with one of the world's universalist religions. From time immemorial all West Africans had followed the religion of their fathers which some, for lack of a better term, have called Paganism. Then from AD 632 Islam gained a foothold in Egypt and from there set out to conquer the rest of North Africa. The ancient North African urbanized cities were relatively easy to conquer, but the Berbers of the desert put up a stout resistance. Rather than submit, some of them started to migrate, the Lemtuna taking the lead in this. But the Arabs and Islam followed them on; refugees and their pursuers followed the beaten track of the ancient trade routes across the Sahara. By the eighth century the Sanhaja had got to what is now Mauritania; by that same century a Muslim state of southern Algeria, Tahert, was already trading with Awdaghast, a Sanhaja city. From the latter place Islam penetrated further south into the Sudan proper, the ruling dynasty of Takrur being the first black dynasty to embrace the new religion.

This new factor which entered West Africa through the trade routes eventually proved a more permanent and dynamic historical force than the trade which brought it. At first, however, its role in shaping events appeared subordinate to that of trade. Only in the nineteenth century did Islam become the chief determinant of political change in the Sudan.

In other spheres of life Islam also represented a factor of change. The pilgrimage which it encouraged brought the élite of the Sudan into contact with the most advanced ideas of the time and so kept them up to date and progressive. Idris Alooma of Borno (1571–1603), for instance, learnt of the use of firearms in the course of his pilgrimage, introduced their use into the Borno army and thus won himself a place in history as a military reformer and conqueror. Islam also introduced into the Western Sudan the mode of dressing now considered traditional in the Sudan belt, and, more important, the Arabic script.

This latter event is perhaps, from the historian's point of view, the most important innovation by Islam in West Africa, for it made the keeping of written records possible.

The state of Islam in the Sudan by about 1800 is now a matter for dispute amongst historians of West Africa. According to one view Islam had, by 1800, gone to sleep in the courts of petty monarchs, that is, it had become the religion of lukewarm and pleasure-loving princes and of the rich commercial classes. It had grown very formal, attaching a lot of importance to institutions and titles rather than to purity, piety and simplicity. It had not made, and was not making, any noticeable impact on the peasants and their rural way of life. It was not based on a living knowledge of the Quran. Consequently even the urban Islam that existed had absorbed many of the practices and symbols of the traditional religions of the Sudanese peoples.

But other scholars have pointed out that this unfavourable view of the state of Islam around 1800 derived from an uncritical use of the works of propaganda produced by the jihadists of the nineteenth century about whom more will be said. It has also been argued that the career and work of the jihadists, which go back to the last few decades of the eighteenth century, show something of the life and capacity for self-criticism which continued to characterize West African Islam even during periods when it appeared to have lost its zeal for rapid expansion.

Development of European trade

Earlier in this chapter, it was indicated that the role of the trans-Saharan trade as an important historical force was not limited to the Sudan. Directly and indirectly it determined political and economic development in the forest. European merchants, especially from Italy, the Iberian peninsula and France, were early participants in the trans-Saharan trade, but only indirectly. The merchant princes and kingdoms of the Maghreb succeeded in creating for themselves middlemen's monopoly of this trade. To preserve, and benefit from, this position they prevented their European customers and rivals from going into the interior with them to participate directly in the Sudanese trade. One or two Europeans succeeded in breaking through the middlemen's cordon and penetrated the interior along these routes. A merchant from Toulouse, Anselme d'Isalguier, is said to have got as far as, and lived in, Gao between 1405 and 1413, while a Genoese merchant was able to get to Touat in 1447. But such cases as these remained exceptional. By and large, what Europeans knew about the interior came to them second hand. Fed on stories of fabled cities of gold and the like they grew all the more anxious to participate directly in this trade. It was this desire that was partly responsible for the European bid, starting in the fifteenth century and led by the Portuguese, to reach West Africa by sea. The Europeans hoped that when they got to West Africa they would be able to divert this trade towards the south to their incalculable advantage. In a sense, therefore, the trans-Saharan trade gave rise to the impulses which created the trans-Atlantic trade which first competed with it and then stifled it.

But the European exploration of the West African coast derived not only from this economic motive. There was also a missionary motive. From about the eighth century, when the Muslims gained control of the Mediterranean and seriously embarked on the conquest of southern Europe, especially the Iberian peninsula, Christian Europe had been involved in a seemingly endless conflict with Islam. From the internal crusade for the liberation of Portugal and Spain the struggle had developed into the crusade against Islam in the Holy Land during which Christian Europe for a while actually seized the initiative. By the fifteenth century the crusading ideal had died in the rest of Europe but not in Portugal and Spain, the two countries which had suffered most from the

Muslims. As part of their offensive against Islam the Portuguese now had the ambition of side-stepping the Muslims of North Africa to reach the (pagan) black Africans of West Africa, whom they hoped to convert to Christianity. Along with this ambition went the even vaguer hope of making contact with Prester John, a legendary Christian potentate whom they hoped would come to the aid of the Christians.

Spurred on by economic ambitions as well as these vague dreams, the Portuguese in about 1417 launched their plans to reach West Africa. With the able management of Prince Henry the Navigator they achieved startling success in a short time, considering the navigational difficulties they encountered and dealt with. They reached Cape Verde in 1444 and the Bight of Benin in 1475. Seven years later, in 1482, they arrived at the Zaire (formerly Congo) river.

On getting to West Africa the Portuguese set out to put their discoveries to their advantage. Contacts for trade were made in the regions of what are now Senegal, The Gambia, Ghana, Benin and Nigeria, and adventurers were sent inland to find the gold mines that supplied the trans-Saharan trade. Hand in hand with the trade went missionary effort. In the key islands off the shores of the Windward Coast and the Gulf of Guinea, Portuguese colonies were planted to serve as centres for the exploitation of the continental trade. In this trade at first emphasis was on products such as gold, ivory, and pepper. But early in the history of Portuguese contact with West Africa there was also a small volume of trade in slaves who were sent to Portugal. The first of the unfortunate Africans who were shipped to Portugal were not actually captured as slaves. They were to be trained for missionary work in West Africa. But then it was discovered they were useful as farm hands in the underpopulated areas of Portugal and so the trade grew in volume.

With the Spanish colonization of America, and the discovery that Africans were better able than the native Indians to work the Spanish mines and plantations, the trade progressively acquired a new importance and grew in scale. By about 1650 slaves had become West Africa's main export.

The first effective challenge to the Portuguese came only in the 1590s from the Dutch. In 1642 and 1647 the Danes and the Swedes respectively entered the race for West African trade, while the British and the French intensified their participation in the trade from the 1650s. The Prussians were the last on the scene, entering as they did in 1682. In any case by the middle of the sixteenth century the trans-Atlantic trade with Europe had become an established concern. Like the trans-Saharan trade in the Sudan, this international trade with Europe proved an important historical force in the West African forest.

The influence of European trade on West African states

The forest lands of Ghana inhabited by the Akan-speaking peoples were rich in gold and kola, two of the principal items of the northern trade. From here trade routes radiated northwards via Begho to Jenne and Hausaland. In consequence of this northward trade the earliest Akan state, Bono-Tekyiman, rose on the forest fringe some time after AD 1450, and perhaps the foundation of a number of petty principalities was laid in the forest zone proper and along the coast. Then, about 1470, the Portuguese got to the coast of Ghana and in 1482 built the castle of Elmina to establish effective exploitation of the trade of the region. With the establishment of this trade there developed more intense rivalry amongst these petty kingdoms for its control than there had ever been for the more remote northern trade. Up to about 1650 among the more successful of the older states were Denkyira, Fante, Akyem and Akwamu. Then about 1670 the Asante kingdom was founded with its capital at Kumasi. While fully exploiting the northern trade it sought also to control the coastal trade. In this process it swallowed up Denkyira in 1701, Akyem in 1742, and then got ready to engulf Fante.

In modern southern Nigeria west of the Niger an identical event led to the rise of Oyo. Benin's case was a little different since it was already a flourishing state by the time the European trade was established. Its rise

West African peoples mentioned in the text

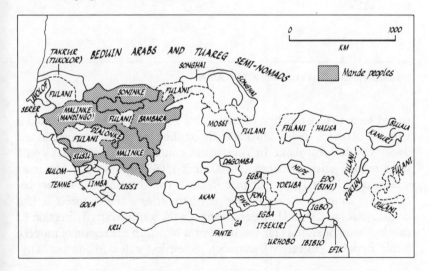

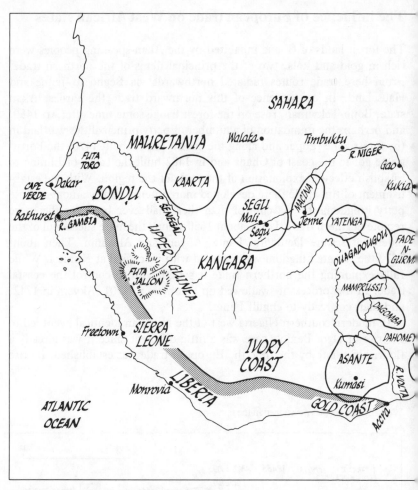

States, towns and physical features of West Africa

would seem to owe much to its trade with Yorubaland which connected it with the northern trade. Edo oral traditions link the rise of Benin's historic dynasty with Yorubaland. In Yorubaland a number of principalities would seem to have arisen between AD 1000 and 1500. Of these Oyo, the most strategically located to participate in these two international trades, became pre-eminent. Being on the northern fringe of the forest it had commercial links with Hausaland, while in the south-western direction its cavalry could operate as far south as Porto Novo. In the region of modern Benin Republic (formerly Dahomey), the earliest states, Allada and Why-

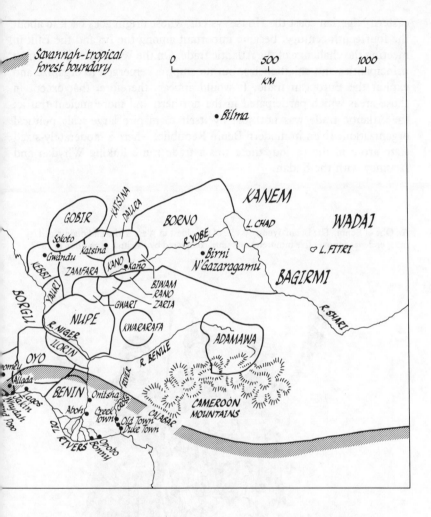

Savannah-tropical forest boundary

0   500   1000

KM

dah, arose along the coast after 1550 and must have done so largely in response to the Atlantic trade. Abomey, the youngest of the Aja states, rose after 1620 and in direct response to the challenges of the coastal trade, thereby creating the state known as Dahomey. The rise and expansion of this last Aja state resulted directly from the attempt of the Fon of Abomey to organize themselves for defence against the Oyo, Allada and Whydah, who constantly raided them to supply the trans-Atlantic slave trade.

The regions of Guinea to the east of the Niger and to the west of Ghana were isolated from the direct impact of the northern trade. Political developments here were inspired largely by the Atlantic trade. Along the eastern Nigerian coast the House system, whose origin goes back to about the fourteenth century, became important among the Ijo and the Efik in meeting the challenge of the Atlantic trade. On the Windward Coast small principalities and chieftaincies, but no empires, emerged to organize and exploit the European trade. It would appear, therefore, that except in those areas which participated in the northern and more ancient traffic, the Atlantic trade was not able by itself to inspire large-scale political organization. Even in modern Benin Republic, where a moderately-sized state arose in the period, there was a trade route linking Whydah and Abomey with the Sudan.

An Oba of Benin. The Benin dynasty is one of the oldest in West Africa and maintained its independence for over five hundred years until conquered by a British expedition in 1897

Trans-Saharan trade and the trans-Atlantic trade compared

On the economic side, the Atlantic trade ended the isolation of Guinea as well as the period when it lay in the economic backwaters of West Africa. But, contrary to Portuguese expectation, this trade was not able, until the twentieth century, to stifle completely the northern traffic and focus attention on Guinea alone. The trans-Saharan routes were still important by the nineteenth century, so important in fact that, as will be shown, Europe at times seriously thought of using North Africa (in particular Tripoli) as the gateway to the West African interior. Indeed the attraction of these routes remained strong enough to make Sir Frederick Lugard contemplate seriously, between 1900 and 1906, exporting the produce of Northern Nigeria across the Sahara. The Atlantic trade, unlike the northern trade, was not an unmixed blessing for those who participated in it. From about 1650 the slave trade was its lifeblood. This trade was not only morally bad for the Africans and Europeans alike, it also caused a heavy, and for West Africa unprofitable, transfer of population from Guinea to the New World. The total loss to West Africa in human beings in the course of the trade has been variously estimated as between ten and forty million souls. Even the latest efforts to resolve the debate on how many slaves were actually shipped across the Atlantic have only brought more heat to the controversy. However, as most of those sold were the most vigorous sections of the population, their enforced emigration was a severe loss to the land of their birth. It was partly because of this and partly because of the insecurity and destruction caused by the forcible recruitment of the slaves that many productive indigenous industries declined, or at least stagnated, with the triumph of the trade.

Like its northern counterpart, the Atlantic trade brought with it to Guinea another universalist religion, Christianity, which was subsequently to contribute immensely in shaping the destiny of West Africans. Up to the nineteenth century, however, it was of even less account than Islam. Portuguese missionary efforts on the Windward Coast, at Benin and Warri, achieved nothing, partly owing to lack of well-trained missionaries and partly owing to the stifling influence of the slave trade.

In West Africa, therefore, before 1800 the factors that determined much of the history of the indigenous peoples were international trade, and alien universalist religion. With varying emphasis they remained the same in the period covered in this book. European commerce and Christianity led first to the exploration of West Africa and then to its colonization by France, Britain, Germany and Portugal. West African nationalism and the achievement of independence were the results of African reaction to this new form of economic exploitation. But even before these forces had unfolded themselves, Islam had inspired a series of attempts at empire-building in the Sudan. The subsidiary effects of this, allied with the militant advance of European economic exploitation, led to the fall of the Guinea states which had survived into the nineteenth century. In the following chapters these new developments of the nineteenth and twentieth centuries will be dealt with. They should be seen in perspective as the further unfolding of forces already present in West Africa by 1800.

But there was some difference. Whereas it was the northern trade that dominated life in West Africa before 1900, after that date the Atlantic trade gradually took over the leadership and eventually completely destroyed the northern trade. Whereas Islam and Christianity in the main played a subsidiary role to the economic factor before 1800, after that date they assumed an importance of their own. Christianity in particular became more central than previously in the political, social and moral evolution of West Africa. And finally whereas international trade, especially the European trade, did not threaten the independence of West Africans before 1800, except the few occasions when some states of the Maghreb had designs on Songhai and Borno, after that date it became more and more evident that for some time, at least, the two things could not exist side by side.

2 The growth and character of European influence (c.1800–61)

Introduction

For nearly three centuries European interest in West Africa had two main features. In the first place it was dominantly commercial. In the second place it was limited to the coast, despite the fact that the climate of the West African interior was healthier than that of the malaria infested coast along which Europeans conducted their trading business for over three centuries. The Europeans remained at the coast for so long because of the nature of the trade in which they were primarily interested. The slave trade did not need European intervention inland to maintain the steady flow of captives.

In the fifteenth century the Portuguese, who had hopes of discovering the gold mines that supplied the northern trade, had tried to penetrade the interior. On the Senegal, for instance, they had gone as far inland as the Felou falls, while on the Gambia they had reached the Geba river. In 1485 they got to Benin City. But these early voyages inland proved uniformly unrewarding. Unlike South America, with its rich mines of Peru, the West African interior had no dazzling attractions for the Europeans, at least until the nineteenth century.

It has often been contended that it was indigenous opposition that kept the Europeans off. It would seem, however, that if the latter had seriously wanted to penetrate the interior they could have done so in spite of local African obstruction. The African communities of Guinea were certainly better organized and better armed in the nineteenth century than they were in the sixteenth and seventeenth centuries, when the Europeans had the monopoly of the musket and the cannon. Yet African opposition in the nineteenth century could not keep off the Europeans.

Until about 1800 therefore the European nations did not seriously consider the conquest and colonization of West Africa for economic exploitation. The Portuguese colonized the Canary Islands, Madeira, San-

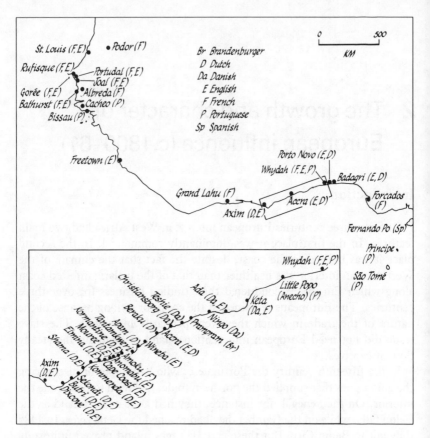

European forts and trading posts

tiago, São Tomé and some other offshore islands but these were used as centres from which to tap the continental trade. São Tomé was in addition a plantation colony which by the middle of the sixteenth century was an important source of sugar for Europe. The French between 1687 and 1702, and the British in 1763 had sought to plant colonies in the Senegal and Gambia areas respectively. All these efforts were tentative and not vigorously pressed. In consequence, in spite of three centuries of European presence, trade along the West African coast was conducted as between equals. The Africans remained their own masters, and lived their own lives according to their own standards and traditions. Even when they copied European ways they did so at their own wish. They were in fact responsible for seeing that law and order were maintained on the coast in order to protect trade. On the coast of modern Ghana they were able to

The Danish fort at Christiansborg (Osu) before the nineteenth century

enforce the payment of rents by the Europeans for the pieces of land on which the latter's forts stood. And in spite of these forts the Europeans found themselves devoid of any real political power or influence over the coastal Fante. From time to time they managed to exploit rivalries amongst African chiefs, and used bribes to establish some influence, but by and large it was the Africans who were politically supreme. In 1786, for instance, the commandants of the forts of Tantamkweri, Sekondi and Mouree were kidnapped, stripped and flogged for insulting Africans, while in 1812 the commandant of Winneba was killed. On both occasions the Europeans lacked the power to avenge this drastic treatment.

On the coast of Dahomey the *Yevogan* – the representative of the Abomey king – dictated to Europeans and Africans alike the regulations guiding trade and had the means of securing obedience to his master's will. There, as on the coast of the Oil Rivers (the name by which the creeks of the Niger delta were known) and elsewhere, Europeans had to pay harbour and trade duties before being allowed to engage in the coastal trade. A detailed study of the relationship which existed about 1800 between Africans and Europeans along the coast shows that the latter were neither feared nor liked but tolerated by the former. They were tolerated because Africans realized that Europeans were useful in providing goods which could not be manufactured locally and which, from being luxuries, had become necessities, especially amongst the richer classes.

But in the course of the nineteenth century this relationship, based on

47

equality and mutual advantage, was undermined and superseded by a new one which increasingly approximated to that between a master (the European) and his servant (the African). At heart European interest remained economic. But revolutionary changes which took place in European society caused a shift of emphasis from trade in human beings to trade in natural produce. This shift in emphasis dictated a new trading strategy which in time called for direct political domination. For some time, however, the full implications of this change were obscured by apparently harmless interests in the abolition of the slave trade, the exploration of the interior and the propagation of Christianity. It is with these three movements that we shall now deal.

The campaign against the slave trade

The reasons behind the abolition of the slave trade were many and various, but the most important of them was economic. To some extent the slave trade destroyed itself. By the middle of the eighteenth century surplus capital, part of which came from the slave trade, had helped to bring about the Industrial Revolution in Britain. In the other parts of Europe the same changes were slower in taking place. Fundamental to the Industrial Revolution was the application of science to industry which made it easier and quicker to turn raw materials into manufactured goods. The economic implications of this were far-reaching. More raw materials were needed to keep the machines fully and profitably employed and it was discovered, or in any case seriously believed, that of these raw materials West Africa could supply vegetable oils, rubber, indigo, cotton, ivory, timber and the like.

Hand in hand with the quest for raw materials went a quest for new and expanding markets to absorb the products of the industries. With regard to this it was again discovered that West Africa had great promise because of her size and population.

The old relationship between Europe and West Africa based on the slave trade came to be seen as unsuitable in the new circumstance. The slave trade not only carried away from West Africa men and women who could help in raising the new crops needed by British industries and in providing an ever-expanding market, but also the raids and wars associated with it were believed to create such chaos and insecurity as would hamper agriculture and peaceful trade. In the light of these new needs the slave trade appeared outdated and so had to be abolished.

There was also another side to the economic factor. About this period there arose in Europe a group of economic thinkers who propagated and popularized the idea that free trade, free competition and free labour were more profitable than rigidly regulated trade and forced labour. Slavery was forced labour and so, according to these thinkers, was unproductive and wasteful. The slave could not give of his best because he was made to work against his will. Furthermore, he was generally not a skilled worker. Here again, the slave trade was shown to have become an anachronism.

But it was not the economic arguments alone that gave birth to the campaign against the slave trade. In fact it was not the rational economists and the new trading interests which launched and carried through the movement. The importance of these new interests lay rather in the fact that, without their support, the spearheads of the abolitionist movement would have achieved little. For, at the same time as the economic developments sketched above were taking place, a group of men generally known as humanitarians began to campaign against the slave trade and other forms of oppression in many parts of Europe and America. These men opposed the slave trade and gave their lives to its abolition not on economic grounds but because it caused too much human suffering. It was these men who never tired of collecting for publication stories of atrocities committed in the process of the trade. In their effort they were supported by churchmen who at about the same time developed a keen interest in the propagation of Christianity amongst Africans and Asians. Members of this group, known as the Evangelicals, opposed the slave trade mainly on religious grounds. They argued that slavery was evil because it contravened a divine law, according to which all men should be brothers and equal under the Fatherhood of the Almighty Creator.

It was these economic, humanitarian and evangelical arguments which, in the second half of the eighteenth century, combined to give rise to the British anti-slavery movement. The detailed story of the struggles and campaigns of the movement belongs properly to British domestic history. Only the outlines will be given here. The foremost leaders of the movement were Granville Sharp, Thomas Clarkson and William Wilberforce, the last being the representative and spokesman of the movement in the British Parliament for many years. Apart from these, however, there were other participants in the crusade whose roles have not yet been properly assessed or even widely recognized. Among this later group was a former Igbo slave, Olaudah Equiano, also known as Gustavus Vasa the African. Equiano (Ekwoanya?) who was born either at Essaka in mid-western Nigeria or at Isieke in eastern Nigeria, was kidnapped and sold into slavery early in the eighteenth century. After a most startling life of adventure and travel which took him to America, the West Indies, Europe and Turkey he purchased his freedom and settled in Britain. With the rise of the anti-slavery movement he plunged himself wholeheartedly into it.

Olaudah Equiano, the ex-slave who became prominent in the British anti-slavery movement

He organized public lectures at various centres in Britain in which he ventilated the evils of the slave trade and told the British public what rich material reward they could reap if they suppressed the slave trade and developed the natural resources of Africa. He embodied these ideas in his autobiography which he published in 1789. This book contained one of the earliest enunciations of the idea that only legitimate commerce, agriculture and Christianity could effectively destroy the slave trade.

The anti-slavers achieved their first success in 1772 when Granville Sharp brought a case about a runaway slave to an English court. In dealing with the case Chief Justice Mansfield declared that English law did not recognize slavery and that as soon as a slave set foot on English soil he became free. This decision had an important consequence for West Africa which will be dealt with later in this chapter. From this time the campaign grew in volume and intensity. After a long and hard struggle in and outside the British Parliament by Sharp and others a law was passed in 1807 which made the trade illegal for British subjects. After this the scene of the campaign shifted from Britain, where it had been carried out by means of public lectures, parliamentary lobbies and highly coloured pamphlets and newspaper articles, to West Africa, where these methods were replaced by naval force, diplomatic persuasion and pressures, legitimate commerce and missionary propaganda. All these methods, with the possible exception of the last, were interrelated, and the campaign in West Africa must be seen as a piece. Its outlines are bold and clear.

Until the later 1830s Britain concentrated her effort on getting other European nations and America to give up trading in slaves. She sought to achieve this by the use of diplomacy, and in addition a detachment of the Royal Navy (often called the West African, or the Preventive, Squadron) was stationed permanently in West Africa for the purpose of seizing slave ships. The two instruments of diplomacy and naval force were complementary. The British Foreign Office negotiated treaties banning the trade with nations which had not yet done so, while the Royal Navy enforced the terms of these treaties. In theory all those nations which either outlawed the slave trade completely or restricted the area in which it could be carried on by their nationals were expected to co-operate with Britain in capturing and bringing to justice those who continued the trade; but in practice it was only Britain that was both able and willing to assign a reasonable naval force to this patrol.

Since Britain was not at war with the other nations of Western Europe and America, her gunboats could not capture their slaving ships on the high seas without breaking international law. Hence the British Foreign Office took pains to negotiate treaties with the chief slave-trading nations which would give British warships the scope to do their duties without fear of creating international crises. Thus Britain persuaded France and Brazil to ban the trade for their nationals in 1815 and 1830 respectively although the ban was not at all seriously enforced until 1831. Meanwhile, Spain (1817) and Portugal (1819) were persuaded to restrict their slave-trading activities in Africa to areas south of the equator. Britain also negotiated Reciprocal Search Treaties with Spain (1817) and Portugal (1819), under which British warships could stop and search north of the equator any ship flying the flag of either of these two countries which was suspected of carrying slaves. Spain and Portugal enjoyed similar rights with regard to ships flying the British flag. If a ship was found to be carrying slaves it was seized and taken either to Sierra Leone or to some port in America where special courts known as Courts of Mixed Commission were established to deal with such activities. These were courts whose membership comprised judges from countries which had agreed by treaty to co-operate in this matter. In 1831 France signed a similar treaty.

Soon it was found that the Reciprocal Search Treaties did not give sufficient scope to the British Preventive Squadron to deal with slavers, because they contained the provision that only ships *actually carrying* slaves could be seized. But many ships were seen which, though not carrying slaves at the time, were certainly slaving ships since they carried equipment for the purpose. To make the naval patrol more effective the Foreign Office bent its energies to negotiating treaties which covered this loophole. This was the origin of the so-called Equipment Treaties which British negotiated with France in 1833, with Spain in 1835, and with Portugal in 1842, under which ships could be caught and condemned if they carried equipment used by slaving ships.

This method of fighting the slave trade by persuading or forcing Euro-

British anti-slavers attack a settlement of slave traders

pean and American nations to give it up did not prove very effective, as many of the nations were not prepared to co-operate with Britain. This was partly because they suspected that the British zeal was not entirely the result of humanitarian intentions but was also connected with a desire to promote her economic interests. Some of the nations were jealous of British naval power and feared that Britain would misuse rights granted her under the Reciprocal Search and the Equipment Treaties. The United States, for instance, refused to sign any of these treaties.

There were other reasons which helped to make the campaign ineffective. There were not enough gunboats in the Preventive Squadron. As mentioned above, Britain alone maintained a naval force of any consequence in West Africa, yet up to 1832 the British West African Squadron never had more than seven ships at a time; often it had less, and sometimes it had only two. Since these few ships had to watch the entire coast between Cape Verde and the equator it is not surprising that many slave ships escaped and that in this period more slaves were carried from West Africa annually than in any year before. It has in fact been suggested that not more than 25 per cent of the slavers were caught. Moreover not all the ships used in this strenuous watch were suitable. Some of them were old and rotten, while the class of ships known as frigates were not only too large and too slow but had the extra handicap that their masts were easily seen from long distances by slave ships, which naturally made good their escape. Also the ships which now engaged in slaving were built to suit the difficult times and were relatively fast.

There was only one place on the West African coast, Sierra Leone, where captured slavers could be sent for trial. This meant that even if a ship was caught at the southernmost end of West Africa, it had to be taken on a journey of nearly 3000 kilometres before it could reach the nearest place where it could be tried. What was worse, the members of the Courts of Mixed Commission did not always co-operate. The non-British members carried their national jealousies to the sittings of the Court, and their intrigues not only caused delays but often led to the acquittal of guilty ships.

African attitudes to abolition

The ineffectiveness of the methods used to stop the trade was to some extent the result of African opposition. It was not easy for West Africans to abandon overnight a trade which had lasted for so long that they had come to regard it as part of the normal way of life. The slave trade was accepted as part of their economic, social and even ritual life. The coastal peoples in particular had become so entirely dependent on the trade, had invested so much capital in it, that they could not abandon it without serious economic loss. Throughout West Africa the trade had come to be the normal means of getting rid of thieves, bankrupt debtors, witches and other undesirables; it was also the means of procuring the men and women who were used in satisfying some of the demands, for instance human sacrifice, of ritual life. In Dahomey it was the basis of economic life. The royal plantations depended on it and part of the army received its training in military tactics during the annual slave raids. Throughout West Africa slaves were also economically useful in the sense that they were used as currency, and by acting as carriers played a great part as a means of transport in an area that had no wheeled carriage. At the time of the abolition it was not easy to think of a ready economic substitute for the slave trade. The British talked of ivory, vegetable oil, timber, indigo and so on, but profitable trade in these needed time to develop. By the 1830s much of the coast of modern Nigeria had built up a viable substitute to the slave trade in the palm produce trade. The coast of Dahomey was soon to follow. But in other areas the story was different. In what later became Ghana the gold trade failed to expand and it was not until the 1880s that cocoa was introduced. And even then whatever promise it held as an item of profitable export still lay in the future. In the Senegambian region, the groundnut was to become an important item of legitimate trade but not before the active intervention of the French. One coastal chief, when persuaded to sell ivory in place of slaves, pointed out that slaves were easier to catch than the elephants from which ivory came.

African traders wondered what right the British had to dictate to them about their trading practices. Many simply refused to consider abolition, because the slave trade had become traditional in their society. In 1863 King Glele of Dahomey told Commodore E. Wilmot of the West African Squadron that slave trading was the custom of his ancestors. As a king, it was held, he could not break with custom without bringing disaster on his people. Much later, in the 1890s, the Aro of eastern Nigeria told a British political officer that they would not give up slave dealing because it was the custom of their fathers. There were other aspects of the problem. Those African chiefs who signed the treaties of abolition did so unwillingly rather than because they had suddenly become more enlightened than their fathers. So whenever they felt they could break the treaties and export slaves without being found out and punished, they did so gladly and very profitably. There were also the fact that the nineteenth century was a particularly turbulent one. There were, for instance, the great and small jihads of the Western and Central Sudan, the Yoruba wars and the Dahomean invasions of Yorubaland. These disturbances yielded a rich harvest of captives whom their captors were anxious to dispose of through sale.

African objections to abolition were strengthened by the activities of the Portuguese, Spaniards, Cubans, Brazilians and others. While the British told West Africans to abhor the slave trade and to patronize the oil trade, these others persuaded them to do the opposite. This was very confusing. Africans took the conflicting attitudes of the different European powers to mean that Britain was at war with the other nations of Europe and America, and as the quarrel did not concern them, African middlemen did not see why they should ruin their business by siding with Britain. Some of the coastal middlemen were able for a long time to ignore the menace of the British gunboats because of the nature of the coast along which they lived. On the coast of Nigeria, for instance, there is such a maze of creeks and water channels that, while gunboats watched one port closely, traders could ship their slaves through another which was quite unknown to the British. When, for instance, the British boats watched Bonny too closely Bonny men transferred their slaving business to Brass. For similar reasons the slave trade in the region which became modern Guinea (Conakry) proved particularly difficult to abolish.

Anti-slavery treaties

In the late 1830s, therefore, Britain was forced to re-examine and modify this method of fighting the slave trade. As a result of the reassessment the campaign was extended to the West African interior. First Britain signed slave trade treaties with a number of West African chiefs. Under this kind of treaty the African chief undertook to abolish the slave trade in his territory and to encourage trade in palm oil and the other products of the forest. In return he received annual subsidies from Britain for a fixed term of years. Britain reserved the right to say when the treaty was broken and to mete out punishment in consequence. Two chiefs of what is now Cameroon entered into this type of treaty with Britain in 1840 and 1842. In what is now Nigeria the Calabar villages of Creek Town and Duke Town made treaties in 1843, as did Bonny in 1848. The Bond, which bound Fante chiefs to abolish 'barbarous' customs, seems to come under the category of slave trade treaty (though this treaty will be discussed in detail later). Treaty-making as a means of fighting the slave trade was not limited to the coast. It became in fact a permanent feature of European strategy in West Africa throughout the nineteenth century.

By the 1840s the practice had penetrated the interior. The British 'civilizing mission' of 1841, for instance, concluded such a treaty with a prince as far inland as the Ata of Igala. One interesting revelation of these treaties is that the Africans who opposed the abolition were not necessarily morally bankrupt. On the contrary they were hard-headed businessmen whose concern was that there should be good business. Bonny's treaty with Britain came so late for a coastal state because over and over again Britain would not live up to the terms of the contract. Since this occasioned financial loss for Bonny she too over and over again ignored the treaty and revived the slave trade. Another illuminating example was the attitude of King Obi Ossai of Abo in 1841. This king did not need much persuasion to sign the treaty. His first request was that British men and ships should visit Abo in large numbers to buy Abo's natural produce. These treaties gave Britain the excuse to intervene in the affairs of many West African states, even in matters which lay beyond the scope of the treaty. As another way of dealing with the slave trade, British missionaries and legitimate traders decided to push into the interior, establish their posts there and cut the root of the slave trade by persuading Africans to embrace Christianity, legitimate commerce and agriculture. The details of this development will be given later.

The founding of Sierra Leone

Both in the short and long run the campaign against the slave trade had far-reaching consequences and significance for West Africa, Europe and America. The earliest and most tangible of the results was demographic. The enforced exodus of blacks from West Africa was checked. What was more, an attempt was made to reverse the migration through shipping former slaves from Europe and America back to West Africa. This did not happen to many, but it led to the foundation of first Sierra Leone and then Liberia. How this came about needs to be told in some detail, in view of the places which Sierra Leone and Liberia occupy in West African intellectual and political history.

For long it had been the practice of British planters in the West Indies who were going home to England either on leave or on retirement to take along with them their black domestic slaves. In this way by 1772 there were about 14 000 such slaves in Britain. When therefore Chief Justice Mansfield gave his celebrated decision in 1772 on the place of the slave and slavery under the English law and constitution all these men became free. Their owners, who were not happy with Mansfield's judgment, turned them out. Since these ex-slaves had not been previously prepared for emancipation they could not all fend for themselves effectively, with the result that many of them resorted to begging and thus became a nuisance in English society. Soon their state aroused the pity of the humanitarians who in 1786 formed the Committee for Relieving the Black Poor to organize the giving of alms to these destitute men. The Committee soon found that the numbers of those needing its help grew daily, and was forced to think of another way of tackling the problem. As early as 1783 Granville Sharp had thought of settling the 'Black Poor' somewhere along the coast of West Africa. Now his scheme was taken up seriously. Dr Henry Smeathman, who had once visited Sierra Leone, recommended it as suitable for such a settlement. As the Committee prepared for the venture the British government undertook to contribute towards the cost of the project at the rate of £14 for each settler. In February 1787 the first party, 411 in number, left the British Isles for West Africa, and arrived in Sierra Leone some time in May.

It proved very difficult to establish the settlement on a firm basis. To start with, the party got to Sierra Leone in the wet season, that is at a time when it was too late to start the planting of crops or the building of houses. Without good shelter and care, disease soon spread, and by March 1788 only about 130 of the 411 original settlers were alive. The others had died from fever. What was worse, the two coastal chiefs who had sold the settlers the land they occupied had done so without consulting their paramount ruler, Miambana, King of the Temne. The infant settlement now faced the rage of this king. The other European traders on the coast, especially members of the Royal African Company, were also hostile. Though Sharp sent a new party of settlers with fresh supplies in May 1788, the future of the settlement remained gloomy.

Sharp and his friends, who now realized that a new arrangement was needed if the colony was to survive, formed a company, first known as St George's Bay Company, to take over the affairs of Sierra Leone. By forming such a commercial company, Sharp and his friends hoped to persuade wealthy businessmen to invest in the project. To some extent they were successful. On receiving a charter from the British government the company was renamed the Sierra Leone Company. Somehow the affairs of the colony began to improve. In 1792 about 1200 former slaves, known as Nova Scotians, arrived to swell the population of the settlement. These men had sided with the British against the Americans in the American War of Independence. After the war the British had settled them in Nova Scotia in Canada where they found life very difficult and as a result applied for transfer to Sierra Leone. In 1800, 550 Maroons, a batch of ex-slaves who had been involved in a slave revolt in Jamaica in 1796 and had been sent to Nova Scotia, also arrived in Sierra Leone.

In spite of this growth in population the Sierra Leone Company failed to prosper and found the work of defending and administering the colony

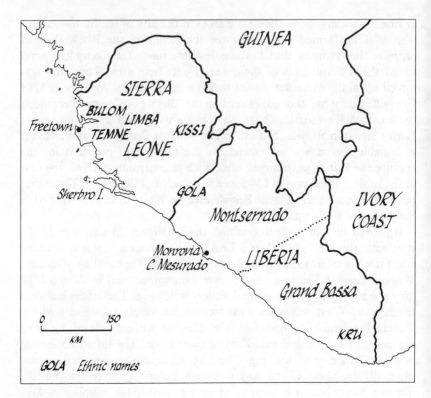

Sierra Leone and Liberia

beyond its resources. Revenue was restricted because the company did not engage in the slave trade, which was the only lucrative business at that time. Legitimate trade in which alone it was interested was only being pioneered, and was as yet unpopular with Africans and Europeans alike. The company therefore appealed to the British government to take over responsibility for the settlement. In 1807 Britain abolished the slave trade and committed herself to the difficult task of preventing other nations from continuing it. As she needed a naval base in West Africa from which to carry out the campaign, Sierra Leone, with its good natural harbour, was the obvious choice. As a result on 1 January 1808 Sierra Leone became the first British Crown Colony in West Africa. The same year a Vice-Admiralty Court was established in Freetown for the purpose of trying slave traders whose ships were seized by the Preventive Squadron. When later Britain persuaded Spain, Portugal and France to abolish the trade, a Court of Mixed Commission was established in Freetown to try ships of these nations caught carrying on the prohibited trade. Sierra

Leone benefited immensely from all this. Her population was greatly augmented since the slave cargoes of many of the arrested ships were liberated and settled there. In order to ensure that Sierra Leone's economy benefited from this rapid growth of population a Liberated Africans Department was established to do the work of settling the new arrivals either by apprenticing them to trade or by grouping them in villages to pursue agriculture.

The founding of Liberia

The successful issue of the Sierra Leone venture was to some extent responsible for the American experiment in settling free blacks on the portion of the West African coast now known as Liberia. In the early decades of the nineteenth century the United States faced problems which were in some ways similar to those which Britain faced as a result of Mansfield's famous judgment, but which were more acute. There were in the United States in 1800 about 200 000 free blacks. Some of these were people freed by masters who in course of time had become convinced that slavery was evil and contrary to the divine law, some were those who by their own hard work had purchased their freedom, some were those freed on the death of their masters, others were simply runaways. Many of the free blacks became small businessmen and were able to find honourable means of living; others lived by less honourable ways, including theft, not so much becaue they were lazy but because they could find no employment.

The existence of this large and growing community of free blacks presented a serious problem to the United States. It was thought, for example by Thomas Jefferson, that the best solution lay in settling the blacks somewhere, preferably outside the United States. This view was shared by the large section of the community which still owned slaves, and argued that free blacks were a nuisance in society because they endangered the institution of slavery. Especially in the Southern states, laws were passed designed either to make it impossible for more blacks to become free or to force those already free to return to slavery. The Northern states, most of which had emancipated their slaves, feared that the free blacks in the South would flock into their territories, and so passed laws to prevent this.

About this time there arose in the United States a movement which was both humanitarian and evangelical, and which aimed at helping the poor and oppressed and at applying Christian principles to social life. The members of this movement, out of sympathy, came to favour the idea of transporting the free blacks back to Africa. This step, they hoped, would save the blacks the humiliation and degradation they suffered in America, while enabling them to be the instrument by which 'civilization' and Christianity would spread to the 'darkest' parts of Africa.

It was these different groups of people who in 1816 formed the American Society for Colonizing the Free People of Color of the United States, more popularly known as the American Colonization Society. In 1818 this society sent Samuel J. Mills and Ebenezer Burgess to Sierra Leone to survey the possibilities of carrying out its intentions. These men picked on Sherbro Island about 50 kilometres south of Sierra Leone. It was here that the first party of 88 landed in 1820. It was soon found that the site was very unhealthy for within a short space of time 22 of the settlers died. The remaining 66 ran to Sierra Leone in panic. When the second batch of settlers arrived in 1821 they took local advice and moved lower down the coast to Cape Mesurado where they secured a piece of land from the local chiefs and founded a settlement in 1822. A few months after this another batch of 55 settlers arrived under Jehud Ashmun, who was to prove himself the real founder of Liberia. One General Harper now suggested the name Liberia (Land of the Free) for the settlement, and Monrovia, after President Monroe of the United States, as the name of the capital city.

When the settlers first arrived the local chiefs, not knowing that they had come to settle permanently, welcomed them enthusiastically. When these chiefs discovered their mistake they became hostile and sought to wipe out the settlement, partly because it interfered with their slave-dealing activities and partly because the settlers adopted an irritating and superior attitude towards the established people. The Spaniards and Cubans urged the local chiefs on, and even helped to provide them with the arms and ammunition with which to attack the colony. The stability and progress of the colony was also threatened by the fact that many settlers refused to undertake agriculture. They preferred trade which yielded quick profits and they spent these profits on foreign goods. The economy of the country was thus unstable.

Though Liberia was many years younger than Sierra Leone its political development was more rapid. This was largely because the United States government was not prepared to carry the burden of administering Liberia and so did not interfere, while the American Colonization Society, which was responsible for the welfare of the settlement, was also liberal. The officials of the colony were white men up to 1841, after which blacks took over. In 1828 the elective principle was introduced. In 1830 the *Liberia Herald* was published and it remained for 25 years the only newspaper in West Africa. In 1838 Liberia was divided into two counties, Montserrado and Grand Bassa, each of which had a national council of ten elected members who, with two officials called the Agent and the Vice-Agent, formed its governing authority.

All this while, the authorities of Sierra Leone remained hostile to Liberia and their hostility was one of the factors which forced the infant settlement to declare its independence rather prematurely. By 1830 Liberia laid claim to about 500 kilometres of the coast, most portions of which were hardly populated. But European traders and the authorities of Sierra Leone who made fun of the idea of a black government refused to recognize Liberia's claims to the whole of the area, or her right to levy harbour and customs duties at any point of it. Liberia's attempt in 1845 to collect customs dues from an English trader, Captain Davidson of Sierra Leone, only provided an occasion for humiliation, for the Sierra Leone government sent Commander Jones of the West African Squadron to seize from a Liberian port a vessel belonging to a Liberian subject. The United States government was not prepared to take up the case of Liberia with Britain, or with any other power. The American Colonization Society was powerless to assist and so advised Liberia to declare her independence in order to ensure recognition as a sovereign nation. In June 1847 the Liberian authorities summoned a constitutional convention and on 26 July of the same year proclaimed Liberia a sovereign republic with a constitution modelled on that of the United States.

Economic consequences of abolition

The suppression of the slave trade also brought about an economic revolution in West Africa, a revolution which not all the former participants in the coastal trade – European and African – could survive. The slave traders who had invested heavily in the business by way of equipment suffered heavily. True, these men were already familiar with the techniques and tricks of business in West Africa, and some of them had also accumulated capital, but the transition from slave running to legitimate commerce was painful and profits at first were low and uncertain. The changeover estranged former friends. The arrangements for the trade throughout the period of the slave trade recognized and respected the position of the middlemen. But the rise of legitimate trade demanded a new arrangement which would enable the Europeans to penetrate the interior. The Europeans wanted to go inland partly to increase their profit margin and partly to establish collecting centres for produce which were more efficient than those existing along the coast. In the event a war ensued between the middlemen and the European merchants. By the time the conflict died down the middlemen had lost their pre-1800 privileged position. For those communities along the coast this loss of economic position also meant loss of political stability. The history of the trading states of the Oil Rivers in the second half of the nineteenth century provides the best illustration of the truth of the above analysis. There the House system which had served the needs of the slave trade largely went down with that trade.

European exploration and penetration

During the last two decades of the eighteenth century European interest in West Africa began shifting from the coast to the interior. Explorers sent out by private European organizations and governments made determined attempts to penetrate and explore inland. The earliest attempts in this direction were dictated perhaps more by scientific than by commercial interests. The eighteenth century witnessed the exploration of the interior of many continents and countries. For instance southern Asia, the basin of the Amazon and the interior of Australia were all explored in this period. In view of this progress being made in the exploration of other parts of the globe, some scientifically minded men in Europe felt that their prevailing ignorance of the interior of Africa was a challenge. They wanted to know more about Africa's river systems, especially about the course of the Niger, about Africa's botany and natural history, about its peoples and their ways of life.

But there was also an economic motive for the enterprise even from the beginning, and as the business of exploration progressed this motive acquired greater importance and even came to overshadow all others. One of the results of the Industrial Revolution, as already noted, was Europe's pressing need both for new markets and for raw materials. For Britain in particular, which took the lead in exploring the African interior, this need became more pressing after the loss of America in 1783. In fact it was only five years after this event that the African Association, which at first led the movement for exploration, was founded. It is also significant that the Association, though a scientific organization, was not slow to call the attention of British businessmen to the economic promises held out by its discoveries.

The third important factor partly responsible for this growing interest in the interior of Africa was the movement for the abolition of the slave trade. This did not influence the promoters of African exploration until after the second decade of the nineteenth century. Before that time Britain, as already shown, had thought that her plan to abolish the slave trade could be achieved through naval patrols off the coast of West Africa and diplomatic negotiations in the courts of European nations and America. But experience later showed that this hope was exaggerated. It was only then that a number of far-seeing men, the first of whom was James McQueen, started to argue that the only way to abolish the trade effectively was to persuade Africans to turn from it to agriculture and legitimate commerce. Since it was believed that Africans could not do this by themselves, it was urged that European traders, agriculturalists and missionaries should penetrate the interior and teach the people how to earn a living by exploiting the natural produce of their country. For many years McQueen was a lone voice crying in the wilderness. Though he advocated this policy in the book *A Geographical and Commercial View of Northern and Central Africa*, published in 1821, it was not until 1841 that the first really organized attempt was made to carry out the programme.

British penetration

The exploration of the West African interior was the affair of the few private individuals who formed the African Association before it became a government-sponsored enterprise. The Association was formed on 9 June 1788 and with that the European drive to penetrate the interior of West Africa could be said to have begun in earnest. Between 1788 and 1805 the Association sponsored all the British exploratory missions into the interior. There were six of these. Then the British government stepped in and took the lead. The African Association had taken time to publicize the successes of its agents and to advertise the possibilities for profitable trade in the Western Sudan which these agents had found. This propaganda captivated the commercial and industrial classes who were becoming progressively influential in British politics and public life. If the mouth of the Niger, for instance, were to be discovered, it was argued that British commerce would have a highway into the Western Sudan. Also about 1800 it came to be known that the French were showing serious interest in the region of the Senegal. This caused some concern; if Britain did not act fast enough the French would reap the benefits of the labours of the African Association. In the light of these new developments it became clear that the work of African exploration was too weighty an issue to be left in the hands of private men who had no authority to act on behalf of the nation.

The problem of exploring West Africa was tackled from two main directions, from the west coast and from North Africa, especially Tripoli. The first and second attempts were made from Cairo and Tripoli respectively. When penetration from here seemed to hold no promise whatever,

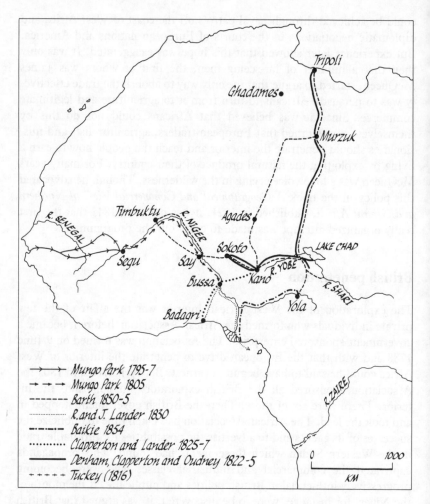

European exploration of West Africa

both explorers having died before they reached the Sahara, Britain decided to use the southern approach through the coast. In a sense this seemed the natural route of approach. British business here was already about three centuries old and there was no single barrier as great as the Sahara to be encountered from the south. What was more, British business along the coast was already immense and it would not be difficult to organize trade after initial exploration, since what was already established could be extended. However, it soon became clear that the southern approach could easily turn out to be the graveyard of British explorers.

The leaders of the three expeditions sent out between 1805 and 1816 died, and this loss of life led Britain to the conclusion that the west coast was not the best base from which to explore the Sudan.

Once again attention turned to Tripoli in the north, which now showed promises of providing the long-sought-for gateway to the Sudan. For one thing, Tripoli stood at the narrowest crossing of the Sahara. Secondly, Tripoli now had an able and energetic ruler, Yusuf Karamanli, who had established peace in the interior. Furthermore, this prince was on good terms with Shaikh Muhammad al-Kanemi of Borno and Sultan Muhammad Bello of Sokoto, the two men who controlled the southern half of the route from Tripoli to the Sudan. Karamanli could thus guarantee safe conduct to all travellers crossing the Sahara with his consent. Though the attempt to use this route in 1819 failed, the leader of the expedition having died at Murzuk, the next attempt in 1821 was a success. The explorers reached the Sudan, and of the three members only one died. But the expedition which followed this failed, the leader, Major Gordon Laing, dying in circumstances which caused estrangement between Britain and Tripoli. In consequence, attention shifted to the Niger waterway, whose mouth had been discovered in 1830, but this route soon proved as treacherous. Two expeditions which sought to use it in 1821 and 1841 suffered severe loss of human life.

Britain once more turned her attention to the northern route which had meanwhile come under the control of friendly Turkey. The preparations she made for return to this route gave the impression that, if things went well, the route would be in use for a long time. For instance she established a vice-consulate at Murzuk in 1840, and another at Ghadames in 1847, which soon became centres for spreading British influence and acquainting the people with British goods. Then in 1854 the Central African Mission was sent to open up a secure way of communication with the interior of West Africa across the Sahara. But this expedition, which held out so much hope and promise, sealed the fate of the northern route. Two-thirds of its members died, while a supplementary expedition sent to help it lost four of its five members. There were also other factors which helped to resolve the choice between the northern and southern approaches in favour of the latter. Dr William Balfour Baikie, leading a government expedition up the Niger in 1854, showed that the dangers posed by malaria on the southern route could be effectively met by using quinine as a prophylactic. Furthermore, as the southern route became more frequented, more European goods got to the Central Sudanese empires – Nupe, the Hausa cities and Borno – from the south. This meant that much of the trade which hitherto travelled between Hausaland and North Africa via the Sahara was diverted to the south. The rivalry between the northern and southern approaches was to some extent another side to the old rivalry between the trans-Saharan trade and the Atlantic commerce. By resolving it in favour of the southern approach the British achieved what the Portuguese had aspired to long before but failed to achieve.

The list of West Africa's explorers and would-be explorers is long and impressive. It is headed by John Ledyard who sought to penetrate through Cairo but died before he could leave the ancient city. He was followed by Simon Lucas who made the first attempt to use the route through Tripoli but had to abandon the idea owing to the disturbed political situation in southern Tripoli. The third on the list was Major Daniel Houghton who, starting from The Gambia, explored the region of modern Senegal and Mali and then disappeared without trace. More famous are Mungo Park, Walter Oudney, Hugh Clapperton, Major Dixon Denham, Major Gordon Laing, Richard and John Lander, James Richardson, Dr Heinrich Barth and Dr Adolph Overweg.

The first major success in the exploration of West Africa was achieved with Mungo Park's first journey which was sponsored by the African Association. He was charged with finding the course and if possible the termination of the Niger, about which there was great ignorance in Europe at the time. One theory about the Niger, for instance, maintained that this great river rose in the east, flowed to the west and entered the Atlantic as

Mungo Park (1771–1806), the Scottish explorer of the upper and middle Niger

three rivers. It was also hoped that Park might get to Timbuktu, about which Europe had heard so much but knew nothing that was reliable.

Leaving England in May 1795 Park entered West Africa through The Gambia and reached the Niger at Segu in July 1796. His plans to move further down the river could not be implemented, partly because a state of war existed between the Bambara states of Segu and Kaarta, partly because his resources were running short, and partly because the rainy season was getting more severe. He therefore went back to England in 1796 with reports of his travel which excited so much public interest that in 1805 the British government sent him back to Africa. Park got to Segu from where he set out down the Niger and to his death. Later reports revealed that he perished at the Bussa rapids. Park's travels were a landmark in the history of West African exploration in the sense that he was the first European in centuries to set eyes on the Niger and thus establish beyond any dispute that the river existed. His testimony that the Niger flowed west to east disposed of the earlier belief that it flowed in the reverse direction. But it also created a new complication. Some armchair geographers speculated, on the basis of this, that the Niger joined the Nile somewhere, or disappeared into an inland sea in the desert.

The other great landmark in West African exploration was the discovery of the estuary of the Niger by Richard Lander. Lander had been introduced to the field of West African exploration by Captain Hugh Clapperton, who had been a member of the expedition also comprising Walter Oudney and Dixon Denham which for the first time, in 1821, showed that the northern gateway through Tripoli was a possible route into the Sudan. When sent back to Africa to follow up the results of this expedition Clapperton took Lander as his personal servant. This expedition had not only failed but had also seen the death of Clapperton. Lander got back to Europe only to be sent back by the British government to complete his master's half-finished assignment. Taking his brother John with him, Lander first got to Bussa by land and then, travelling down the Niger, emerged into the Atlantic through the river Nun in the Oil Rivers. The Landers thus solved the puzzling geographical problem of the course and termination of the Niger.

The significance of these journeys was mainly twofold. The first was scientific. Europe came to know more about the geography and topography of the interior of West Africa than she did before 1800. For instance, the sources of West Africa's main rivers as well as the estuary of the Niger were discovered. The explorers brought back much useful and detailed information on the peoples of the region they visited, on their commerce and civilization as well as on the flora and fauna of the interior. The explorers' narratives, especially Heinrich Barth's five volume *Travels and*

A Kanembu spearman from an engraving by Major Dixon Denham. This is a detailed drawing typical of those that nineteenth-century explorers made on their travels, before the invention of photography

Discoveries in North and Central Africa, constitute a rich source of information on the geography, history, languages and peoples of the Western Sudan.

The second importance of these journeys was economic. The explorers painted an attractive picture of the opportunities which existed in the Sudan for profitable business. To the mercantile interests in Britain this was perhaps more important than the scientific information brought home by the explorers. Thus each major advance in the exploration of the interior was followed up with grandiose schemes and plans for the introduction of British commerce. The best illustration of this point was the reaction of the British business class to the discovery of the mouth of the Niger by the Landers. They considered it, and rightly, as opening a highway for British commerce into the interior and immediately set about exploiting it. A Scottish merchant, MacGregor Laird, led the formation of the African Inland Commercial Company, which declared that its purpose was to penetrate the interior and establish a commercial depot at the confluence of the Niger and Benue, as a centre for collecting the produce of the Sudan. The first expedition of the company left in July 1832 under Richard Lander, but the project failed hopelessly. Many of the members, including Lander, died from malaria. The African Inland Commercial Company wound up in 1834. For about six years after that only individuals like John Beecroft and Robert Jamieson attempted to trade up the Niger, but they did not actually go beyond the Oil Rivers. This was not the end of organized attempts at the commercial exploitation of the discoveries of the explorers. In fact the drive received further justification from humanitarian impulses.

By the 1830s it had become abundantly clear that diplomacy and naval blockade were not enough as measures against the slave trade. What was more, the bid to reach the Sudan through the northern gateway had brought the British face to face with the internal slave trade from the Sudan to North Africa. In consequence of this the humanitarians, now led by Thomas Fowell Buxton, the author of *The African Slave Trade and Its Remedy* (1839), started pressing for the implementation of the programme which McQueen had put forward in the early 1820s. In 1841 an expedition directed towards the attainment of these two purposes – the commercial exploitation of the interior and the supplanting of the slave trade with legitimate commerce backed by agriculture and Christianity – was organized on a large scale by the British government and sent up the Niger. This also turned out to be a failure. About fifty of the Britons who took part in it died within three months and the expedition had to be abandoned.

But the attempt continued. The British were not to be cheated of the profits of their labours by a capricious climate. The next organized attempt to tap the resources of the Niger was made in 1854. In that year a goverment expedition under Baikie was sent up the Niger. This expedition eventually became famous for two achievements. Firstly, through the use of quinine as a prophylactic, Baikie was able to prevent the loss of even a single life among the members of his party. This expedition thus turned out to be the first up the Niger during which nobody died. Secondly, the *Pleiad* the ship in which the expedition was made, navigated the Niger without great difficulty. This showed that the technical problems connected with navigating the Niger were being satisfactorily met.

In 1857 the British government entered into a five-year contract with Laird under which it agreed to pay him an annual subsidy in return for his maintaining a steamer service on the Niger. Between 1857 and 1859 Laird and his agents established trading stations at Abo, Onitsha and Lokoja on the Niger. From now on European enterprise and influence started to penetrate the various sections of our region of study.

French penetration

Though they certainly dominated hinterland exploration, it was not the British alone who were active at this time in the business of exploring the West African interior and exploiting its resources. France, Britain's great rival in West Africa from the eighteenth century, not only played some part in the exploration, but was also concerned with tapping the resources of the interior from the Senegal, the other important waterway of West Africa. In the field of West African discovery France's two most distinguished travellers were G. Mollien and René Caillié. Mollien discovered the sources of the Gambia, the Rio Grande and the Senegal in 1818, while Caillié was, perhaps, the first European to reach Timbuktu and return alive to relate his experiences. In many British circles, however, it was believed that Caillié did not enter Timbuktu but had merely stolen the journals of the English explorer, Major Gordon Laing, who reached Timbuktu but later died in the Sahara.

With regard to exploiting the resources of the interior the French concentrated their activities on the Senegal, where their interests had been dominant since 1659 when an agent of the Compagnie Normande established the city now known as Saint Louis. A little later, in 1672, a French admiral drove the Dutch from Gorée, while another chartered company, the Compagnie du Sénégal, occupied such coastal towns as Rufisque and Joal. In 1818 the French returned to the posts on the Senegal from which they had been expelled by the British in the course of the Revolutionary and Napoleonic wars. As part of the attempt of the restored Bourbons to strengthen the economy of France they conceived a grand programme of establishing on the Senegal large plantations of tropical crops like groundnuts, cotton and indigo. To this end they appointed Colonel Schmaltz as governor. The experiment, however, proved a failure owing to hostile climate, lack of labour, poor soil and indigenous opposition.

Still the attempt continued. The French obtained land from the Walo kingdom in return for an annual subsidy. On this land they established experimental farms and gardens under the charge of experts specially sent out from France. But this again ran into trouble. The Traza branch of the Moors, who inhabited the right bank of the Senegal, claimed that the Walo had no right to the land they leased to the French and so ravaged the plantations and drove off the planters. Also the problem of labour remained unsolved. At one time the French government thought of an arrangement with the Spanish government under which the latter would send labour from the Canary Islands. But this plan was soon dropped and about 220 black prisoners were sent down from Martinique (a French island in the West Indies) to work on the farms. Indigenous Senegalese prisoners were also made to work there. Still the labour was not enough. Attempts to raise free labour failed. Meanwhile the Traza continued to ravage the farms. The French attempt to punish them only led to the further destruction of the farms. Disillusioned, the French abandoned the dream of flourishing tropical plantations on the lines of the Dutch Indies and turned to commerce.

Nor did this flourish. For many years the only profitable trade was that in guns. French penetration of the interior was made hazardous by the Traza who through a system of alliances with the African peoples ringed the French colony with a hostile combination. The rise of al-Hajj Umar in the 1840s made the penetration of the interior even more difficult. Moreover there was the fear that Umar would soon issue a call to all Muslims to take up arms against the French 'infidels'. This, it was felt, would make the French position even more untenable. Governor Bouët-Willaumez (1844) advocated the use of force to solve the problem of interior penetration, but since the French treasury had no money for this the home government did not support him. French presence on the Senegal remained precarious and economically unrewarding until the appointment of Louis Faidherbe as governor in 1854.

Faidherbe turned out to be a very able soldier and administrator as well as a clear-headed diplomat. His first period as governor of the colony (1854–61) transformed its history and brightened its prospects. On his arrival he started a number of public works, and founded the Ecole des Otages for the training of interpreters and French emissaries into the interior. By means of military demonstrations on the river he firmly established French prestige. In 1855 he brought the Walo kingdom under direct French control, while in 1858 he defeated the Traza and forced them to cease their molestation of French traders in the interior. To open up the overland route connecting Dakar and Saint Louis he intervened in the politics of the state of Cayor and deposed the Damel in 1861. To defend the colony and offer effective protection to French traders he built forts at Medina, Joal and Kaolack.

Towards al-Hajj Umar he adopted a wise policy. He was not, like many of his contemporaries, full of blind prejudice against Muslims, perhaps owing to his wider experience with Muslims in Algeria. Therefore he was not prepared to blame Umar for every indiscretion committed by his over-zealous supporters and admirers on the Senegal, who at times acted without his direction. All the same he was not opposed to showing Umar that French enmity could be dangerous. Thus when his garrison at Fort Medina was attacked by Umar's forces he first relieved it by force before talking of negotiation. Faidherbe knew he had not the forces to pursue a policy of confrontation against Umar and so did not seek to follow up his victory. He was also lucky that at the time Umar's eyes were fixed on Segu and Macina. In 1860 the two reached a peaceful settlement delimiting their frontiers. Faidherbe left Senegal in 1861, the most successful administrator the colony had so far had. He came back a second time (1863–5) but with less dramatic results. Thanks to his achievements Senegal became the base for French advance into West Africa.

African reactions to European penetration

What, one is bound to ask, was the reaction of Africans to this growing European invasion of their fatherland? What the common people thought about this we do not know, but the vested interests in traditional African society were plainly hostile. A few examples can easily be given. During his second expedition Mungo Park got into Segu with an odd assortment of goods. He displayed these in a small shop and sold them at great profit. In doing this he aroused the hostility of the Mandingo traders from Jenne and of the Moors who had hitherto monopolized all the trade here. They decided to make things difficult for Park, and even tried to bribe the authorities to kill him.

The same attitude was typical of the middlemen traders in the Oil Rivers. Part of the difficulties which wrecked the 1832 expedition of the African Inland Commercial Company was the opposition of these men. They wanted to protect their position by preventing direct European trade in the interior, and the Liverpool merchants who had long been established on the coast joined the African middlemen in opposition to their fellow Europeans. They feared that if the trade shifted to the interior they would sustain heavy losses in consequence of their having already spent much money in equipping themselves for the coastal trade.

African rulers were generally enlightened and friendly in their attitude to the explorers. Park's journals record the hospitality and readiness to help displayed by the chiefs of the territories through which he passed. The king of Segu, for instance, was deeply impressed by Park's arguments on the advantages of establishing direct trade with Europe. In spite of the hostility of the traders in his territory he was prepared to give Park an escort. Clapperton's relations with Sultan Muhammad Bello of Sokoto and Muhammad al-Kanemi of Borno on his first mission tell the same story. But the chiefs, concerned with the safety and peace of their territories, were also suspicious and on their guard against the intruders. The attitude of Bello was a case in point. When Clapperton on his first journey talked of the advantages of European traders coming to trade directly within the caliphate, Bello warned him against 'big capitalists'. On his second mission Clapperton came at an inauspicious time, when relations between the Sokoto and Borno empires had worsened. Without knowing of this changed relationship Clapperton included in his gifts for al-Kanemi guns and pistols. Bello confiscated these weapons on seeing them and forbade Clapperton and Lander to go to Borno. Bello's first duty was to protect the caliphate which he had inherited from his father Usman dan Fodio.

The coming of the Christian missions

At the beginning, European interest in West Africa was not only commercial, it also had a missionary motive. This was particularly true of the Portuguese who in the fifteenth and sixteenth centuries attempted to introduce Catholic Christianity into the Senegambian region, Sierra Leone, Benin City and Warri. However this missionary aspect of European interest was soon blighted by the slave trade. With the onset of this traffic in human beings, slave traders not only maintained that Africans were such inferior beings that their miserable position in life would not be bettered by admission into the Christian fold, but also opposed any attempt by missionaries to convert Africans along the West Coast. Although in 1800 there were European priests in many of the coastal forts, they were there to cater for the souls of the European agents, and to carry out a meaningless baptism of African slaves before shipment. In places like Benin City and Warri what remained of the earlier attempts at planting Christianity were memories preserved in oral traditions, the motif of the cross which had been adopted by indigenous artists, and ruined temples.

In the nineteenth century the attempt to Christianize West Africans was revived, first by Protestant missions and then by Roman Catholics. The Evangelical Movement which had supported the abolition of the slave trade and slavery also took steps to introduce the Christian message to the non-Christians of Asia and Africa. The first missionary society to arise out of this movement was the Baptist Missionary Society, founded in 1792 by William Carey. Others followed: the London Missionary Society (1795), the Glasgow Missionary Society (1796), the Church Missionary Society (1799), the British and Foreign Bible Society (1804), and the General Missionary Society of the Methodists (1818). The movement was not limited to Britain. Societies were being founded at the same time in America and Europe. In the United States the American Board of Commissioners for Foreign Missions was founded in 1810 and the General Missionary Convention of the Baptist Denomination in 1814. On the European continent the Netherlands Missionary Society was founded in

1797 and the Basel Missionary Society in 1815. Catholic missionary societies came much later. Among the earliest was the branch of the Society for the Propagation of the Faith founded in Lyons (France) in 1822. Fifteen years later the missionary society of the Holy Ghost Fathers was founded in Paris, then came the Society of African Missions founded by Father de Bressilac in 1856.

Before the end of the eighteenth century British missionary societies, led by the Baptists, began work in West Africa, starting with Sierra Leone; but by 1800 none of these missions had a solid outpost in West Africa. The real beginning of the new missionary effort in West Africa can be taken to be 1806 when the Church Missionary Society (CMS) was established in Sierra Leone. From then on mission stations grew apace along the coast. By 1853 the CMS had other stations at Abeokuta (1844), Lagos (1851), and Ibadan (1853); the Wesleyan Methodist Missionary Society at Sierra Leone (1811), in the Fante states (1833) and at Abeokuta (1844); the Basel Missionary Society among the Fante (1827); the Church of Scotland Mission at Calabar (1846) and the Bremen Society among the Ewe of Ghana (1847). The American missions, also led by the Baptists, concentrated on Liberia.

For many decades and for a variety of reasons missionary enterprise in most of West Africa was limited to the coast. Until the discovery made in the 1850s that quinine could be used in preventing malaria, the missionaries, like other European visitors to the coast of West Africa, died in large numbers, with the result that there was a perpetual shortage of the qualified men needed for expansion inland. The tendency therefore was to concentrate on the coast. Also, African rulers and elders in the interior, unlike their counterparts along the coast, often proved very hostile to the new religion. It was only after they had been forcibly brought under European rule that they were compelled to allow missionaries a free hand in their territories.

In Sierra Leone the missionaries had more than enough to do as a result of the continued addition to the population of the colony of thousands of liberated slaves who needed conversion and education. In Liberia the hostility, open or veiled, between the Americanized settlers and their indigenous neighbours in the interior was an obstacle to the spread of the influence of the missions beyond the boundaries of the republic. On the coast of Ghana the incessant war between the Asante and the British made it unsafe for missionaries to venture inland, though it must be mentioned that Thomas Birch Freeman, who was half-black West Indian and half-European, opened a Wesleyan outpost at Kumasi in 1839. The reputation of Dahomey for barbarism and bloodthirstiness, whether merited or not, warned missionary intruders off her interior for a long time.

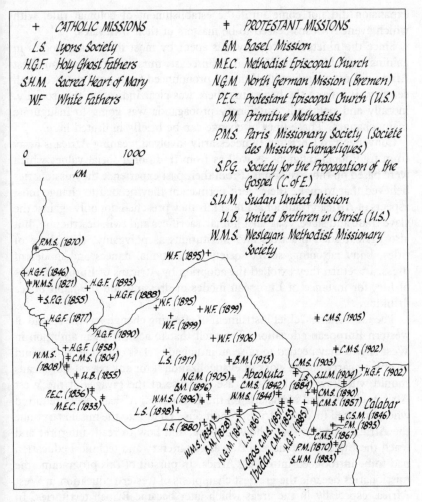

The spread of missionary activities in West Africa

In Yorubaland, where by 1853 the CMS had gone as far as Ibadan, about 150 kilometres from Lagos, the situation was different. The rivalry among the states which emerged after the collapse of Oyo in 1830 made many Yoruba states willing to accept any group of Europeans, traders or missionaries, as each state hoped to strengthen itself through alliance with Europeans who brought the guns it needed for war. The Egba found the CMS missionaries who settled amongst them a great asset in their wars with Dahomey. Otherwise indigenous opposition to missionary activity was the rule in the interior. As a result the great age of missionary expansion did not come until the establishment of colonial rule, with which event Africans ceased to be masters of their own fates.

Since the nineteenth century was spent by most missionary bodies in gaining toeholds on the West African coast, missionary impact on West Africa did not manifest itself in any pronounced form until the twentieth century. But from the beginning there was clear indication that socially, morally and politically missionary propaganda was going to inaugurate many changes. These lines of change can be briefly indicated here.

Conversion to Christianity necessarily involved weaning Africans away from traditional religions as well as from traditional social values which were based on those religions. From their past experience the missionaries believed that to make their work permanent they needed to change most aspects of African traditional life. Thus they preached not only against the slave trade and slavery, against human sacrifices and twin destruction, but also against such practices and institutions as polygamy, the taking of titles, body tattooing, secret societies, traditional dances and modes of dress. In return they extolled the adoption by Africans of European ways of life, for instance of European modes of dressing and the habit of tea drinking.

The missionaries' chief instrument of effecting change was the spread of western European education. They felt that to achieve their ambition in West Africa they needed to raise an indigenous class of people who would be able to carry on the work of evangelization if for any reason Europeans should withdraw. And in any case, because of the ravages of the West African climate and of malaria on the Europeans, Africans were required who were used to West African conditions. To fit into the missionary shoe the Africans had to know how to write, and how to read, interpret and teach the Bible. To achieve this, western literary and technical education had to be introduced into West Africa. In pursuit of this programme the missionaries became the greatest champions of western education in West Africa, especially in the areas which later became British territories. In Sierra Leone, for instance, by 1861 the CMS already had 21 elementary schools. During the following four yearss it founded a secondary school for boys and another for girls. The Fourah Bay College, now the University of Sierra Leone, was founded by the same missionary body in 1829. The other missionary bodies were not as energetic as the CMS in this period, but they all contributed towards the establishment of educational institutions in West Africa. Moreover, since the missions were confined to the coastal areas until much later, the impact of the education they provided was felt most in Lagos, Accra, Freetown, Bathurst (now Banjul) and like places.

The missionaries also initiated the scientific and systematic study of

West African languages and gave most of them a written form. The missionaries needed a thorough knowledge of the languages of West African peoples in order to approach them directly instead of through interpreters, and also in order to translate the Bible or sections of it into vernacular languages for the use of the people. The missionary study of West African languages was born in Sierra Leone between 1830 and 1832 when the CMS Missionary, Rev. J.T. Raban, began a study of Yoruba with a view to effectively reaching the increasing Yoruba population of the colony. When the 'civilizing mission' of 1841 was being projected the study of Nigerian languages was intensified under Rev. J.F. Schon in order to raise interpreters. From these small beginnings the study of indigenous West African languages had made rapid progress by 1862. By that year many primers, dictionaries and grammars of indigenous languages had been produced by the missionaries. Rev. S.W. Koelle produced in 1854 a *Grammar of the Bornu or Kanuri Language* and *African Narrative Literature in Kanuri*; Schon published a *Hausa Primer* in 1857 and his *Grammar of the Hausa Language* in 1862. In the latter year also the Rev. Hugh Goldie of the Presbyterian Mission produced his *Principles of Efik Grammar and Specimens of the Language*. In the years that followed the missionaries not only deepened and broadened their achievements in the fields indicated above, but also extended their services to providing such social amenities as hospitals and maternity homes.

The African educated élite

As a result of this spread of education there arose in West Africa a new class of people generally called the western-educated élite. They came to occupy leading positions in West Africa because they could read and write, and had learnt many of the ideas and techniques which were responsible for the progress of Europe in the nineteenth century. These people dressed in a new way, thought in a new way, and led their people when it came to dealing with white men. The missionaries and other Europeans expected them to spread western civilization, western commerce and western Christianity among their people. For many years members of this class believed that they and the missionaries and European traders were all pursuing the same goals in West Africa, that is promoting progress and spreading civilization. It soon became evident, however, that many Europeans who came to West Africa were concerned more with their own gain than with serving West Africans. It shocked many educated Africans to discover that there were even missionaries who were sometimes ready to help those who wanted to deprive West Africans of their independence. With this discovery relations between the educated Africans and Europeans soon turned into mutual hostility.

The beginning of this quarrel could be seen in the politics of Sierra Leone in the 1850s. Sierra Leone, like Liberia, produced many members of this new élite; in fact it was from there that many of them spread to Ghana and Nigeria. In Lagos in the 1860s nearly all the members of this class came from Sierra Leone. Most of them were freed Yoruba slaves who, after their stay in Sierra Leone, started, from about 1839 onwards, to go back to the land of their birth. In the 1850s the educated class in Sierra Leone were disappointed by British unwillingness to introduce representative government into the colony, though the British themselves enjoyed parliamentary government at home. These educated Sierra Leoneans became all the more discontented when they compared what was happening in the colony with what was happening in Liberia, where the people governed themselves. They therefore started to attack the Crown Colony system of government which was imposed on them. In 1853 they formed the Sierra Leone Committee of Correspondence to ask for more political rights and for a change in the existing situation. Here we can see that, from the beginning of the quarrel between the new élite and the Europeans, the former adopted the method of grouping themselves together which in later years led to the growth of the highly organized political parties which helped to bring an end to European rule in West Africa.

One other consequence of the introduction into West Africa of western Christianity with its hallmark of literacy in the Roman script, remains to be mentioned. This was the rift it caused in African communities. Mention has already been made of the rise of a new élite who became the rivals of the traditional élites of chiefs, priests, diviners, artists and the like for the leadership of society. In those societies where European rule at the local level later took the form of indirect rule, this rivalry was to loom large, at times becoming bitter in tone. This was all the more the case as the first converts to Christianity, and therefore the first members of the new élite were usually ex-slaves, or in any case from the underprivileged sections of society.

There was another side to this tendency for Christianity to introduce or reinforce divisions within African society and thus weaken African resistance to alien invasion. From purely accidental and historical and logistical reasons, Christianity sought to penetrate West Africa from the coast. Consequently it achieved its greatest success in the southern forest areas. The Sudan or the northern regions remained largely the domain of Islam. The result was, as time went on, a north–south religious dichotomy which went far to reinforce differences of outlook arising from differences of geography, economy, and political experience. The problems posed by this fact are best seen in contemporary Nigeria.

Even in the forest or southern regions which were more or less the domain of western Christianity, the introduction of that religion helped to emphasize long-standing divisions between ethnic and political units. There were too many rival Christian denominations soliciting for converts in the region. This fact enabled each small community to ensure that it did not embrace the same denomination as any of its neighbouring rivals or enemies. In this way ancient lines of rivalry and conflict were baptized and dressed up in the idioms and symbols of the new age.

3 Revolutions and wars

Introduction

The first eight decades of the nineteenth century brought great and often violent changes to many areas of West Africa. In the Sudan the period saw the forcible establishment of new states by men who claimed to be inspired by the desire to ensure that relations between man and man, as well as between man and state, were guided by Islamic codes of law, justice and morality. In Guinea it witnessed the disintegration of one of the greatest empires of the forest region, as well as attempts at military expansion by two of the remaining three. It is with these happenings and how they helped to shape the history of many West African peoples that this chapter deals.

The jihads of the Western Sudan

The jihads, which were among the most significant events in nineteenth-century West African history, were brought about by factors which were so many, so varied and so complex that historians are not yet agreed on their true nature. However, they may be seen as resulting from tensions which had existed in Sudanic society for some time before the nineteenth century.

In the first place there was a conflict in most Sudanic communities between Islam and the traditional religions of the peoples. Though by 1800 Islam was many centuries old amongst most Sudanic peoples, it had not succeeded in displacing the traditional cults. This was an explosive situation, for Islam, although it recognized Christians and Jews as 'people of the book', did not recognize the validity of any other religion. In orthodox Islamic doctrine the only way to the good life in this world and to salvation in after life was provided by the teachings of the Prophet Muhammad. Furthermore Islam commanded that all faithful believers had a duty to persuade, and if need be to force, all non-Muslims who were not 'people of the book' to embrace the faith. The parallel existence of Islam and the traditional religions in the Sudan was thus very unsatisfactory and challenging to orthodox Muslims.

Moreover Islam was not just a religion to be practised privately by individuals; it was also a way of life and so had its own codes of law, justice and morality, which it held should guide all properly ordered societies and states. At the opening of our period of study the ways of life pursued in many Sudanic states and societies were a contradiction of this ideal. Some of the states, like Segu and Kaarta, were ruled by adherents of traditional religions. Other states like the Hausa Bakwai were nominally Muslim in the sense that their dynasties were Muslim, but did not enforce the code of laws known as the Malikite code which most orthodox Muslims in the Sudan expected them to follow. Since there were Muslim communities in most of the Sudanic states it meant that orthodox Muslims were made to live under conditions which did not satisfy their religious consciences. What was more painful to such Muslims was that states ruled by followers of traditional religion or nominal Muslims often forced them to pay tributes and to undertake other obligations which were either not commanded by the Quran or were forbidden by it.

From the above general sketch it becomes clear that if some determined Muslim reformers were to come into existence at any time in the Sudan there would be open conflict between them and those who did not want the existing state of society to change. This was precisely what happened in the nineteenth century.

There were also political reasons for the jihads. Generally the Muslim clerical class were better educated than their traditionalist or nominally Muslim neighbours and rulers, with the result that they believed they knew more about the world in which they lived than their illiterate neighbours. As educated men they were often employed as secretaries and advisers by rulers; they also had a high reputation as makers of powerful charms which could protect their wearers from evil-minded people and dark forces, or ensure victory in war. These Muslim clerics enjoyed a great deal of influence in the communities in which they lived. This was another source of trouble between them and the non-Muslim or nominally Muslim groups in the Sudan. The clerics felt superior to their neighbours and rulers who depended so much on their services, and also became politically ambitious after having tasted power as advisers and secretaries. The rulers on their side not only became jealous of the influence which their advisers accumulated but they also grew very suspicious of their political intentions.

Fulani Muslims

These tensions started coming to a head from about 1725 when the reforming Muslim clerics began pressing their points of view. Most of these men came from among the Fulani, especially from the town Fulani who were often fanatical Muslims. The Fulani led in these movements not only because they were good Muslims, but also because they had economic grievances against the Sudanic peoples, who saw them as strangers and discriminated against them in matters of land ownership and rights of trade. Because they were scattered throughout the Sudan the movement spread over the whole region. Some other Sudanese peoples, such as Tuareg, certain branches of the Songhai and Mande-speaking peoples who had been associated with Islam for a long time and some Hausa, also took part in the jihad. Though the participants in the revolution thus differed in their ethnic origin, they were united in the fact that they had a common ideology (Islam) and were generally from sections of the people who could be described as politically underprivileged.

Open conflict between the Muslim reformers and the non-Muslim or lukewarm Muslim dynasties of the Sudan began in the eighteenth century in the western half of the Western Sudan. In 1725 some Islamic reformers led by a Fulani called Alfa Ibrahim bin Nuhu successfully rose against the pagan rulers of Futa Jallon and established there an imamate, that is a state under an imam, a religious leader who claimed to rule in the name of his maker. A little later a similar move occurred in Futa Toro, a state west of Futa Jallon and on the southern bank of the river Senegal. There the reformers, led by a man called Suleiman Bal, declared a jihad against the pagan rulers of the state in 1769. In 1776 the latter were overthrown and a state along the lines of Futa Jallon was established by the victorious reformers. Later still another imamate was founded at Bondu in the region between Futa Jallon and Futa Toro.

Usman dan Fodio

But the most important of these jihads were fought in the nineteenth century, and of these the most successful and the one with the most enduring results was that fought in Hausaland under the leadership of Usman (Uthman) dan Fodio.

Usman dan Fodio, a Fulani of the Toronkowa clan, was born in December 1754 at Maratta near Birnin Konni in the then leading Hausa state of Gobir. At the early age of 7 he was taught to read and copy the Quran by his father who was himself a scholar and teacher of some note.

After this, like other young Muslim students, he started wandering from place to place in search of distinguished teachers under whom he could further his education. In the process he passed through the hands of many sheikhs who introduced him to the rich intellectual heritage of Islam. Abdul-Rahman ibn Hammada taught him syntax and grammar; Uthman Binduri imparted to him his zeal for right living and action; while a third cleric, Jibril, also infected him with his zeal for radical religious, social and political reform. Jibril had got so exasperated with what he considered social injustice and irreligion in the Hausa states that he had at one time planned a jihad but had been thwarted.

By the time he was 20 Usman dan Fodio had finished his studies and settled down to teach (1774–5). With his centre at Degel, he travelled far and wide in Hausaland teaching the Islamic religion and pleading for social reform. His preaching journeys took him especially to Kebbi and Zamfara. By the time he completed these travels he had become so famous that he decided to settle at Degel while those in need of instruction flocked to him. It did not take long before the king of Gobir, Bawa, recognized the political danger in Usman dan Fodio's activities and sought to control him by appearing to conciliate him. But it was with Bawa's successor, Nafata, that the clash between the reformer and established authority came into the open. In a bid to counter Usman's influence, Nafata issued decrees which laid down that only those born as Muslims could practise the Muslim religion and that all those who had been converted to Islam as a result of the recent propaganda of Usman should return to the faith of their fathers. Some of the decrees denied any cleric except Usman dan Fodio the right to preach, and forbade such Islamic practices as the wearing of turbans by men or of veils by women. This conflict deepened when Yunfa, a former pupil of Usman dan Fodio, succeeded Nafata as King of Gobir. The final break came when Usman released a group of Muslims who were about to be sold into slavery by Yunfa's men, for according to the Quran Muslims should not be slaves. This action of Usman angered Yunfa, who gave orders that his former teacher should be seized for trial. Before this could be done Usman dan Fodio and his followers fled to Gudu on 21 February 1804, and from there declared a jihad against Gobir. At the same time Usman dan Fodio was proclaimed *Amir al-Muminin* (Commander of the Faithful) by his followers.

Yunfa was quickly defeated by Usman's brother, Abdullah. Fearing that the Fulani would support Usman, other Hausa states attacked the Fulani in their areas. This step made matters worse, since it forced the cattle- and town-Fulani to unite against their Hausa oppressors. The jihad thus spread beyond Gobir and covered all Hausaland. One after the other the Hausa states fell into the hands of Usman and his followers. By

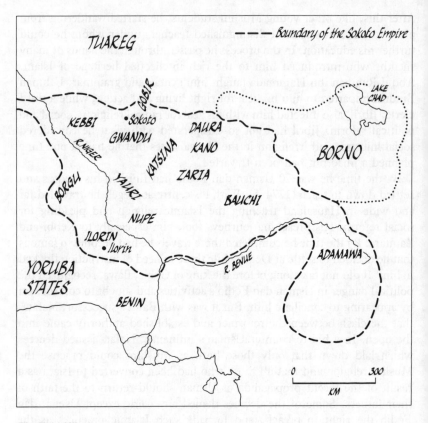

The Fulani jihad

1810 most of Hausaland had come under the control of the Fulani who formed them into an empire (caliphate) under a caliph with his capital at Sokoto, which was founded in 1808 to mark the dawn of the new era.

After seeing the jihad through its early years Usman dan Fodio retired from active politics to resume his life of contemplation and scholarship which the wars had interrupted. Before doing so he divided his empire in two with capitals at Sokoto and Gwandu. The Sokoto part he gave to his son Muhammad Bello who was later to succeed him as *sarkin musulmi* (Leader of the Faithful); Gwandu went to his brother Abdullah.

Reasons for the success of the jihad

Why, one might ask, did the Fulani rebels find it so easy to overthrow the

Bludgeon of wood

Wrist dagger

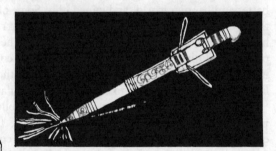

Sword

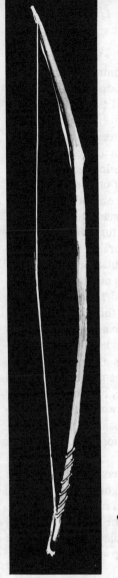

Bow

Knife with sheaf

Quiver and arrows

A selection of northern Nigerian weapons. It should be remembered that the majority of the soldiers fighting in the jihads had no firearms. Much skill and care was thus taken with the manufacture of traditional weapons, as can be seen from these drawings

old Hausa aristocracy? The reasons were many but the main one was the inability of the different Hausa states to unite in a common effort against Usman dan Fodio and his followers. The states had risen as rivals and they remained rivals to the end. Neither the invasions of the Songhai in the early sixteenth century, nor of the Borno from the fifteenth century nor of the Jukun of Kwararafa in the seventeenth and eighteenth centuries, nor the unceasing raids of the Tuareg of the desert over the centuries, had succeeded in inducing the Hausa states to co-operate. Instead they gloried in their independence and often went to war against one another. Thus, when Yunfa appealed to the other states for help, he received no response. The mutual jealousy and suspicion among the Hausa rulers gave the Fulani the opportunity to attack and defeat each in turn. In contrast the Muslim leaders in the Hausa states responded favourably to Usman dan Fodio's call for support. So did the great leader's Fulani kinsmen.

Another reason for Usman's success was that it was not the Fulani alone nor Muslims alone who resented the rule of the old Hausa aristocracy. Different sections of the Central Sudanese society at this time felt discontented for different reasons. Some resented over-taxation, while others resented the moral and religious laxity of their rulers. All these discontented elements saw Usman dan Fodio's uprising as a chance to build a better and happier world, and joined him. Some of them were later to find that Fulani rule was no less irksome than Hausa rule, but not before they had helped to destroy the Hausa city states. There were some who supported the Fulani because they saw the ensuing confusion as an opportunity for loot and rape. At the time of the conflict, therefore, the Hausa kings lacked enough supporters to overwhelm the Fulani.

What was more, Usman dan Fodio and his followers, convinced of the purity and righteousness of their own cause, fought with a zeal and enthusiasm which the bewildered Hausa rulers could not match. Finally, from a strategic point of view, the wide dispersal of the Fulani in previous centuries worked to their advantage. The Hausa rulers had to deal not with foreign invaders but with organized rebel groups within their gates.

Repercussions of the jihad

The echoes of Usman dan Fodio's jihad were not restricted to the Hausa states; on the contrary they were heard with varying intensity and results in three other neighbouring states and beyond. In 1808 a section of the Fulani in the Borno empire rose in sympathy with Usman against the Sefawa; as a result that ancient but decadent dynasty lost its western provinces, which became emirates of Hadejia (1808) and Katagum (1810) under Fulani lieutenants of Usman within the Sokoto caliphate. The Sefawa dynasty and empire already seriously weakened by the attacks of the Tuareg of the desert, the Mandara kingdom of the mountainous south and the states of Wadai and Bagirmi to the east were only saved from complete ruin by a remarkable Islamic scholar and soldier from Kanem, popularly known as Muhammad al-Kanemi. It was not al-Kanemi's military genius alone that saved the Borno empire. He was also a reformist Muslim, and his puritanical reforms in Borno made the religious propaganda of the Sokoto jihadists sound hollow in the ears of the Kanuri. He also wrote books, in which he accused Usman and his followers of self-seeking and hypocrisy and defended the stand of Borno. But, although the Fulani failed to capture the whole of Borno, their jihad affected that empire seriously. The jihad not only deprived it of its Hausa satellites and of some of its western provinces, but was also responsible for the rise of al-Kanemi and his children to positions of political importance. The latter development was to end in the total eclipse of the Sefawa. After saving the Borno empire, al-Kanemi came to enjoy a great deal of political authority and influence in Borno as the commander-in-chief of the military forces and as a great religious leader. What was left for the Sefawa was simply the title of *mai* (ruler). Al-Kanemi died in 1835, to be succeeded by his son Umar who in 1849 completed the political revolution which his father had started by dethroning and killing the last of the Sefawas and stepping into his shoes as the undisputed ruler of Borno.

The jihad of Usman dan Fodio also affected the fates of the non-Muslim states of Nupe and Oyo lying to the south. We shall deal with Oyo and the jihad later. In Nupe there were Fulani Muslims, led by Mallam Dendo who, like their counterparts elsewhere, wanted to benefit from the revolution started by their kith and kin in the Hausa states. Fortunately for them at this time the Nupe state was in the throes of a disputed succession. The Fulani supported first this and then that contestant and after they had weakened the old dynasty sufficiently, quietly installed themselves as rulers and brought Nupe under Gwandu.

Ahmadu Lobbo

The second of the three great jihads of the nineteenth century in the Western Sudan took place in Macina, which lies west of Hausaland around the great bend of the Niger. Here it was led by a reforming Fulani Muslim called Shaikh Ahmadu (Ahmad, Hamad, Hamadu) Lobbo. This man had taken an active part in Usman dan Fodio's jihad in its early stages. Fired with the spirit of this movement he returned west to Jenne from where he was soon expelled for subversion by the conservative Islamic scholars of the city's ancient mosque. He had accused them of ignoring the strict practice of Islam which enjoined prayer and simple living in favour of futile philosophical disputations. From there he fled north to Sebera where he established a school and rallied men around him. In addition to his routine teaching, Ahmadu tried to persuade his fellow Muslims that in the present corrupt state of society the only course open to a faithful Muslim was the jihad. In 1808 he said he had a vision in which he was instructed to establish a Caliphate along orthodox Islamic lines. He did not, however, meet with much success until the writings of Usman dan Fodio on his own jihad reached the region, and those who doubted whether Ahmadu was correct in his view read these works and were convinced. Meanwhile Ahmadu had sent to Usman dan Fodio for a flag, which was the accepted symbol that a jihad had Usman's blessing; but before this could arrive Ahmadu and his followers had fallen out with the Bambara ruler of Segu, who was their overlord, and had declared a jihad and defeated the armies sent after them.

Feeling confident of his ability to stand on his own, Ahmadu rejected the flag when it eventually arrived. From Sebera he conquered Macina, Jenne and Timbuktu and the neighbouring areas. He pitched his capital at Hamdullahi, from where he organized his theocracy to which he recruited the advice and help of Muslim scholars from the whole region. The empire of Ahmadu Lobbo of Macina was perhaps better organized than that of Usman dan Fodio though much smaller in size. Within it a more determined attempt was made to abide by the dictates of Islam on how to run a rightly guided state. Detailed regulations were made on environmental hygiene and many other aspects of life. For instance married people were not allowed to loiter around town after dark, horses and donkeys were to be treated kindly, horse riders were not to look over fences lest they should catch the women off guard.

Still the empire had its internal weaknesses and internal critics. Islamic zeal and Ahmadu's simple life were not enough to unite the diverse elements in the state who had not forgotten their old rivalries going back to the eclipse of the Songhai empire in the sixteenth century. Many ancient families in Jenne and Timbuktu resented his rule, criticizing it as harsh just like the ones it superseded. On Ahmadu's death in 1845 his son Ahmadu Seku was able to maintain his inheritance intact. But Ahmadu Seku's son Ahmadu, who succeeded to the caliphate in 1852, was unable to do the same. What was more, under him the Macina caliphate came into conflict with another – that of al-Hajj Umar – which had arisen further to the west. Indeed the Macina caliphate was destroyed by al-Hajj Umar's in 1862.

al-Hajj Umar

This other caliphate grew out of a similar movement led by another Muslim reformer known popularly as al-Hajj Umar, but his full name was Umar b. Said Tall, who, in all probability, was a Fulani, though some scholars have described him as Tukolor. Umar, born either in 1794 or 1797, was a great soldier as well as a scholar of considerable ability. Like Usman dan Fodio he started his studies under his father, Saidu Tall, who was in his own right a learned man. After graduating from his father, Umar travelled widely in the Sudan in search of learned scholars under whom he would finish his studies. This took him to Mauritania, Futa Toro (his home) and Futa Jallon. In the latter place he met the Tijani scholar Shaikh Abdul-Karim al-Naqil who initiated him into the Tijaniyya sufi brotherhood. In 1826 he undertook the pilgrimage to Mecca where he met Sidi Muhammad al-Ghali who gave him further instructions in Tijani lore. At Mecca Umar came into contact with the revolutionary ideas which agtitated the Islamic world at this time. He travelled extensively in the east, visiting Egypt where he met the sheikhs of al-Azhar University in Cairo. After leaving the east Umar passed through Borno where he met the reformer al-Kanemi, and Sokoto where he spent twelve years in close touch with the court of Muhammad Bello. He married two Sokoto women, one of them a sister of Bello.

In 1838 Umar left Sokoto for Macina soaked in the revolutionary ideas of his time and world. His stay at Macina was short since his relations with Ahmadu Lobbo were strained. From there he renewed his wanderings, going to Segu and Futa Jallon preaching reform, making friends as well as enemies. Finally he withdrew to Dinguiray with his followers to lay deep plans for the jihad which he eventually launched in 1851, succeeding in conquering Kaarta by 1854. His plan would seem to have been to create a caliphate on the Senegal but he was thwarted by the French who drove him from Medina which he had invaded in 1857. He then decided to strike eastwards against the Bambara states and by 1861 had conquered Segu and Kaarta. In capturing Segu, Umar alienated Ahmadu Ahmadu of Macina, who regarded Segu as falling within his sphere of influence. The Macina authorities had in fact sent forces to aid Segu against al-Hajj Umar. The latter, regarding this as justifying war, invaded Macina and captured it in 1862, killing Ahmadu Ahmadu in the process. For the next two years Umar found himself entrapped in Macina trying to suppress local rebellions.

At his death in 1864, Umar's far-flung empire had no administrative system to hold it together. Ahmad Seku, his son and successor as caliph, inherited administrative problems which he never succeeded in solving.

Ahmad Seku, the son of al-Hajj Umar. No picture of al-Hajj Umar himself was apparently ever produced but he must have worn similar clothing and perhaps bore some family resemblance

Unfortunately he did not inherit his father's great influence and prestige, which had helped to keep the conquests together and his followers under control. As soon as Umar's death was announced the empire broke up into three virtually independent states. One part was under Ahmad himself who ruled from Segu, the others were respectively ruled from Hamdullahi and Nioro by Umar's brother, al-Tijani, and a slave, Mustafa. Mustafa and al-Tijani, while they acknowledged Ahmad Seku as caliph, remained practically independent. In addition to these problems there was the threat posed by the French based on the Senegal, who had developed an appetite for the whole of the Sudan and looked upon Ahmad's empire as a mere obstacle to their advance. Had the French heeded his advice and concerned themselves only with trade while he established himself as the ruler of the Senegal basin, he would have had no quarrel with them.

Umar's jihad differed from the other jihads of the Western Sudan in two ways. Firstly it was centrally organized. Its military campaigns were carried out from the centre according to previously laid plans, while Usman dan Fodio's jihad, for instance, had depended on uncoordinated risings by his Fulani brethren who sympathized with his cause. Secondly this jihad depended on the use of firearms to a greater extent than any of the preceding ones. It was to obtain these arms that Umar encouraged trade even with European unbelievers.

The effects of the jihads

In spite of the ease and rapidity with which some of these caliphates disappeared, the jihads of the nineteenth century in the Western Sudan made a great impact on the lives of the peoples in the region. On the political plane they brought appreciable sections of the Western Sudan under large empires, a feature that recalled the glorious days of Ghana, Mali and Songhai. Usman dan Fodio's jihad brought about 466 200 square kilometres of territory under the allegiance of the caliph at Sokoto. The jihad of Shaikh Ahmadu Lobbo of Macina created a state of about 145 000 square kilometres, while that of al-Hajj Umar created an empire 388 500 square kilometres in area. To a great extent within these states, at least within the states of Usman dan Fodio and Shaikh Ahmadu Lobbo, this meant the re-establishment of order and good government over a wide area, leading to the expansion of trade.

The Macina caliphate was the most centralized of these states. The Sokoto caliphate, though a loose confederation of practically autonomous states acknowledging allegiance to the *sarkin musulmi* at Sokoto, was also able to ensure a certain measure of law and order. The explorers of West Africa who entered the Central Sudan and lived to tell their story were full of admiration for the peace which reigned within the caliphate. But with al-Hajj Umar's empire, the story was different. Umar died before he had organized an administrative system. His son and successor had not sufficient energy and drive to provide one. In consequence, unregulated and apparently purposeless wars and raids rendered life here nasty, brutish and short. To some extent the French were regarded by many communities here as deliverers from an intolerable state of affairs.

On the religious side these jihads led to extensive conversions of non-Muslims to Islam, while strengthening the faith of those nominally attached to Islam. In northern Nigeria for instance, places like Bauchi and Adamawa were for the first time brought within the influence of Islam. Further west the wars and rule of Shaikh Ahmadu Lobbo of Macina brought about extensive and permanent conversions. In the empire of al-Hajj Umar things were again different. Extensive conversions were achieved or enforced at the point of the sword. But when that sword was withdrawn there were equally large-scale reversions to the traditional

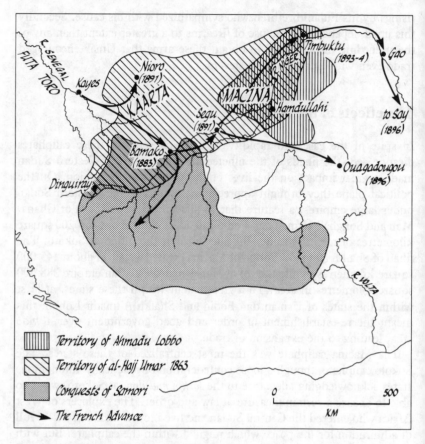

The empires of Ahmadu Lobbo, al-Hajj Umar and Samori Ture

religion, especially among the Bambara. Although the jihads on the whole strengthened Islam, they also weakened it in some areas, especially within Umar's caliphate. Umar made no distinction between outright non-Muslims and Muslims who did not belong to the Tijaniyya brotherhood. His Tijani exclusiveness and arrogance alienated many Muslims, especially those who belonged to the older Qadiriyya brotherhood. This explains why they did not support him, and in fact were sympathetic to the French. Even in the central Sudan the two Islamic states there, Sokoto and Borno, remained irreconcilable. Co-operation between them was impossible even in the face of foreign aggression.

Socially the jihads were revolutionary. The old aristocracies of the states against which the jihads were fought were overthrown, and in their place rose new groups who hitherto had been among the unprivileged in society. In particular, the Fulani underdogs of previous centuries became the arrogant aristocrats of the future.

On the cultural plane the jihads were important mainly in the ferment of intellectual activity they encouraged and created. The jihadists felt called upon to produce written justifications of their actions, especially of their attacks on supposedly fellow Muslims. Usman dan Fodio and his son Muhammad Bello were particularly productive in this field. So was al-Hajj Umar, but not on the scale of the former two. In other spheres of culture the movement does not seem to have been very significant. In the central Sudan, for instance, the Hausa, who suffered political defeat at the hands of the Fulani, culturally conquered the latter. Even in political and administrative fields, the Fulani merely took over Hausa institutions. In language too most of the settled Fulani ruling group lost their language and adopted Hausa.

By and large, however, the jihads caused much dislocation, much confusion and much suffering, especially among the non-Muslims who were raided to swell the volume of the trans-Saharan slave trade. The distinction in Islam between the 'abode of war' and the 'abode of Islam' provided philosophical and religious justification for raids against non-Muslims. This was at least so in northern Nigeria where raids against non-Muslims stopped only with the imposition of British rule in the early part of the twentieth century. The exact purpose of these raids which had become a normal state of existence is a matter of dispute.

Samori Ture

A similar state of dislocation existed in the upper Niger region and it was to some extent this which enabled Samori Ture, the son of a Malinke farmer, to establish an empire for himself there from the 1850s onwards. Samori, who was born about 1830, became a trader, until in 1852 he joined the army of Sori Birama, King of Bisandugu.

It was immediately obvious that Samori was a brilliant soldier, and it soon became his ambition to create a force strong enough to establish an empire and impose peace throughout Malinke-land. With peace, trade would flourish. After a few years in the army of Sori Birama, Samori felt strong enough to establish himself independently, and his abilities as a leader attracted many to serve under him; those who were less willing to join him he persuaded, by force or diplomacy, to rally to his side.

Sanankoro became the main town of his new army and from the later part of the 1860s and through the 1870s, Samori's armies campaigned regularly. By 1879 he controlled an area from Sierra Leone in the west to

Ivory Coast in the east, and from a point near Bamako in the north, to the Liberian frontiers in the south. His capital was at Bisandugu.

The system Samori gradually built up to administer this empire was to split it into provinces; the three central provinces were directly controlled by Samori and his ministers, while each outlying province was governed by an appointed military official, who shared his authority with a *qadi* (judge) who was also the local head of the religious community. This direct control was carried down to the level of the village, groups of which formed a district within each province.

But Samori depended on the army to acquire, and then to hold, his empire. His power rested in the loyalty of the army and not, as for example with al-Hajj Umar, on his authority as a religious leader. The ranks of this army were filled mainly with captives, who were trained as rifle-carrying infantrymen, and were known as *sofa*. These men formed a standing army directly loyal to Samori, while in times of need a conscripted reserve was also available, as well as a volunteer militia made up of those who owned horses. Samori's flexibility in using his forces – as raiding parties, as protection for caravans or towns, or to lay siege to

A drawing based on a contemporary print of Samori's arsenal. When Samori's supply of firearms from the coast was cut off he was compelled to manufacture and repair his own arms

fortified enemies – lies at the heart of his genius as a soldier. In addition the army was supported by a highly organized administration which ensured that supplies of all sorts were readily available. Apart from food, Samori established groups of metalworkers to manufacture rifle parts, cartridge cases and other military requirements.

Up to the year 1882 Samori's armies continued to expand his empire. Then, while they were laying siege to the village of Keniera (near Siguiri in modern Guinea), there came the first clash with the French. This was ultimately to result in the defeat and capture of Samori, and the destruction of his empire, but his military genius enabled him to resist the French for a long time, so that it was not until 1898 that he was finally overwhelmed.

Samori's career has been the subject of controversy. He has been regarded by some as a national leader fighting to maintain his empire in the face of a colonizing power, and by others as a ruthless and cruel tyrant who brought suffering to very many people, especially through his wars and involvement in slave trading. Some have been impressed by the gestures he made to Islam. He embraced the religion in 1850 just before he took to professional soldiery. But it was not until the 1880s, after he had become sure of his power base and with the increasing threat from the French, that he began to identify his empire more closely with Islam. First he changed his title from *faama* which was pagan to *almamy* (imam) which was Muslim. Then in 1886 he issued a decree calling on all his subjects to embrace Islam. But when this evoked spirited resistance, he withdrew it. That was after 1888. In spite of all this, however, he cannot be numbered amongst the great religious revivalists of the century. His Islamism would appear to have drived largely from reasons of state.

Rabih ibn Fadlallah

Another empire builder cast somewhat in the Samori mould was Rabih ibn Fadlallah, who started his career in what is now the Sudan, where he had served under a slave dealer called Zubair Pasha. Like Samori, Rabih broke away from his former master, and built up a strong and well-organized army of his own, with which he invaded the Chad region around 1891. Rabih invaded and conquered Borno but, before he could consolidate his conquests around Chad, he was challenged by the French in Bagirmi. He was defeated by them and killed in 1900, after which his empire collapsed. It had been held together only by his own ability as a soldier and, although he tried to associate himself with the Mahdist movement in the Sudan, religious zeal was not a notable part of his career.

The collapse of the Oyo empire

The Yoruba empire of Oyo, founded about the fifteenth century, reached the height of its power about the middle of the seventeenth century and then disintegrated in the nineteenth century. Its collapse can be traced to constitutional and administrative breakdown going back to the mid-eighteenth century. The strength and peace of the Oyo empire depended on the readiness and ability of the *alafin* and the *Oyo Mesi* (State Council) to keep each other in check. Some time in the eighteenth century the balance between the two was upset as the *alafin* lost more and more control over the army and the administration to a number of chiefly lineages. The well-known career of Bashorun Gaha was only one of the signs of the evil times into which the office of *alafin* had fallen. A politician of great ability, influence and fame, Gaha used his traditional position as chief king-maker to bring a succession of *alafin* and his fellow members of the *Oyo Mesi* under his control. In this way he made himself the virtual ruler of the empire. Though his tyranny was later ended in 1774 by Alafin Abiodun, who destroyed him and almost his entire family, the events associated with the years of his ascendancy left a lasting imprint on the fortunes of the empire.

In the years before the eighteenth century some of the chief officials of the Oyo empire were usually slaves of the *alafin's* household. This was particularly the case with certain offices at the metropolis, especially with the élite corps of 70 warriors known as *Eso* who had command of the Oyo army. Since these slaves were usually eunuchs they had no children and so never raised families which could be in rivalry with the royal lineage. The slave officials knew that they owed their position to the *alafin* and so obeyed him implicitly. But during the course of the decline of the central authority in the eighteenth century this tradition was quietly set aside and the *alafin* were compelled to give important offices of state to some powerful Yoruba families of free status who did not owe all they possessed to the *alafin*. Thus the chief officials of the empire became less dependent on the *alafin*, with the result that the office of *alafin* became weakened by a continuous struggle for power. As the *alafin* and his advisers and lieutenants were preoccupied with the constitutional crisis at the centre, the provinces of the empire were less effectively governed. The provincial residents (the *ajele*) did as they liked and became corrupt and oppressive, while the local population of the provinces became restive and independent and rebelled at the earliest opportunity. For instance the Egba took the opportunity of the conflict between Abiodun and Gaha in 1775–80 to rebel against the oppression of the *ajele* and to throw over the yoke of Oyo. All subsequent attempts to bring the Egba back to Oyo rule failed. The trouble between Gaha and the *alafin* had led to the neglect of the army, which therefore decayed.

The Oyo empire thus entered the nineteenth century afflicted with a serious constitutional and administrative crisis which rendered it incapable of effectively facing external threats to its existence. But in 1804 Usman dan Fodio had launched his great jihad, and the triumphant Fulani advance towards the south which followed threatened the northern provinces of the Oyo empire. To meet this threat *Alafin* Abiodun appointed Afonja, a descendant of the Yoruba royal line, to the post of *Are-Ona-Kakanfo* (an *ad hoc* commander-in-chief of provincial forces), with headquarters at Ilorin and the duty of defending the empire against the Fulani. But following the example of many other nobles at the metropolis, Afonja treacherously proceeded to use his office to strengthen himself against the central government. Abiodun's successor, *Alafin* Awole therefore decided to destroy him in the traditional way by setting him an impossible task which he had to accomplish or commit suicide, Afonja not only refused to tackle the task or to commit suicide he also rose in revolt against a later *alafin* in 1817. At once all the discontented people, of whom there were many in the empire, joined him. Unfortunately for the Oyo empire the hands of the *alafin* were weakened by a struggle with the *Oyo Mesi* at this time. What was more important, Afonja further strengthened himself by allying with the Fulani and in doing so opened the gate into the Oyo empire for the Fulani jihadists. First the Fulani helped Afonja to establish the independence of Ilorin, and then they overthrew and killed him in order to become the rulers of the province, which now became an emirate under Gwandu. The extension of the jihad into Ilorin was the immediate cause of the collapse of Oyo. It touched off a chain of events which kept Yorubaland disturbed by wars and rumours of wars for the rest of the nineteenth century.

These events greatly affected the outcome of the Owu war which broke out in 1820. The people of Owu had quarrelled with the Ife and the Ijebu over trade matters, as a result of which the Ife and the Ijebu began a combined attack on Owu in 1820. About this time the war between Oyo and Ilorin was causing the inhabitants of northern Yoruba towns to flee to the south for safety. These displaced men thronged the highways and the paths, seeking for means of livelihood and spreading panic and unrest as they went. When they got to Owu they joined the Ife and the Ijebu, thus helping to bring about the fall of the invested town. The fall of Owu did not mean the end of the disturbance in Yorubaland, since the army that destroyed Owu contained many homeless refugees, who had become accustomed to live by plunder and who were not ready to demobilize and settle down. This army therefore continued southwards from Owu until it got to the place now occupied by Ibadan, where it destroyed Egba towns and villages, thus forcing out the Egba who had to start a new settlement at Abeokuta. About the same time the war between the Fulani of Ilorin and the Oyo empire grew in volume and intensity. In 1830 the *alafin* made a great effort with the aid of the Bariba of Borgu to recover Ilorin. The attempt not only failed hopelessly but led to the destruction of Oyo, the capital of the empire, by the Fulani. The *alafin* and his court fled in panic into the forest town of Ago-Oja to the south, where a new capital was built and named after the old. This is the present Oyo, which lies about 50 kilometres north of Ibadan. The old Oyo empire had thus completely collapsed. The aftermath was a series of wars waged by a number of states which sought to occupy the position of pre-eminence which Oyo had hitherto enjoyed in Yorubaland.

The Yoruba wars

Though Ariba, the first *alafin* to rule in new Oyo, tried to revive the time-honoured traditions of the empire and to maintain the prestige and dignity of the royal court, Oyo ceased to play an important part in Yoruba politics after 1830. The *alafin* was forced to recognize that Oyo was no longer a military power, and that the defence of Yorubaland against the outsider had passed to the towns which were either founded or grew in importance as a result of the confusion following the Fulani invasion. The best he could do was to confer traditional imperial honours and titles on the leading chiefs of these rising towns in the hope of using them for his purposes.

There were four principal Yoruba states involved in the struggle for ascendancy. The first was Ijaye which was situated between Oyo and Ibadan, and which was dominated by Kurunmi, one of the ablest Yoruba generals of the day. Ijaye was responsible for defending the western provinces of Yorubaland against Dahomey which now threatened to conquer the Yoruba. In order to keep Ijaye within the imperial system Atiba conferred on Kurunmi the title of *Are-Ona-Kakanfo*.

Then there was Ibadan which began as a war camp but soon became one of the leading powers in Yorubaland. Here Oluyole was supreme. To control him Ariba made him *Basorun*. Ibadan had the duty of defending the northern and north-eastern provinces against the Fulani.

The Egba with their new capital at Abeokuta were also in the struggle for supremacy in Yorubaland. They were not interested in the reconquest of the provinces which the Fulani had seized, but only wanted to defend themselves first against Ijebu and Ibadan and then against Dahomey and

Ibadan. For this they wanted an outlet to the coast from where they could get the necessary European weapons.

Lastly there were the Ijebu. These shrewd businessmen were keenly interested in the confusion in the interior, since it offered them immense opportunities for profitable business. Success in these wars depended greatly on the availability of guns and powder, which came from the coast through Ijebu. The wars also produced a large crop of slaves which passed through the hands of the Ijebu to those Europeans on the coast who still traded in the commodity in spite of the British naval blockade. The Ijebu therefore were determined to preserve their monopoly of the trade between the port of Lagos and Benin. They were thus hostile to the Egba who were trying to get a port on the coast. But when later Ibadan threatened to swallow up all the rest of the Yoruba states the Ijebu were frightened and allied with the Egba to frustrate this ambition.

Yorubaland at the time of the wars

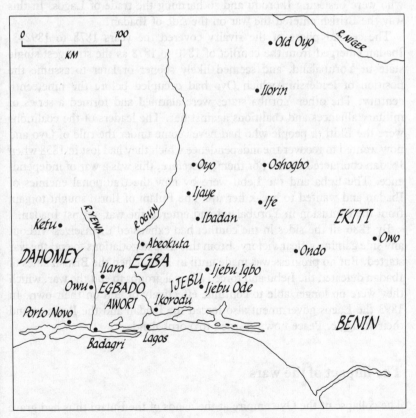

The struggle between these states grew very intense after the battle of Oshogbo (1840), where the Ibadan defeated the Fulani and put a check to Fulani advance towards the south. The history of this struggle falls into two clearly marked phases. The first phase was dominated by the struggle between Ibadan and Ijaye in which the latter enjoyed the support of the Egba. The rivalry between Ibadan and Ijaye led first to the battle of Batedo (1844) which neither party won; and then to the more famous Ijaye war (1860–2) in which Ijaye was destroyed.

The disturbances and skirmishes associated with this war lingered on until 1878 as an engagement between the victorious Ibadan and the Egba. One important development in this period was the fact that the British became involved in the conflict. The British had seized Lagos in 1861, not only as a means of stopping the slave trade but also in order to benefit from the trade of Yorubaland. Their hopes were disappointed as the wars in the interior disturbed the flow of trade, and they therefore became interested in the restoration of peace. In 1865 they sent soldiers to expel the Egba, who were besieging Ikorodu and so harming the trade of Lagos. In this way the British entered the war on the side of Ibadan.

The second phase of the rivalry covered the years 1878 to 1892–3. Ibadan emerged from the conflict of 1840 to 1878 as the strongest single state in Yorubaland, and seemed likely sooner or later to assume the position of leadership which Oyo had occupied before the nineteenth century. The other Yoruba states were alarmed and formed a series of military alliances and coalitions against her. The leaders of the coalitions were the Ekiti, a people who had never come under the rule of Oyo and now wanted to recover the independence which they had lost in 1858 when Ibadan conquered them. For them, therefore, this was a war of independence. The Egba and the Ijebu were by now the traditional enemies of Ibadan and wanted to break her up. The Fulani of Ilorin sought to gain from the confusion in Yorubaland and entered the war against Ibadan.

By 1886 all the sides in the conflict had exhausted themselves without any side gaining a clear victory. From this time negotiations to end the war started. But no progress was made until in 1892, when the British allies of Ibadan defeated the Ijebu and forced all rival groups to end the war, which they were no longer able to continue effectively or end on their own. In 1893 the Lagos government also forced the Ibadan and the Ilorin to end their struggle. Peace now returned to Yorubaland.

The impact of the wars

The collapse of the Oyo empire at the hands of the Fulani thus had grave consequences for the Yoruba people. First, it brought about a massive shift in population. As the Fulani advanced from Ilorin the Yoruba fled from the more open lands of the north to the thickly forested lands of the south in search of shelter. This flight of population southwards led to the growth of new towns. Here two good examples were New Oyo and Abeokuta. Old settlements and towns also benefited from this development and expanded both in area and population.

Secondly, it brought the full impact of the slave trade to Yorubaland. Before the events of the nineteenth century most of the slaves from the west coast came from the Niger Delta ports, Dahomey, the area of modern Ghana, and the region to the west of it. The influence of the *alafin* was somehow able to limit the extent to which the Yoruba caught and sold each other, with the result that most of the slaves sold by the Yoruba came from the markets to the north of Yorubaland. When the Fulani conquest of Ilorin closed the northern markets to the Yoruba the slave demands of Ijebu and other coastal groups had to be met by increased raiding in Yoruba country. The interstate rivalry which followed the fall of Oyo supplied these needs. Thus, though the desire for slaves did not cause the wars, the fact that the wars produced slaves provided an extra reason for prolonging them unduly. The wars were lucrative business.

Thirdly, the wars were a landmark in the history of Islamic expansion in Yorubaland. Even before the nineteenth century, there were Muslims in the Oyo empire. But they were mainly Hausa slaves who were kept as horse attendants and veterinarians. Their support was an important factor in the success of Afonja and his Fulani allies against Oyo. With Ilorin becoming an emirate within the Sokoto caliphate, Islam gained a firm foothold within the Yoruba culture area. And as people fled from the north to the south many important elements in society – soldiers, long-distance traders, charms specialists – who were already attracted by Islam, penetrated further into Yorubaland. The result was that by 1858, the Timi of Ede was Muslim while such towns as Iwo and Iseyin were considered strong centres of Islam. Then, in 1871, Ibadan got its first Muslim *Bale* while by 1878 Oyo was said to have about 12 mosques.

Fourthly, the wars caused a military revolution in Yoruba society. As the crisis deepened and spread, warriors began arming themselves more and more with firearms imported from Europe in place of traditional weapons. This change compelled people to become professional as leaders spent time training their followers in marksmanship, camouflage and other aspects of tactics. It was with the new importance attached to firearms that interest in the coastal trade grew. The guns and the powder were bought from the Europeans at the coast. This was one reason why neither the Ijebu nor the Egba could have stayed out of the war even if they had so wished for they controlled the access to the coast where these purchases could be made.

Fifthly, the wars created the opportunity for British intervention in Yorubaland. Since the Yoruba were divided amongst themselves the British found it easy to have their way. While appearing to be bringing peace to the Yoruba people the British actually deprived them of their independence.

Dahomey

From about 1840 to the end of the nineteenth century the kingdom of Dahomey made a number of military incursions into Yorubaland. These invasions have sometimes been treated as part of the internal history of Yorubaland, and in particular as a phase in the Yoruba wars of the nineteenth century. Here, however, they will be examined as part of the history of the Dahomean state from which the invasions originated.

There were two main reasons behind the invasions. The first was political. Ever since Dahomey rose to greatness in the first half of the eighteenth century it had been a dependency of Oyo. Various attempts by its kings to become independent of Oyo had only brought severe punishments at the hands of the Oyo army. Oyo overlordship at times meant for Dahomeans subordination to irritating laws and regulations. For instance the *alafin* of Oyo regarded the Dahomean army as part of his military forces which should be placed at his service as he wanted. Also the *alafin* from time to time passed regulations forbidding the kings of Dahomey to use certain materials for clothing because those materials were considered as only fit to be used by the *alafin* himself. Though the Oyo were never really able to enforce obedience to these rules, they were humiliating to Dahomean national prestige. Then Dahomey had to pay tributes to the *alafin* throughout the eighteenth century. It was thus certain that any king of Dahomey who could do so would end this subservience to Oyo, which the proud Dahomeans found uncongenial. Also it must be remembered that at the beginning of the nineteenth century Dahomey was still an energetic state full of imperial ambitions. It thus had a mission not only to win its independence from Oyo, but if possible to expand at the expense of that empire.

The second reason behind the invasions was economic. From about the 1740s the Dahomean economy rested mainly on slavery. Some of the slaves were sold to Europeans on the coast, from whom the kings of Dahomey got the manufactured goods needed by their people, especially the arms and ammunition which were required for the army. Of those slaves who were not sold overseas some were used in working the extensive royal plantations while others served as the unfortunate victims of the human sacrifices for which the kings of Dahomey were notorious. It was to provide the slave needs of the state that the Dahomean army was constantly in action to the west and north of the kingdom. By the beginning of the nineteenth century these traditional raiding grounds had been seriously depopulated. Dahomey thus had to turn to the country to the east and south-east, that is to a section of the Yoruba country. This change was made possible by the break-up of the great Oyo empire which had hitherto frightened Dahomey off Yorubaland.

In the nineteenth century the economic motive for expansion in the direction of Yoruba country was reinforced. In 1807 Britain prohibited her subjects from engaging in the slave trade and started a campaign to abolish the trade throughout the world. By the end of the first half of the nineteenth century the volume of the slave trade across the Atlantic was being drastically reduced. For Dahomey this meant economic ruin. It became essential to find a substitute for slaves as an export. This meant that Dahomey had to find new tracts of fertile territory in which to grow the products which the Europeans now required. The region to the west and north was dry and infertile. It was the area to the east and south-east, the Yoruba country, that once again answered Dahomey's needs. Thus whether it was slaves or land that Dahomey needed she had to look to Yorubaland. Nothing could have prevented the clash between the Dahomeans and the Yoruba in the nineteenth century. The Dahomeans themselves were conscious of this fact as shown by their war song which asked:

> Yoruba and Dahomey
> can two rams drink from one calabash?

For Dahomey the conditions appeared favourable: 1817 was the year of Afonja's revolt at Ilorin which opened a gate into Yorubaland for the Fulani; 1820 was the year of the Owu war which started a civil war in Yorubaland which lasted for 80 years. On the other hand Dahomey was as strong as ever. In 1818 Gezo, a very energetic and ambitious man, came to the Dahomean throne. When he saw that the time was ripe he declared Dahomey independent of Oyo. This claim was not contested and it looked as if nothing would prevent Dahomey from overrunning the country to the east and south-east, occupied by the Egbado and Awori Yoruba. Until the 1850s the Dahomeans financed this programme from the proceeds of the slave trade which grew in volume in the 1840s through the encouragement of the Brazilians. After the collapse of that evil trade in the 1850s attention was shifted to the trade in palm produce. The Dahomean kings had established extensive palm plantations. But the proceeds from the new trade could not be compared to the yields of the slave trade. Contemporary visitors to Dahomey contrasted the wealth and splendour of Gezo's court (1818–58) with the rather drab court of his son and successor Glele.

The political situation was complex. As a result of the confusion arising from the Owu war the Egba had been expelled from their ancestral home around Ibadan and forced to found the new town of Abeokuta. The nature of politics in Yorubaland at this time made the Egba develop ambitions in the direction of Egbado and Awori. To be able to defend themselves against their enemies, the Egba needed a port on the coast through which they could obtain the guns which were changing the nature of warfare in Yorubaland. Since they could not hope to control Lagos, which was held by the Ijebu, their enemies at the time, they hoped to gain control of Badagri. To do this they needed to control the roads leading from Badagri to Abeokuta. This in turn meant they had to control the Egbado and Awori country. In this way the Egba came to stand in the way of Dahomey.

It was these rival interests that soon brought the Egba and Dahomey into conflict. Dahomey opened the aggression by sending forces to help Egbado and Awori towns which the Egba were trying to seize. The Egba bitterly resented this Dahomean intervention and retaliated in 1844 by ambushing a Dahomean army which was going to attack the Egbado town of Ilaro. In the scuffle that followed, the Dahomeans suffered more than the Egba. King Gezo narrowly escaped capture but lost his royal umbrella, stool and war charms. It was in that year that Gezo made up his mind to destroy Abeokuta as a punishment for the insult. To prepare the way he destroyed Oke Odan in 1848. The Egba retaliated two years later by sacking Igbeji which was under Dahomey. The following year (1851) Gezo undertook his long-expected, full-scale invasion of Abeokuta only to be beaten off with severe losses. He was not able to return to the attack before his death in 1858. But his son and successor, Glele, regarded the destruction of Abeokuta as his life's assignment and refused to complete the ceremonies connected with his coronation until he had achieved this ambition. But events proved him no luckier than his father for when he attacked Abeokuta in 1864 he suffered a severe defeat. After this attempt Dahomey did not again try to seize Abeokuta by storm, but resorted to isolated raids and forays against the Egba. Glele, however, met with better luck in his attack on Ketu, a Yoruba kingdom, which he devastated in 1883 and took by siege in 1886.

Abeokuta's victory over Dahomey was to some extent the result of British aid. The Lagos government in particular supplied the Egba with guns and powder and sent trained soldiers to educate the Egba on how to

King Behanzin, the last independent nineteenth-century king of Dahomey. He succeeded Glele in 1888 and was deposed by the French in 1894

repair their defences and how to fire some of the new guns they supplied. The CMS missionaries who at this time were settled at Abeokuta identified themselves with Egba interests. In their writings they presented the Dahomeans as devils against whom the British should help the harmless Egba to defend themselves. This propaganda proved very effective as a means of evoking the help of the Lagos government.

Asante, Fante and the British

As already shown in an earlier chapter the rise of the Atlantic trade had precipitated intense rivalry among the numerous Akan principalities for its control. By 1800 Asante, the youngest of these, had emerged as the greatest power in Akan-land. It had a buoyant economy based on flourishing agriculture, richly diversified village industries and crafts, gold and kola nut trade with the Sudanese states, and gold and slave trade with the Europeans at the coast. The southern trade was particularly important as it was the source of firearms on which the formidable Asante army was coming to depend more and more. This was why the effective suppression of the slave trade here after the 1820s created a serious economic and political crisis for the empire.

Along with a rich economic base Asante entered the nineteenth century with a fairly strong monarchy. There was increasing use under Asantehene Osei Bonsu (1801–24) of professional civil servants who took control of taxation, provincial administration and foreign affairs from the traditional office holders. Because of their family connections these latter had not always been very loyal, nor were they always very efficient or honest. This trend towards the building up of a bureaucracy had actually started in the last few decades of the eighteenth century. Osei Bonsu improved on it and even made use of foreigners like Muslim clerics from the Sudan and even renegade Europeans. The use of Muslim clerics was indicative of the spread of Islam into the empire. Again this was another trend traceable to the eighteenth century. Indeed Osei Kwame (1777–1801) is said to have been overthrown in a coup partly because he patronized Islam too openly. Osei Bonsu continued to use Muslims and to express a deep liking for their religion while wisely avoiding conversion.

On the face of it, therefore, Asante, now at the height of her power, was poised to conquer and annex all the remaining neighbouring petty independent states, especially the Fante and Ga states of the coast. However, contrary to expectation the history of nineteenth-century Akan-land is not the story of the triumphant achievement of the Asante ambition and the universal reign of Asante peace throughout Akan-land. On the contrary it is a monotonous story of a series of wars fought between the Asante and the British. One interesting aspect of these wars is that neither the British nor the Asante really desired them. Both parties wanted to trade peacefully with each other, yet they constantly found themselves at war with each other. The main causes of these wars and their results for those involved will be briefly sketched here.

On the side of the Asante there were two factors which drove them into war with the British. The first was political and derived mainly from the nature of the Asante constitution. The Asante Union or Confederacy was a great military power, but never a highly centralized state in spite of the increasing use of professional servants. In fact this reform created distrust, at times expressed in rebellion, between the Asantehene and his provincial chiefs. Administratively speaking the union consisted of three concentric rings of divisions under varying degrees of control. At the centre was the state or province of Kumasi which was the capital of the Asantehene who ruled it directly in his capacity as Kumasihene, that is as the original king of Kumasi before the union. Here the power of the Asantehene was extensive and effective. After Kumasi came the other states of Ofinso,

Nsuta, Dwaben and Kokofu which with Kumasi had originally brought the Asante Union into existence. Each of these states had its own king who before the union was equal to the Kumasihene. He ruled his state with his own council of chiefs, but recognized the Asantehene as his overlord. Within this circle the supreme authority was the Asante state council or Asante Kotoko of which all the chiefs of the above states were members. In this council if the Asantehene was not merely the first among equals, neither was he a dictator. The council dealt with all important matters of war and peace; it was the supreme court of the realm before which even the Asantehene could be tried. It was also responsible for crowning and removing the Asantehene. The great bond of union within this wider circle was the fact that all these states descended, or believed that they descended, from the Oyoko matrilineal clan; also all of them recognized the Golden Stool as embodying the spirit of their nation.

Outside this circle was one more, occupied by the conquered provinces of the Union such as the states of Akyem, Akwamu, Akwapim, Denkyira, Wassa and Ga in the south, and Dagomba and Gonja in the north. This circle had an ever-changing radius, shrinking when any of these states rebelled, and expanding when new conquests were made. The provinces in this group were not effectively integrated into the Asante Union. Their kings had no seats in the Asante Kotoko and though they might be under the supervision of Residents appointed by the Asante, they practically ran their affairs without reference to Kumasi. The Residents were often absentees.

Being under so loose a control, and not having forgotten their ancient independence and greatness, while also living near their kith and kin who were still independent of Asante and who often encouraged them to rebel, these states were constantly in revolt. This was a situation that forced the Asante state to be constantly at war in order to punish rebellious chiefs and provinces, and to conquer those neighbouring groups who were still independent and who instigated rebellion against the Asantehene. In the nineteenth century the Fante states of the coast were notorious for aiding and abetting rebellions within the Asante kingdom. Partly for this reason it became necessary for the Asantehene to bring the Fante under his control.

The other factors which helped to determine Asante policy towards the Fante and the British were economic. Asante was an inland power and wanted to gain free access to the coastal forts in order to trade directly with the Europeans. In particular the Asante wanted to ensure a steady supply of arms and ammunition which they needed for their wars. By 1800 Asante had gained access to the forts of Appollonia and Accra, but still wanted direct business with the Europeans at the forts of Anomabu,

Kormantine, Cape Coast and Mouree. It was in these places that the Asante came into conflict with the Fante. The latter had built up a strong and prosperous position as middlemen in the trade between Europeans on the coast and their fellow Africans in the interior, and since they did not want to lose this lucrative position, they insisted that the Asante should continue getting the European goods they wanted through them. To this end they tried to prevent the Asante from getting to the forts. If the Fante succeeded in doing this the Asante would then buy imported European goods in the interior markets at prices fixed by the Fante. For the Asante to prosper economically the Asantehene had to incorporate the Fante into his empire.

Since the British on the coast were all traders, one would have expected them to co-operate with the Asante to promote trade. For instance the British could have helped the Asantehene to assert his authority in his empire in order to maintain peace in the interior, which would help to promote trade. But this the British would not do. They believed that the Asante empire was a savage state, and after the abolition of the slave trade came to regard the Asante as incorrigible slave dealers. For humanitarian reasons the British therefore adopted the policy of giving protection to rebels against the authority of the Asantehene. The result was that the British intervened in the internal affairs of Asante against the authority of the Asantehene and his council.

Also one would have expected the British to welcome direct trade contact with the Asante and try to promote it, especially as it was common knowledge that the Asante wanted the goods which the British brought to the coast. The British therefore might have been expected either to have allowed the Asante to conquer the Fante, or to have controlled the Fante themselves in order to deal directly with the Asante. But they saw the Asante empire as a tyranny and would not allow their Fante allies to be made part of it. More importantly they were afraid that if the Asante held the entire coast of modern Ghana the Asantehene would control the Europeans as strictly as the king of Dahomey did along his own coast, and this might have meant high tolls and less profit for them. The existing situation along the coast, in which the Fante were disunited and weak, suited the British because it allowed them to have their way by playing off one Fante chief against his neighbour. Up to the 1870s the British did not seek to gain control themselves; for the most part they were not interested in acquiring colonies along the West African coast since colonies were considered expensive to maintain.

For all these reasons the British and the Asante found themselves repeatedly at war. The story of the origin of the first Anglo–Asante war is sufficient to show how most of these wars came about without either side wanting to fight the other. In 1807 two Assin chiefs rebelled against the Asantehene. The rebellion was easily put down but the chiefs managed to escape to the Fante for protection. The Asantehene asked the Fante to surrender the refugees but the Fante would not. If the Asantehene had allowed them to keep the refugees his authority would have been greatly endangered, because all other rebels could easily run to the Fante to escape punishment. When the Fante refused to surrender the rebels the Asantehene had to invade the coast. In the battle which followed the Fante were easily defeated. But once again the two chiefs in question managed to escape capture and fled to the British fort of Anomabu for protection. Though the British did not want a war with the Asante they would not surrender the fugitives because they did not believe they would receive a fair trial. Nor would they allow the Asante to continue their slaughter of the Fante since it might end in the Asante controlling the coast and imposing their will on the Europeans. The British therefore came to the defence of the Fante and the refugee chiefs. The result was the first of the Anglo–Asante wars.

Within a hundred years the British and the Asante fought wars in 1807, 1811, 1814–16, 1823–4, 1826, 1863, 1873–4, 1896 and 1901. In all these it was only on three occasions, in 1873–4, 1896 and 1901, that the British invaded Asante. On the remaining occasions it was the Asante who invaded the coastal districts. This does not mean that the Asante were bloodthirsty. On the contrary they were essentially a peace-loving people who did not resort to arms unless diplomacy and negotiation failed In fact many of their invasions of the coast came after weeks or even months of fruitless attempts to achieve peaceful settlements of outstanding quarrels.

The Anglo–Asante wars started because the British would neither control the Fante nor allow the Asante to do so. When they ended, the British had annexed not only the Fante but the Asante as well. The process by which this came about is interesting. At the beginning of the wars the affairs of the British forts were in the hands of merchants. After the third Asante war of 1814–16 it was felt that there would be no peace on the coast as long as merchants, who were preoccupied with ways of maximizing gain and minimizing loss, were in charge of British interests on the coast. The Company of Merchants was therefore dissolved in 1821, when all the British possessions on the west coast were taken over by the Crown and placed under the Governor of Sierra Leone. In 1822 Sir Charles MacCarthy, the Governor at that time, visited his Gold Coast provinces to see Britain's Fante friends. In the process he treated the Asante shabbily, thus precipitating the war of 1824, in which he lost his life. Two years later the British managed to avenge the death of MacCarthy by defeating the Asante at Katamansu, near Dodowa. The British government then recons-

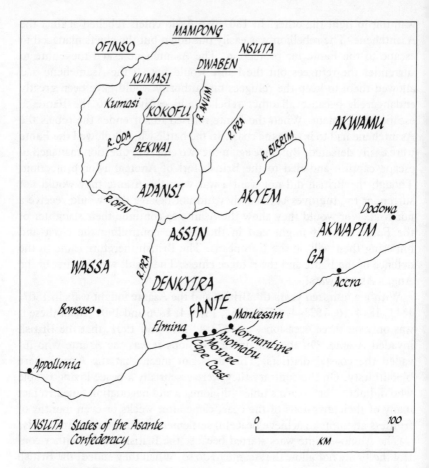

MAMPONG

OFINSO NSUTA

DWABEN

KUMASI

Kumasi KOKOFU R. ANUM R. PRA AKWAMU

R. ODA BEKWAI R. BIRRIM

ADANSI AKYEM

Dodowa

ASSIN AKWAPIM

GA

WASSA DENKYIRA

Accra

Bonsaso FANTE

Mankessim

Elmina Kormantine

Anomabu

Mouree

Cape Coast

Appollonia

NSUTA States of the Asante
        Confederacy

0   100

KM

Asante and the coastal states

idered the whole question and having found that it was not easy to
maintain the peace decided to abandon the forts. But the merchants on the
coast persuaded it to hand the forts over to a committee of three London
merchants, who formed themselves into a company in 1828 and appointed
a governor, Captain George Maclean, to administer the affairs of the forts
with the aid of a council of merchants resident on the coast.

Maclean arrived on the coast in 1830 and the following year signed a
treaty which maintained peace between the British and the Asante for over
30 years. He raised a small body of men whom he used as policemen and
soldiers as the occasion demanded, and with this was able to make sure
that the Fante did not provoke the Asante. He maintained peace along the
coast by patiently listening to and settling all disputes that might lead to

trouble. Though this administration was cheap and effective, complaints against it soon arose. Some traders who did not like Maclean accused him of not fighting slavery on the Gold Coast, others accused him of misusing his powers. A Select Committee of the House of Commons appointed to look into the matter found that Maclean was not guilty of the charges made against him, but recommended that since his administration of the Fante was illegal, it should be legalized.

Once again the British government took back the forts and placed them under a Lieutenant Governor who was responsible to the Governor of Sierra Leone. Maclean, who was made the chief justice in the new administration, negotiated a series of treaties with the Fante chiefs in 1844–5 which gave the British the loophole through which to intervene in Fante affairs and help the chiefs in settling cases of murder and robbery. These treaties are known in history as 'The Bond' and did not in any way hand over Fante territory to the British.

The British now tried to face the problem of raising money locally to cover the cost of administration. After an attempt to levy taxation had aroused so much opposition that it had to be abandoned, the British sought to raise money by imposing customs duties. But if they imposed duties on goods passing through their forts, then traders would divert their activities to Dutch forts. The British therefore sought a way of buying out the Dutch, the Danish having been bought out earlier in 1850.

Before this could be arranged the British and the Asante blundered into war again in 1863. The British had once more refused to surrender an Asante refugee. For the second time the British government started wondering whether it had acted wisely in assuming responsibility for the affairs of the Gold Coast, for the whole business was costing too many men and too much money. Since at the same time Britain was finding it difficult to administer her other possessions along the west coast, a Select Committee of the British Parliament was appointed in 1865 to investigate the whole question. The Committee recommended that the British government should, if possible, stop getting involved in West African politics, except perhaps in the affairs of Sierra Leone.

The news spread quickly along the coast that the British were about to withdraw. If this happened the Fante would have to face the Asante alone. The Fante then decided to make their own defence arrangements. In 1869 about thirteen of their chiefs came together and formed the Fante Confederacy. With the aid of some educated Africans these chiefs in 1871 drew up a constitution at Mankessim under which they would govern themselves and raise forces to defend their territory against the Asante. The British, who had said they were about to go, turned round and said the drawing up of the constitution was a rebellion against their authority. The leaders of the movement were arrested and thrown into prison and the scheme collapsed.

As these things were happening the British succeeded in buying out the Dutch from the Gold Coast. This meant that the people of Elmina, who had been the allies of the Asante, were handed over to their British enemies. The result was an Asante invasion of the coast in 1873. The British replied by sending a force under Sir Garnet Wolseley, which marched to Kumasi and destroyed it. Then the British turned round, and without consulting the people, declared Fante territory their colony. This was how the Fante lost their independence 32 years before the Asante.

The end of Asante independence

The British sack of Kumasi in 1874 was a great blow to the Asante empire from which it never recovered. Many of the chiefs of the northern and southern provinces seized the opportunity to declare their independence. The British did nothing to discourage the rebellions; in fact they encouraged the rebellious provinces by promising some of them protection. At the same time the power of the central government declined as a result of disputes between the Asantehene and his council. One Asantehene was destooled in 1874 for breaking an ancient tradition. After some struggle a successor was enthroned, only to be removed in 1883 for not being in favour of war to reconquer the southern states which had broken away. Then there followed a period of confusion during which the member states of the empire could not agree on a successor. In 1888, however, Agyeman Prempe, then a young man of about 16 years of age, was elected as Asantehene.

The Asantehene-elect succeeded to a difficult inheritance. After so many wars, with their interruptions of trade and dislocation of normal life, the Asante kingdom was not only impoverished, but also depopulated as people fled southwards to the coast either to escape punishment for crimes or to pursue their business in peace. Also, on his accession Prempe was faced with rebellion from several provinces – Kokofu, Nsuta and Mampong. Two events of the early years of the reign clearly indicate to what depths the fortunes of the empire had sunk. First the Asantehene sent a personal message to the Governor of the colony requesting a loan of £320 towards the cost of his enstoolment though when this was made public he denied it to save his face. Then in 1890 the Asante war machine was reduced to such impotence that the Asantehene asked for troops from the colony to help him quell rebellions against his authority. While Prempe was turning and twisting helplessly to keep the empire together, the

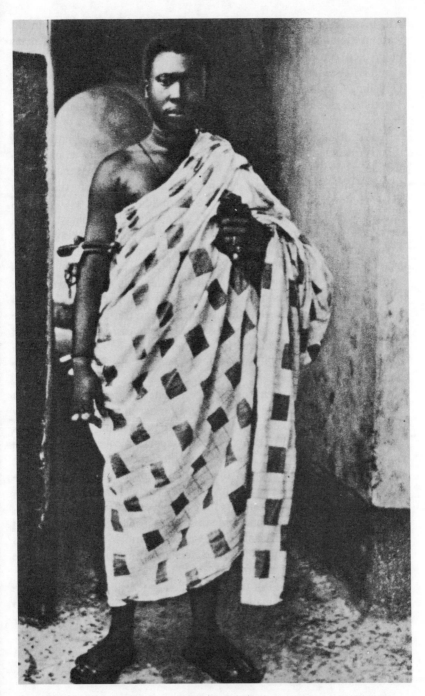

Asantehene Agyeman Prempe I. Asantehene from 1888, he was deposed and exiled by the British in 1896

British came to the conclusion that the only effective way to maintain peace in the interior was to bring the Asante Union and its dependencies under their control.

In 1891 the Governor of the Colony, Brandford Griffith, sent his Acting Travelling Commissioner, H.M. Hull, to Asante with a letter inviting the Asantehene to place his kingdom under British protection; but this Prempe refused with firmness and dignity. In 1894, the year of Prempe's enstoolment, the British again asked the Asante to accept the stationing of a British Resident at Kumasi. In 1895 Joseph Chamberlain became Colonial Secretary and pressure on Asante increased. The Asantehene in despair sent an embassy to London to get a guarantee from the British government that Asante independence would be respected, but this embassy was disgraced and ridiculed. Even while the embassy was still away the British sent an ultimatum to the Asantehene asking him to explain his failure to fulfil all the terms of the Treaty of Fomena, imposed on the Asante Union in 1874. Prempe wanted to hear the result of his embassy before replying. The British regarded this as a refusal of the ultimatum. The forces in the colony were put on a war footing. In 1896 they occupied Kumasi without resistance. Behind this occupation lay the fact that the French were advancing from west to east in the Sudan, and seizing territories as they went. It was therefore feared that if the British did not act fast enough the French or even the Germans would seize Asante.

There was a sequel to this event. The Asante had decided not to resist the British in 1896 because they hoped for a peaceful settlement. But they had been disillusioned. The British seized Prempe and his principal chiefs and courtiers and exiled them. The Asantehene's court was looted, a Resident was stationed at Kumasi, and then the British proceeded to encourage the disintegration of the Asante Union by treating each province as an independent state. This hurt the pride of the Asante. Therefore when in 1900 the Governor of the Colony, Sir Frederick Hodgson, asked for the Golden Stool of Asante to sit on, a privilege not even enjoyed by the Asantehenes, the Asante rose against the British. The uprising was put down after nine months of dogged resistance. In 1901 the Asante state was annexed to the British crown.

These wars thus ended in the loss of their independence by the Fante and the Asante. The dream of a union of all the Akan under the leadership of Asante vanished. On the side of the British, the wars drew them deeper and deeper into the politics of what was then the Gold Coast and is now Ghana. In consequence by the time of the Scramble they already had a strong excuse for the conquest of what remained of Akan-land.

114

4 The establishment of European rule in West Africa (c. 1880–1900)

The origins of European rule in West Africa

As their interests and influence changed in character and expanded in scope in the course of the nineteenth century, European nations, especially Britain and France, began to develop outright political ambitions in West Africa. Britain was the first European nation to acquire a West African territory over which she exercised direct political control. British interest in the campaign against the slave trade and in the protection of legitimate commerce necessitated her seizure of some territories along the West African coast from which to supervise these interests effectively. In 1808 she took over the Sierra Leone colony as a base from which the West African Squadron would carry on the campaign against the slave trade, while in 1843 she finally took over control of certain forts on the coast of Ghana in order to give effective protection to her commerce and her Fante allies against what was considered the Asante menace. For the same reason she bought out the Danes (1850) and the Dutch (1870) from the coast of Ghana. In 1874 she sought to consolidate her control of the Ghanaian coast by annexing the Fante states.

It was the same desire to protect her interests that led Britain to assume political control in one or two areas along the coast of what later became Nigeria. In this region she took the first step towards political power in 1849 when she appointed John Beecroft as consul for the Bights of Benin and Biafra. Supported by the then much-dreaded British gunboats this official started meddling in the politics of the coastal states. In 1851 he interfered in a succession dispute in Lagos, an act which helped to prepare the way for British rule. In 1861 Britain seized this little Yoruba kingdom as a means of controlling the activities of Brazilian slave traders there and the overland trade route which ran from Lagos, through the heart of Yorubaland to Hausaland via Jebba on the Niger.

Meanwhile the new developments in the trade and politics of nineteenth century West Africa had weakened the city states of the Bight of Biafra with the result that these states became increasingly unable to maintain order between the European and African traders as effectively as they had done in centuries past. The white traders immediately seized the opportunity of the new development to usurp part of this waning political control. About 1832 those of them in Bonny formed what in 1854 was named the Court of Equity which assigned itself the duty of regulating relations between African and European traders. This court, which was presided over by Europeans, was soon brought under the control of the British consul. From Bonny the institution spread to the other states of the Niger delta and the Cross River estuary. Though this method of political control in the Bight of Biafra remained informal for a very long time, it was nonetheless real. The consul, the gunboat and the Court of Equity became very important factors in the politics of the region throughout the rest of the century.

With the French, political activity was concentrated in the region of the river Senegal, an area in which they had shown great interest even in the days of the slave trade. If in the course of the eighteenth century France had lost the greater part of her colonial empire to Britain, she now sought to build a new empire in Africa. Thus in 1817 she occupied the mouth of the Senegal where she established an administration and sought to encourage the cultivation of export crops like cotton and groundnuts. By 1865 French rule had reached the upper Senegal, where her influence covered an even wider area.

In spite of these early political developments, however, European rule in West Africa remained severely limited in its territorial extent up to about 1880. There were many reasons for this. For the greater part of the nineteenth century, indeed up to about 1879, French governments were very unstable and throughout that period France could not entertain a vigorous extension of the area in West Africa over which she exercised political rule. Britain, which had more stable government, was busy colonizing Australia and New Zealand which she found more attractive than West Africa. Also at this same time British economic thinkers, known as the free traders, preached against colonization. They argued that colonies were very expensive to maintain and that disputes over them often led to unprofitable international wars. They were confident that given a fair chance Britain would be able to dominate any market through peaceful competition with other nations. What was more, until about 1854, Europe had no answer to the problems presented by malaria in West Africa. In these circumstances European rivalries in West Africa declined. The Dutch and the Danes were even prepared to withdraw, and no other European power rose to challenge the West African interests of either the

French or the British. For all these reasons therefore, though European political ambitions in West Africa were born early in the nineteenth century, they did not achieve an appreciable growth for nearly eighty years.

However, from about 1880 the European attitude to colonies in Africa changed remarkably and as a result within a space of only twenty years nearly the whole of the African continent was under European rule. The factors which caused European nations to scramble for colonial possessions in Africa are discussed in the Conclusion to this volume. Here we are concerned only with the form which that scramble took in West Africa.

To a large extent the scramble in West Africa was a straight fight between the French and the British. As we have already seen, Denmark and Holland had withdrawn from West Africa in the period when colonial possessions in Africa were not very much in favour with European powers. Portugal, which preceded all the other European nations in West Africa, showed very little interest in expansion there. In consequence she was confined to the small enclave of Portuguese Guinea, the conquest of which taxed her resources and determination until about 1915. It was only the intervention of Germany that tended to make the scramble in West Africa a three-cornered fight. Except on the coast of Togoland German interest in West Africa was very negligible by 1880. But in 1884 Germany quickly seized not only Togoland but also the Cameroons, the latter being an area where British interests had been clearly dominant for some time. After this swift move Germany did not attempt to acquire more territories in West Africa but settled down to giving precise definition to the boundaries of these two protectorates, an exercise that involved long negotiations with Britain and France.

The French

The two latter powers thus had the rest of West Africa to fight over. Each not only held what she already had along the coast but from there sought to expand into the interior. Thus French expansion was directed largely from Senegal. This, however, does not mean that the French were not active elsewhere along the West African coast. On the contrary, from the beginning of the scramble they reasserted their control over all their forts along the coast which they had tended to neglect in the previous decade. In 1878 they formally took possession of Cotonou. Four years later they declared a protectorate over Porto Novo. In 1886 they reoccupied their forts on the Ivory Coast which they had abandoned in 1871. From these forts they extended their control over the whole coast between

Liberia and Ghana through treaties with the local chiefs. Higher up the coast they occupied Conakry and from there claimed the whole region between Sierra Leone and Portuguese Guinea. In 1893 they formally proclaimed the Ivory Coast and French Guinea their colonies and undertook the conquest of Dahomey, a task which they completed in 1894.

But in spite of all this Senegal was the main base for French expansion in West Africa. Since the 1850s the French had entertained the ambition of obtaining the undisputed control of the Western and Central Sudan whose ancient fame and glory as a region rich in commerce attracted them very much. To them Timbuktu was still the centre of this trade which they greatly wanted to capture. In consequence they regarded their stations elsewhere along the coast as merely providing alternative routes to the Sudan rather than as bases from which independent expansion could be made. Even their colony of Algeria in North Africa was seen as providing a gateway into the Sudan. From 1880 the French started sending out from Senegal a series of military and exploratory expeditions into the heart of the Sùdan with the object of seizing the whole Sudan and linking it with other French bases along the west coast. By 1883 the French had gone as far as Bamako. In 1890 they started the conquest of the empire of Ahmad Seku, the son and successor of al-Hajj Umar. By 1893 they had succeeded in over-running the whole of this empire. Then they launched an attack on the empire of Samori in the region of Upper Guinea and Ivory Coast, driving him from pillar to post until 1898 when they captured and exiled him. In 1894 the French occupied the ancient and romantic city of Timbuktu. In 1896 they occupied Say. As the French advanced they developed even wider territorial ambitions. At one stage they had plans for a great and glorious French African empire that would stretch across the whole continent from the Senegal to the Nile, thus embracing the whole of the Sudan. This empire was to be continuous with Algeria in North Africa, with French Guinea, the Ivory Coast and Dahomey on the west coast as well as with French possessions in Equatorial Africa. It was to be served by a network of modern railways which would tap the resources of this whole region to the everlasting benefit and glory of metropolitan France.

The British

The British on their part concentrated mainly on the forest region of West Africa since they did not fall victim to the ancient romance of the Sudan. They set out to expand their holdings in the forest zone where they could

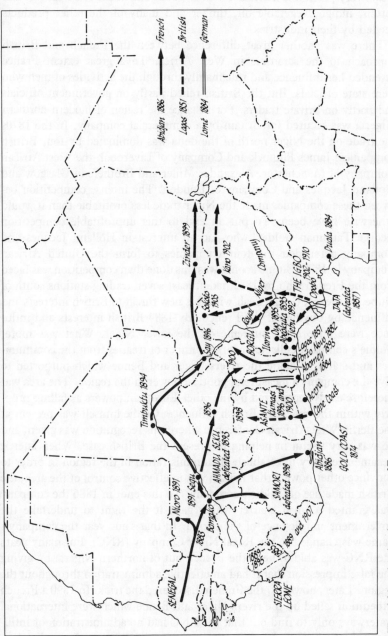

West Africa, showing the progress of European penetration

create very profitable markets for their goods and at the same time obtain cotton, indigo, vegetable oil, timber and many of the other products needed by their industries.

There was another great difference between the French and British approach to the scramble in West Africa. To a great extent France extended her influence and rule mainly through the activities of men who were state officials. But the British relied partly on government officials and partly on private traders. For instance the region of modern northern Nigeria was secured for Britain by a commercial company. In the 1870s the trade on the Niger north of the delta was dominated by four British companies: James Pinnock and Company of Liverpool, the West African Company of Manchester, Alexander Miller and Brothers of Glasgow and Holland Jacques and Company of London. The intense competition between these companies made the Niger trade less profitable than it would otherwise have been. To put an end to this unprofitable competition George Taubman Goldie, who had an interest in Holland Jacques and Company persuaded the four companies to form the United African Company in 1879. But no sooner was this done than competition was faced from the French who by 1882 had at least seven trading stations south of Nupe. However, Goldie dealt with this new threat to British interests and influence by buying off the French. By 1884 British interests and influence were once again supreme on the lower Niger. What was more, Goldie's company collected a large number of treaties from the communities and states all along the rivers Niger and Benue which purported to give the company a measure of political power in the region. The area was therefore easily recognized by the other European powers as falling properly within the sphere of British influence. Goldie himself was present at the Berlin West African Conference where this recognition was given, and he was very useful in helping to present the British case. When later it became necessary to establish an administration in the region in order to convince other powers that Britain was in effective control of the area, the British made use of Goldie's company. To this end, in 1886 the company was granted a royal charter which gave it the right to undertake the government and defence of the region. In that same year the company's name was changed to the Royal Niger Company (RNC). For many years the RNC was able to keep the French out of northern Nigeria by giving the false impression that it had an effective administration throughout the region. Later, however, the French discovered the trick. In 1890 a French expedition sailed up the rivers Niger and Benue which were international waterways only to find out that the RNC had no administration or influence whatever in a place like the emirate of Adamawa. Immediately struggle for the control of this region ensued. The RNC, however, successfully met the challenge and secured for Britain not only Yola, the capital of Adamawa, but also much of the extensive Borno empire. But the company was able to meet successfully all such challenges. Thus after the conquest of Dahomey in 1894 the French started moving up towards the Niger, and in the process discovered that the company had no influence or establishment whatsoever in Borgu and much of the area around it. The French again made a determined effort to seize the region. In the course of the ensuing struggle for Borgu the British government realized that the RNC had not the resources with which to meet this fresh and more serious challenge. The Borgu question brought Britain and France to the brink of war and Britain was forced to create the West African Frontier Force under the command of Frederick Lugard in 1897. It was this direct intervention of the British government that resolved the Borgu crisis and kept the region under British rule. On 1 January 1900 the RNC was deprived of its charter and Northern Nigeria was declared a British Protectorate. Nevertheless it can be said that the RNC served Britain well in winning for her the extensive area of Northern Nigeria.

Elsewhere in West Africa the establishment and expansion of British rule was in the main the result of official action. As soon as Germany seized the Cameroons the British consul in the Niger delta, Edward Hewett, took steps to ensure that Britain was not pushed out of the Oil Rivers. He collected treaties of protection from various chiefs and villages on the basis of which Britain proclaimed the whole region between Lagos and the Cameroons the Oil Rivers Protectorate in June 1885. This protectorate which extended as far inland as Lokoja on the Niger and Ibi on the Benue had no real administration until 1891, the year when its name was changed to the Niger Coast Protectorate. British acquisition of Yorubaland was the work of the Lagos government, which since the 1860s had been deeply involved in Yoruba politics. In 1888 the Lagos authorities made a treaty with the *alafin* of Oyo who is said to have placed all Yorubaland under British protection, even though the *alafin* never controlled more than a fraction of Yorubaland during the peak period of his empire. In the region of modern Ghana, Asante was occupied in 1896 and forced to admit a British resident to Kumasi. From there the authorities of the colony proceeded in 1898 to annex the Northern Territories of Ghana to Britain. In 1896 the Freetown government extended British rule to the Sierra Leone hinterland. British expansion on the Gambia was in like manner the work of British officials rather than of private businessmen.

After the scramble

By 1900 the scramble was virtually over, and all West Africa, except the small Repubic of Liberia, was now under European rule. Even then Liberia was not unaffected by the scramble for she lost a considerable portion of the coast to which she had laid claim since the 1830s. Furthermore she lost all opportunity for expansion into the interior. Of all the powers involved France emerged from the scramble with the lion's share of the territory. Whereas Britain, her nearest rival in West Africa,

The treaty made between Consul Hewett and Jaja of Opobo in 1884

TREATY with Kings and Chiefs of *Opobo*

Signed at *Opobo*

HER Majesty the Queen of the United Kingdom of Great Britain and Ireland, Empress of India, &c., and the Kings and Chiefs of *Opobo* being desirous of maintaining and strengthening the relations of peace and friendship which have for so long existed between them;

Her Britannic Majesty has named and appointed E. H. Hewett, Esq., Her Consul for the Bights of Benin and Biafra, to conclude a Treaty for this purpose.

The said E. H. Hewett, Esq., and the said Kings and Chiefs of *Opobo* have agreed upon and concluded the following Articles:—

ARTICLE I.

Her Majesty the Queen of Great Britain and Ireland, &c., in compliance with the request of the Kings, Chiefs, and people of *Opobo* , hereby undertakes to extend to them, and to the territory under their authority and jurisdiction, Her gracious favour and protection.

ARTICLE II.

The Kings and Chiefs of *Opobo* agree and promise to refrain from entering into any correspondence, Agreement, or Treaty with any foreign nation or Power, except with the knowledge and sanction of Her Britannic Majesty's Government.

ARTICLE III.

It is agreed that full and exclusive jurisdiction, civil and criminal, over British subjects and their property in the territory of *Opobo* is reserved to Her Britannic Majesty, to be exercised by such Consular or other officers as Her Majesty shall appoint for that purpose.

The same jurisdiction is likewise reserved to Her Majesty in the said territory of *Opobo* over foreign subjects enjoying British protection, who shall be deemed to be included in the expression " British subject " throughout this Treaty.

ARTICLE IV.

All disputes between the Kings and Chiefs of *Opobo* , or between them and British or foreign traders, or between the aforesaid Kings and Chiefs and neighbouring tribes, which cannot be settled amicably between the two parties, shall be submitted to the British Consular or other officers appointed by Her Britannic Majesty to exercise jurisdiction in *Opobo* territories for arbitration and decision, or for arrangement.

ARTICLE V.

The Kings and Chiefs of *Opobo* hereby engage to assist the British Consular or other officers in the execution of such duties as may be assigned to them; and, further, to act upon their advice in matters relating to the administration of justice, the development of the resources of the country, the interests of commerce, or in any other matter in relation to peace, order, and good government, and the general progress of civilization.

ARTICLE VI.

The subjects and citizens of all countries may freely carry on trade in every part of the territories of the Kings and Chiefs parties hereto, and may have houses and factories therein.

White

ARTICLE VII.

All ministers of the Christian religion shall be permitted to reside and exercise their calling within the territories of the aforesaid Kings and Chiefs, who hereby guarantee to them full protection.

All forms of religious worship and religious ordinances may be exercised within the territories of the aforesaid Kings and Chiefs, and no hindrance shall be offered thereto.

ARTICLE VIII.

If any vessels should be wrecked within the *Opobo* territories, the Kings and Chiefs will give them all the assistance in their power, will secure them from plunder, and also recover and deliver to the owners or agents all the property which can be saved.

If there are no such owners or agents on the spot, then the said property shall be delivered to the British Consular or other officer.

The Kings and Chiefs further engage to do all in their power to protect the persons and property of the officers, crew, and others on board such wrecked vessels.

All claims for salvage dues in such cases shall, if disputed, be referred to the British Consular or other officer for arbitration and decision.

ARTICLE IX.

This Treaty shall come into operation, so far as may be practicable, from the date of its signature, *Article VI as herein printed being expunged.*

Done in Duplicate at Opobo this nineteenth day of December in the year one thousand eight hundred and eighty four

Edward Hyde Hewett

JaJa

Cooksey Gam

Prince Saturday Ja Ja

Finebourne   *His X Mark*

acquired a total area of 1 243 200 square kilometres, France's empire in West Africa measured about 4 662 000 square kilometres, Germany came third with Togoland which measured 854 700 square kilometres, and the Cameroons which had an area of 518 000 square kilometres, Portugal came last with a colony measuring 36 300 square kilometres in area. To some extent France achieved her ambition which at first appeared visionary. She secured most of the Western Sudan and linked this up with all her territories on the coast. Furthermore, she was able to link her West African empire with her possessions in North Africa. But she failed to link all this up with the Nile. The Anglo-Egyptian Sudan stood in her way. The main rivers of West Africa fell into French and British hands. Britain controlled the lower Gambia, the lower Niger and the navigable portions of the Benue, while France controlled the whole of the Senegal, upper Gambia, the upper and the middle Niger. These rivers were useful as gateways into the areas of West Africa which they drain. Though Britain's four colonies, The Gambia, Sierra Leone, Ghana, and Nigeria were all widely separated, each of them enjoyed the advantage of having direct access to the sea. But whereas the French could travel from one end of their West African possession to the other without passing through any other power's colony or entering the sea, the British could not.

Reasons for the conquest of West Africa – treaties, force and African disunity

The ease with which the European powers partitioned West Africa without fighting among themselves should be explained. In the first place before the scramble had started in earnest the European nations had held the Berlin West Africa Conference (1884–5) to set down the rules of the game. This conference did not partition West Africa, or any other part of Africa, as is often popularly believed. Among other things it declared the Niger and the Congo (now Zaire) international waterways, which meant that these rivers were to be free for navigation by all nations of the world. Though this principle was soon infringed on both the Niger and the Congo, no international crisis resulted because no nation seriously took it upon herself to challenge the action of those who controlled the two rivers. The conference also set down the conditions under which the occupation of a territory by one power would gain the recognition of the others. An occupying power was not only required to notify the others of the fact of her occupation but also was to set up an administration as a visible evidence of her effective presence. By and large this principle was adhered to. As a result no power deliberately trespassed against the established rights of her neighbour. Germany, who had offended the British by her seizure of the Cameroons, soon withdrew from, and lost interest in, further territorial expansion in West Africa. There was therefore no opportunity for them to clash again in West Africa. Britain and France seemed most likely to clash but did not actually do so because their interests were not really in conflict except perhaps in one place. France for the most part wanted the savanna belt, Britain the forest region. It was only the British 'intrusion' into the Sudan by way of her interest in Northern Nigeria that nearly brought the two countries to war over Borgu. There would have been a crisis over the imamate of Futa Jallon in which the French had shown interest since 1860, but the French suspicion between 1880 and 1882 that Britain wanted to annex Futa Jallon to Sierra Leone, turned out to be unfounded.

European rule was imposed on West Africans by 'diplomacy' and war. What is described as 'diplomacy' here, would be better described as 'trickery'. Britain, France and Germany claimed to base their rule in many areas on treaties of protection which they said they had signed with the local chiefs. In these treaties the chiefs are said to have signed away for ever their territories and peoples. Since no West African ruler ever had the right to give away his people and their land, it is doubtful whether these so-called treaties were treaties in fact. If any chief ever signed such a treaty it was invalid in traditional law. A critical study of some of these treaties seems to reveal that many of them were fake. In 1880 a French officer, J.S. Gallieni, visited the empire of Ahmad Seku of Segu (the successor of al-Hajj Umar) and came out with a treaty which claimed that Ahmad had agreed to place under 'the exclusive protection of France' the basin of the Niger passing through his empire. This copy of the treaty did not carry Ahmad's signature or the seal of his empire. The Arabic copy of the same treaty which bore Ahmad's signature and imperial seal did not mention that Ahmad had made any such grants to the French. The Arabic copy merely reveals that Gallieni and Ahmad Seku signed only a treaty of peace and friendship. But in order to keep off possible European rivals Gallieni must have tampered with the contents of the original treaty. This is perhaps a good example of how many of the so-called treaties of protection were obtained.

If some of these treaties were actually signed by African chiefs, there is reason to believe that such chiefs did not know the full implications of what they were asked to do. When Consul Hewett was touring the Niger, 'hunting' for treaties with African chiefs, he came to Opobo which was then under King Jaja. He asked this delta chief to sign a treaty of 'protection' and 'free trade' with Britain. Jaja, who was a very intelligent man, asked him to explain what he meant by 'free trade'. When the explanation which Hewett gave did not satisfy him, Jaja refused to sign the treaty unless the section referring to trade was removed. This section was duly removed before Jaja signed the treaty. It is unlikely that, if the Europeans had explained the full meaning of these treaties to the people, most West African chiefs would have signed them.

In most places, however, sometimes even in places where they claimed to have obtained the so-called treaties of cession, Europeans had to impose their rule by force. Though West Africans often clamoured for European goods, they did not clamour for European rule, and never trusted Europeans. One of Ahmad Seku's lieutenants told Gallieni in 1880: 'We like the French but do not trust them, they trust us but do not like us'. Most West Africans knew that their way of life was different from that of Europeans, and that European rule would tamper with this way of life. They also did not want to lose the right to govern themselves. When the Mogho Naba of Mossi was informed that the French would civilize his country, he told them he was satisfied with his country as it was. For these reasons West Africans could not accept European rule with enthusiasm. The Europeans therefore had to conquer them in order to rule. It was by force that the French established themselves in Dahomey, Futa Jallon, Upper Guinea, Upper Ivory Coast, Kaarta, Segu and Macina. The British also had to fight many wars in order to subject the people in their West African colonies to their rule. They fought the people of Sierra Leone Protectorate (1898); fought the Asante throughout the nineteenth century; in Nigeria they fought Ijebu (1892), Brass (1895), Ilorin and Bida (1897), Benin (1897), Arochukwu (1901–2) and Northern Nigeria (1900–4). In certain parts of West Africa armed resistance lasted till the second decade of this century. By 1919 the British were still fighting to subdue certain villages in the Igbo and Ibibio areas for the first time. Military resistance in the French colony of Niger lasted until 1922. In Portuguese Guinea military action became an aspect of normal government. Thus the first problem which the Europeans faced in ruling West Africa was to get the West Africans to accept their rule. In this they never wholly succeeded. West Africans never accepted European rule with all their heart.

Though the opposition to European rule was widespread in West Africa the Europeans succeeded all the same in bringing West Africans under their rule. This was so for two reasons. Firstly, the Europeans were better armed and had better trained soldiers than any West African people. The Maxim gun and incendiary rockets which played a major part in these wars were weapons the like of which no West African people had ever seen or heard of before. They therefore had no answer to them. Secondly, West African opposition was not co-ordinated. Each kingdom, and sometimes

127

each village, fought its own battle and suffered defeat without any help from its neighbours. Even the Muslim states of the Sudan which had many common ties failed to combine against the European invaders. Samori of Guinea and Ahmad Seku of Segu were so opposed to each other, that Ahmad sometimes preferred co-operation with the French to co-operation with Samori. Futhermore, many of the better-organized African states were in decline at the time. Borno started to decline again after al-Kanemi. After the death of Muhammad Bello in 1837 the Fulani empire lost its vigour. The empire of Ahmad Seku of Segu was never properly governed, as a result of which the provinces were already breaking away when the scramble started. The French exploited this situation by posing as the liberators of the rebellious provinces and in so doing weakened Ahmad Seku. The empire of Samori was still rising when the scramble started. The Asante state had been severely weakened by a century of continuous warfare. The Oyo empire was already in disarray by the second decade of the century while the states which rose after its fall were engaged in mutual destruction. The kingdom of Dahomey was probably the strongest and best-organized West African state on the eve of the scramble. But then it had been very much weakened by its wars with the Egba, and in any case fought without any help from its neighbours.

Then there was the co-operation which renegade West Africans gave to the invaders. The armies which conquered West Africa were made up largely of West Africans, with a sprinkling of West Indians, trained and led by European officers. In Nigeria, for instance, the British used mainly Hausa troops to conquer the south, and mainly Yoruba and other non-Muslims to conquer Hausaland. Even the educated elements did not all speak with one voice in defence of African independence. Some of them considered a period under European tutelage necessary for Africa. Bishop Samuel Ajayi Crowther, for instance, is said to have strongly recommended the British annexation of Lagos. There were many other similar cases.

There is no doubt that African leaders did not fully recognize the extent of the dangers they had to cope with, especially in those areas where European Christian missions were already well established. These missions and their agents formed the vanguard of the invaders' intelligence network and thus supplied much of the information the armies needed. On occasions they provided personnel such as doctors and nurses, and facilities such as hospitals, for the treatment of wounded colonial troops. In the campaign against the Aro of south-eastern Nigeria, for example, Presbyterian missionaries in Calabar provided these facilities and more. They allowed their river crafts to be used in the movement of troops, thus directly assisting the process of colonial conquest and occupation.

128

5 Egypt from the Napoleonic invasion to the British occupation

Egypt, an Arab nation

As was pointed out in the Introduction, Egypt had lived under a series of foreign rulers ever since the defeat and conquest of the last dynasty of pharaohs in 341 BC. Of these foreign rulers the Arabs who conquered the country from the Eastern Roman (Byzantine) empire in AD 639 made the most profound impact on its life. From the Arab conquest began the process which led to the adoption of Islam as the religion of the overwhelming majority of the population. As Islam is not just a matter of personal beliefs but a comprehensive way of life, the adoption of the religion has influenced every aspect of the peoples' existence. The administrative and legal systems, family life, education and the attitude of the people to life and to other peoples have all been profoundly influenced by Islam. This, together with the fact that Arabic became the language of the people, almost completely replacing the native Egyptian tongue, and the considerable admixture of Arab blood, accounts for the situation in which Egypt to this day regards itself as an Arab state with ties to the Middle East as well as Africa. Islam is still such a powerful force in the country that many, especially the fanatical religious organization called the Muslim Brotherhood, would like to take the country towards a system of government based on Islamic fundamentalism after the pattern of Iran.

Although Egypt after the Arab conquest became, and has remained, an Islamic society there always survived a substantial community of Christians who are known as the Copts. These Christians, who are still a large community today, occupied an ambiguous position in Egyptian society. Under Muslim law they were entitled to protection but could not be full members of an Islamic state. They often held important posts in the service of the state but they were distrusted because of their religion and disliked by their Muslim fellow subjects.

The Mamluks, 1249–1517

After the Arab conquest Egypt was at first part of the vast empire established by the early caliphs, but with the break-up of the political unity of Islam it fell under a number of different dynasties in succession. In 1249 the slave bodyguard of the ruler (who belonged to a dynasty known as Ayyubid) seized power. This was the beginning of a long period in which Egypt was governed by a military class of slaves of foreign origin. These slave rulers were recruited from Turkey and South Russia and were known as Mamluks. They gave Egypt one of the most glorious periods in its history and the magnificent buildings erected under the Mamluks are still among the wonders of modern Cairo. But the Mamluks weakened their power and wasted the resources of the country in internal struggles for power. They divided up the land of Egypt between themselves and forced the peasants to pay heavy taxes. They failed to keep up with progress in the rest of the world and in 1517 they were utterly defeated by the forces of the Ottoman sultan of Turkey.

Egypt under the Ottoman empire

Thereafter Egypt became a part of the Ottoman sultanate. At first the new rulers introduced many welcome improvements. Regular centralized administration was established, taxes were lightened, irrigation canals were cleared and improved and the country became prosperous again. But in time the Ottoman sultanate fell into decline. The sultan's administration became weak and corrupt, and the generals and other officers in the provinces were left to do much as they pleased. In these circumstances the Ottoman officials in Egypt began recruiting their own slave bodyguards and the Mamluk system was revived in a new form. By the eighteenth century Ottoman authority had so declined that the sultans had virtually no influence in the country which was still officially part of their empire. The real rulers of the land were the Mamluks headed by officers known as *beys*. Only the bitter rivalries between the *beys*, which gave the Ottoman ruler the chance to play one faction off against another, prevented the Mamluk *beys* from establishing complete independence. Inside Egypt one Mamluk band fought against another to make its leader the most powerful figure in the country. Bloody battles were fought in the streets, the shops of merchants were looted and the peasants (*fellahin*) were unmercifully overtaxed to support the fighting bands of their overlords.

In these grim circumstances the peasants began to neglect the cultivation of the land, the irrigation system deteriorated, merchants were unable to make improvements in commerce or industry, and the once prosperous country became steadily poorer, falling far behind the developments that were taking place in western Europe. The Mamluks themselves were so absorbed in the continual struggle for power that they did not even keep abreast of changes in military methods and continued to cling to long-outdated methods of warfare on horseback. To complete the miseries of Egypt the land was subject to repeated epidemics of plague and the population dwindled from about 8.5 million in the fourteenth century to about 3 million at the beginning of the nineteenth century

Napoleon invades Egypt

In 1798 the course of Egyptian history was suddenly and violently altered when Napoleon with his French forces landed on Egyptian soil. His reasons for making this move were complex. Amongst the ideas of the French Revolution, of which he considered himself the leader, was the belief that there should be a universal law for all humanity, and that the whole human race sould be liberated to enjoy the ideals of Liberty, Equality and Fraternity as well as other aspects of the French revolutionary system. Although a soldier, Napoleon had a real interest in, and respect for, the ancient Egyptian civilization, and his army included a large team of scholars and experts to study the monuments of the land he was about

The Battle of the Pyramids, 1798

to conquer. His deeper reasons were less unselfish. As he told his government in France, his main objects were to ensure the exploitation of the riches of the country for the benefit of France and to use it as a stepping stone for the conquest of the British empire in India.

When Napoleon's forces reached Egypt power was in the hands of two notoriously quarrelsome *beys*, Murad Bey and Ibrahim Bey. The mass of the people, long used to being passive spectators as one group of foreigners after another seized their country, and worn out by the oppressions of their Mamluk overlords, could hardly be expected to rally to the defence of their masters, even against an infidel invader. The Mamluks themselves were militarily years out of date and in no position to offer serious resistance to the French army. Their magnificently clad horses and riders fell in heaps before the accurate musket and cannon fire of the French at the Battle of the Pyramids (1798), and Napoleon made himself the master of Egypt.

Consequences of Napoleon's invasion

The Napoleonic conquest of Egypt, even though it lasted for no more than three years, had important consequences for the history of Egypt and the entire Arab world. Ever since the ending of the Crusades (towards the end of the thirteenth century) the heart of the Islamic world in Egypt and the Middle East had been free from serious attack from Christian Europe. During the later Ottoman period the whole area had become increasingly backward and out of date in contrast with Europe. But because of belief in the superiority of the Islamic religion this was not obvious to the peoples of those areas, who had continued to drift complacently downhill. The unexpected conquest of Egypt, a key province of the Ottoman empire, by Christian forces suddenly made the real situation painfully clear. Thereafter the whole Islamic world began to be agitated by reforming movements of one kind and another, which had begun with the rise of the Wahhabis in Arabia fifty years before Napoleon. Some aimed at the adoption of European ideas and their reconciliation with Islam, others at sweeping away corruption and a return to the purity of the original faith. All were aimed at wiping out the shame of the weak position of Muslims in relation to Christian Europe and restoring the power and prestige of Islam. This movement was felt throughout the whole Ottoman empire and as far away as Afghanistan and northern India. In Africa it influenced not only Egypt itself but the eastern Sudan, Somalia, Libya and the Sudanic belt of West Africa. It was the beginning of a revolution in thought and attitudes as well as in techniques and political systems which is still in progress in much of the Islamic world.

In Egypt the short period of French rule brought many important developments. In the attempt to win the support of the Egyptian masses, Napoleon proclaimed that he had come to Egypt to deliver the Egyptians from their Mamluk oppressors, whose greed and injustice had ruined the once prosperous land. He would give Egyptians freedom, respect Islam and help all Muslims, including the Ottoman Turks, to fight against Christian 'infidels'. He ended his proclamation by saying: 'Let every qadi, imam and sheik in Egypt proclaim these truths from his mosque. Glory to the Sultan, glory to the brave French army, curses on the Mamluks and happiness to Egypt.' The Egyptian populace could not be expected to accept these sentiments wholeheartedly from the mouth of an 'infidel' conqueror. However much they had disliked the Mamluks, their deep religious beliefs made them hate Christian invaders even more. Violent riots broke out in Cairo which were severely suppressed. Nevertheless, Napoleon still attempted to take Egyptians into partnership in the administration of their country by setting up local and district councils on which native Egyptians – as opposed to alien Mamluks – were represented. He also established a central council called the Diwan to advise him on matters of state. Two newspapers were founded, one of them in the Arabic language. This was the first Arabic newspaper in the Nile valley, and was an important development, considering the role which newspapers subsequently played in the growth of Egyptian nationalism and its struggle against British rule. Another significant innovation of the French period was the founding of the Institut de l'Egypte (Egyptian Institute) to study the rich past of the country. It played an important part in the development of the study of ancient Egypt, now known as Egyptology, and in reminding Egyptians of their cultural heritage. The same idea can be seen in many countries of modern Africa where institutes of African studies have been established.

The British force Napoleon to leave Egypt

The French occupation of Egypt was seen in Britain as a direct threat to the British possessions in India and it became the object of British policy first to prevent Napoleon from carrying out his plans to use his conquest as a base for an attack on India, and secondly to force him to withdraw from Egypt altogether. British forces sent to the Syrian fortress of Acre prevented Napoleon from advancing through the Middle East on his planned invasion of India from the north and Nelson destroyed the power of the French navy in the Mediterranean by defeating the French fleet at

Abukir Bay in August 1798. This meant that the army in Egypt could easily be cut off from its supplies and the French were forced to leave the country in 1801. This struggle between the British and the French was only the first step in a long process which resulted in the British occupation of Egypt. The basis of the struggle was a conflict of strategic interests. Britain could never feel that her position in India was safe if another powerful European country which might at some time become hostile had a dominant influence in Egypt.

The rise of Muhammad Ali

When the French departed, Egypt returned to a state of chaos. The Mamluk *beys* resumed their rivalry, the British gave their support first to one and then another, and the Ottoman sultan sent forces to the country in the attempt to make his rule effective. This confused situation provided the opportunity for a remarkable man to come to the fore and make himself the real ruler of the country. His name was Muhammad Ali. An Albanian born in 1769, he had taken to the career of soldier of fortune in the sultan's army. Though fully trained in the principles of the Ottoman regime under which he lived, he clearly saw the need for the Muslim world to adopt and apply the methods and techniques of western Europe. It was to be his role to wake Egypt from its slumbers, and to attempt to bring it in one great leap into the modern world. Though many of his plans resulted in disastrous failure, and though some of the policies which he initiated resulted, when they were later carried on by less able men, in Egypt coming under foreign rule, there are few who would deny him the title of founder of modern Egypt.

Muhammad Ali first showed his political genius in triumphing over the numerous factions struggling for power in Egypt. At first he played the two main Mamluk factions – Bardisi and Elifi – off against one another. Then he threw his weight behind the official Ottoman governor (*pasha*), Kirshid, against both Mamluk groups. Then as Kirshid became unpopular both in Cairo and Constantinople, Muhammad Ali led the people of Cairo against him. Kirshid was deposed and his successor lasted for six months. Having weakened all the powerful factions that were struggling for power Muhammad Ali then seized the leadership of the country for himself, taking care to win the Sultan's approval for his action. By 1805 he was effectively in control of the country. In 1806 Muhammad Ali was officially confirmed in the position of *wali* (governor) by the Sultan.

Once in power he consistently pursued a number of closely related policies. Firstly he sought to strengthen his own position in Egypt, to

Muhammad Ali, effective ruler of Egypt from 1805 until his death in 1849

destroy all possible rivals and to ensure that this power would be handed down hereditarily to his descendants. This inevitably involved the policy of establishing the independence of Egypt from the Ottoman sultanate because as long as the country was in theory just a province of the Ottoman empire he was legally no more than an Ottoman official, liable to dismissal at any time and with no guarantee that his children would be allowed to succeed him. This in turn meant that he must strive to make Egypt a rival to Turkey as the centre of the Muslim world and was related to the most famous and deeply cherished of Muhammad Ali's policies, namely the attempt to turn backward and poverty-stricken Egypt into a fully fledged modern state.

Destruction of the Mamluks and social reforms

One of Muhammad Ali's first and most significant acts was to stamp out the Mamluks and put a final end to a system which had lasted since AD 1249. In 1807 the Mamluk *beys* rose in an unsuccessful revolt against the new master of Egypt and were suppressed with the aid of Muhammad Ali's Albanian soldiery. In 1811 he invited a large part of the surviving

Mamluks to a great banquet in Cairo. Then when his guests had assembled he gave the order and they were all put to death. This crushing blow was followed by an all-out attempt to hunt down and destroy the remaining Mamluks in the provinces. Only a small number escaped to take refuge in the lands of the Funj sultanate higher up the Nile valley. Having destroyed the Mamluks, Muhammad Ali abolished the system of land ownership under which they had exploited the peasantry and declared the land returned to the tillers of the soil.

Military reforms: the creation of a national army

The elimination of the Mamluks meant that Muhammad Ali had to base his military power on other means. To rely exclusively on his Albanian troops would have been too dangerous, for they were soldiers of fortune in a foreign land. Having put him in power they might have easily turned against him and removed him. He was thus led to take the momentous step of recruiting native-born Egyptians into the armed forces and laying the foundations of a modern national army. This was a step of tremendous importance for the future for it meant that the native Egyptians, who for centuries had been unarmed and helpless under successive foreign rulers, would be in a position to decide their own destiny. It is not too much to say that the creation of a truly Egyptian army meant the beginning of effective Egyptian nationalism. This was first seen in the nineteenth century in the career of Arabi Pasha, and more recently in the career of Gamel Abdul Nasser. At the time, however, the move was not at all popular. For more than a thousand years the Egyptian *fellahin* had taken no part in the military defence of their country. Army life was something that was alien and dreaded. What is more the Egyptians recruited to the army were taken only into the lowest ranks; the officers remained Albanians or Turks. Thus the peasants had to be forced most unwillingly into the armed forces and Muhammad Ali was anxious to find alternative sources of military manpower.

Muhammad Ali's new army (Nizam Jadid) was an innovation. He deliberately set out to equip and train it in the most modern fashion. A French military instructor, Captain Seres, was appointed to take charge of the training programme and the latest military equipment was imported from Europe. To the astonishment of the world, which tended to regard the Egyptians as incapable of fighting, the new army went on to distinguish itself in a number of very difficult and laborious campaigns.

Land forces were not Muhammad Ali's only concern. He clearly realized the importance of sea power and with speed and determination set about building up a modern navy.

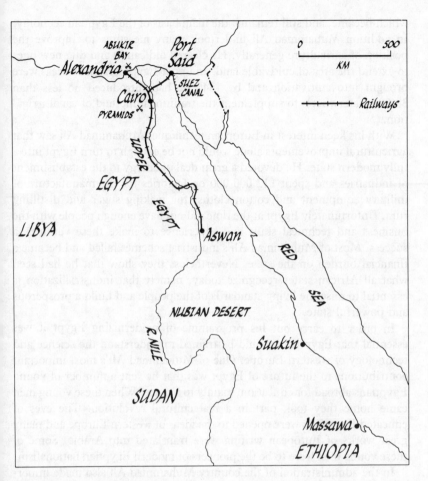

Egypt in the nineteenth century

Attempts to modernize the Egyptian economy

To support these new and expensive forces and pay for the campaigns on which he used them, Muhammad Ali required a greatly increased revenue and he devoted himself with as much energy to the modernization of the Egyptian economy as he did to the improvement of the armed forces. By far the most important of his innovations in this field was the development of cotton growing as a major agricultural activity. Seeing the economic value of the crop he introduced a strain of cotton grown in the upper Nile valley previously little grown, if at all, in Egypt itself. A tremendous campaign was launched to persuade the peasants to plant the new crop

137

which became, and still remains, the main basis of the Egyptian economy. In addition Muhammad Ali undertook many measures to improve the position of agriculture generally. He cleared old canals and dug new ones to extend the area of cultivable land. In upper Egypt large new areas were brought into cultivation and by 1844 he had introduced no less than 38 000 waterwheels to supplement the traditional method of canal irrigation.

With his keen interest in European techniques Muhammad Ali saw that agricultural improvements alone would not be enough to turn Egypt into a fully modern state. He devoted a great deal of energy to the establishment of industries and spent £12 000 000 on factories for the manufacture of military equipment and cotton cloths, for making sugar and distilling rum. Unfortunately Egypt at the time did not have enough people with the business and technical skills and experience to make these ventures a success. Most of Muhammad Ali's industrial schemes failed and became a financial burden on the state. Nevertheless they show that he had seen what all African states recognize today, namely that industrialization is essential to raise the living standards of the people and build a prosperous and powerful state.

In order to carry out his programme of modernizing Egypt it was essential that Egyptians should be trained to understand the science and technology of western Europe. One of Muhammad Ali's most important contributions to the future of Egypt was that he sent a number of young Egyptians abroad for education, mainly to France. When these young men came home they took part in a real cultural revolution. The eyes of educated Egyptians were opened to the ideas of western Europe and many great works of European writing were translated into Arabic. Some of these young men were to be the pioneers of modern Egyptian nationalism.

In the administration of the country Muhammad Ali also made important reforms which gave the native Egyptians some say in the running of their country. Some Egyptians were employed in the civil service, though usually under better-educated Turks, and Egyptians were appointed as village heads, district heads and tax collectors.

In spite of his modernizing and Europeanizing schemes Muhammad Ali was well aware of the strength of tradition and took care not to offend the religious beliefs of his subjects too deeply. He himself built one of the most magnificent mosques in Egypt on the top of the citadel in Cairo. The Islamic judges (*qadis*) and *muftis* were also kept in office to dispense justice in accordance with Muslim law. Realizing that Egypt was becoming cosmopolitan, however, he established two courts for foreigners. These courts were dominated by merchants, not by Muslims. The one at Alexan-

The Citadel Mosque, Cairo

dria had nine members; four of them were Arabs and there was one Frenchman, a Jew, a Greek, and two Middle Eastern Christians. Muhammad Ali was liberal in religious matters and allowed freedom of worship to the Copts and other Christians and to the Jews.

Muhammad Ali's foreign policy

Foreign policy was probably Muhammad Ali's greatest interest. Unless he could win a considerable degree of independence for Egypt from the Ottoman empire he could in theory be deposed at any time by the Ottoman sultan, and all his plans might be undone. He therefore tried to strengthen Egypt's position as an Islamic power and to win more independence from the Ottoman empire. At first he set out to achieve his aims by co-operating with the Ottoman sultan. The Ottoman sultan on the other hand was afraid of the growing power of his overmighty subject and hoped to weaken him by getting him involved in difficult and expensive military campaigns.

In 1812 the Ottoman sultan asked Muhammad Ali to undertake the suppression of a rebellion by the fanatical Wahhabi sect in central Arabia. Egyptian forces were sent to Arabia and in spite of the extreme difficulties of fighting in that mountainous and desert area they succeeded in defeating the Wahhabis and establishing Muhammad Ali as the dominant power in the neighbourhood of the Holy Cities of Islam.

The next task for which the Sultan asked Egyptian aid was to help suppress the Greeks, who had risen against the Ottoman empire in a war of independence. Muhammad Ali's forces, led by his son Ibrahim, almost turned the tide of the war, but the British and French navies came to the aid of the Greeks and destroyed the new Egyptian navy at the battle of Navarino in 1827.

Muhammad Ali's military schemes were not all outside Africa. He set out to extend his power up the Nile valley, where the ancient Egyptians had had their gold mines. He also hoped to recruit large numbers of black slaves to strengthen his army and to obtain timber from the tropical areas of the Upper Nile for his navy. In 1820 his armies invaded the area which is now the Republic of the Sudan. That area was then under the Funj sultanate (see Introduction) but the Funj kingdom was in the last stages of decline. A number of different claimants to the throne were struggling for power, many chiefdoms had asserted their independence from any central government and the position was made worse by the squabbles and intrigues of the Mamluk refugees who had fled into the area at the time of Muhammad Ali's destruction of Mamluk power in Egypt. The people of the Sudan were therefore not able to offer a united resistance and Muhammad Ali was able to establish his authority. He introduced a number of important reforms in the Sudan which will be discussed in the next chapter. He found that the gold of the Nubian desert had been largely exhausted in ancient times but he did succeed in forcing large numbers of blacks from the Sudan into his army.

Muhammad Ali had undertaken his campaigns in support of the Ottoman sultan as a way of winning greater autonomy for Egypt but the sultan was unwilling to grant this and the Egyptian ruler then tried to strengthen his position by taking possession of the Turkish province of Syria. His son, Ibrahim, began the campaign in 1832 and the Egyptian forces easily gained the upper hand. He was hailed by the Syrians as a deliverer from the corrupt and oppressive rule of the Ottoman Turks and there seemed to be nothing to prevent him attacking. But this campaign involved Muhammad Ali in the politics of the major European powers. The Ottoman empire had been declining for a long time and Russia was hoping that when it collapsed its territories would be divided between the European powers in such a way that Russia would gain control of the Bosphorus and access to the Mediterranean. She did not wish to see a more powerful ruler take the place of the Ottoman sultan as he might revive the Ottoman state and deny Russia the chance of gaining her ambition. As the sultan's armies had been defeated and there seemed a possibility that Muhammad Ali might advance on Constantinople the sultan appealed for Russian aid. In the Treaty of Unkiar-Skelessi of 1833 Russia promised to give military support to the Ottoman sultan in case of need in return for access to the Bosphorus. This treaty was much disliked by Britain; for in the interests of safeguarding her trade routes, Britain had always tried to bolster up the Ottoman empire to keep Russia from gaining too much influence in Constantinople. Britain was therefore anxious to prevent the sultan from making use of the Russian offer and hoped to win the Turks away from a pro-Russian policy. For this reason Britain was anxious to prevent Muhammad Ali from putting the sultan in a position where he had to ask for Russian military assistance under the terms of the treaty. Faced with this international situation Muhammad Ali stopped his forces and fell back on trying to get his way by negotiation.

In spite of the weak position of the Ottoman empire, however, the sultan refused to give him what he wanted. In 1839 fighting began again and Muhammad Ali's forces easily defeated the Turks and began to advance rapidly towards Constantinople. His forces reached as far as Konieh and the way seemed open to the Ottoman capital. This move created great alarm amongst the European powers, with the exception of France which was particularly friendly to Muhammad Ali and hoped to gain trading advantages.

In 1840 the European powers, with the exception of France, signed a treaty in London in which they agreed to limit Muhammad Ali's territorial ambitions. They agreed to maintain the sovereignty of the Ottoman sultan over Egypt but they also agreed that Muhammad Ali should be recognized as the hereditary governor (*pasha*) representing the Ottoman sultan in

Egypt and life governor of Acre in Syria. France refused to sign the treaty and continued supporting Muhammad Ali. The British navy then began bombarding Syrian ports and landing troops to cut off Muhammad Ali's advance forces from their base. He had the wisdom to see that he could not hope to fight against the combined forces of the major European powers and therefore agreed to accept the London treaty.

Achievements of Muhammad Ali

Muhammad Ali thus failed to achieve his ambition of winning complete independence from the Ottoman empire. But at least he ensured that his descendants would succeed him in the rulership of Egypt and he had taken the country a long way on the road to complete independence. Like his foreign policy his internal schemes in Egypt were also a mixture of success and failure. His industrial plans were unsuccessful and the heavy expenses involved in maintaining his armed forces and using them on major campaigns meant that the Egyptian peasants had to be very heavily taxed. This did a great deal to undermine the value of his agricultural reforms. Peasants began to refuse to plant the new crops as the taxes were so high that they received very little profit. Some of them abandoned the land altogether. Muhammad Ali then began to grant land to individuals on a large scale. This was done to bring land which had fallen into neglect back into cultivation, but it brought into existence a class of wealthy landlords to replace the Mamluks whom he had earlier destroyed. Muhammad Ali's own family was naturally prominent in this class and acquired enormous estates. This landlord class was later to gain a great deal of political influence until its power was greatly reduced by the reforms of Gamel Abdul Nasser.

It should be remembered that the mass of the Egyptian peasants had lived for more than a thousand years under oppressive foreign rulers. Poverty-stricken, uneducated and overtaxed they were little interested in government. They were intensely conservative, and ill-disposed towards any improvement in their age-old methods. It was simply not possible to change all this in the course of a single lifetime.

Nevertheless Muhammad Ali's achievements are amazing. He had put Egypt on the way to modernization and independence. He had established her as a major cotton producer. He had built a national army and showed that Egyptian soldiers could be the equal of any in the world. He had given Egyptians some place in the government of their country and laid the foundations for the growth of a western-educated class. Under him Egypt had suddenly appeared on the world stage as a power to be reckoned with, and he had done all this without taking any loans from the European powers which might have committed him to them.

Abbas I

Muhammad Ali died in 1849 and it was the tragedy of Egypt that none of his successors had his ability. Abbas I who ruled from 1849 to 1853, was almost his exact opposite. He was deeply conservative, and lacked Muhammad Ali's understanding of the modern world. Under his rule the factories were abandoned, schools were shut and many European advisers dismissed. This did mean, however, that state expenses were reduced. This large cut in state expenses in turn lightened the burden of the *fellahin*, for Abbas found it possible to lower their taxes. Moreover Abbas endeared himself to the *fellahin* by treating them kindly.

Said and the Suez Canal agreement

Abbas I was succeeded in 1853 by Said. He had received a French education, was highly westernized, and loved to surround himself with European friends. He fully shared Muhammad Ali's desire to modernize Egypt but he lacked his shrewd sense of political realism. In his reign Egypt became a happy hunting ground for the promoters of various schemes of improvement and for the agents of European bankers who were only too eager to advance the money on conditions favourable to themselves. The greatest of these schemes was the project for building a canal at Suez to link the Mediterranean and the Red Sea. This idea had been put forward some time before, but it became a practical reality when the Frenchman Ferdinand de Lesseps persuaded Said to give his support on terms very unfavourable to Egypt. Under the agreement Egypt was to provide the labour for the construction of the canal as well as a substantial proportion of the other costs. Egypt was also to give up to the International Company of Suez a stretch of territory through which a sweet water canal was to be cut for irrigation. At the same time the control of the Company and the bulk of the profits were to remain with the French shareholders. It was a clear case of swindling. In order to fulfil his part of the bargain as well as to finance other expenses Said resorted to European bankers who gave him huge loans in return for heavy interest. By the time Said died in 1863 Egypt had borrowed £14 million from foreign bankers.

Ismail Pasha and his extravagance

Said was succeeded in 1863 by Ismail Pasha, the man who is often held responsible for allowing Egypt to fall under British rule. His character is difficult to judge. To British imperialists like Lord Cromer and Sir Alfred Milner, Ismail was a weak, cunning and selfish pleasure-seeker who borrowed money from Europeans and later turned against them and ungratefully refused to pay his debts. An American writer, Pierre Crabitès, however, described him as a shrewd, progressive and enlightened ruler with the best interests of Egypt at heart and a victim of the swindling tricks of unscrupulous Europeans. Neither of these views is entirely right or entirely wrong.

Ismail's main failing was that while he sought to carry out a policy very similar to that of Muhammad Ali he lacked the cleverness and sense of proportion to carry it out successfully. He tried to do everything too quickly and on too big a scale for the economy of the country. He was too easily tricked by the moneylenders and their agents who flocked around him. In the attempt to modernize Egypt overnight he built over 13 000 kilometres of irrigation canals, almost 1500 kilometres of railway, 8000

The procession of ships at the opening of the Suez Canal in 1869

kilometres of telegraph lines, 450 bridges, 4500 elementary schools and a modern port at Alexandria. Enormous sums were also spent on personal and prestige affairs. He spent £1 million on entertaining guests at the formal opening of the Suez Canal in 1869. He built luxurious hotels and patronized art on a lavish scale. Like Muhammad Ali he sought to extend his power in Africa. He employed European explorers to search for the sources of the Nile, and he despatched costly expeditions to Ethiopia which met with complete defeat. To carry out his schemes he employed ever-increasing numbers of Europeans who rose from 5000 in 1836 to 100 000 in 1875.

Towards self-government

One project in which he was fairly successful was in winning further concessions from the Ottoman sultan. Unlike Muhammad Ali, his grand-father, he did not use force but bribes of silver and gold with which he persuaded the sultan to increase the independence of Egypt. In 1863 the sultan conferred the administration of Egypt on Ismail and his heirs and gave the important Red Sea ports of Suakin and Massawa to Egypt. Then in 1867 the Sultan gave Ismail the title of *Khedive* and the right to enter into administrative and commercial conventions as well as to make laws and regulations for internal government. The measure of self-government which Egypt had gained was internationally recognized in 1874 at the Conference of Berne, when Egypt was admitted to the General Postal Union and became one of the original signatories of the Berne Convention.

Ismail's character was a strange mixture. He was strongly attracted to European culture but still deeply attached to the traditional Islamic way of life, and he could never work out how to combine the best of both. Thus he remained a traditional Muslim landlord while at the same time he tried to abolish the system of slavery which was the basis of that type of landownership. To impress Europeans that he was a modernist he intro-duced a constitution that laid the foundations for a parliamentary system but at the same time he went on behaving as an autocrat whose authority should not be questioned.

British purchase of Suez Canal shares

As a result of his grand schemes and lavish spending Ismail accumulated enormous debts for Egypt and as he was careless in financial matters he was easily cheated. By 1879 Egypt had acquired debts of £100 million. Of this the country had only actually received £65 million, the rest going to swindlers. As the debts grew Ismail inevitably reached the situation where he was unable even to pay the interest on outstanding loans. It was this situation which made him sell Egypt's shares in the Suez Canal to Britain.

Ever since the Napoleonic invasion of Egypt, Britain had been aware of the danger that if the country were dominated by a hostile European power it could be used as a stepping-stone for an attack on India. At first Britain did not want to get politically involved in the country but merely wished to prevent French influence getting too strong. When the project for the Suez Canal was launched Britain expected it to fall and took no part, but when it proved a success the British government saw that Egypt had become very much more important to her than before, as the shortest way to India was through the Canal. The British Prime Minister, Benjamin Disraeli, seized on the chance offered by Ismail's financial difficulties to buy Egypt's shares in the Canal for the sum of £4 million, which was only a fraction of the amount Egypt had spent on the project. Disraeli's purchase of the Canal shares was not simply a clever business deal. It was a deliberate attempt to establish a foothold in Egypt and control of the vital Canal which was becoming the lifeline of the British empire. Disraeli told the British Parliament on 21 February 1876 that his motives in buying the shares were political and imperialist. He said: 'I have never recommended and I do not recommend this purchase as a financial investment ... I do not recommend this purchase as a financial speculation ... I have always and do now recommend it to the country as a political transaction, and one which I believe is calculated to strengthen the empire.' Disraeli's motives in buying the Canal shares can be compared in some ways with the imperialist motives of the Royal Niger Company in Nigeria or the British South Africa Company in Rhodesia. Once Britain had come to feel that Egypt was vital to the survival of the British empire it was clear that she would stop at nothing to prevent the country falling under the influence of any other power. The weakness of Ismail and Tewfik, his son and successor, were convenient excuses for further intervention. The days of Egypt's independence were numbered.

International control of Egyptian finances

From 1876 onwards Egypt's independence began to disappear. As the *Khedive* was unable to pay his debts, Britain and France, the countries with the largest stake in the country, began to exert increasing pressure to ensure that debts to their citizens were paid. During 1876 the British government sent Stephen Cave, the Paymaster-General, to investigate Egypt's financial situation. Then in 1878 Britain and France, acting together, forced the *Khedive* to place Egyptian finances under joint Anglo-French control on the grounds that Egypt could not be relied upon to fulfil her obligations to the European moneylenders. The scheme of joint control was a convenient device whereby Britain and France could both secure their essential interests in the country without coming into conflict with each other. As Lord Salisbury, the British Foreign Secretary, explained: 'When you have got a neighbour and faithful ally who is bent on meddling in a country in which you are deeply interested – you have three courses open to you. You may renounce – or monopolize – or share. Renouncing would have been to place the French across our road to India. Monopolizing would have brought very near the risk of war. So we resolved to share.'

Nationalist reaction and the rebellion of Arabi Pasha

With joint Anglo-French control over Egyptian finances, Egypt virtually lost her independence and this provoked a powerful reaction, which brought the system of joint control to an end and led to outright British occupation. Educated Egyptians began nationalist agitation through the press and the General Assembly, demanding that Ismail and his son, Tewfik, together with a number of corrupt Turkish office holders be removed from office. They denounced British and French interference with the affairs of the country and insisted that if allowed to control their country's financial affairs, they could fulfil Egypt's international obligations. The British and French, however, did not trust the nationalists and were not prepared to surrender control of the Egyptian finances. They were also anxious to preserve the power of the *Khedive* so that they could continue to control the country through him.

As the nationalist agitation grew it spread to the army and a man emerged who was to become the leader and inspirer of the whole movement. His name was Arabi Pasha and he was one of the few senior army officers of pure Egyptian descent. He had joined the army at 17 and like many other true Egyptians in the armed forces he suffered a great deal at the hands of Turkish officers. He thus fully shared the growing hatred of the mass of the *fellahin* for the privileged class of wealthy Turks, relatives of the Khedival family, court favourites and a few wealthy landlords. Arabi Pasha was an embodiment of the growing spirit of nationalism, with its demand of Egypt for the Egyptians and its hatred of both external European interference in the country and of the dominance of a small,

Arabi Pasha

Ismail Pasha

largely Turkish class in Egypt itself. He was so popular that Egyptians nicknamed him 'The Only One'.

Arabi Pasha was far-sighted enough to see that in order that Egyptian independence could be re-established, thorough reform would have to be undertaken before abolition of the monarchy and the introduction of a republican constitution. His movement was very nearly successful and Lord Cromer, who became British ruler of Egypt for twenty-four years from 1883 to 1906, confessed: 'Had he been left alone there can be no doubt that he would have been successful. His want of success was due to British influence.'

British occupation of Egypt

As the nationalist movement grew the *Khedive's* position became weaker and weaker. It was obvious that unless something were done the system of joint British–French control of Egyptian finances would collapse, and Arabi Pasha and the nationalists would emerge as the effective rulers of the country. Both European governments were under pressure from those of their own citizens with financial interests in Egypt, and Britain was anxious to ensure that whatever happened the French should not be allowed to act first and establish a position which would endanger the route to India. The excuse for armed intervention came in June 1882 when nationalist riots broke out in Alexandria and about fifty Europeans were killed. Britain decided that a show of force was necessary if the collapse of European authority in the country was to be prevented. The French were asked to take part but they refused to take immediate action before their National Assembly had given its consent. Thus the British fleet alone mounted the show of force. On 10 July the warships bombarded Alexandria and when this did not put an end to the nationalist movement, troops were landed. The British Parliament lost no time in voting money for military occupation. On 13 September the British forces under Sir Garnet Wolseley, who was already famous for his victory over the Asante in 1874, met Arabi Pasha's forces. The Egyptian army could not stand up against the well-trained and well-armed British forces. Arabi was defeated and three days later the British occupied Cairo. Egypt became for all practical purposes a part of the British empire until 1922.

6 The Sudan and Ethiopia in the nineteenth century

Egypt and the Sudan

As we have seen, the life of Egypt is, and always has been, dependent on the river Nile. This great river has two main sources. The White Nile starts from Lake Victoria and flows through the modern Sudan. The Blue Nile rises in the Ethiopian uplands and flows westward to meet the White Nile at Khartoum, the capital of the modern Sudan Republic. The two rivers then unite their waters and flow on northwards through the desert to reach the sea at the Nile delta. Both branches of the Nile are of great importance to Egypt. The White Nile maintains the flow of water down the Nile valley throughout the year and provides most of the water that is now used for irrigation in the summer months. The Blue Nile is responsible for the annual floods which until recent times provided the most important means of irrigation. The Blue Nile also brings down from Ethiopia the rich silt which is left behind when the flood waters dry up and which produces the great fertility of the Egyptian soil. Egypt, the Sudan and Ethiopia are thus linked together geographically and have a joint interest in the use of the Nile waters.

In addition to the geographic link the three areas have longstanding historical relations. The ancient kingdom of Kush in the Sudan arose under the influence of Egyptian civilization and then for a brief period kings of Kush ruled in Egypt itself. Much later Kush suffered from the rivalry of the kingdom of Axum in Ethiopia, and about AD 350 it was destroyed by the Emperor Ezana, the first Christian ruler of Axum. Christianity was introduced into the northern part of the modern Sudan from Egypt and by the sixth century two Christian kingdoms, Maqurra and Alwa, had come into existence. In Ethiopia Christianity was introduced by Greek traders, but the Ethiopian Church affiliated itself to the Church in Egypt and received its Patriarchs from Alexandria.

After the Arab conquest, Egypt was gradually converted to Islam and inevitably the new religion tended to spread up the Nile along the routes of trade which linked Egypt with the upper Nile area. By the fourteenth century due to the infiltration of Islam and the immigration of Arab peoples moving up the Nile, Maqurra had ceased to be a Christian kingdom. The kingdom of Alwa, further south, survived for another century.

The Funj sultanate in the Sudan

In 1504 the remains of the kingdom of Alwa were destroyed by the conqueror Amara Dunkas, who built in its place an Islamic kingdom, the Funj sultanate, with its capital at Sennar. This state survived until 1821 and was known as the Black Sultanate. Its founders, the Funj, were blacks though their origin is not precisely known. Some writers believe that they were Shilluk, a people who are still important in the Sudan.

At the height of its power the Funj sultanate controlled a very large area, from the neighbourhood of its capital at Sennar to as far north as the first cataract of the Nile. It did not, however, include the Dinka, Azande and other peoples of the southern area of the modern Sudan.

Within the large territory of the Funj sultanate many areas enjoyed considerable independence. This was particularly true of the Arabs along the Nile valley north of the confluence of the Blue and White Nile, who were ruled in the name of the Funj Sultan by an Arab viceroy called the Abdullab. It was also true of many chiefdoms in the southern part of the kingdom, who kept their own chiefs and merely accepted the paramountcy of the Funj ruler. This type of kingdom was naturally very fragile and could not be held together if the power of the sultans remained strong. This power depended on a well-trained cavalry force and an infantry force made up of slaves who were captured in the Nuba mountains. The strength of the Funj kingdom was shaken when the Shaiqiya who lived around the great bend of the Nile rebelled against the Sultan's viceroy and succeeded in asserting their independence. This revolt damaged the trade of the Funj sultanate and in compensation the sultans attempted to expand into Kordofan. This led to too much power being given to the army commander Abu Likeilik and he marched on Sennar and deposed the Sultan. Thereafter the sons and grandsons of Abu Likeilik fought one another for power, each of them supporting one or other member of the Funj royal family as puppet sultan. In these conditions of civil war many chiefdoms broke away from the kingdom and its authority became confined to a very small area. After 1811 the position was further worsened by the arrival of quarrelling bands of Mamluk refugees from Egypt.

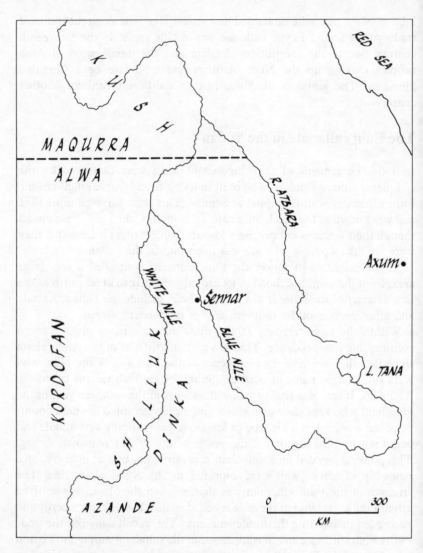

The area of the Funj sultanate and the Nile confluence

Turco–Egyptian conquest and administration of the Sudan, 1820–81

It was this weak and confused territory that was invaded in 1820 by the army of Muhammad Ali under the command of his third son, Kamil Pasha. The Funj sultanate was in no position to make an effective stand

and the 4000 troops under Kamil Pasha met with little severe resistance except from the Shaiqiya. Muhammad Ali's objectives in conquering the Sudan were to find the gold mines of the ancient Egyptians, and to acquire sources of timber for his fleet and manpower for his army. The first proved a complete disappointment and the second of relatively little value, but Muhammad Ali did succeed in forcibly recruiting large numbers of Sudanese blacks into his army. In addition he and his successors introduced into the Sudan much of their modernizing programme.

Between 1820 and 1881 the Sudan was administered by Turco–Egyptian governor-generals known as *likimdars*. The area was divided into a number of provinces administered by provincial administrators called *mudirs* and the provinces were in turn divided into districts called *qisms*, each administered by an officer called *qism naziri*. Finally each of the *qisms* was divided into still smaller units called *khatts* ruled by *khatt hakimi*. The Turco–Egyptian government was maintained by a large army of 10 000 infantry recruited from the Sudanese blacks and known as the Jihaniyya, and about 9000 cavalry largely recruited from the Shaiqiya.

Muhammad Ali's conquest of the Sudan naturally led to a greatly increased flow of trade between that country and Egypt. Egyptian cultivators were also sent into the area to teach new farming methods and introduce new crops. Cotton growing was started on a substantial scale and now provides the Sudan's major export crop. New lands were brought under irrigation and plantations of indigo and sugar were established. Improvements in communications were also made in the Turco–Egyptian period. A telegraph system was introduced which by 1866 linked Wadi Halfa to upper Egypt. In 1874 this was extended to Khartoum. Another line was built linking the Sudan to the Red Sea and another extended westward through El Obeid to the borders of Darfur. Nile steamers speeded up communications and helped the administration. The foundation of Khartoum, capital of the modern Sudan, was also an achievement of the Turco–Egyptian administration. In 1825 it was a mere village near the confluence of the Blue and White Niles but by 1833 it had expanded so much that it was made the administrative capital of the country. By 1837 its population was estimated at 20 000.

The Turco–Egyptian government expanded its area of authority far beyond the limits of the Funj sultanate. The 'pagan' blacks of the southern Sudan were conquered and for the first time brought under common government with the Muslim peoples of the north. The rulers of Egypt employed many European administrators and experts in the territory in their efforts at modernization and they engaged European explorers to investigate the hinterland with a view to further extensions of territory. One of these, Samuel Baker, discovered the sources of the Blue Nile and confirmed that the White Nile did rise in Lake Victoria. Another European employee of the Turco–Egyptian regime, a German called Emin Pasha, reached as far as the northern part of modern Uganda with a number of Egyptian soldiers, and the Turco–Egyptian regime might have been extended into the heart of East Africa if it had not been for the outbreak of revolt in the Sudan itself.

Unpopularity of the Turco–Egyptian government

Though modern Sudanese patriots like to dwell on the seamy side of the Turco–Egyptian regime, there can be doubt that it conferred many benefits on the peoples of the Sudan. Nevertheless, it was far from popular. In the first place, like most conquerors, Muhammad Ali and his successors were concerned first and foremost to exploit the Sudan for their own benefit rather than in the interests of the Sudanese. In the attempt to profit from the area they imposed heavy taxes which were much resented. This was particularly so in the reign of Khedive Ismail (1863–79) who tried to increase his revenue from the Sudan as much as possible to help meet his ever-mounting debts to Europeans. The administrators who were sent to the Sudan disliked being sent there. They tried to get away as soon as they could. Between 1821 and 1885 there were no less than 23 *likimdars* serving for an average period of two years. Only one of them, named Kurshid, served for a substantial period – 13 years. During their stay many of the administrators at all levels engaged in corrupt practices in the hope of making quick money. The administration was strongest in the reign of Muhammad Ali himself and afterwards fell into a sad state of decline. The Khedive Ismail managed to restore efficiency to some extent but after 1876 he became so preoccupied with his European debts that he could only think of the Sudan as a source of revenue. In addition to their maladministration the Turkish administrators belonged to the Hanafite school of Muslim law, the most lax of all the Islamic codes. Many of them were open wine-drinkers, and this was particularly shocking to the Sudanese, who belonged to the strict Malikite school. The religious feelings of the Sudanese were also disturbed by the employment of European Christians in important positions and the belief grew that the country was to be handed over to Europeans. The position was not helped when in 1877 Ismail Pasha appointed an Englishman, Charles George Gordon, as governor-general. Gordon's active opposition to the slave trade and the steps he took to punish slave traders disturbed the traditional economy of the Sudan and aroused bitter opposition. The fact that he employed increasing numbers of Europeans in administrative posts under him further increased the bitterness.

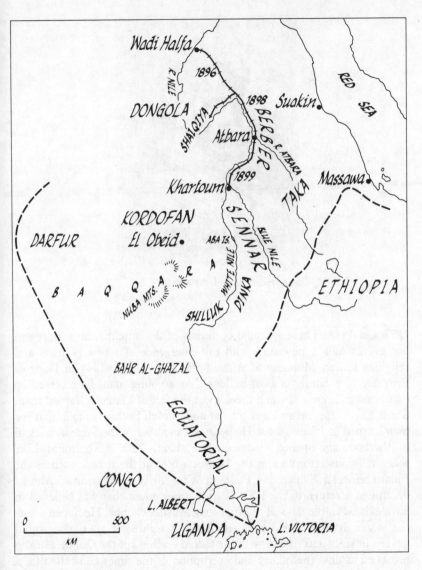

Sudan under Egyptian rule

Muhammad Ahmad, the Mahdi

Almost immediately after the 1820 conquest there were revolts against the taxes imposed by the new masters. There were uprisings in Darfur against the new administration in 1838 and 1878, and in the Bahr el-Ghazal in

Muhammad Ahmad, the Mahdi

1877 and 1878. These sporadic outbursts of discontent were suppressed but events took a new turn with the emergence of a new political and religious leader, Muhammad Ahmad. He was born in 1844 in Dongola Province to a family of boat-builders. As a young man, he received an education in Islamic law and theology at the feet of a famous learned man, Sheik Tayib. He was an eager scholar and himself became a *faqih*, that is a man learned in Islamic laws. He became a member of the Sammaniya sufi brotherhood and opened a lodge on Aba island, south of Khartoum. Like other religious reformers in the Islamic world at the time – such as the Fulani reformer Usman dan Fodio in West Africa – Muhammad Ahmad dreamt of a return to the ideal Islamic government that was believed to have existed in the days of the first four Muslim caliphs. He hoped to see the whole Islamic world reunited under a righteous ruler who would govern in strict accordance with the sacred teaching of the Quran. He also preached against the luxury and corruption of the times and called for a return to the purity and asceticism of the ideal Islamic life. He saw the Turks as ungodly and corrupt and condemned the Sudanese sheikhs for their lax and luxurious way of life and their acceptance of offices under the Turco–Egyptian regime. He began to see himself as the heaven-sent deliverer destined to rule the entire Muslim community and restore it to godliness and purity. In 1881 his followers proclaimed him as the *Mahdi* (The Guided One).

156

Collapse of the Turco–Egyptian regime and triumph of the Mahdi

The proclamation of Muhammad Ahmad as the Mahdi alarmed the Turco–Egyptian administration and he was summoned to Khartoum. He refused to come and an expedition sent against him was defeated. The news spread rapidly among the masses that Allah had fought on the side of the Mahdi and that he had defeated his enemies without military effort. Support for the new leader grew rapidly and soon became too much for the Turco–Egyptian forces. The Mahdi conducted his campaign on Islamic lines modelled on the life of the Prophet Muhammad. He began by performing a *hijra* (or flight from the ungodly) like Muhammad's flight from Mecca to Medina. This flight took him to Kordofan in the west where most of his supporters were to be found at first. There the numbers of his followers, who were called the *Ansar*, increased rapidly. In Kordofan and Darfur he won several military successes and then began to extend his power eastwards. By 1883 he was not only ruling over Kordofan and Darfur but was also master of areas around the Bule Nile. The eastern part of his conquests was governed in his name by Osman Digna.

The Turco–Egyptian administration was in a particularly weak position for, as we have seen, the British had occupied Egypt in 1882 to support the authority of the Khedive and ensure the payment of Egypt's international debts. In 1883 the British decided to support their puppet regime in Egypt in its attempt to restore Turco–Egyptian control of the Sudan. A mainly Egyptian army led by an English commander, Hicks Pasha, was sent to capture the Mahdi in Kordofan. The invaders were decisively defeated and the Sudanese, who interpreted the victory as another miracle and a sign that Muhammad Ahmad really was the Mahdi, hesitated no longer in rallying to his side. Lord Cromer, the British Consul-General in Egypt, was in a difficult position. The Khedive, whose government the British occupation was officially intended to support, was naturally anxious to regain control of the Sudan, but W.E. Gladstone, the British Prime Minister, was opposed to what he regarded as unnecessary extensions of British responsibility and had often spoken of the rights of the Sudanese to struggle for their independence. The British cabinet was divided, and there were some who felt that as Egypt was dependent on the Nile, British strategic interests in Egypt demanded that she should control the upper Nile valley.

An official decision was taken to evacuate the Sudan and leave it to the Mahdi, but those who disliked this decision managed to ensure that the man sent to carry out the evacuation should be the eccentric General Gordon, a man who could be relied upon to disobey his official instruc-

General Gordon

tions. When Gordon reached Khartoum he refused to proceed with the evacuation and announced his intention to smash the Mahdi. His forces were far too small, however, to face the massive following of Muhammad Ahmad and he found himself cut off and besieged in Khartoum. Gladstone, who was furious at Gordon's behaviour, refused for a long time to do anything to rescue him. Finally, however, a relief expedition was organized under General Wolseley and fought its way to Khartoum. By the time it arrived the town had fallen to the Mahdists and Gordon was dead. The relief column therefore retreated, leaving the Mahdi in complete control of the Sudan (1885).

Muhammad Ahmad did not live to enjoy the fruits of his victory for long. He died soon after his troops had occupied Khartoum. During his short reign he had tried conscientiously to put into practice his ideals of Islamic government. He collected only taxes that were laid down in the Quran and based his administration of justice on the *sharia*. He tried to purify society and administered severe punishments for theft, adultery, drunkenness, smoking and bringing of false accusations. He succeeded in enforcing the law requiring women to wear veils, though he was unable to suppress some traditional Sudanese practices of which he disapproved, such as the wearing of amulets, elaborate wedding ceremonies and mourning customs at funerals. During his reign he minted gold and silver coins. To help him in his campaigns the Mahdi appointed three deputies or *khalifas* named Abdullahi, Ali and Muhammad Sharif. The title is the same as that used by the political successors of the Prophet Muhammad,

158

Khartoum in the nineteenth century

the early caliphs who ruled the whole Islamic world. The three *khalifas* were army commanders during the life of the Mahdi and on his death soon after the capture of Khartoum one of them, Abdullahi, succeeded to the supreme position in the Sudan.

The Sudan under the Khalifa 1885–98

The rule of the Khalifa has been described in the past by European writers, some of whom were anxious to justify the subsequent British conquest and others who had suffered as prisoners of the Khalifa, as one of unrelieved brutality and barbarism. Recent researches have shown, however, that it was in fact a remarkably successful system. The death of the Mahdi created a crisis for his followers. As the Mahdi was supposed to be immortal his death led many to doubt whether he was really the Mahdi at all. Abdullahi also found it difficult to make the other two khalifas accept his position as the supreme head of state, and members of the Mahdi's own family felt that they should hold the highest offices in the land.

The Mahdist movement was one of religious as well as political reform. Muhammad Ahmad, by virtue of his claim to be the Mahdi, denounced all

159

The Mahdist state

the traditional law schools of the Islamic world and prepared his own code; though he had himself been a member of a sufi brotherhood he also denounced all the sufi orders. These moves were naturally unpopular among the more conservative learned men and the leaders of the powerful sufi groups in the country. The reforms were much more difficult to maintain when the Mahdi himself was dead. The movement had grown up very quickly under the inspiration of the Mahdi's personality and brought many societies together in common opposition to the Turco–Egyptian rule. Once the hated foreign government had been overthrown and the Mahdi was gone, traditional hostilities were soon renewed.

Abdullahi thus had to struggle against many difficulties. In 1888 and 1892 he was faced by revolts led by members of the Mahdi's family. A more serious source of trouble, however, was the attempt of some of the chiefdoms to establish their independence from central government control. Abdullahi's own chiefdom, the Baqqara, a cattle-keeping people near Darfur, were among the most obstinate. Expeditions had to be sent against them in the first three years of the Khalifa's reign. In 1889 he sent one of his relatives, Uthman Adam, to administer them and when even this did not put an end to the troubles he forced a number of them to leave Darfur and settled them in the Omdurman district.

In addition to internal problems there were also questions of foreign policy. Although the British government had at first decided on a policy of non-intervention in the Sudan the Egyptian rulers had never abandoned hope of recovering the territory. A large section of the Egyptian army was stationed near Aswan, not far from the frontier and this forced the Khalifa to maintain a large army in preparedness for an attack. In 1889 he took the initiative and himself invaded Egypt but he was repulsed.

On the eastern frontier of the Sudan lay the Christian empire of Ethiopia. As a religious leader the Khalifa was duty bound to make war against the 'infidels' and a jihad was declared against Ethiopia. Sudanese forces invaded Ethiopia in 1889 but were severely defeated at the battle of Metemma, where the Ethiopian Emperor Yohannes (John) was killed. This did not mean the end of the struggle, however, and tension continued when Menelik came to the throne of Ethiopia and began a policy of vigorous expansion. In this he had the tacit support of Britain, France and Italy, with whom he had treaty relationships. Menelik was regarded with particular hostility by the Khalifa as he openly claimed Fashoda and Khartoum as part of his empire. Between 1892 and 1897 Menelik made overtures to the Khalifa suggesting that they unite their forces to resist the designs of European imperialists but no permanent alliance between the Christian empire and the head of an Islamic reforming movement proved possible.

By about 1892 Abdullahi had succeeded in solving most of the country's internal problems. The capital was established at Omdurman on the other bank of the Nile from Khartoum and a metropolitan area grew up around Aba island which the Khalifa ruled directly. The rest of the state was divided into provinces governed by *amils* (agents) who in accordance with the practice of the early Caliphate were both governors and tax collectors. It was the Khalifa's policy to appoint *amils* who were not necessarily members of the peoples over whom they ruled. The attempt to purify society in accordance with Islamic beliefs, which had been such a marked feature of the Mahdi's policy, was continued, and a high moral tone was maintained in the administration, where corruption was severely punished. Taxes were much lighter and more honestly collected than in the Turco–Egyptian period and the people paid them much more willingly. The necessity for the state to maintain a large army meant that most of the revenue was spent on defence and relatively little was done in the way of economic improvements. The army was provided with firearms, some of which had been captured from the defeated Egyptian army but most of which were made in Omdurman. The men came largely from the Nuba mountains where Muhammad Ali had previously recruited soldiers for his Egyptian forces. They were brave fighters and remained loyal to the state to the end.

Ethnic disturbances were eventually brought under control. The Baq-qara, who gave most trouble of all, were finally converted into a group of the Khalifa's most ardent followers; a number of its leading men were taken to Omdurman and given high positions in the government. The Khalifa had succeeded in establishing a theocratic system which might have proved satisfactory to the Sudanese people if it had been left alone by the European powers.

The British conquest of the Sudan, 1898

In the last decade of the nineteenth century the imperialist designs of several European powers were moving towards the upper Nile. The Germans were heading towards it from Tanganyika, the British from Uganda and Kenya. The Belgian king, Leopold II, was extending his possessions in that direction from the Congo Basin. The Italians were looking inland from the Red Sea coast and the French were thinking of seizing a stretch of territory right across Africa from their possessions in Equatorial Africa and Senegal to the Red Sea. In South Africa, Cecil Rhodes was dreaming of a great chain of British territories from the Cape to Cairo, linked together by a transcontinental railway and telegraph system.

As already stated, Britain was concerned first and foremost with the strategic position of Egypt and realized that she could not hold her position there if a strong and possibly hostile power controlled the upper

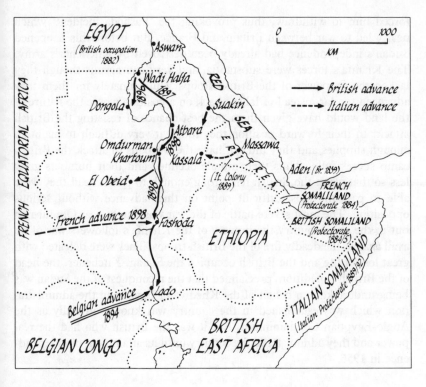

The European advance on the Sudan

Nile valley. The British government therefore did its best to keep other powers out of the area and bought off the threat from Belgium, Italy and Germany by agreeing to recognize the sovereignty of those nations where they already had interests, at the price of their agreeing to leave the upper Nile valley alone. The French, however, refused to be bought off. They had always regarded Britain's occupation of Egypt as a treacherous act and hoped to undermine the British position there. Accordingly the French prepared a grand programme for a march on the Nile. They planned to send expeditions from the French Congo and North Africa. In 1896 the French explorer, Major J.B. Marchand, set out from the Upper Congo and achieved the difficult task of reaching Fashoda on the Nile, a frontier town of the Sudan. Britain became thoroughly alarmed, and the government decided that it could no longer leave the Sudan as a tempting bait for another European power. Plans for an invasion of the Sudan were hurriedly prepared, a railway line was built and troops armed with the most modern weapons marched under the command of General H.H. Kitchener into the country. In 1898 Kitchener faced Marchand at Fashoda and forced him to withdraw, thus provoking the 'Fashoda incident' which nearly led to war between Britain and France. But before this happened Sudan's independence had already been destroyed by Kitchener's army. The Khalifa's forces were substantial and very courageous though they lacked the firepower of the British troops. Unfortunately for them they advanced too far instead of falling back on a position where the nature of the land would have given them the best chance of resisting the British attack. In their forward position they found it very difficult to maintain enough supplies and they did not have the weapons to attack the British camp successfully. Thus their morale declined and their numbers grew less so that when the British felt strong enough to push ahead they were able to pass the most difficult point on their advance without serious opposition. The most severe battle of the war was fought near Omdurman but in the open country the bravery of the Khalifa's followers was of no avail against the deadly fire of the British troops. They were defeated with great loss of life and the British occupied the Sudan. Kitchener, the head of the British expedition, proclaimed that the reconquest of the Sudan was being undertaken on behalf of the Khedive of Egypt and the administration which was established in the country was known officially as the Anglo-Egyptian Condominium. But it was the British who had the real power and they administered the country until its attainment of independence in 1956.

The Ethiopian empire at the beginning of the nineteenth century

Ethiopia, as we have seen in the Introduction, is the centre of one of Africa's most ancient civilizations. From the beginnings of the empire of Axum more than two thousand years ago until today the Ethiopian highlands have had a continuous history. From about AD 350 when the Emperor Ezana adopted Christianity as the official state religion, and throughout the history of the empire the Church played a vital role as the guardian of Ethiopia's culture, just as the authority of the emperor, who was held to be descended from King Solomon of the Holy Scriptures, was a symbol of unity and political identity. Geography has played a double part in Ethiopian history. On the one hand, the great height of its flat-topped mountains, ranging from 1500 to 3700 metres, with great valleys and gorges, and the semi-desert lowlands which surround them, have made Ethiopia a land very difficult for a foreign aggressor to attack. These natural features have isolated the Ethiopians from other peoples and made it possible for them to continue developing their own unique culture. On the other hand the mountainous country and the difficulties of communications have placed obstacles in the way of the development of a strong and highly centralized kingdom. There has always been a tendency for rulers of provinces (*rases*) to take advantage of any weakness of the central government to establish themselves as virtually independent kings.

At the beginning of the nineteenth century the kingdom was in a very weak state. Ever since the invasion of Ethiopia by the Somalis under Mohammed Gran in the sixteenth century the position of the emperors had been growing weaker. The Muslim invasion led to the emperor inviting Portuguese aid. With this help the Somalis were defeated but the coming of the Portuguese brought religious controversy into the country. The conversion of one of the emperors to the Roman Catholic faith and the civil wars which followed before the traditional church was restored, weakened the emperor's position. Worse still, they distracted attention from a more serious problem, the gradual movement onto the plateau of the cattle-keeping Oromo (Galla). In the end the Oromo overran almost half the area traditionally belonging to the Ethiopian empire and their raiding activities made travel difficult even in the areas they did not occupy. In these circumstances the provincial *rases* broke away completely from the central government and fought each other in endless little wars for the almost worthless dignity of the imperial crown. Nevertheless in spite of the sad state to which the country was reduced the traditional civilization did not collapse entirely. The Church still survived and succeeded in preserving the values of traditional Ethiopian culture. The Oromo began to settle down and adopt much of the Ethiopian way of life. Some of them became Christians, others became Muslims. Finally, even though the emperors had lost almost all their power and there were often several persons claiming the title at the same time, the tradition that there should be an emperor who was the rightful ruler of all Ethiopia still survived. It was in these circumstances that three great rulers arose who succeeded in restoring the power of the monarchy, reuniting Ethiopia and making it a powerful state once more.

Emperor Tewodros (Theodore)

The first of the three great Ethiopian rulers of the nineteenth century was the son of the governor of the small frontier province of Kwara. His childhood was very poor but he grew up a brave and adventurous lad and began his climb to power by building up a band of followers who helped him in plundering trading caravans. Eventually his following became so powerful that he was in a position to intervene in the struggle for power

165

Emperor Tewodros II of Ethiopia

that was going on between the great *rases*. The two main contenders for
the imperial title at the time were the *rases* of the two large provinces of
Gondar and Shoa. He defeated them both and forced the Abuna or
Patriarch of the Ethiopian Church to crown him as emperor in 1855. He
took Tewodros (Theodore) as his imperial name and soon showed that he
intended to make his imperial position a reality in a manner that had not
been attempted for more than a hundred years. For this purpose he
maintained a very large and well-paid army which he used to put down the
numerous rebellions which broke out from time to time. He attempted to
destroy the independent power of the *rases* completely and to turn them
into salaried officers to be appointed and dismissed at will. He also tried to
improve the taxation system, to regulate the power of the Church, to
suppress the slave trade, and to enforce monogamy.

In foreign affairs Tewodros had sweeping ambitions. He dreamed of
conquering the Sudan, Egypt and Jerusalem and wiping Islam from the
face of the earth. In particular he was determined that Ethiopia should be
given the respect she deserved from the great powers. Tewodros saw the
advantages of modernization, particularly in the field of weapons, and
many Europeans were attracted to his court. Two of them, John Bell and
Walter Plowden, became his trusted advisers and encouraged his programme of reforms. Others were not such worthwhile persons, and contributed to turning the emperor's mind against the Europeans.

166

As Tewodros's reign continued he ran into increasing difficulties. He tried to do too much too fast. His attempts at centralization naturally aroused bitter opposition from the provincial *rases*, and this opposition was increased by resentment at the heavy taxes needed to maintain his inflated army. As a result Tewodros became more and more unpopular and steadily lost control over growing areas of the country. This in turn produced a sense of bitter frustration which affected his personality until by the end of his reign he had become almost insane.

The crisis which ended in the fall and death of Tewodros began when he addressed a letter to Queen Victoria proposing the opening of an Ethiopian embassy in London. Unfortunately the letter was given no serious attention and no reply was sent. Tewodros took this as a calculated insult from a ruler whose subjects he had always befriended. In his rage he threw the British Consul, Charles Cameron, into prison. When the British sent an agent to demand Cameron's release, with a message condemning the emperor's action as uncivilized, he threw the agent and 60 other Europeans into jail also. The British government then felt in honour bound to rescue its subjects and in 1867 an expedition under Sir Robert Napier was sent out for the purpose. The British expedition found great difficulties in surmounting the geographical obstacles in the way of an invasion of Ethiopia but they met with no serious military opposition. By this time the great majority of the Ethiopian people were in opposition to their ruler and as the British made it clear that they did not intend to occupy the country permanently but merely to rescue their own subjects the *rases* were inclined to encourage them. Indeed the progress of the British force was made much easier by the fact that for much of their journey one of the *rases* provided them with free food for men and animals. Tewodros was deserted by all but a small fraction of his once massive army. He decided to make a stand at his capital of Magdala and on 10 April the remnants of his followers were easily defeated by the British troops. The unfortunate emperor shot himself rather than fall into the enemies' hands.

After the successful achievement of their purpose the British left the country again, taking the released prisoners with them. The British expedition to Ethiopia created a quite false impression about the strength of the country. It looked as if the kingdom had been very easily defeated when in actual fact the only fighting had been between the British and the small remnant of Tewodros's bodyguard. The mass of the people had been neutral or actively supported the invaders. To conquer Ethiopia in face of a real national resistance would be quite a different matter.

Tewodros's reign could thus be said to have ended in failure but from the point of view of Ethiopian history this was not really so. Even though he became so unpopular that he was deserted by the majority of his

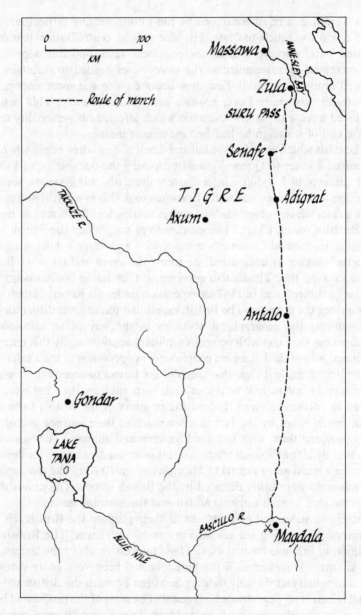

Napier's march from Zula to Magdala

subjects, and even though his schemes for centralization of government were unsuccessful he had restored the position and prestige of the monarchy. Henceforward no one doubted the power of whoever occupied the imperial throne. Indeed the throne became a precious jewel which the *rases* coveted and struggled among themselves to win.

The reign of Emperor Yohannes (John) IV

The death of Tewodros left three great rivals for the imperial throne. They were Gobaze the *ras* of Amhara, the *ras* of Tigre and Menelik, the *ras* of Shoa. Gobaze proved the strongest at first and was crowned as emperor in 1868. He ruled for four years only, and his reign was uneventful. The end of his reign in 1872 left the two great *rases* of Tigre and Shoa face to face. Of the two, the *ras* of Tigre proved the most successful and was crowned as the Emperor Yohannes (John) IV. Menelik remained largely independent, however, and it was not until 1878 that Yohannes was able to force him to renounce the imperial title of Negus Negast (King of Kings) which he had claimed ever since the death of Tewodros. Yohannes was a skilful diplomat and with wise statesmanship he did not attempt to crush Menelik completely. Instead, in return for recognition of the emperor's paramountcy, Menelik was given a free hand to extend his territorial possessions in the southern part of the empire over provinces which had long been overrun by the Oromo. In 1882 the relationship between the two great men was further strengthened by a marriage alliance between two of their children, coupled with an agreement that the succession should pass to Menelik after Yohannes's death.

The energies of the Emperor Yohannes were largely absorbed by the necessity to defend the empire against a succession of aggressors. The threat came first from Egypt. Amongst the grandiose plans of Ismail Pasha was the idea of building a great empire in Africa, and included in this was the design to invade and occupy the Christian empire of Ethiopia. The Turco–Egyptian government had a base on the Red Sea coast at Massawa which had originally been seized by the Turks in the sixteenth century. With the aid of European advisers and the most up-to-date weapons two attempts were made to invade Ethiopia, in 1875 and 1876. In spite of the superiority of weapons in the hands of the Egyptian forces and the presence of expert European military advisers, both these invasions were decisively defeated. Large quantities of arms and equipment were captured by the Ethiopians. The defeat of the second Egyptian expedition, the Egyptian financial crisis and the outbreak of the Mahdist revolt in the Sudan, meant the end of the threat to Ethiopia from Egypt.

But the withdrawal of the Egyptians from the scene was followed by the appearance of an even more serious danger. The French had acquired the Red Sea port of Obok as early as 1862 and this was destined to become the nucleus of French Somaliland. The Italians acquired a coaling station in the Bay of Assab in 1869 and thereafter began to take an increasing interest in Somaliland and the interior. With the collapse of the Egyptian schemes the Italians began to emerge as the chief contenders for control over the Ethiopian kingdom. They established themselves on the coast of the area now known as Eritrea in 1885 and began to push inland in the direction of the Ethiopian province of Tigre. At the same time the Italians did their best to weaken the kingdom by playing Menelik against Yohannes. Menelik took the arms and money they offered him as he had previously accepted aid from the Egyptians, but he gave no real help to the invaders. In 1887 Italian forces clashed with Ethiopians at a place known as Dogali. The Italians were defeated and forced to fall back on Massawa. It was clear however that it would not be long before the Italians tried again.

The dangers which Yohannes IV had to face did not come only from the direction of the Red Sea. The fanatically religious government of the Khalifa in the Sudan declared a jihad against its Christian neighbour and the Sudanese forces overran a large part of Ethiopia before they were decisively defeated by the Ethiopians at the battle of Metemma in 1889. In this battle the Emperor Yohannes lost his life and Ethiopia was left without a ruler at a critical time.

Emperor Menelik II and the Italians

Throughout the reign of the Emperor Yohannes IV, Menelik, the *ras* of Shoa continued to take every opportunity to strengthen his position. He allowed first the Egyptians and then the Italians to believe that they might be able to use him in their attempts to gain control of the country, and by this means he acquired large quantities of up-to-date firearms which he used to extend his conquests over the Oromo areas. He had, however, no intention of being used as a tool to establish foreign rule over the empire to which he hoped to succeed, and in spite of the aid he received he did nothing to help the invaders. With the death of Yohannes the question of succession arose. Under the agreement which had been made between Yohannes and Menelik, Menelik was entitled to the succession but Yohannes had a son, Mangasha, who hoped to establish his claim to the throne. The Italians, who had been intriguing with Menelik for some time, believed that he would be a useful puppet ruler and at first gave him

Emperor Menelik II of Ethiopia

their support. He realized that Ethiopia's chances of survival depended on the possession of modern armaments and found it convenient to allow the Italians to continue believing that he would be a willing tool for their ambitions. Thus Menelik and the Italians entered into the Treaty of Wichale (Ucciali) in 1889 under which the Ethiopian emperor received huge supplies of arms and ammunition.

The clause in the treaty for which Italy had been prepared to pay so heavily was one which stated that Ethiopia consented to use Italy as her intermediary in foreign affairs. This could be interpreted to mean that Ethiopia was no longer an independent state but under Italian protection. The Italian government exploited this and informed the European powers that she had established a protectorate over the Ethiopian kingdom. Thus the kingdom of Ethiopia disappeared from maps produced in Europe and was replaced by Italian East Africa. In preparing to accept the Treaty of Wichale, however, Menelik had taken care to see that there should be nothing in it which could be interpreted as a surrender of independence to the Italians. Two versions of the treaty had been drawn up, one in Italian and one in Amharic, and the wording of the two versions was subtly different in an important way. It was only the Italian version which said that the emperor consented to use the services of the Italians in foreign affairs; the Amharic version merely said that he *might* do so if he wished. Menelik wisely signed the Amharic version only. Thus when he heard of the way in which Italy was exploiting the treaty he was in a position to

171

respond. In 1891 he sent a circular letter to the European powers pointing out that Ethiopia had not surrendered any part of her independence. In the same letter Menelik claimed very wide frontiers for the Ethiopian empire, including Khartoum and Lake Rudolf (now Lake Turkana), and stated that he did not intend to sit idly by while distant powers came to partition Africa.

By the time Italy realized that she had herself been cheated by the Ethiopian monarch she had hoped to cheat it was already too late. She fell back on giving support to Mangasha who was still holding out in Tigre but it soon became clear that he would be no more willing than Menelik himself to buy a throne at the price of placing his country under foreign domination. Thus Italy was faced with the fact that she could only hope to establish her claims by a direct attack on a ruler who she herself had armed and strengthened. Plans were therefore made for an invasion of Ethiopia. The example of the British expedition led the Italians to believe that the conquest of Ethiopia would be a relatively easy task for a modern European army. They forgot that they had themselves supplied the emperor

The Italian campaign in Ethiopia in 1896

172

The Battle of Adowa: a drawing based on a picture in Addis Ababa University

with arms at least as good as those they intended to use against him. They gravely underestimated the numbers of men that he could assemble for battle, and above all they failed to realize that while the Napier expedition had only had to fight against a small bodyguard, their invasion would be opposed by the whole mass of the people. Indeed as the menace of an Italian invasion grew nearer Menelik whipped up the sense of national patriotism. *Rases* who had hitherto been dissidents gave him their support and even Mangasha rallied to the national cause. The Italian army which invaded Ethiopia in 1896 was thus inferior in numbers and no better armed than the defenders of Ethiopia. Its commanders had very little conception of the gravity of the task before them and were deceived for some time by false rumours, deliberately put about, that the emperor had died suddenly of a snake bite. They allowed themselves to be brought to battle on most unfavourable ground at Adowa by the whole Ethiopian army under the personal command of the emperor. The result was an overwhelming Ethiopian victory. The Italians were completely and disastrously defeated. Most of their armaments fell into Ethiopian hands and large numbers of their troops were taken prisoner. Italy was forced to abandon her claims and recognize Ethiopian independence in return for the release of her subjects. This humiliation, the greatest ever suffered by a European power in Africa, continued to rankle in Italian hearts, and one of the reasons behind Benito Mussolini's invasion of Ethiopia in 1935 was the desire to wipe out the memory of this disgrace.

The victory of Adowa established Ethiopia's independence beyond question and Menelik was free to continue his policy of consolidating and extending his rule. In a series of campaigns led by Hapta Giorgis, Tessama and Ras Makonnen, the frontiers of the empire were pushed outwards and during his reign Menelik is said to have more than doubled the territory under effective Ethiopian control.

With the dramatic defeat of Italian claims Ethiopia appeared once more on European maps and the European powers hastened to establish diplomatic relations with the Ethiopian court. In the year following the battle of Adowa, Britain, Russia and Turkey opened legations in Ethiopia. When Britain was about to engage in the conquest of the Sudan she was very anxious to ensure that Menelik did not give aid to the Khalifa which

The provinces of Ethiopia after Menelik's conquests and European colonization

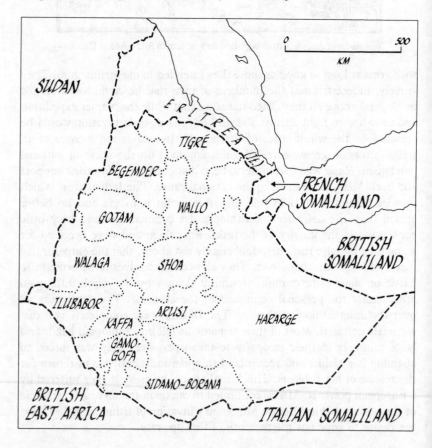

might make the reconquest more difficult, or even impossible. Britain accordingly sent the Rodd mission to Ethiopia, which in return for the promise not to give aid to the Khalifa or allow arms to pass through Ethiopia to the Sudanese, recognized all Menelik's conquests and gave him a further 39 000 square kilometres in the settlement of the Somali frontier. Finally in 1906 Britain, France and Italy signed a Tripartite Treaty formally recognizing the independence and territorial integrity of Ethiopia. However, the treaty makers – in the expectation of Menelik's imminent death and a subsequent period of disunity and possible outside intervention – also stated their respective spheres of influence in Ethiopia.

Thus at the end of the nineteenth century, whilst the Sudan lost the independence she had won from Egypt in 1885, Ethiopia had her independence strengthened and was recognized – if somewhat ambiguously – by the colonial powers.

7 The Maghreb and European intervention

Introduction

Broadly speaking, in the opening years of the nineteenth century, the Maghreb was divided into two administrative and political systems. On the one hand was the independent Maghreb el Aksa (Morocco), under the Sherifian dynasty of the Alawites or Filali, a dynasty founded in 1664 and still on the Moroccan throne. On the other were the semi-independent administrations of the Regencies of Algeria, Tunisia and Libya, under the effete suzerainty of the Sultan of Turkey. Located between Mediterranean Europe, the Middle East and Africa south of the Sahara the Maghreb has for centuries been influenced by, and in turn has influenced, sometimes decisively, events occurring in these three areas. For instance by 1800 the Berber–Arab inhabitants of the Maghreb were culturally identified with the Middle East. Islam had been embraced for centuries and Islamic institutions adopted; the cult of the saints had become strong, particularly in Morocco, and the sufi brotherhoods had begun to attract a larger number of adherents. Arabic was becoming the language of learning, of religion, of government and of administration. The people, Berber–Arabs as they may be called, were agile and abstained from alcohol; they had already begun to bathe frequently and to wear the cylindrical tobe with a coat; they had begun to veil their women and to nurse contempt towards Christians.

Morocco: the monarchy and *baraka*

The political and administrative state of affairs at the beginning of the nineteenth century was as follows. Starting from the west to east is Morocco, a country in which the monarchy has for centuries been of the greatest significance. The monarchy, through Islam, came to be the focus for Berber sentiments of nationality and solidarity. Before the Islamic invasion of the eighth century the Berber inhabitants of the Maghreb had had no form or emblem of unity. But the majority of them having embraced Islam, the Berbers came to have a mystical reverence for the Prophet Muhammad and his descendants. The first of the Prophet's descendants who came to Morocco and established a dynasty was Idris, whose dynasty, the Idrisids, lasted for about a hundred years into the tenth century. Henceforward one dynasty followed the other in Morocco, and although the centrifugal forces in the country undermined the power and efficiency of the monarchy, the fact that the monarchical institution persisted helped to make it the hub of the country's unwritten constitution. But what ensured its permanence and the veneration in which it was held, was the belief of the Moroccan people in *baraka*, the celestial unction which the Prophet was believed to have in an inexhaustible abundance, and part of which was transmitted to his descendants and to saints.

For the cult of saints with its belief in *baraka* came to be central to the lives of the Moroccan Berbers, the logical extension of the idea of the cult of ancestors traditional to the Berbers before Islam was introduced to the Maghreb. The saints were believed to possess supernatural powers to foretell the future and to say extraordinarily potent prayers and utter dreadful curses. In a sense these saints held the same position in Muslim thought as that held by Catholic saints. Saints acquired their *baraka* by communion with the deity, by holiness of life, by the performance of good works and by leadership in the holy war against the 'infidels'. In many cases *baraka* could be inherited. The great saints transmitted to their descendants, known as marabouts (*murabitin*) the *baraka* with with they had been so richly endowed. But the most fortunate in this regard were the *sherifs*, the descendants of Prophet Muhammad. No one had approached the Prophet in the amount of efficacy of the *baraka* with which he had been possessed, and to the *sherifs* this priceless inheritance had been transmitted unimpaired, although diffused and unequally distributed.

By their genealogical connection with the Prophet and their inheritance of *baraka*, the celestial unction which the Prophet was believed to possess in inexhaustible abundance, the Filali sultans came to be venerated by the Moroccans. The sultan's person was sacred; he was the first of all Muslims, 'Lord of the Believers', the great Imam, Commander of the Faithful and the viceregent of God on earth, whose faults should be excused and attributed to a divine inspiration which ordinary mortals were incapable of understanding. It was the sultan's duty to prevent a diminution of his *baraka* from the action of the sun's rays, and to this effect his sacred person was shielded by a magnificent umbrella, which thus became the

177

symbol of royal authority. The welfare of the whole Moroccan community was thought to depend on the sultan's *baraka*.

The Berbers

The significance of the divinity that hedged the sultan lies in the fact that it provided him with the spiritual qualifications with which he commanded the obedience of the entire Berber-Arab population of the country in specified circumstances. For politically the Berbers, particularly those of the Sanhaja, Masmuda and Zenata groups living in the *Bilad es Siba* ('the country of disobedience'), were traditionally unsubmissive. They eschewed centralization in any form and would not transfer their loyalty to any unit larger than the clan except when the entire race was threatened by

The Maghreb in the nineteenth century

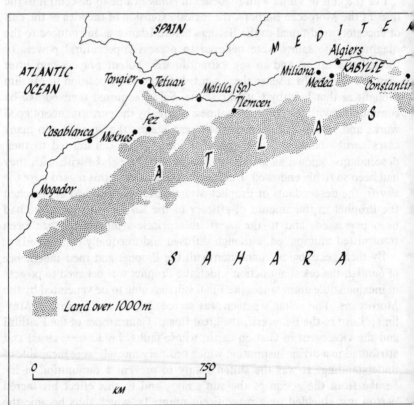

external aggressors. Semi-nomads, these Berbers who lived in the mountainous interior had an intense aversion for the descendants of Arab invaders in the lowlands, for Arab culture and for the Berber agriculturists living in the *Bilad es Makhzen* (Land of Order) who were law-abiding and tax-paying citizens, and who were prepared to accept the Sultan politically. By contrast, the Berbers of the *Bilad es Siba* (Land of Disorder) had the habit of repudiating the sultan's political claims. They would pray for him in their mosques every Friday and follow him in the holy war; they might allow him to represent them in dealings with foreign powers and sometimes to settle quarrels among them; their chiefs might even accept investiture from him as his officials. But to him they paid neither taxes nor troops, except for services in the holy war. Even the supremacy of the sultan in the *Bilad es Makhzen* was not always complete. It was only in an ineffectual way that the sultan's authority was diffused, administratively,

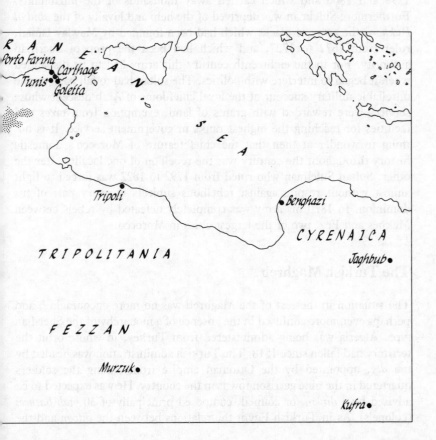

throughout the country. He was the head of the *Makhnes* or Council, which in turn had supervisory control over the *caids* or tribal chieftains, the sheikhs or village heads and the khalifas, the local administrators.

From the ninth century, when the Idrisids began the welding of the Berber groups into a Moroccan nation, to the period of imposition of French colonial rule, the preoccupation of the various governments was how to bind the various societies together under one ruler in a territory where geography aided particularism, factiousness and sectionalism.

In the circumstances the extent of the power of a sultan depended on his ability and military power. And indeed only three monarchs in Moroccan history before 1800 ever succeeded in welding the various societies into one. No nineteenth-century sultan succeeded in achieving this end. It is not surprising then that Mawlay Suleiman, the occupier of the throne in 1800, was weak, in the face of the political confusion that engulfed the country, a situation worsened by the plague which visited the territory in 1799 and 1800 and which carried away thousands of the inhabitants. Furthermore Suleiman was deprived of the help and loyalty of the *abid al Bukhari*, the army of blacks which had been founded by Mawlay Ismail, ruler from 1672 to 1727, and which had been the prop of Sherifian authority. For in the eighteenth century this army had to be disbanded when it began to interfere with politics. The sultan had to fall back on the unreliable military succour of the loyal chiefdoms of Arab descent whose services were rewarded with grants of land, exemption from taxes and facilities for reaching the highest ranks in government service. It is nothing to wonder at then that the chief feature of Morocco's domestic history throughout the century was the rebellion of one locality after the other. Sultan Suleiman who ruled from 1792 to 1822 was forced to fight almost without respite against rebellious subjects in every part of his dominion. In 1820 his army was completely defeated by rebels between Meknes and Fez, two of the largest cities in Morocco.

The Turkish Maghreb

The situation in the rest of the Maghreb was no more encouraging, and perhaps even more confused in the absence of a monarchy of the Sherifian type. Algeria was being administered from Turkey, in whose orbit the territory had fallen since 1518. The Turkish administration was headed by the *dey*, appointed by the Ottoman empire from among the soldiers quartered in the nine garrison towns in the country. He was expected to be advised by a *diwan*, or council, composed principally of 30 *yiah bashees* (colonels). As in Turkish Egypt the relations between the *diwan* and the *dey* were anything but cordial. Continual struggle for power among the colonels characterized Turkish administration. But more often than not the latter reduced the *dey* to a mere cypher. The struggle for power among the colonels, all of whom could legitimately aspire to the position of the *dey*, made the Turkish administration in Algeria more chaotic than in Egypt. Unlike in the latter country where the Mamluk *beys* who were in virtual control of the administration had a stake in the country, the Turkish officials, all of whom came to Algeria from Anatolia, cared little for the interests of Algeria *per se* and remained an exclusive group speaking a language different from Berber and Arabic. The Regency was divided into three administrative provinces, viz, western, Titan and eastern, with headquarters respectively at Oran (after 1792), Medea and Constantine. Outside the administrative and garrison towns Turkish ascendancy in Algeria existed more in theory than in practice. The Berber groups, fanatical lovers of their independence, were allowed to rule themselves and many of them found refuge in the physically difficult Aures, Kabylie and other mountains. Whatever influence the Turkish officials – who are said to have numbered about 20 000 – had over the country was owed to their tactic of siding with the stronger factions among the Berbers against the weaker factions in the eternal clan warfare characteristic of the people.

Tunisia, like Algeria, had been a *beylik* of the Ottoman empire since the end of the sixteenth century. But in 1705 Husayn ibn 'Ali Agha', a janissary (infantryman) of Cretan origin, usurped the supreme authority and founded the Husaynid dynasty which ruled over the country until 1957. Unlike the Algerian *deys* the Husaynid dynasty was hereditary and had some root in the sentiment of the Berbers. For in the eighteenth century the Husaynid *deys* acquired Berber blood and established genealogical connection with the Hafsid dynasty, the purely Berber dynasty which had ruled Tunisia from the thirteenth to the sixteenth century. The Husaynid dynasty attempted to enforce the authority of the central administration against the centrifugal forces of tribal life.

Libya was in 1800 being administered by the most powerful of the Karamanli dynasty which had established itself, independent of the Turks, in 1711. This dynasty of *kuloghus* (descendants of Turco-Arab marriages) remained on the throne till 1835. And yet it was during Yusuf's reign that the centrifugal forces in the territory were fully unleashed. Yusuf had to face revolt upon revolt in a territory where the social structure was conducive to the growth of localized parochialism. For to the east of the territory were the fierce descendants of the Banu Suleiman of the notorious Hilalian invasion of the eleventh century. In the interior, nearest to the desert, were the factious Berbers and in the towns were the Jews, some blacks, *kuloghus* and Turkish elements. The Beduin, semi-nomads, were not only averse to town life but were relentless opponents of taxation. It was natural that Yusuf's attempt to impose centralized authority over them failed. From 1803 to 1804 he had to fight against rebels in Gharyan, against Ghadames from 1806 to 1810, against Mahmud Sherif, governor of Fezzan in 1812, against the Djabal Nafusain in 1815–21 and against his own son, Muhammad, in the east of the country from 1821 to 1822.

European influence in the Maghreb before 1830

But the internal political weakness and problems and the tendencies towards political disintegration in the Maghreb notwithstanding, all the governments were sovereign *vis-à-vis* the European powers. For centuries the 'Barbary corsairs' and European countries had indulged in mutually beneficial piracy on the Mediterranean waters and the former had established their superiority over the Europeans. They captured Europeans as slaves, a situation that contrasted with that on the Atlantic seaboard of West Africa; they compelled the European slaves to erect their palaces, till their land and row their galleys. The European powers recognized the sovereignty of the Maghreb governments. This sovereignty was more than just paper recognition. For instance by 1783 there were no less than eight consular representatives in Tripoli, including consuls from the Netherlands, Sweden, Denmark, Spain and the Italian states. When in 1798 Sweden did not want to pay the usual tribute to the Libyan government, the Libyan navy compelled her to do so. About the same time Napoleon signed a treaty with Yusuf Karamanli against Portugal. When the French army invaded Egypt under Napoleon, Hamouda Bey, ruler of Tunisia from 1782 to 1814, declared war on France because she had invaded a province of the Ottoman empire. However in 1802 he concluded peace with the French government without reference to the Ottoman government. Morocco had ambassadors at St Petersburg, London, Berlin, Madrid and Paris at the beginning of the nineteenth century, while as late as 1811 Yusuf Karamanli placed the British consul, W.W. Langford, under house arrest with impunity.

The sovereignty being exercised by the Maghrebian rulers over the Europeans and Americans was not palatable to the latter. From 1800 onwards they began to undermine the sovereignty of the rulers either by refusing to pay customs duties or 'exactions' or by bombarding their coast or by supporting rival candidates to the thrones. The undermining of the sovereignty of the Maghreb rulers by the European powers was a manifestation of European economic imperialism in Mediterranean Africa, a factor of decisive importance in North African history throughout the nineteenth century. Also the 'suppression' of 'piracy' and non-payment of tributes to the authorities meant a loss to the revenue of the Maghreb states. Then the activities of European powers in these early years of the century were a prelude to the actual subjugation of North Africa and active interference in the politics of the Maghreb. In Egypt, it may be noted, France and Britain were already interfering in the internal politics of the country towards the end of the eighteenth century. Both countries acted in this way in the furtherance of their political and commercial interests. And as early as 1804 the United States had made an attempt to remove Yusuf from the Libyan throne in favour of a puppet by the name of Hamed.

Indeed the doings of the British consul in Libya in the second and third decades of the nineteenth century show the loosening of the Maghrebian rulers' grasp of affairs. Hanmer Warrington, the British consul in Tripoli from 1814 to 1835, became friendly with Yusuf Karamanli in a way that made the former wield considerable influence. In 1816 he introduced vaccination into Tripoli and suggested ways and means of increasing the agricultural output of the territory. In order to push British influence far into the interior he proposed to the British government that a vice-consular post should be established at Murzuk, the capital of the oasis of Fezzan conquered by Yusuf in 1811.

By 1824 Yusuf had been driven into such financial straits that he asked for a loan of 200 000 Spanish dollars (about £40 000), to be repaid in six years. Yusuf Karamanli thereby established a precedent which in most cases provided the excuse for the displacement of traditional rulers in North Africa by European powers. In many respects foreign and domestic policies bore the unmistakable marks of Warrington. By 1825 those European countries which had no diplomatic relations with Tripoli entrusted him with their affairs. By that date he was acting in the capacity of a consul for Austria, Hanover, the Netherlands, Portugal, the two Sicilies and Tuscany. Between 1815 and 1827 he used his good offices to settle differences between Tripoli and Denmark, Sardinia, Tuscany and Sweden. Indeed, to all intents and purposes Warrington became, in the late 1810s and throughout the 1820s, the *de facto* Secretary of State for Foreign Affairs of Tripoli. In domestic affairs Warrington persuaded Yusuf not to increase the tributes by the chief, and converted the consulate to a sanctum for 'oppressed' subjects and slaves. Yusuf was later to regret the confidence he had reposed in Warrington who in 1832 plotted with rebels to effect his overthrow, which event Warrington hoped 'would establish British influence for the next half century in Libya.'

The French occupation of Algeria, 1830

Traditionally the Regency of Algiers and France were on friendly terms. Since the eighteenth century the French connexion had been economically beneficial to Algeria, the latter producing grains and olive oil for France. Moreover, in the *deys's* view, the French were, of all the European powers, the least hostile to the Turks before the nineteenth century, a situation that was likely to temper the traditional hostility of the Berber and Arab Muslims to France. Franco–Algerian commercial relations improved during the Napoleonic wars when Algeria supplied provisions for the armies of Egypt and Italy. Indeed Louis XVIII entered into commercial treaties with the *deys*. Franco–Algerian friendship was reinforced by Algieria's hostility to the growing naval strength of the British in the Mediterranean.

Friendship foundered over the joint economic interests of two influential Jews and some Frenchmen in Algeria, and over the insulting behaviour of Deval, the French consul, a man of questionable character. As in Morocco and other parts of the Maghreb the Jews were financiers and traders of considerable importance in Algeria. And towards the end of the eighteenth century two Jews, Bacri and Busnach, had attempted to monopolize all Algeria's export trade. The *dey* who was a creditor to France and who expected to be paid the debt owed him saw himself swindled and presented as a debtor to the two Jews. The latter connected themselves with the French administration somehow and made a deal with Talleyrand. After the Restoration the interrupted negotiations over the payment of the debt were resumed, and a commission finally reduced the sum outstanding from 24 million to 7 million francs. Bacri and Busnach were only interested in getting their own share, and the *dey*, Hussein, who had lost his grip of the situation, was left with the general impression that he had been swindled.

The appointment of Deval as French consul in Algiers did not improve the situation, for he had the reputation for shady transactions. Several times Hussein had in vain asked for his removal, but the French government persistently ignored his requests, and refused to investigate the charges he brought against the consul. Hussein began to suspect that the French were not sincere in their friendship, for while they were anxious to have Algerian grain they refused to strengthen the Algerian navy as the *dey* demanded. In 1827 Deval and Hussein quarrelled over the supply of grain to France. Tension was already high before the celebrated meeting which took place on 29 April 1827 between Deval and the *dey*. The latter struck the French consul with a fly-whisk because, according to the *dey*, he had been provoked. Deval had said in an insulting manner that the *dey* could not expect the French government to reply to his letters, and then added insulting remarks about Islam. This episode led to the French attack on and occupation of Algeria in 1830, an event which marked a turning point in North African history.

The fly-whisk incident was no more than an occasion for the invasion of Algeria by the French, for worse treatment had been meted out to Europeans continually for three centuries. Nor can the French declaration that the invasion was undertaken to suppress piracy be taken seriously, for piracy was until the Conference of Paris in 1856 recognized by France and Britain as a legitimate form of warfare. More to the point was the fact that Charles X, the last of the Restoration Bourbons, wished to turn the Algerian issue to advantage in an effort to revive the prestige of his regime. He sent a fleet that blockaded Algiers for three years but General Bourmont's victory of July 1830 over Hussein was too late to influence the elections which overthrew him.

At first the French prime minister, the Prince de Polignac, fearing the reaction of Britain to any French attack on the Regency, wished Muhammad Ali to occupy Tripoli and Tunis and punish Algeria. In this enterprise the French were to aid the Egyptian *pasha* with a naval fleet and financial encouragement. Britain persuaded Muhammad Ali to refrain from such an adventure and advised the Ottoman sultan to punish the *pasha* should he venture westwards. Later, when Polignac advised a show of strength, he indicated that he had been dreaming of a scheme 'to establish the influence of France on the African shores of the Mediterranean and right into the heart of Asia'. The Minister of War, General Gérard, justified the conquest of Algeria by the 'need to open up a vast outlet for our surplus population and for our manufactured products in return for other products foreign to our soil and to our climate'. Louis Philippe, who came to power only a few weeks after the expedition landed near Algiers, declared that it was France's intention to found 'an important colony' in Algeria.

As they had claimed on the occasion of their Egyptian invasion the French issued a proclamation in which they announced that their attack was not directed at the Berbers and Arabs but against their Turkish taskmasters. The reaction of the Algerians to the French invasion was different from that of the Egyptian fellahin. Unlike the latter the former did not look upon the French as liberators, but as 'infidels' against whom the holy war should be fought. So far as the Berbers were concerned it was the entire race and their patrimony that were threatened and they spoke with one voice, in a manner unexpected by and disconcerting to the French. Berber nationalist feelings and sense of common identity rose to heights unknown since the days of Kusailah, Princess Kahina and the

Kharijite movement against Arab cultural and political imperialism in the seventh and eighth centuries. The Berbers reacted sharply and swiftly against the French. They saw their resistance as a jihad against the French 'infidels'. The man on whom Berber nationalism and resistance to the French invasion devolved was Abdel Kader. The almost universal spontaneous support given to this man in Algeria from 1832 to 1847 and the continuation of resistance to the French by the Berbers after his capture by the French, were a clear testimony to the fact that, in a sense, Algeria was a living political entity before the advent of the French. The view often expressed by French writers that the Algerian nation was exclusively the creation of the French is not substantiated by facts.

Abdel Kader and resistance to the French occupation

Abdel Kader is one of the few African personalities of the nineteenth century whose qualities and career have attracted the attention of foreign biographers. Abdel Kader emerges from these works as a patriot, a soldier, a religious leader, a statesman, an administrator, a learned man and a diplomat – all rolled into one. In many ways he can be compared and contrasted with Muhammad Ali of Egypt, a man whom he met and of whom he was enamoured. But unlike the Albanian adventurer who had no Egyptian blood in his veins but seized power by plots and counter-plots and forced himself upon the masses, Abdel Kader was a Berber–Arab called to power by popular acclamation. He used the occasion of the French danger to weld together eternally factious chiefdoms. The groups who submitted to his authority included the Banu Yakub, the Banu Abbas, the Banu Amer, the Banu Mejaher and the Banu Hashem. But although not all the groups submitted to his rule at all times – many withdrawing their loyalty whenever the French aggression receded – perhaps no one before him ever administered centrally as large an area in Algeria as Abdel Kader did. Administratively he divided the country into eight *khalifaliks*, the most important of which were those of Tlemcen, Mascara, Miliana and Medea. Tekedemt, a town 100 kilometres southeast of Oran, was made the capital. Fortified, it became a centre for the manufacture of muskets, for minting and for learning.

Every group was held responsible for the peace and good order of its locality. Weekly reports on the state of affairs were expected from every *khalifa* who was given a number of soldiers to help him. The Quran was the basis of his administration and he himself has been described by all his biographers as a genuinely pious man who observed punctiliously the ceremonies and rituals of the Muslim faith. He sent salaried *qadis* to all districts for administration of justice and he punished crimes severely. Himself an ascetic and hater of luxuries, he forbade men from using gold and silver ornaments, proscribed alcohol and tobacco and attempted to put an end to prostitution. As he moved from place to place he constituted himself the sole dispenser of justice. He indicated his punishment with a gesture. If he raised his hand the victim was carried back to prison; if he held it out horizontally, the victim was executed; if he pointed to the ground the victim was caned. He himself presided over a tribunal of *ulema* (learned men) which was the final court of appeal, but sometimes he referred doubtful cases to Egypt and Morocco.

Abdel Kader never demanded anything outside the Quranic taxes of *ashur* (one-tenth of agricultural produce) and *zakat* (two and a half per cent of one's property to be given to the poor by all faithful believers). He attached importance to education, opened schools throughout the territory, where students were taught the principles of Islam, reading, writing and arithmetic. Those who wanted higher education were encouraged to enter into the *zawaya* (singular: *zawiya*) (similar to the monasteries of medieval Europe) and mosques.

The military resistance organized by Abdel Kader stupefied Europe as that of Abdel Karim in the Rif war of the present century in Spanish Morocco was to do. Although in terms of weapons and numbers Abdel Kader's forces were inferior to those of the French, the Berbers enjoyed the advantage of local knowledge. By persuading the Berbers to deny sale of any form of provisions to the French, who depended mainly on local supply, the French were in many instances starved into submission. The Algerian forces used British and French muskets purchased at Tlemcen, Mascara, Miliana, Medea and Tekedemt. And at the seat of government of each of his *khalifas* he placed tailors, armourers, and saddlers, to make the clothing for his troops, repair their arms, and maintain their cavalry equipment. Swift French incursions into the interior were generally followed by swift retreats, largely because of lack of provisions which, on Kader's orders, the Berbers buried beneath the surface of the ground. Kader also employed the tactics of luring the French into the mountain passes and into trenches he had dug for them. He was also militarily strong so long as his lines of communication were not menaced by the French.

Much against their will the French had to concede victory to Abdel Kader twice, in 1834 and 1837. In the former year General Desmichels, the French commander, decided to negotiate with him, without prior consultation with Paris. The Desmichels Treaty of 26 February 1834 indicated the extremities into which the French had been driven by Berber resistance. Abdel Kader had compelled the French to sue for peace; he had dictated his terms. By this treaty Abdel Kader was to pay no tribute and his territory was not limited. The French general acknowledged his independence by offering him the power to appoint and receive consuls. The French were to load at one port alone, and to submit to his tariff. Kader felt he had in fact obtained a mandate to organize the trade of Algeria on a state monopoly basis. Certainly he had scored a major diplomatic triumph.

But the Desmichels Treaty was not a complete victory for Abdel Kader and the Berbers. It gave tacit approval to a French presence on Algerian soil by recognizing French rights to the maritime area of the territory. Some of the more fanatical Berbers became disappointed at a treaty which they regarded as a gross betrayal of the sacred cause of the jihad. However to Abdel Kader negotiation with the 'infidels' was a realistic policy. Like Muhammad Ali of Egypt in his foreign policy and like Bismarck in the way he united Germany in stages, Abdel Kader knew when, where and how to stop. He was aware that henceforth French imperialism had come to stay, and that the Berbers must learn to live with it. He knew that the French had superior arms and that if the French were to mobilize all their military resources the French could easily crush the Berber resistance. In Abdel Kader's view, it was better to salvage as much as he could of Algeria's sovereignty and territorial integrity. In a war such as the Berbers were engaged in, ultimate and complete victory by them was out of the question. In Abdel Kader's judgment he had obtained concessions for Islam and its culture. In any case he needed some breathing space to grapple with the problems of administration and the centrifugal tendencies among the groups who found his stringent application of Islamic laws unpalatable.

In fact the French government regarded the Desmichels Treaty as a great humiliation and its architect was instantly recalled. His successors, particularly General Bugeaud, sought either to reduce the power given to Abder Kader in the Desmichels Treaty or neutralize it completely. The Algerian sultan – he had become sultan by the wish of the people – was able to stand up to the French generals. Through the French newspapers, which he read often, he was able to measure the barometer of public opinion in France. He employed spies and agents who organized propaganda in his favour among influential people in France. The French were persuaded to believe that it would be in France's interest to befriend, rather than alienate, such a revered person. These agents, it is said, extolled Kader's merits and enlarged upon his talents for administration. General Bugeaud, who took over the French army in 1836, at first decided to appeal to arms, but after reviewing his resources he agreed to peace with Kader as a humiliating necessity. After a meeting with the Berber leaders Kader handed over the plain of Algiers to the French.

On 30 May the controversial Treaty of Tafna was made. In the copy to which Abdel Kader did not affix his seal, the sultan acknowledged the sovereignty of France. But according to the Arabic text which he signed Abdel Kader said only that he acknowledged that there was a French sultan, and that he was great. Still according to the French version the frontiers of France in Algeria were delimited, consisting mainly of the plains of Algiers. Kader was recognized as the sultan, to administer the provinces of Oran and Titteri and part of the province of Algiers not yet occupied by the French. The sultan was not to exercise any authority over the Muslims who resided on the territory reserved to France, but these should have the liberty to go and reside on the territory under the sultan's jurisdiction; the Arabs living in French territory were to enjoy the free exercise of their religion; they might build mosques, and follow their religious discipline in every particular, under the authority of their spiritual chiefs. In addition, the sultan was to give the French army 30 000 measures of corn, 30 000 measures of barley, and 5000 head of oxen; he should be empowered to buy in France powder, sulphur, and the arms he required; commerce was to be free between the Arabs and the French; and the farms and properties which the French had acquired, or might acquire, on the Arab territory would be guaranteed them. The sultan also engaged not to give up any part of the coast to any foreign power whatsoever, without the authorization of France; the commerce of Algeria should be carried on only in French ports and France should maintain agents near the sultan, and in the towns under his jurisdiction, to act as intermediaries for French subjects in any commercial disputes they might have with the Arabs. The sultan would have the same privilege in French towns and seaports.

It is clear that the Treaty of Tafna severely modified that made with Desmichels. The independence of Algeria was already compromised politically and economically. The French in effect became a state within a state. Algeria's independence in foreign affairs was bartered away. Nevertheless the French were not satisfied with the attenuated power granted to the Algerian sultan. General Bugeaud had been strictly enjoined by Paris to confine Abdel Kader to the province of Oran only; on no account, he was instructed, must he cede to the sultan the province of Titteri, and he must insist on his paying tribute. Indeed the Treaty of Tafna confined the French substantially to a few towns on the sea coast, with very circumscribed adjacent territories, whilst all the fortresses and strongholds in the interior were left in the hands of their victorious adversary.

There is nothing to wonder at then that within two years of the Tafna agreement differences over the text and interpretation of the treaty by France and Algeria led to a resumption of war. Apart from the dispute over sovereignty there was the boundary question. Marshal Valée, who had assumed the functions of governor-general in Algiers in November 1837, was asked to discuss the details of the treaty with the Algerian sultan. In 1839 Abdel Kader occupied a territory also claimed by the French. This country, lying to the south-east of the province of Algeria, was one of the greatest utility to the French since the garrison of Constantine drew its provisions from it, and they could not help feeling that Abdel Kader could now at any moment stop the supply. Marshal Valée wanted the Treaty of Tafna modified; Abdel Kader would not budge. And as European powers were to do in other parts of Africa in the course of the century, the French began to violate the treaty, firstly by assailing Abdel Kader's agents in the areas occupied by the French with studied affronts and by preventing Muslims in the French territory who wanted to settle in Abdel Kader's territory from doing so, as had been sanctioned in the treaty. Abdel Kader's agent in Algiers, through whom he obtained ammunition and other supplies from France, was suddenly arrested by the French, put in chains and sent to France. Then recognition was withdrawn from Abdel Kader's consul at Algiers, an Italian called Garavan, and the French attempted to instruct Abdel Kader whom he was to appoint. Also the French deliberately violated Abdel Kader's territory. The sultan declared war on 18 November 1839.

The French decided to seize the bull by the horns. A big military offensive was launched, granaries hidden underneath the ground were scouted out and corn was milled by machines carried about by the troops. A systematic dislodgment of Abdel Kader's infantry was undertaken. Attempts were made to cut Abdel Kader's communications with Morocco and Tunisia and assistance was given to those tribes who opposed Abdel Kader. The cupidity of the Tijaniyya sufi brotherhood was satisfied and it began to side with the French against the Berber resisters.

By 1843 the backbone of the Berber resistance was already broken. Many of his *khalifas* were either captured or dead and many of the Berber groups not only surrendered to the French but openly fought with the latter against Abdel Kader. Abdel Kader's state had lost cohesion. The sultan himself fled to Morocco, whose sultan was persuaded by the French to put a price on his head. In the circumstances Abdel Kader was betrayed by Sultan Abdel Rahman, after the French had defeated the Moroccan army at the battle of Isly in 1845. In fact the Moroccans and Abdel Kader's forces fought each other in many engagements. In December 1847 Abdel Kader saw that he could no longer rouse the Berbers to continue the holy war. He was at the end of his tether. Rather than surrender to the Moroccan sultan he decided to hand himself over to the French. This he did on 23 December 1847, on the condition that he was taken to another country annd treated generously. The French gave all these guarantees, and were relieved at the removal of this remarkable soldier, statesman, administrator and patriot from Algeria.

Exemplary punishment of the most brutal kind was meted out to the Berbers; land and animals were seized, fines were imposed, many people were executed, others were deported and many were transferred to France as hostages. War was waged on plantations and several thousand olive trees were destroyed, hundreds of villages were burned down and supporters of Abdel Kader had their throats cut. Well could General Bugeaud declare to settlers in Algiers after an expedition in 1846: 'We have burnt a great deal and destroyed a great deal. It may be that I shall be called a barbarian, but as I have the conviction that I have done something useful for my country, I consider myself as above the reproaches of the press'.

Not only were the Berbers punished physically but they were also forced to pay for the punishment. The casbah treasury was found to contain a treasure worth 49 million francs, of which 43 million francs were dispatched to France. With other booty the entire sum captured was 55 million francs. This covered the 48 million francs which the expedition had cost, leaving France with a profit of 7 million francs.

The punishment meted out to them notwithstanding, the Berbers did not down their arms with the surrender of Abdel Kader. Kabylie, the mountain land guarding the interior, was not occupied by the French until 1857. Here in 1871 a violent insurrection broke out again, the last great attempt by the Berbers in the nineteenth century to win back their independence. Even by 1860 there had been little consolidation of the areas occupied by the French, and, to 1869, Algeria had cost France the lives of 150 000 soldiers and a large number of colonists.

European settlement in Algeria

The French invasion of Algeria was a turning point in the history of the Algerian Berbers and struck terror in the rulers of the other parts of the Maghreb. 'Infidels' began to settle in the best parts of their country from which they had either been forcibly removed or bought out by questionable means. Algeria became the receptacle of all kinds of European settlers – soldiers, wealthy investors, Spanish, Italian, Maltese and Corsican peasants and fishermen. After the 1848 revolution, for instance, no less than 13 500 unemployed from Paris, who were considered a threat to the maintenance of law and order, sailed for Algeria under an official scheme, though few preparations had been made for their reception. Even a group of German emigrants stranded in one French port *en route* to the United

States was diverted to North Africa and settled in the countryside. In 1878 some of the winegrowers who were affected by the blight that had hit French vineyards went to Algeria to retrieve their fortunes. In 1839 there were 25 000 *colons*, of whom 11 000 were of French nationality. In 1849 the figures were 109 000 and 47 000. By 1871 the French element had increased to just over half the total European population and numbered 130 000 as against the 115 000 of other nationalities. By 1912 the Europeans numbered nearly 800 000 in the country.

The consequences of this influx of Europeans into Algeria were tremendous and far-reaching. The Berbers were systematically deprived of their lands, to the tune of 8–9 million hectares, the equivalent of four-fifths of the area available for cultivation in the Tell and on the High Plateaux. The objective of the settlers was, in the words of a general, 'deportation of the Muslim population to other selected areas in order to dispose of the land freely'. In the words of another general, 'colonization and the exigencies which it implies will be the proof that submission [of the Berbers] is genuine'. As in Kenya, South Africa and the Rhodesias the settlers began to look upon the Berbers who owned land as unprogressive cultivators withholding from mankind enormous resources that they, the settlers, were best able to develop. The local communal concept of land was dealt a mortal blow.

French legal policies

The Algerian Berbers suffered also in matters of justice. The original aim of the French was to uproot the Berber past and replace it with French ideas and machinery of justice. The French idea was that French institutions were not only just – absolutely just – but were also universally applicable. French justice was beyond question and good everywhere and therefore any Berber form was simply an obstacle to be brushed aside in order that the supposedly backward Berbers could the better experience the freedom and equity of the French forms. Therefore the Muslim *qadis* and their tribunals were suspended and the Code Napoléon introduced for both civil and criminal cases. Later the native penal law (the *code de loi Indigénat*) was promulgated and customary law continued to prevail in the Kabylie.

Clearly opposed to this French concept was the Berber–Arab viewpoint. For Muslims the Quran was the basis of their religion and their law; its precepts were immutable and sacred; to violate them was to assail their religion and liberty, and might result in a holy war. They held the view that the law, as declared by Muhammad, was fixed and they could not accept the French contention that the law had to keep pace with the changing conditions in Europe. In their view the French were disseminating heresy. The Berbers, absolutely powerless before their masters, swallowed the humiliation. After the Kabylie revolt of 1871 the French attempted a clean sweep of the customs and institutions of the Berbers of Kabylie.

Politically the Berbers were not taken into partnership. Administration remained under the control of the white colonists, usually hot-headed, opinionated, arrogant men but influential with the French administration, through their connections in the world of business and politics. They regarded Algeria as a mere extension of France, a view consistently endorsed by the French government until the advent of Charles de Gaulle. The Berbers were considered as backward, uncultured, ineducable and almost irredeemable, and were consequently excluded from the administration of the country. They did not qualify for French citizenship, the only citizenship recognized in Algeria, though in 1870 the Jews were naturalized *en masse*. Jules Ferry, a French Prime Minister, said of the indigenous Algerians in 1892: 'The Moslems have no notion of the political mandate or of limited and contractual authority; they know nothing of a representative *regime* or of the separation of powers, but they have in the highest degree the instinct and need and ideal of a strong power and just power'.

The Algerian Berbers' reaction to the repressive policy of the French taskmasters was one of sullen resignation to their fate. Their past was being uprooted, their present miserable and their future bleak. They had no love for French rule; they despaired and disaffection began to seethe among them. The eloquent silence of the masses was misconstrued by the French as evidence of satisfaction with their rule, and in later days when the *effendiya* (educated élite) launched the nationalist movement, the French began to argue that these nationalists did not represent the wishes and aspirations of the apparently apathetic masses.

European pressure on Morocco

The French invasion and occupation of Algeria had effects on North Africa as a whole and on the Maghreb in particular. The rest of the Maghreb saw the writing on the wall. It became clear that the occupation of the rest of Mediterranean Africa by the European powers was only a question of time. European imperialism had evidently come to stay. What postponed the evil day for many of the North African states was the mutual jealousy arising out of the conflicting interests of the various

European powers who had interests in the appropriation of this part of the continent. For many decades the interest of one power cancelled out that of the other, until they agreed among themselves on how to share the spoils. The postponement of the establishment of European rule was also partly due to the role played by many North Africans. The Maghreb produced many shrewd rulers who exploited the differences among the European powers to knock the head of one power against that of the other, thereby postponing the inevitable doom.

The situation in Morocco and Tunisia showed this clearly. In this area the imperial interests of Britain, France and Spain converged. For Britain Morocco was of the highest strategic value. The northern coast, and especially that part of it forming the southern shore of the straits of Gibraltar, guarded the entrance to the Mediterranean. British interests in Greece, the rise of Muhammad Ali and French activities in other parts of Mediterranean enhanced the importance of Morocco for the British. British trade with the territory was substantial. The British fortress of Gibraltar depended on the territory for provision. To France too Morocco was of first-class interest, particularly after the Algerian invasion of 1830. The boundary between Algeria and Morocco was purely an artificial one, having been determined by fortuitous historical events. The border chiefdoms, who were naturally anti-French, could not be made to recognize its existence. Moreover there were linguistic, cultural and religious ties which the border chiefdoms of Morocco and Algeria shared. For instance there were the sufi brotherhoods which knew no international boundaries. The French had observed the power of the brotherhoods in the movement led by Abdel Kader. Of the brotherhoods the most important was the Taibiya whose leader was the Grand Sherif of Wezzan in Morocco. Should he command the faithful in Algeria to rise up against the French, would the faithful not obey him? Moreover establishment of French influence in Morocco was absolutely necessary in the plans of the French to extend into the desert and semi-desert regions of the Algerian coast. The French feared that Morocco could become a sanctuary to those Berbers who might resist their penetration into the Sahara. Spain's interest in Morocco of course dated back to the fifteenth century. To all these powers Morocco was potentially promising for financial investment. The rivalry of these three powers became the strength of the sultan, guaranteeing the independence of the territory until the French and British concluded the agreement which gave to the former a free hand to annex Morocco in the first decade of the twentieth century.

Sultan Abdel Rahman's (1822–59) weakness and domestic problems were exploited by the European powers. In 1828 the British blockaded Tangier; the following year the Austrians bombarded Arzila and Tittawin, as reprisals for the seizure of some merchant ships by Morocco, thus putting an end to the sultan's corsair navy. The French attack on Algeria was a real crisis for Morocco. Immediately after the French attack the Arabs of Tlemcen appealed to the sultan for help. Abdel Rahman seized the chance to extend his influence into western Algeria by appointing *khalifas* to Tlemcen, Miliana and Medea. Between 1832 and 1834 the sultan also gave moral and material support to Abdel Kader. By 1842 the French had begun to consider the invasion of Morocco. In 1844 war broke out between Morocco and the French over the help the former was believed to be offering to Abdel Kader. Fiqq, a territory claimed by Morocco, was peremptorily annexed by the French and Mogador and Tangier were bombarded. The battle of Isly, mentioned earlier, compelled Abdel Rahman to accept French wishes. France claimed no territory, no indemnity, not even the expenses of the war. The sultan was merely asked to deliver Kader to France. The treaty stipulated that should the French capture the Algerian leader they should treat him generously; but should Morocco capture him the sultan should restrict him to one of the towns on the western coast of Morocco until the two governments could decide how best to prevent Abdel Kader continuing to be a menace to them.

But the battle of Isly strained Franco-Moroccan relations. In 1851 the French bombarded the port of Sale, following the capture of some French vessels by the Moroccans. The weakness of Morocco was exploited by the Spanish who in 1859, at the accession of Sidi Mohammed IV, declared war on the sultan, after a dispute over the Spanish fortification of Mellila. With an army of 30 000 men Spain took Tetuan and was only prevented from advancing into the heart of Morocco by British intervention. A convention was signed in 1860 by which more territory around Mellila was ceded to Spain, the latter's right to avenge any Berber attack on the Spanish without hostility from the sultan was acknowledged and Morocco was to pay an indemnity of £4 million. This latter sum was obtained from the territory's customs receipts until the 1880s. A most-favoured nation convention was also signed by which no trading privileges were to be granted to other powers except they were granted to Spain as well.

The commercial privileges forced on Morocco by Spain opened the way to France and Britain, both of whom soon extracted the same demands. In 1865 Moroccan goods were allowed to go free of duty to Algeria. Nevertheless Franco–Moroccan relations did not improve and during the 1871 rebellion in Algeria, France violated Morocco's territorial integrity by pursuing some of the rebels into Moroccan territory. In order to meet the European challenge the sultan established an artillery school, revived sugar plantations in the south and began a sugar refinery. The Muhammadiyah Printing Press was also founded.

Hassan III

The successor to the Sherifian throne in 1873, El Hassan III, was a dignified, well-respected strong man who attempted to halt the unhappy developments in the country. He was in a sense a modernizer who carried out some reform of the administration and judiciary. He appealed to pan-Islamism and renewed diplomatic relations with the Ottoman sultan. But the situation was beyond repair. European influence had come to stay and could not be driven out as he wished. All he could do was to play one power against the other. He was fortunate that the French were preoccupied in other parts of the globe. There was reconstruction in France; Egypt and Tunisia were of greater immediate attention, and it was not until the 1890s that France could concentrate on Morocco in a forceful fashion. In these years too Anglo–Moroccan relations improved, and Morocco looked to Britain to safeguard Morocco's interests against the intrigues of other European powers, in return for commercial concessions. Britain was given a monopoly of the merino wool and exploited Moroccan iron and phosphates. Morocco also imported a great deal from Britain. This is not to say that Britain keep other European powers out of Morocco's trade. In fact Spain's commercial interests enlarged during the period and Germany and Belgium also entered the commerce of the territory in the last decade of the century.

In the meantime Hassan had to deal with internal problems. It took him ten years to consolidate his kingdom and to obtain undisputed possession of the country. Nevertheless, with the exception of Mawlay Ismail, none of his Filali predecessors ever succeeded in exercising authority over the Berbers of the south as he did. Throughout his reign he was constantly engaged in military expeditions in parts of the country where rebellion occurred. He succeeded in compelling the *caids* of the south to pay him tribute regularly. The main consequence of his constant involvement in the pacification of his country was that he did not have the time to carry out administrative, economic and military reforms, such as those carried out by Muhammad Ali for the modernization of Egypt. He tried to introduce an army trained by Europeans, but Arab aversion to professional soldiery led to the failure of the scheme. Many who received arms from him deserted to the dissident chiefdoms and fought against him.

It may be asked why, in spite of his strong character, Hassan did not obtain the co-operation of his people. In the latter's view all the nineteenth-century sultans had committed a heinous crime by associating themselves in any manner with Europeans. For instance Abdel Rahman had betrayed the interests of the country by not supporting Abdel Kader. The masses came to believe that their sultans were selling their country to rapacious 'infidels'. Hence in 1878 and 1887 there were Berber demonstrations against Hassan when foreign men-of-war in the ports demonstrated, ostensibly to protect their nationals. What could this be, asked the Berbers, but a combined design on their independence?

In 1894 Hassan died and was succeeded by Abdel Aziz who did not reach his majority until 1900. Until the latter date the real ruler was Bou Ahmad, a strong ruler and the son of a black slave. Abdel Aziz was the opposite of his immediate predecessor, a timid and idealistic ruler. Nor was he a powerful religious dignitary. His chief mistake however was that he allowed himself, like Said and Ismail of Egypt and Muhammad es Sadek of Tunisia, to be unduly fascinated by European gadgets. One man who influenced him in this respect, simply to improve British commerce in Morocco, was Maclean, an enterprising British ex-officer from Gibraltar, who came to make a fortune in Morocco. He became the sultan's instructor and colonel of his bodyguard. He came to be nicknamed Caid Maclean. Maclean introduced the youthful sultan to sport of all kinds, including bicycle races at court, to the delight of spectators. He spent a great deal of money on lawnmowers, cameras, cigarette-lighters, musical boxes, silk dresses and ostrich-feathered Parisian hats. His court came to be known as the court of amusements and he was nicknamed 'the mad sultan' who was believed to have been bewitched by the foreigners.

The significance of the extravagance of this 'mad sultan' lies in the fact that he was soon compelled to do what other rulers in North Africa had done, and which became the pretext on which European powers occupied their territory – borrow money. By 1900 the establishment of French rule over Morocco was only a question of time.

Tunisia and the French occupation of Algeria

The *bey* of Tunisia's first reaction to the French attack on Algeria was one of delight partly because the *dey* of Algiers was his traditional enemy and partly because he felt that by allying with France the latter would allow him to annex Constantine in eastern Algeria. In fact at one time it seems that the French toyed with the idea of handing over the administration of Algeria to a Husaynid prince. A treaty was signed with France on 8 August 1830, a clause of which ceded to France a conspicuous spot on the coast for the erection of a memorial chapel in honour of Louis IX and another article of which restored to France the coral fishery on the coast. However the *bey* was soon disappointed in the French who were embarrassed by the support which the Tunisians began to give to Abdel Kader. The *bey* had to maintain a policy of strict neutrality.

Indeed the *bey* soon began to regret his pro-French manifestations. For the British lost no time in encouraging the sultan of Turkey to reassert his suzerainty over Tunisia. The permanent presence of the French fleet at Goletta, a Tunisian port, the influence the French were believed to be wielding in the *bey's* court and the gifts made to the *bey* by the French from time to time – all these alarmed the British. Rather than have French influence increase in Tunisia the British government decided to encourage the Turks to neutralize French influence in Tunisia, as the Turks had been persuaded to do with Muhammad Ali in Egypt. For just as they had encouraged Muhammad Ali's intransigence in Egypt the French wished to encourage the *bey* to assert his independence of the Ottoman empire, and thereby depend on France even more than before.

The reign of Ahmed Bey

During the reign of Ahmed Bey, 1835–55, French influence in Tunisia increased considerably. In 1842 the *bey* was successfully persuaded to abolish the slave trade. In 1846 he went on a state visit to Paris and was received with great pomp. The French government asked him to relieve the Jews of the disabilities they were suffering and to grant concessions to Roman Catholic schools in Tunisia. The *bey* acceded to these requests in an attempt to please the French, whose support he felt he needed for the maintenance of his independence against the Turkish threat.

Ahmad Bey also decided to become a modernizer in order to prevent annexation of his country on the grounds of his country's 'backwardness'. Like Muhammad Ali of Egypt, he attempted to modernize his army and navy. In 1840 he founded a military academy where Italian, British and French teachers instructed the cadets in sciences, in military strategy, and in history, geography and languages. At this academy about forty books in these various fields were translated into Arabic. He also attended to the navy. Porto Farina became the naval base and 12 ships were built for the use of the navy. It is estimated that on the whole Ahmed Bey spent not less than two-thirds of the country's revenue on defence alone. Like Muhammad Ali too, aware of the political implications of borrowing, he kept Tunisia solvent and was cautious in yielding to European pressure for social and constitutional reforms. At his death in 1855 he left 120 million francs in the treasury.

Muhammad es Sadek and the growth of European influence

His successor, Muhammad es Sadek, 'the Magnificent', was comparable

Muhammad es Sadek, Bey of Tunis

to Ismail Pasha of Egypt. He dissipated the Tunisian revenues on beautiful Georgian, Turkish and Circassian slave girls, leaving only a small surplus to be swallowed up by French engineers in bringing pure water to Tunis over the aquaduct of Adrian. On 24 October 1855 Muhammad es Sadek signed his first convention with France for the construction of electric telegraph lines throughout Tunisia. By 1862 the Treasury was empty, and in May 1863 a loan was negotiated in Paris for £1 400 000 from Messrs Oppenheim and Erlanger. The terms imposed on this loan were so onerous that the *bey* only received in cash one-seventh of the sum. By 1869 the financial condition of the country had become so desperate that an international commission was established to consolidate the debt and arrange for its service. On this commission the British, French and Italian interests were represented, though the greater part of the debt was in the hands of the French creditors.

In the meantime the European commercial and financial interests were scoring one success after the other. The British held a concession for an important railway from the city of Tunis to Goletta. After 1870 the Italians joined in the scramble for opportunities and soon began to outbid the British in competition with the French. The interest exacted on the various loans the *bey* was encouraged to take varied from 12 to 15 per cent. The financial burden on the state could be alleviated only by increasing taxes. A special tax called *majba* of 36 *rials* was levied on all able-bodied men and this provoked a popular rebellion led by Ali ibn Ghadhahim, who was styled 'the Bey of the People'. The struggle to suppress this uprising

199

plunged the *bey* still further into debt.

Not only were inroads being made into the sovereignty of the *bey* by the loans he had taken, but he was compelled to grant economic concessions as well. In 1870 he granted an Italian agricultural company an estate at Jedeida, while a French citizen, the Count de Saucy, was put in possession of the fruitful domain of Sidi Tabet. The latter concession was destined to provide one of the excuses for the French occupation of Tunisia in 1881. Indeed the Italian *concessionaires* were hardly installed at Jedeida when they put forward claims to exercise such jurisdiction over the inhabitants as would effectively constitute them into an independent state within the state. And the concession to Count de Saucy for the improvement of 'the breed of horses, cows and sheep' was 1400 hectares of the most fertile land in Tunisia.

The position of the *bey* in Tunisia became very weak as a result of his prodigality. The prime minister from 1837 to 1873, Mustapha Khazinda, who was behind the foreign loans, was not only corrupt but also encouraged the *bey* to rule despotically. Despotic rule was however against European interests. For the narrow sea that separates the territory from Sicily made the Europeans fear that a despotic ruler in Tunisia identified with the Ottoman empire could easily make Tunisia a part of the 'Eastern Question'. If this were to happen, it was feared, the balance of sea-power would be overturned by any power that had Tunisia on its side. For many years therefore the Europeans were incessant in pressing the *bey* to liberalize the constitution of the territory. In 1857 and 1861 the *bey* made abortive attempts at constitutional reforms. In the former year religious reform was proclaimed, the immunities enjoyed exclusively by the Muslims were abolished, a mixed commercial court was set up, liberty of commerce was announced and monopolies were abolished. In 1861 the *bey* announced a liberal constitution and established a 'representative' chamber. The *bey* was henceforward to act only on the advice of his ministers, who were in turn to be responsible to the Assembly. The financial administration was to be improved by the introduction of a budget and civil list, and a court of appeal and a criminal tribunal were to be instituted. This 1861 constitution (*Destour*) later became a rallying cry for twentieth-century nationalists (the *Néo-Destour* party of Habib Bourguiba, who later became President of Tunisia).

By 1871 the *bey* began to find French relations irksome and he began to feel that Tunisia was being milked by the French. Against the wishes of the French he decided to cultivate the goodwill of the Ottoman sultan. To this end an imperial *firman* was issued by the sultan, declaring Muhammad es Sadek Pasha as *wazir* of Tunisia and conferring upon him 'the right of hereditary succession', renouncing the annual tributes Tunisia had been obliged to pay for centuries and binding Tunisia to give positive support to Turkey in case of war between the latter and any other power. It stated further that the *bey* was not to conclude any treaties with any foreign powers, the prerogative of which was to remain in the hands of the Ottoman empire. The *bey* furthermore alienated the French by flatly refusing to entertain Ferdinand de Lesseps' suggestion of an 'inland sea' in Tunisia. Finally in 1880 the *bey* refused the French harbour concessions at Goletta.

The French occupation of Tunisia, 1881

France was enraged at these events and began to look for pretexts to justify the occupation she had been entertaining for a long time. Up till 1878 it was British opposition that had prevented France from declaring her suzerainty over Tunisia. In this year, however, the British gave the French a blank cheque in return for French recognition of British occupation of Cyprus. At the Congress of Berlin in which Britain gave the French a free hand in Tunisia, Bismarck was also favourably disposed towards a French occupation of Tunisia, hoping thereby to draw France's attention away from Alsace-Lorraine which had been annexed by Germany in 1870.

The only remaining formidable opponent of France over Tunisia was Italy. Tunisian friendliness to Italy as a counterpoise to the dangerous aspirations of the French made the latter decide in 1880 on an occupation. In that year the *bey* was actually asked to sign a protectorate treaty, a proposal sponsored by the Tunisian ruler. After 1860 the Italians began to establish themselves in Tunis, which was just across the sea from Italy. By 1880 there were 20 000 Italians settled in Tunisia, as opposed to 200 Frenchmen. This flow of population was accompanied by a growing agitation in Italy for the acquisition of Tunisia. For, according to nationalist Italian writers, Tunisia was a part of the old Roman empire which the new unified Italy was expected to revive in a modern form. In fact in 1870 the Italian government had been tempted to take advantage of France's disasters in the Franco–German war to seize the territory of the *bey*. On that occasion it was only the unveiled threat of the French provincial government which deterred Victor Emmanuel from taking action.

At the Berlin Conference of 1878 Italy had concentrated attention on *Italia Irredentia*, the Trentino and Trieste, which it expected Austria might grant to it. Andrassy, the Austrian foreign minister, had called Count Corti's attention to the Mediterranean as the area on which Italy should concentrate its aspirations. But for Corti the territory in Europe was the more important. He returned to Italy only to regret that he did not follow up the suggestions as to Tunisia. It is said that the indignation in Italy was so great that Corti was almost stoned in the streets and soon after resigned his position as foreign minister.

But in the French-Italian scramble for Tunisia the Italians were the weaker power. So far as the Italians were concerned the struggle was really a hopeless one. For the French had much greater resources, financial and military, at their disposal, and what was more, they had the other great powers behind them. Nevertheless the Italians made a last bid to neutralize French influence by allowing Italian interests to continue the competition with the French. The two governments clashed in the matter of the Tunis–Goletta railway, which the British owners had offered for sale. By the lavish use of money the Italian Rubattino Company finally secured the line, after which the Italian Parliament passed a bill granting the new owner an annual subvention. The incident led to a sharp exchange of notes between Paris and Rome, and the French would probably have proceeded to take action in the summer of 1880 had it not been for the opposition of prominent French leaders. Even so, Charles de Freycinet, the French premier, appears to have considered the establishment of a protectorate just before his ministry fell from power in September 1880.

However the French still hesitated, for there was little sentiment in Paris in favour of colonial adventure, and there was much disagreement in

The European advance into the Maghreb

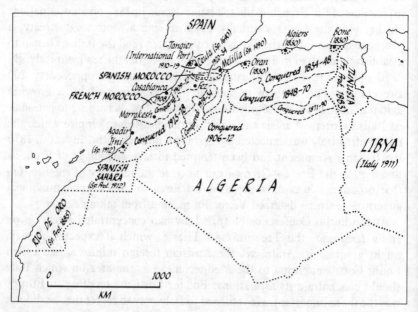

government circles as to what should be done. President Grévy maintained that Tunis was not worth a cigar while Léon Gambetta felt that Bismarck was driving the French towards Africa in order to make France forget the humiliation of 1870. But the incident of 10 January 1881 precipitated events. At Palermo, the brother of the *bey*, leading a delegation of Italians resident in Tunis, met King Umberto of Italy. High-sounding speeches were made and the Italian press took care to point out the political significance of the visit. These demonstrations, naturally, had an electrifying effect in Paris. Even Gambetta was forced to admit that action was imperative. Efforts appear to have been made almost immediately to induce the *bey* to sign a treaty with France and accept some form of protectorate. The *bey* refused to entertain these ensnaring proposals.

It was too late for the French government to turn back. A pretext for military action was found in a raid on the Algerian frontier by the Krumirs in March 1881. There was nothing unusual about these raids. Indeed it is said there had been over 2000 of them between 1870 and 1881. In 1879, the French also alleged, the Krumirs had provided the Berber rebels in the Aures with ammunition. Moreover the French liked to believe that the pan-Islamic movement in North Africa – including the Arabi Pasha revolt in Egypt, the Mahdi movement in the Sudan, the killing of Flatters, a French colonel, in the desert and the insurrections of South Oran — was most active in Tunisia. Moreover, although the pan-Islamic movement was directed against the Christian powers of Europe generally, it was organized 'specially' against France. This Muslim fanaticism, the French contended, endangered the lives of the French nationals in Tunisia and demanded French intervention.

After a 'military promenade' the *bey* surrendered in May and signed the Treaty of Bardo which established what amounted to a French protectorate over Tunisia. By the articles of this treaty France was to control Tunisian foreign policy. By another treaty, the Treaty of Marza, signed in 1883, the French established control over the internal affairs of the country as well, including finance and the judiciary.

The French occupation of Tunisia was similar in many ways to the British occupation of Egypt. The relationship between the *bey* and the resident-general was similar to that between the *pasha* or *khedive* and the governor in Egypt. The local administrators in Tunisia, who supervised the *qadis* and *sheiks* in the interior, were counterparts of the British *muffatash* in Egypt. There was, however, a difference. The *bey* appointed his own ministers who had limited functions, while there were departments under the French resident-general alongside. In Egypt the governor appointed ministers.

But the treaties of Bardo and Marza are not a true guide to the power actually wielded by the French. Tunisian 'independence' was in reality fictitious,.for the protectorate was one in which the authority of the *bey* was gradually usurped by French administrators. Armed opposition to the presence of the French continued into the last years of the nineteenth century, by which time the Ottoman sultan had finally relinquished his sovereignty over Tunisia.

Nevertheless the protectorate status of Tunisia made it impossible for the French to administer Tunisia in the same way they were administering Algeria. By the very circumstances of the occupation of the former, the so-called policy of assimilation was out of the question. The difference is best expressed in the words of S.H. Roberts:

> [Algeria] was a colony assimilated to France, [Tunisia] a protectorate which retained an Oriental organization: the one was a country of small settlers, the other of *entrepreneurs* alone; the one was essentially rural, the other equally urban; the one saw everything native shattered and priority given to European codes and methods, while the other retained the old native policy as the basis of future organization; the one thus had the natives driven back, the other left them predominant; the one had its trade subordinated to France, the other kept its development free.

Libya under the Turks

Unlike the other parts of the Maghreb, Libya was much less subject to the threat of European imperialism in the nineteenth century, but imperialism came all the same – from Turkey. France's attitude towards Yusuf Karamanli stiffened after the Algerian invasion. One month after the event Admiral Rosamel forced a treaty on Yusuf. By this treaty Yusuf was to apologize to the French consul, Rousseau, for previous humiliations, trade monopolies were abolished, enslaving of Christians (Europeans) was to cease, all forms of exactions from the French were to cease, Libya's navy was not to be strengthened any further and Yusuf was to pay 80 000 francs as war indemnities on amounts lost by French nationals in Tripoli. The French and British encouraged rival candidates to Yusuf's throne, Warrington living among the rebels and the French consul supporting the legal heir, Ali Pasha. In the circumstances, under pretence of sending reinforcements to restore law and order in Libya, a territory then composed of the three loosely administered areas of Cyrenaica, Tripoli and Fezzan, the Ottoman government sent a punitive expedition under Mustapha Nedgib to Tripoli. The general landed without any opposition, arrested all members of the royal family, declared the Karamanli dynasty entirely abolished, and then proclaimed himself governor of the Regency.

But Turkish rule was confined in the main to the coastal areas, and it was not an efficient administration. Between 1835 and 1911, the year of the Italian invasion of Libya, 33 *walis* (governors) ruled the territory. Three of them held office for about thirty years, leaving the others with an average term of just over one year. Evidently the frequent change of governors impaired administrative efficiency. Nor were there large forces to control so vast a territory. Moreover Constantinople had no desire to have strong *walis* in Libya, lest the latter became strong enough to assert independence.

The Sanusiyya brotherhood

But Turkish rule in the country was very weak. It was in this circumstance that a sufi brotherhood came to exercise the greatest influence in the interior of Libya. In Islamic history religious brotherhoods have been of considerable importance. Although essentially religious and spiritual in their purpose, the brotherhoods often assumed a political complexion. A phenomenon which often impelled them to perform political functions was a threat from the 'infidels'. In Morocco for instance the brotherhoods' *zawaya* or lodges, were among the focal points of Moroccan patriotism and resistance in face of the Spanish and Portuguese danger in the fifteenth and sixteenth centuries. In Arabia in the nineteenth century the Wahabbis rebelled against Constantinople and for a time founded their own state. And in the last years of the nineteenth century until 1932 the Sanusiyya became anti-French and anti-Italian. But a branch of a sufi brotherhood in one territory might behave differently from one in another territory. For example in the nineteenth century the Quadiriyya were fiercely and uncompromisingly anti-French in the Maghreb, while the Tijaniyya became pro-French and pacific. But in Northern Nigeria the Tijaniyya became the spearhead of the anti-British resistance, while the Quadiriyya remained conservative and soft-pedalled with the British.

The brotherhoods' *zawaya*, besides being centres of religious activities, often served also as schools, infirmaries and charitable institutions, and might be compared with the monasteries of medieval Europe. For many important religious and political figures in Islamic Africa were influenced one way or the other by one of the brotherhoods. Usman dan Fodio, for instance, was a member of the Qadiriyya and the Mahdi of the Sudan was influenced by the Mirghaniyya.

The Sanusiyya was named after the founder, Sayyid Muhammad bin 'Ali al-Sanusi, the Grand Sanusi. He was born in Algeria about 1787 into a distinguished family of sharifs. Well-informed in Muslim theology, juris-prudence and interpretation of the Quran, he became interested in the Moroccan order of the Tijaniyya. In the 1820s he left Fez on pilgrimage for Mecca, probably in order to avoid the hostility of the Moroccan authorities, who were alarmed at the political consequences of his pan-Islamic propaganda. Al-Sanusi's teachings were alarmist to Muslim rulers and seemed heterodox to the *ulema*. From Fez he went to Tripoli and Benghazi, preaching all the way. He had by the 1830s gathered around him his first disciples, *ikhwan*, mostly Algerians, many of whom followed him to Egypt. It is probable that the independence of Muhammad Ali and the cultural and intellectual revival in Egypt at this time left their mark on his mind. Having studied in the Hijaz under a number of sheikhs at Mecca and Medina, he began to preach a return to Islam as practised zealously and genuinely in the days of Prophet Muhammad. The man who influ-enced him most was Sayyid Ahmad bin Idris al Fasi, the fourth head of the Moroccan order of the Qadiriyya, whom the Grand Sanusi followed for two years.

In 1837 the Grand Sanusi established his Order at Mount Abu Qubais, near Mecca. In 1841 he left the Hijaz for North Africa, with his disciples. In 1842 he reached Libya and the following year he established the mother Lodge of the Order at al-Baida on the central Cyrenaican plateau. In 1856 he made Jaghbub, 160 kilometres from the coast, his headquarters. This place became the centre of the Sanusiyya and the seat of an Islamic university, second only in Africa to al-Azhar. This place was chosen because it had certain political advantages. It was out of reach of the Turkish, French and Egyptian governments; it was on the main pilgrim-age route from north-west Africa through Egypt to Mecca, and this pilgrimage route bisected at the oasis one of the trade routes from the coast to the Sahara and the Sudan. By 1856 this predominantly missionary brotherhood had converted the nomad and semi-nomad Beduin chiefdoms of Libya and Egypt.

It was in this oasis of Jaghbub that the Grand Sanusi gathered the learned men, over three hundred of them. Under his personal supervision and that of his disciples, far from worldly distractions, the Grand Sanusi was able to train the future leaders of the Sanusiyya. The shaikhs of the Sanusiyya *zawaya*, established throughout the territory, were appointed by him from among his intimate circle of disciples, many of whom follwed him from Algeria and other parts of the Maghreb. A very learned man and a writer of distinction, he had a library of about eight thousand books, mostly works on Islamic law and jurisprudence, mystic-ism, philosophy, history, Quranic exegesis, poetry, astronomy and astrol-ogy. It was in this oasis that he died in 1859.

In 1859 he was succeeded by his eldest son, al-Sayyid Muhammad al Madhi, after a period of regency. It was under al-Madhi that the Sanusiyya extended into the Sahara and the Sudan. In 1895 he moved the headquarters to Kufra. The choice of this latter place was due partly to its strategic location with reference to Libyan oases and routes, partly because of the rise of the Mahdi in the Sudan and partly because of the military and political activities of the French.

The point has to be emphasized that the Sanusiyya, particularly in its early stages, was predominantly a missionary organization. It aimed not only at reviving Islam and infusing it with new spirit, but at bringing Islam within the reach of people who had not known it. And until the last years of the nineteenth century the Sanusiyya refused to be drawn into the vortex of European conflict with other Muslim states. Hence although the Sanusiyya co-operated with the Turks in the administration of Libya the Sanusi family and the brothers of the Sanusiyya disapproved of their way of life. They resisted Turkish demands for assistance in the latter's war against the Russians from 1876–8; they refused the aid asked for by Arabi Pasha in Egypt in 1882, and by the Sudanese in 1883, against the British. Sayyid al-Madhi likewise rejected diplomatic overtures by the Italians and Germans. It was not until France invaded the Sanusiyya's Saharan territories and destroyed its religious houses, and when later the Italians, also without provocation, did the same in Cyrenaica, that the Sanusiyya resisted militarily the European imperialists.

But within Libya itself the Grand Sanusi and his successors could not resist exercising political authority over the people. For the almost total acceptance of the Sanusiyya by the Beduin was due mainly to political and religious reasons. By virtue of the *baraka* which the Grand Sanusi was believed to possess in great profusion he became a centripetal force welding the factious groups together, as did the sherifian sultans of Morocco. Both the Grand Sanusi and his band of followers, who were mainly foreigners to the Beduins of Libya, thus stood outside the tribal system. They were therefore not involved in the traditional loyalties and feuds inherent in Beduin society. For the missionary organization of the Sanusiyya was separate from the tribal system, and by centering it in the distant oasis of Jaghbub the Grand Sanusi prevented it from becoming identified with any one people or section of the country, as it might have become had it been centred in Cyrenaica, where the brotherhood was strongest. Also many of his immediate lieutenants, the sheikhs, came from outside. The Dardafi and Ismaili families came from Tripolitania, the Ghumari family from Morocco, the 'Ammur, Bu Jibali and Khattab families from Algeria, and so on.

Moreover the tribal groups in the country were made to believe that the

Sanusiyya belonged to them. To this end the distribution of the *zawaya* was based on tribal particularism. The *zawaya* were founded by tribes or tribal sections, and came to be regarded as tribal institutions. But each *zawiya* also came to be a cult centre. Through the Sanusiyya the tribes of Cyrenaica became linked from above in a common, if loose, organization under a single sacred head. Thus a loose federation of tribes was turned into a nation and national sentiment became strong, particularly in face of outside interference by the Turks, and later by the Italians, against whom all the tribes had common hostility.

The Sanusiyya succeeded in establishing peace among traditionally warring tribes. It was the Sanusiyya which established peace between the Tibu and the Beduin Arabs in the north and the Tibu and Uled Sliman in the south, thus rendering the Tripoli-Fezzan-Wadai trans-Saharan route safe. Hussein Bey, an Egyptian Oxford graduate who travelled along the route in 1923, met some Beduin who told him that in the days of al-Madhi, a woman could walk from Berea in Cyrenaica to Wadai unmolested. Hussein wrote:

> There can be no doubt that the influence of the Senussi brotherhood upon the lives of the people of that region is good. The ikhwan of the Senussi are not only teachers of the people both in the field of religion and of general knowledge, but judges and intermediaries both between man and man, and between tribe and tribe... The importance of these aspects of the Senussi rule in maintaining the tranquility and well-being of the people of the Libyan desert can scarcely by over-estimated.

Economically the Sanusiyya took part in the cultivation of land. For like the Christian church in medieval times the brotherhood was endowed with lands. The Sanusi were not mendicants, but they tilled their estates, controlled the trade of their territory and collected gifts. By 1919 the lands of the Sanusiyya totalled more than 200 000 hectares. Moreover its *zawaya*, usually built along the trans-Saharan route, served as hotels for pilgrims and traders. Many of the sheikhs of these lodges even became 'great caravans themselves and gave every stimulus to the trade'.

The Sanusiyya and the Turkish administration

Indeed the Turkish administration appreciated the importance of the Sanusiyya, and recognized its supremacy. In 1856 the Ottoman sultan gave it a charter which exempted its properties from taxation and permitted it to collect a religious tithe from its followers. Another *firman* conferred on the Sanusiyya the right of sanctuary within the precincts of *zawaya*.

The local Turkish officials were content for the most part to sit in the towns, many of them regretting that they had ever been sent to Cyrenaica, where their salaries were low and often in arrears, and to let the Sanusiyya control the interior so long as taxes were paid and no overt act was committed against the Sultan's authority, which might bring them to the notice of Constantinople. And, for its own part, the Turkish government was quite prepared to forget that Cyrenaica formed part of the sultan's dominions so long as there was peace there and it sent annual tribute to Constantinople. The Turks were otherwise indifferent to what happened in Libya, which was a poor province. They had quite enough troubles and they saw no wisdom in alienating to no purpose a powerful sufi brother-hood and the warlike Beduin who supported it. They therefore let the Sanusiyya perform many of the functions of government in the interior, including education, justice and the maintenance of security. Whenever any question which required direct contact with the head of the Sanusiyya arose, it was established through the sheikh of the *zawiya* at Benghazi, or a special messenger was sent from Jaghbub or Kufra to the Turkish gov-ernor at Benghazi, or he sent a messenger to the head of the Sanusiyya in his oasis seat. From time to time the central administration in Turkey sent an envoy to the head of the Sanusiyya with gifts and instructions to report on what was going on in the Sahara.

It is important to note that although the Turks were not much loved by the Sanusi both shared a community of interest in Libya. As Muslims the Sanusi would rather ally with the Turks against the European infidels, than with the latter against Turkey, a lesson which Italy was to learn bitterly. Although the Grand Sanusi and his successors regarded the Turks as usurpers of the Caliphate yet since it had long been in Turkish hands, and since Turkey was the only independent Muslim power capable of protecting Muslim interests in the nineteenth century, the Sanusi felt that the Turks should be respected and the name of the Sultan proclaimed at Friday prayers.

It was certainly in the interest of both the Turks and the Sanusiyya that there should be order, security, justice and trade in the country, and they co-operated to maintain them. Likewise the more prosperous merchants who had dealings with the Beduin or sent caravans to the Sahara and Sudan found it advisable to be received into the Sanusiyya. It is for this reason that in all the towns a small body of the richer and more cultured citizens were affiliates.

The Sanusiyya used the Turks to buttress its position in its dealings with them, and combined with the tribes to resist any encroachments on its prerogatives by the Turkish government. It was in the interest of both the Sanusiyya and the tribes that the Turkish administration should not become too powerful. The Sanusiyya acquired from its central position between the other two parties a pre-eminence in the interior which led to the tribal system becoming even in Turkish times a proto-state with an embryonic government of its own. The tribes first began to see themselves as a nation through Sanusiyya relations with the Turkish administration. They became acutely aware of their separate identity as being all Sanusi *vis-à-vis* the Turkish administration.

The ideology of nationality and the feeling of oneness which the Sanusiyya infused into the inhabitants of Libya assumed a military complexion at the turn of the century when the French attacked the Sanusiyya and when the Italians occupied Libya in 1911. The brunt of the defence of the country against the invaders fell on the head of the brotherhood, Sayyid Ahmad ash-Sharif. When after long-drawn out negotiations with the Italian and British governments, he concluded, in 1920, the Treaty of ar-Rajma, he naturally became the head of a state, recognized by his people as their spokesman and ruler and by the two concerned European powers as such. Even when the Italians destroyed the *zawaya* they came to see that the only way by which their administration might appease the inhabitants was to rebuild some of them. The importance of the Sanusiyya until modern times is clear from the fact that at independence Libya initially became a monarchy under a descendant of the Grand Sanusi, Muhammad Idris, who took the title of King Idris I.

8 Southern and Central Africa at the beginning of the nineteenth century

The geographical features

Southern Africa is not marked off by any clear line of demarcation from the rest of the continent but is simply a continuation of the great African plateau. Around the edge of the plateau there runs a coastal strip separated from the interior highland by an escarpment which is particularly marked on the eastern coast of South Africa where it is known as the Drakensberg. The whole area lies well within the southern hemisphere and has its winter from June to August and its summer from November to February. The severity of the winter is naturally more marked in the extreme south. In South Africa frosts are normal and snow not unknown. Nearer the Zambezi it is much milder.

The whole area has a basic climatic pattern of dry winters, and summer rains brought from the Indian Ocean. In South Africa these rains fall first on the eastern coastal escarpment and then die away gradually leaving the most westerly part of the sub-continent extremely dry and arid. The is the area of the Kalahari desert. In the Cape territory itself the general pattern is disturbed by mountains known as the Cape series and a winter rainfall climate of the Mediterranean type is experienced. Behind the Cape mountains lies a very dry area of semi-desert known as the Karoo.

The Khoisan peoples

Southern Africa was the last area to be settled by the expanding Bantu-speaking peoples and to this day there are still pockets in which the earlier peoples survive. These were the San (known to the Dutch settlers as Bushmen) and the closely related Khoi (the Dutch settlers gave them the uncomplimentary name Hottentots). Both belong to a race with a tawny yellow skin colour and short stature. They both speak languages which

211

A San carrying his bow and arrow, Namibia

contain clicking sounds, unknown in any other human tongues except those of people who have borrowed them through contact. For these reasons, they are often referred to collectively as the Khoisan peoples. Their religious beliefs and practices are also very similar but in other respects the original culture of San and Khoi was very different.

The San were the earliest group and belonged to a people who at one time occupied a great part of the continent. They practised no agriculture and kept no cattle but lived entirely on the wild animals that the men killed with their poisoned arrows, on wild fruits, and on the wild roots and tubers that the women dug up with their digging sticks. They had no permanent houses but lived in temporary shelters made of branches, or in caves which they decorated with beautiful pictures of hunting scenes and animals. Their way of life made it impossible to provide food for a large number of people in a small area and they lived in fairly small groups

House-building in a Khoi settlement, a contemporary engraving

known as hunting bands. These might contain a hundred or more members, usually all related by blood or marriage. Their political organization was very simple, some bands accepted the leadership of a particular individual as chief, in others the adult men took what decisions were necessary after discussion. The San were very attached to their simple but free way of life and were not easily persuaded to abandon it, even for a much richer existence. They could and did enter into trading and other relationships with other peoples, however, and this sometimes led to their taking up new practices such as cattle-keeping. Each hunting band was jealous of its hunting territory. Though the group was always moving in search of animals each band had a definite area within which its members moved. They would resist to the death any intrusion on their hunting grounds.

At one time the San may have occupied most of East and Central Africa as well as Southern Africa but by the nineteenth century they had long lost most of their original homeland to other races. They remained numerous mainly in Namibia, the Kalahari and Angola, though small groups still remained in the northern parts of present Cape Province, southern Orange Free State and Transvaal, and the Lesotho mountains.

The Khoi differed from the San in their way of life. They were cattle-keepers, and their lives centred around their flocks and herds. They probably had their origin from a group of San who adopted the keeping of animals through contact with Bantu-speaking peoples. Like the San the Khoi were always on the move and lived in flimsy shelters which were sometimes carried on the backs of oxen. Though each group had its own home area they were less strongly attached to their territory than the San and were also more easily persuaded to change their habits for material rewards. The Khoi always supplemented the produce of their stock by hunting and gathering. If they lost their animals they could return to a pure hunting and gathering culture like that of the San. One group of Khoi lived very largerly on fish and shellfish. They were known to the Dutch as *strandloopers* (beach walkers) and have left traces of their existence in numerous middens of empty shells on the beaches of the Cape. The Khoi were organized in tribes, each made up of a number of related clans. The head of the senior clan was the tribal chief, but these chiefs had little power. Decisions were taken by consultation among all the clan heads and when there were disagreements tribes often split up. One or more of the clans would simply break away and in time grow into another large tribe. This type of split was often caused by tribes growing too big to keep their cattle together. The Khoi were less widespread than the San. They mainly occupied Namibia, the coastal areas around the Cape of Good Hope, and the eastern coastal strip as far north as modern Transkei. By the nineteenth century they had been driven from much of their original home, but they still occupied much of Namibia and groups of them were found around the Orange and lower Vaal rivers.

The Bantu-speaking peoples

At the beginning of the nineteenth century, as today, by far the largest proportion of the peoples of Southern and Central Africa belonged to the Bantu-speaking group (see Introduction). They had been established as far south as modern Zimbabwe as early as AD 200 and had probably begun to enter the area south of the Limpopo river as early as the fourth century. In South Africa, however, the process of settlement was still not complete as late as the nineteenth century. Bantu-speaking people had advanced furthest on the east coast. There by the eighteenth century they had reached the Fish river and begun to settle in the land between it and the Sundays river which is known as the Zuurveld. It was in this area that they first came into contact with the white settlers who were advancing from the Cape. In the central part of South Africa the Bantu-speaking groups were still north of the Orange river by the nineteenth century, and in Namibia they were still confined to the area north of modern Windhoek.

The Bantu-speaking peoples of South Africa, Zimbabwe and the southern parts of Mozambique were mixed-farmers who kept cattle but also cultivated the land. It is possible that their ancestors may have come from the far north where they would have been in contact with the cattle-keeping Nilotes. They fall into several different language groups. In South Africa one important group is the Nguni-speaking people who live along the eastern coastal strip from Zululand to the Zuurveld. This group has adopted more of the click sounds from the languages of the San and Khoi than any other Bantu-speaking people. The Sotho people occupied most of the central plateau of South Africa as far as the Kalahari desert. The languages of the many different peoples of this group have close similarities though those of the most westerly peoples are rather different; they are called Tswana. In spite of differences of language and culture, Nguni and Sotho peoples were often in contact with and influenced one another. Several Nguni-speaking groups migrated into the mainly Sotho-speaking areas of the Transvaal and Lesotho. In time some of these lost their original languages and came to speak Sotho dialects. West of the Kalahari, two Bantu-speaking groups lived in the northern areas of Namibia; the more southerly were the Herero, whose way of life was rather similar to the Khoi for they relied only on cattle; and further north were the Ambo, who lived by mixed farming.

215

In southern Mozambique the main population belongs to a group called Thonga, who are thought to be related to the Nguni-speaking group of South Africa although they do not use the click sounds. In Zimbabwe there were many different peoples belonging to the group who are now called Shona.

North of these peoples there lived another large group known as the central Bantu-speaking peoples. They are different from the southern peoples because, while all southern Bantu-speaking peoples trace descent from father to son and regard a child as belonging to his father's clan, those in central Africa trace descent through the mother and regard a child as belonging to his mother's people. In their social systems the person a man respects most is not his father but his mother's brother, and the person to whom he leaves his property is not his own but his sister's son. Many central Bantu-speaking peoples did not keep cattle but relied only on farming.

Social and political organization of the Bantu-speaking peoples

The Bantu-speaking peoples lived in larger groups than the San or Khoi and their chiefdoms might contain several thousand members. They moved much less frequently than either of the other peoples though they sometimes shifted their homes to find new land and grazing for their cattle. Their homes were much more substantial. Some were round huts of mud decorated with designs drawn in coloured clay and thatched with grass or leaves, their floors carefully smeared with cow dung to give a smooth surface without dust; some were beehive-shaped structures of woven grass. Usually the family possessed a few simple stools, some mats and cooking pots, and cloaks made of animal skins against the winter cold. Among cattle-keeping peoples the cattle enclosure was the centre of every settlement and grain was carefully stored to last until the next harvest. Though the material standard of living of the Bantu-speaking people was generally very simple their social organization was complex. They had a strong belief in law, and a respect for traditional ways, and they had complicated rules governing the conduct of individuals. Many of these were connected with their family systems which were very strong and linked large numbers of persons. They also believed that the spirits of their ancestors took a close interest in, and exerted an influence on, everyday life. This strengthened their devotion to their traditions and customs. The young men of the southern Bantu-speaking peoples had to go through prolonged and severe initiation ceremonies before they were admitted to manhood and allowed to marry. During the ceremonies the customs of the chiefdoms and the proper behaviour of a man were deeply imprinted on their minds.

Warfare between chiefdoms was frequent and was often caused by quarrels over farming land or the theft of cattle, but these wars did not usually result in great loss of life. They were governed by rules which were known to all and generally respected. The greatest cause of bitterness and loss of life among the Bantu-speaking people of Southern Africa was fear of witchcraft. Many diseases of which the cause was unknown were believed to be caused by the ill-will of witches and when someone, particularly an important person, fell mysteriously sick the witch-doctor would be consulted and the individual he named as responsible would be put to a cruel death. Among the central Bantu-speaking groups, persons accused of witchcraft or other crimes were given a poison called *mravi*; it was believed that if they were innocent they would vomit it but if they were guilty it would kill them. These practices led to much loss of life and gave opportunities for wicked people to take a terrible revenge on their enemies by having them accused of witchcraft. Generally speaking the Bantu-speaking peoples of Southern Africa were peaceful and law-abiding, with few material goods apart from cattle. They were dignified and courteous in accordance with their rules of etiquette and kind to strangers if they respected their customs.

Though there were considerable differences between different peoples, the southern chiefdoms were generally organized on similar basic principles. At the head of each chiefdom was a hereditary chief who was the supreme head of the community. Under him districts of the community's territory were ruled by subordinate chiefs who were often important members of the royal family. The chief was assisted by officials often called *indunas* and among these there was a senior *induna* who acted as deputy chief. Holders of these offices had a great deal of power and were therefore usually chosen from families with no claim to the throne. Although the chief was very powerful he did not rule as an autocrat. The subordinate chiefs were also important and might rebel or break away if the chief behaved in an unpopular way.

Chiefs were careful to discuss their plans with important members of the community before taking decisions. In day-to-day matters they had a small circle of close personal advisers, but before taking major decisions they would summon the subordinate chiefs to a large conference. Amongst the Sotho-speaking peoples public assemblies were also held in which anyone could make suggestions or criticize the chief. The government of subordinate chiefs was very similar to that of supreme chiefs, only on a small scale. They had their own *indunas* and councillors and they sat in judgment over cases which occurred in their own districts, but in these a right of appeal to the court of the supreme chief always existed.

One of the characteristics of the southern political system, especially in South Africa itself, was the tendency for chiefdoms to divide into two or more at frequent intervals. Such divisions usually arose from disputes over succession, but sometimes happened if a chief became unpopular or annoyed some of his subordinate chiefs. They would then break away with their own followers and set themselves up as independent rulers. This process was continually taking place as they moved into and settled new land.

Although the southern political organization seemed to encourage the splitting of chiefdoms it could also work in the opposite direction. If conditions enabled an ambitions chief to conquer a neighbouring community he could add them to his own following and build an enlarged state by simply making the defeated chief a new district sub-chief. In this way extensive empires could be built up without altering the basic system of government. This happened at a very early date in the area of modern Zimbabwe and southern Mozambique. An empire grew up there under rulers of the Kalanga group which extended its authority over some non-Kalanga peoples. In this area trade in gold with Arab and Swahili traders began at least as early as the thirteenth century. Under the stimulus of this trade a powerful chiefdom emerged at the site of the Zimbabwe ruins. By the late thirteenth century a beginning had been made in the construction of the massive stone buildings which have made this one of the most dramatically impressive sites in all Africa. The original chiefdom reached its greatest heights of wealth, artistic and architectural achievement by the beginning of the fifteenth century. By this time its cultural influence had spread over a wide area and many smaller stone buildings built on the Zimbabwe style were erected. By the mid-fifteenth century, however, the area was suffering from shortages of various essential commodities and one of its leaders, Mutota, led an expedition to the north. He established a new centre of power in the Dande area bordering the middle Zambezi. From there he conquered a large number of communities thus building the Mwene Mutapa empire. This, as we learn from Portuguese records, had many provinces and districts governed by chiefs some of whom enjoyed considerable autonomy. They even at times fought minor wars with one another though all recognized the supremacy of the Mwene Mutapa. The original site of the stone buildings was now reduced to a regional centre and fell into a long process of decline, although the stone-building tradition continued at other sites. The Portuguese managed to gain influence in the kingdom by taking part in succession disputes and the power of the kings crumbled away. In the seventeenth century the

Rozvi broke away from the empire. Under their chiefs, who were called Changamire, they began to conquer the Kalanga and drive out the Portuguese. Eventually they reconquered almost the whole of the empire and though the Portuguese were allowed to remain in their main trading posts and trade with the new rulers they lost their influence in the interior. The stone-building tradition was continued under the Rozvi right down to the final destruction of their empire in the nineteenth century.

Amongst the central Bantu-speaking peoples there were many different types of government. Many societies did not feel the need for government systems wider than the organization of the local village. This was the case with the Yao and Makua of northern Mozambique. The Tumbuka, Henga and Tonga of the northern shores of Lake Malawi were also organized in this small-scale way. Other groups built empires along somewhat similar principles to those of the southern Bantu, though each kingdom had its own peculiar and often highly complicated system of government. Amongst these larger states there was the Lozi kingdom of the western province of modern Zambia and the powerful state of the Bemba with its king, the Chitimukulu, which had its centre near Lake Bangweulu in modern Zambia. Both these kingdoms are believed to have been founded by immigrants from the area of Shaba in modern Zaire. In addition, during the eighteenth century Kazembe, a general of the Lunda king, Mwata Yamvo, in the Shaba area, penetrated to the Luapula valley and set up a powerful kingdom. In the same century an adventurous elephant hunter from modern Tanzania visited the Tumbuka people near the head of Lake Malawi and succeeded in uniting many villages into the Kamanga kingdom which was ruled by his successors with the title of Chikulamayembe. The great Maravi group of peoples who live in modern Malawi and the eastern parts of Zambia are believed like most of the central Bantu-speaking peoples to have had their origin in the area of modern Zaire. In the seventeenth century they built up a widespread empire ruled by a chief called Kalonga who had his capital near the Shire river in modern Malawi. This empire broke up within a century of being formed but a relative of the Kalonga named Undi broke away from his overlord and moved westward to establish his capital in modern Mozambique near the eastern border of modern Zambia. There he built up a second Malawi empire covering a very wide area. This empire still existed at the beginning of the nineteenth century but it was not very strongly organized.

The Portuguese in Mozambique

Portuguese influence in the area of Mozambique dates back to the fifteenth century and the opening of the sea route from Europe to India. The Portuguese captured the Swahili/Arab trading settlements on the east coast of Africa including Sofala in Mozambique. They established a base on Mozambique Island and a number of small settlements along the coast and at Sena and Tete on the Zambezi. From these posts they tapped the gold trade of the Shona empire of Mwene Mutapa and other powerful Shona kingdoms. An initial attempt to establish direct rule over the Mwene Mutapa empire was a complete failure. Thereafter the initiative in extending Portuguese influence passed into the hands of private traders. Some of these were Portuguese, others Portuguese citizens of Indian descent from Goa. These traders succeeded in persuading the Mwene Mutapa or other powerful rulers to put them in command of chiefdoms within their states. They ruled these chiefdoms through subordinate chiefs who were generally the traditional rulers of the area. The new overlords maintained their authority with the help of personal bodyguards of slave soldiers who were known as *chikunda*. They used the resources of the chiefdoms for their trading ventures and to support their bodyguards. They could also call on the fighting manpower of the whole population in times of war.

Though they obtained their chiefdoms from African rulers the traders wanted to keep up their Portuguese connections. They therefore formally offered their territories to the King of Portugal and received legal title to them from him. These estates were known in Portuguese as *prazos*. Each *prazo* was in fact a small kingdom with its own army. The *prazo* owners were thus able to use their forces to intervene in succession disputes in the Mwene Mutapa empire. The empire was gravely weakened and its control restricted to a small fractioon of its original extent. The *prazo* owners however weakened their position by over-exploiting their subjects and the gold resources of the area. They received a major setback in the seventeenth century with the rise of the kingdom of Changamire in western Zimbabwe which drove them off the Zimbabwean highveld for good. They still ruled substantial states in the neighbourhood of the lower Zambezi into the nineteenth century however. By this time as a result of intermarriage most of the *prazo* owners were of predominantly African descent. They had some African names, ruled as African chiefs and practised traditional religious rites. On the other hand they were also proud of their Portuguese connection, had some Portuguese names and liked to hold Portuguese titles. They also often practised Christian religious worship.

An early painting showing the landing of Jan Van Riebeeck and the first Dutch settlers at the Cape of Good Hope, 1652

White settlement at the Cape

In 1652 a European settlement was established by the Dutch East India Company at the Cape of Good Hope. The colony was very small at first and was intended merely as a refreshment station for the Company's ships on their way to India. To begin with it consisted only of the Company's servants, but it was soon decided to allow a few of these to settle as free citizens with farms of their own. They would then have the incentive of personal profit to farm diligently and efficiently. The first of these settlers, nine in number, were established on small farms in 1657. Gradually their numbers increased and then under the governorship of Simon van der Stel (1679–1700) a deliberate policy of increasing the population was undertaken to strengthen it against possible attacks by France. More Dutchmen came and a party of French Huguenots, Protestant refugees from religious persecution in France, was also settled in the colony. They were equal to about one-third of the European population and many modern white South African families are their descendants. The French refugees intro-

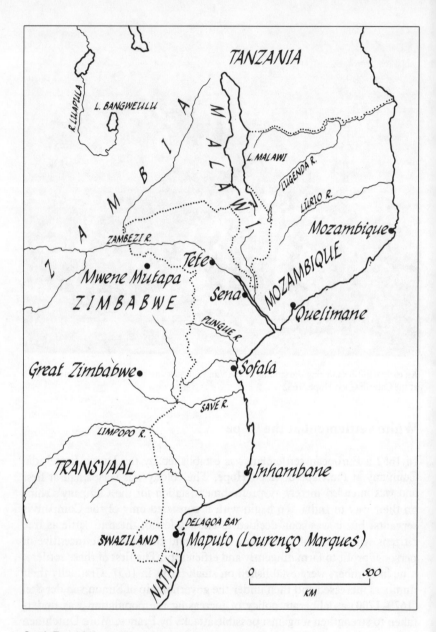

South-East Africa showing modern international boundaries

duced efficient farming techniques but they lost their language and were absorbed into the predominantly Dutch population.

In the healthy climate this little community continued to grow rapidly in numbers and soon began to spread over a vast territory. The majority of the whites were farmers and this meant that as their population increased they would need more land. At first they concentrated on growing vegetables, wheat and wine on fairly small areas and the colony expanded slowly. The costs of production were high, the land was not as fertile as that in Europe and suffered from uncertain weather conditions, and the market for agricultural produce at the Cape was very small. Farmers depended on selling to the Company itself and to passing ships. Attempts to find export markets for Cape produce failed to come up to expectations and matters were made worse by the corrupt practices of Company officials. The notorious Willem Adriaan van der Stel, in particular, used the Company's servants to help him operate a private farm which gave himself and his friends almost a monopoly in supplying provisions to the Company.

In these circumstances only the rich could farm successfully and poorer men found themselves falling ever deeper into debt. Thus while some became rich and comfortable and built substantial houses beautifully decorated with gables in the Dutch style, others were forced to look for another means of livelihood. In comparison with growing wheat and wine at the Cape the life of a cattle trader or cattle rancher in the interior offered fairly easy profits with little initial expense. There was always a market for meat and animal skins. Cattle could be led to market and did not need expensive transport. Unlike perishable agricultural produce they could be kept for another occasion when prices were not high enough. What is more young men in the interior could lead a very inexpensive life with none of the costs of city existence. They could feed themselves and their families to a considerable extent by shooting wild animals, and they could hope to persuade or force Khoi to work for them as herdsmen for very low wages. The life was hard and without much material comfort but it provided a great sense of freedom. The Dutch settlers came to regard it as the happy life.

In spite of all prohibitions to the contrary, settlers began to drift away from the Cape, first trading with the Khoi for cattle, later taking up farming themselves and often forcing the Khoi to abandon their lands. Cattle-keeping required very large areas of land in the dry and often drought-stricken South African conditions; to be successful a cattle farmer in the interior needed at least 10 square kilometres. Once considerable numbers of settlers took to cattle-farming, therefore, the colony was bound to expand at tremendous speed and in spite of its very small white population and large area there was always a shortage of land. The Dutch East India Company disapproved of this expansion, but it needed the meat provided by the cattle farmers, and it lacked the resources and was too inefficient and corrupt to prevent or control it. The main stream of expansion flowed up the east coast where the rains were heavier, and there in the eighteenth century settlers began to enter the area called the Zuurveld, near the Fish river, which the Bantu-speaking people belonging to the Nguni-speaking group were also just beginning to settle.

When the colony was first founded there was no intention on the part of the Company to encourage racial discrimination. To show approval for inter-racial mixture the surgeon of the original tiny settlement was given promotion and a wedding feast in the commander's house when he married a Khoi girl called Eva. Simon van der Stel, the greatest of the early governors, was the son of an Indian woman. The situation began to change after 1716 when the Company decided to allow the free importation of slaves. Blacks were brought from West Africa, Delagoa Bay and Madagascar, and a few Malays came from Indonesia to form the origin of the present Cape Malay community. As manual work became the monopoly of slaves or Khoi, the whites began to develop the attitude that they were naturally superior and entitled to rule over the inferior people.

This attitude was fostered still more on the cattle farms of the interior where the whites felt themselves extremely isolated, surrounded by large numbers of slaves and Khoi servants who might easily turn against them. They believed the only way to protect themselves was to support one another at all times against the non-European peoples and keep them very firmly down. Thus the attitude of white superiority and non-white inferiority was strengthened by fear and established a deep hold on the minds of the settlers. The Calvinist form of religion which the Dutch settlers brought with them supported these attitudes for it taught that all men were divided from birth into the chosen and the damned. Thus although the officials of the Church did not accept it, the ordinary farmer came to believe that the whites were the chosen race and non-whites the condemned heathens, and that the distinction between the races was in accordance with the will of God.

Reaction of the Khoisan peoples to the expansion of the Cape Colony

As the colony expanded it took away the land of the indigenous San and Khoi. Within a few years of the beginning of the colony a war broke out between the Dutch East India Company and a Khoi group which complained that its lands were being taken away. The war lasted from 1658–60 and the Company emerged victorious. After that Khoi numbers were severely reduced by smallpox epidemics. Their political system and culture were undermined by contact with white traders who tempted them to sell their cattle for strong drink, tobacco and other European goods. As they lost their cattle many gave up their land with little resistance and either entered the service of the whites as herdsmen or drifted further into the interior. Others, however, forced by the loss of their cattle to revert to living by hunting and gathering like the San, continued to offer a bitter resistance. The settlers called these groups Bushmen–Hottentots and subsequent historians have tended to confuse them with the San who resisted white encroachment with fierce determination, launching lightning raids on stock and killing herdsmen with their poisoned arrows.

Origin of the Commando system

In response to Khoi and San resistance the settlers developed the Commando system. Local officials known as *veld kornets* were given authority in case of need to call upon the white farmers in their area to come forward, each with his horse and gun, and sometimes armed Khoi servants as well, to form a small mounted force which could take immediate action in response to small-scale raids or cattle rustling. In cases where larger forces were needed the farmers of two or more neighbouring areas would combine under the leadership of a commandant. Where really substantial campaigns were planned the forces of an entire magisterial district or of two such districts could be summoned to form a 'grand Commando'. The Commando system developed in the struggle against San and Khoi was later to be used in conflicts with Bantu-speaking groups. Though it was sponsored by the Dutch East India Company, the government at the Cape, the system once developed could easily be used by private individuals to conduct campaigns without official support. It could even be used by the settlers against the government itself.

Khoisan resistance and the conciliation policy

Though the commandos waged a war of extermination against San and Khoi raiding bands, hunting them down like wild animals, they did not succeed in destroying them. Indeed, their resistance was so fierce that farmers became increasingly reluctant to turn out for such dangerous service offering so little loot. Several districts became so unsafe that they were temporarily abandoned. The farmers turned to buying peace with gifts of sheep and cattle to save the San and Khoi bands from the hunger which led them to fight. In response many San and Khoi raiders settled and in time became absorbed as herdsmen on the white farms. Then, as the settler population increased further, resistance became impossible.

Migration of the Korana

Among the Khoi groups who remained beyond the colonial frontier one of the most important was the Korana (or Kora). They lived around the junction of the Orange and Vaal rivers. In the course of the eighteenth century they expanded northwards along the course of the Vaal and Harts rivers. There they came into conflict with the southernmost of the Tswana. There they were joined by a German deserter from the Company's service, called Jan Bloem. He married several Khoi women and became the head of a Korana clan. With the help of the guns he brought from the Cape he led his people in many raids on the Tswana, robbing them of their cattle which he sold to the Cape. He died in 1790 after a raid on one of the most powerful Tswana chiefdoms and was succeeded by one of his sons, Jan Bloem II, who became an even more daring bandit than his father.

Origin of the Cape Coloured and Griqua peoples

Khoi and San who became servants on white farms were thrown together with slaves and persons of part European descent. In time they lost their original languages and culture. The distinctions between the different groups gradually disappeared and they evolved into the Cape Coloured people. In place of their original cultures they adopted that of their white masters and came to speak a simplified form of the Dutch language which was also coming to be used by the children of white farmers. In this way the Afrikans language was born. In time it became the spoken language of the great majority of the white population as well as of the Cape Coloured community.

In the early days of the colony persons of mixed Khoi–white or slave–white descent had little difficulty in becoming landowners and being accepted in white society. Some Khoi and San who became trusted servants and were employed as farm managers also gained social acceptance and became independent farmers. As colour feeling increased, however, people of this sort who were generally known as Basters or Orlams, found themselves rejected from white society and their rights to land ownership called in doubt. They tended to migrate to the frontier areas where things were less settled and then to move out of the colony altogether. A number of such groups settled along the Orange river where they were associated with Korana and other Khoi groups and some San as well. One such composite group congregated near the confluence of the Orange and Vaal rivers under the leadership of Cornelius Kok and Barend-Barends. Under missionary influence they adopted the name Griqua, drew up a constitution and made laws. In time conflict developed between the missionaries and members of the Kok family. In their place the missionaries persuaded the people to choose a young catechist of San descent named Waterboer. He and his descendants long ruled the first Griqua settlement around Griquatown just to the west of the confluence of the Vaal and Orange rivers. Some members of the Kok family, however, rejected the new leader and broke away to establish two new Griqua communities. One under Cornelius Kok II was established north of Waterboer's community around the village of Campbell. It ceased to exist as an independent community on the death of its founder. The second was established by Adam Kok around Philippolis on the Orange river east of the confluence. It persisted as a separate political community under descendants of its founder until 1861, when they trekked to a new settlement in Griqualand East on the border of Lesotho.

Origin of the Orlam communities in Namibia

Further down the Orange river than the Griqua settlement another group of Khoi and Basters gathered on an island in the river under the leadership of a daring brigand, Jager Afrikaner. Her terrorized alike white farmers within the colony and Tswana beyond the frontier. He beat off all attempts to arrest him until he was finally converted to Christianity by the missionary Robert Moffat. He then visited the Governor in Cape Town, was granted a pardon, and soon afterwards died peacefully. His son Jonker Afrikaner led his people to Namibia and established something of a hegemony over the different Khoi communities there, leading them in conflicts with the Herero. This was the beginning of a long chain of disturbances which in the late nineteenth century were to provide part of the pretext for German annexation of the area. A number of other groups of Khoi and mixed Khoi/white descent migrated independently to Namibia. Like Afrikaner's people they were generally called Orlams.

One such group which has kept the name Baster settled around a village they called by the biblical name Rehoboth. They form a distinct political community in Namibia to this day.

White settlers and Bantu-speaking peoples encounter one another

During the eighteenth century white settlers began to enter the Zuurveld and settle alongside the indigenous Africans who were also just settling the area. The latter belonged to branches of the Xhosa, the southernmost of the Nguni-speaking peoples. This situation did not please the Dutch East India Company which feared rightly enough that contact between settlers and indigenous Africans would lead to trouble. In 1778 Governor van Plettenberg made a tour of the frontier and decided that the two races should be kept apart. After discussion with some chiefs on the Fish river he fixed that landmark as the frontier without realizing that these chiefs had no authority over the people on the Zuurveld and certainly no right to give their land away. Settlers and Xhosa continued to live side by side and soon began quarrelling over land and cattle and in 1779 war broke out between them. This was the first Xhosa resistance war. The Xhosa were temporarily driven from the Zuurveld but soon returned and the tension continued.

In 1786 a magistracy for the eastern districts of the colony was established at Graaf Reinet. After the first magistrate had proved incompetent he was succeeded by H.C.D. Maynier, a sincere and devoted man who tried to bring law and order and a sense of justice to the frontier. He insisted that farmers must not ill-treat their Khoi servants and allowed runaway servants with tales of cruelty to find refuge at his court house. He also tried to regulate the behaviour of settlers towards the Xhosa. When in spite of his efforts war (the second Xhosa resistance war) broke out in 1793 he made terms which permitted the Xhosa to remain on the Zuurveld on condition of good behaviour, and refused to allow farmers to undertake private expeditions against the Xhosa on the pretext of reclaiming stolen cattle. He maintained that the number of cattle reported stolen by Xhosa was grossly exaggerated and that the conduct of the settlers was also responsible for the troubles on the Zuurveld. This made him intensely unpopular with the farmers who accused him of preferring the heathens to Christians. Early in 1795 they rose in rebellion, expelled Maynier and proclaimed an independent Republic of Graaf Reinet. The farmers of the neighbouring district of Swellendam followed their example and also proclaimed a republic.

The Company had not been able to deal with this rebellion when towards the end of 1795 the Cape was seized by the British and the rule of the Dutch East India Company in South Africa was brought to an end.

9 The great nineteenth-century migrations

The first half of the nineteenth century in Southern Africa is dominated by two great upheavals. The first took place amongst the Bantu-speaking peoples. It started in Zululand and gave rise to a chain of movements which affected areas as far afield as the northern part of what is now Tanzania. It is often called the Mfecane, an Nguni word used for the wars and disturbances which accompanied the rise of the Zulu. The second was a sudden movement of expansion of the white settlers at the Cape, known as the Great Trek. It was far less extensive in scale than the Mfecane but is of fundamental importance for the history of Southern Africa. As the Mfecane was the earlier of the two movements and the course of the Great Trek was considerably influenced by it, we shall look first at developments in indigenous African society and later turn back to take up the thread of the development of the Cape Colony which forms the background to the Greak Trek.

Origins of the Mfecane

Zululand and Natal are part of the eastern and coastal corridor which runs between the Drakensberg mountains and the sea. They are favoured by relatively abundant rains and were well suited to support a fairly dense population. We know from the reports of shipwrecked Portuguese in the sixteenth century that the area was already heavily settled by indigenous African peoples at that time. In South Africa moreover the healthy climate and the absence of diseases like malaria encouraged a rapid growth of population, and if we examine the history of South African communities and see how frequently they split into two or more it is obvious that the population was increasing rapidly. The coastal corridor was a narrow area fenced in by the mountains and indigenous Africans were settled along it as far south as the Fish river. If the Zululand communities continued to grow, therefore, they were bound to come into conflict with one another over farming and grazing lands. Involvement in a growing trade in ivory at Delagoa Bay may also have led to conflict between chiefdoms and encouraged the building of expanded political systems. Chiefs were usually able to take a substantial share of the proceeds of such trade and this gave them an incentive to expand the area and the numbers of people under their control and so increase their wealth. During the eighteenth century the Pedi living near the Leoulu mountains in the Eastern Transvaal and on a trade route from Delagoa Bay conquered a number of neighbouring communities and built a substantial kingdom. In the Tswana area the Ngwaketse likewise brought a number of chiefdoms together in an enlarged state. Among the southern Sotho, Motlume temporarily united several chiefdoms under his leadership but they broke up again when he died. Nowhere did the movement acquire such massive proportions as in the Zululand area, however.

This situation of overcrowding and conflict seems to have developed during the course of the eighteenth century. Wars became more frequent and more severe and as they did so great leaders emerged who began to build up enlarged kingdoms. At the same time there was a need for more efficient military organization.

About the middle of the eighteenth century three great figures appeared. One of these was Sobhuza, the chief of a community then known as Ngwane (but now called the Swazi after Sobhuza's successor Mswati). He had his original home near the Upper Pongola river. The second was Zwide, chief of a very powerful chiefdom known as the Ndwandwe in central Zululand. The third was Dingiswayo, chief of the Mthethwa, the most powerful and best known of them all.

Four Zulus in traditional costume (but without weapons) at a modern cattle sale

All these chiefs built up empires and in doing so they developed a new method of military organization. The traditional initiation ceremonies had always created a sense of fellow-feeling amongst young men of similar age who went through them together. The new development in Zululand, which is often said to have been introduced by Dingiswayo, was to abolish the traditional ceremonies altogether and in their place to form the young men of an age suitable for initiation into a regiment of the army. This had great advantages over the older system, in which local chiefs commanded their own local contingents, because it gave the army more unity. It also provided a means of strengthening enlarged states. The young men of conquered communities were put into regiments according to their ages, together with boys from other sections of the empire, so that by fighting together they would develop feelings of comradeship and loyalty to the wider unit instead of just to their home group. During Dingiswayo's time, however, the regiments assembled only in times of war, and warfare remained relatively mild.

As the powerful leaders built up their armies they inevitably clashed with one another. First Zwide clashed with Sobhuza and the latter was driven out with his people to settle in the central area of modern Swaziland. There his people found a large number of small chiefdoms of the Sotho-speaking group. These were conquered one after another and incorporated into what is now the Swazi kingdom.

The rise of Shaka's Zulu kingdom

After Sobhuza had withdrawn from the scene, Dingiswayo and Zwide clashed with one another. Dingiswayo was victorious on several occasions, but at last Zwide succeeded in trapping him. He walked into an Ndwandwe ambush and was taken prisoner in Zwide's home, where he was put to death. Startled by the loss of their leader the Mthethwa army fled and the chiefs who had been conquered by Dingiswayo took the opportunity to declare their independence. Zwide seemed to have emerged supreme, but by this time another leader had appeared on the scene.

His name was Shaka and he was a son of the chief of a small community known as the Zulu. His mother had made herself unpopular at his father's home and been driven away, and Shaka had a very unhappy childhood, teased and bullied by his playmates. He grew up with a fierce determination to gain and exercise power, a reckless bravery and a callous indifference to human suffering. He began his career as a warrior in Dingiswayo's army and won the notice of the great chief by his feats of bravery. When his father died Shaka persuaded Dingiswayo to lend him the military

Shaka

support needed to seize the Zulu throne from one of his brothers who was the rightful heir.

Once established as chief of the Zulu he began to train his followers in accordance with his own military idea. He saw that the traditional weapons, which consisted of shields and throwing spears, were not suitable for close-formation fighting. A warrior who had thrown his spear was bound to fall back. If the warriors kept hold of their spears they could advance in an ordered line, protected by their shields, right up to the enemy and then finish them off. He therefore made his men discard the old weapon and use a short-handled stabbing spear and forbade them on pain of death to leave it on the battlefield. They were carefully drilled to fight in a formation known as the 'cow's horns'. The great mass of warriors would be drawn up in a body several men deep while two regiments, one on each side, advanced in a thin curving line around the enemy. When the two horns met and the enemy was surrounded the main mass would advance to complete the massacre. Such ordered manoeuvres needed considerable training and Shaka introduced a new idea in keeping his age-regiments on permanent duty for many years. They were housed in special military towns each of which was an official homestead of the chief. When not at war they were engaged in practising manoeuvres or ceremonial dances.

When Dingiswayo marched to fight Zwide, Shaka was summoned to go to the aid of his overlord. Whether he deliberately betrayed him, as some believe, or merely arrived too late for the battle, as others maintain, he certainly took no part in the fighting. He withdrew from the scene of the Mthethwa defeat and began at once to build up his own forces by conquering surrounding chiefdoms and putting their young men into his regiments. He even conquered the Mthethwa themselves, killed their new chief and appointed a nominee of his own. As soon as Zwide became aware that Shaka was rebuilding the empire of Dingiswayo for himself he sent an Ndwandwe force to attack the Zulu chief. The superior discipline of the Zulu gave them the victory and the Ndwandwe retired with heavy losses. Zwide then sent his full force in an all-out invasion of Shaka's domain. The Zulu wore them out by constantly retreating, driving away the cattle and destroying the crops as they went. Then as the Ndwande turned homewards tired and hungry, Shaka's troops caught them on the banks of the Mhlatuse river and defeated them in a decisive battle. This was probably in the year 1818.

The victory over the Ndwandwe left Shaka supreme in Zululand. Every year his regiments went out conquering chiefdoms and capturing cattle. They passed right through Natal, forcing almost the entire population to flee to the south, and reached as far as Pondoland. As chiefdoms were conquered Shaka brought them into his expanding kingdom. The conquered communities kept their own chiefs, though sometimes the existing head was killed and Shaka appointed another member of the royal family. These chiefs continued to administer their own people but had less power as all the young men of fighting age were taken into the age-regiments.

The ever-growing army was accommodated at a series of military towns, each under the authority of a military commander. These and the commanders of individual regiments were usually chosen from commoner families and were closely dependent on the king. Each regiment had its own name and its own distinctive equipment. Some had shields of a distinctive colour, others special kinds of head-dress. There was keen rivalry between the regiments for honour in war and the favour of the monarch. The arms and equipment were supplied to the warriors by Shaka and each regiment had a section of the royal herds attached to it. As far as possible these herds were made up of cattle with skins of the same colour as the regiments' shields. Each military settlement was also a royal homestead and contained a section of Shaka's family under the authority of a senior female member who had equal powers with those of the military commander. A large proportion of the marriageable girls in the country were brought to the military towns and formed into regiments corresponding to those of the men. They took part in ceremonial dances and agricultural work. Shaka regarded them as his wards and when a regiment had served long enough to be retired from active service he would dissolve a female regiment at the same time and give the girls as wives to the warriors. Shake himself never officially married and was terrified of having a son who might one day take over his power. Thus the whole way in which his kingdom was organized was designed to increase its military strength and to create among the peoples conquered by his armies a feeling of unity and complete loyalty to Shaka himself.

In 1824 a small party of English traders landed at Port Natal (the site of present Durban) and made their way to see the Zulu king. Shaka received them well. He was delighted with the goods they brought and impressed by the medical skill of one of them, Francis Farewell, who treated him successfully for a stab wound inflicted by a would-be assassin. He was also quick to realize the potential military value of firearms and anxious to remain on good terms with the government of the Cape, which he believed to be very powerful. He allowed the traders to settle in Natal and gather together the pitiful remnants of the Natal population around them. In return the traders fought with their guns in some of his expeditions. The settlement was particularly important because it was through its existence that information about the almost deserted state of Natal and the rich farming land there spread to the settlers at the Cape.

The way that Shaka's state was organized concentrated all power in his hands. The district chiefs who, in the traditional system, could check the actions of a ruler, lost their power when their fighting men were all in the central army. The only persons who could threaten Shaka's power were the army commanders, and they were commoners raised up by Shaka himself. Thus he did not need to consult the traditional type of council but exercised an autocratic authority. As his reign progressed, however he became increasingly despotic until even the loyalty of his devoted soldiers was undermined. The climax came after the death of his mother which upset him deeply. He forced his people to undergo severe deprivations as a sign of mourning. Then at the end of a year's mourning period he sent his army out on a great expedition. They travelled to the south as far as Pondoland and ravaged the Pondo but Shaka was warned by one of the traders that he might come into conflict with the colonial forces. Thereupon he wheeled his army round and sent them off immediately to the extreme north of his territory in southern Mozambique. He himself remained behind at one of his military towns and two of his brothers took advantage of the absence of most of the fighting men to plot his downfall. Together with his most trusted *induna*, Mbopa they stabbed him to death.

The assassins quietened the people by assuring them that they had killed the king to put an end to the never-ceasing wars and the hardships that Shaka had imposed on them.

Dingane, one of the assassins, and a brother of Shaka, succeeded him on the Zulu throne. He was by nature a rather lazy and peace loving man and he tried at first to relax the discipline of the Shaka period, but a revolt led by one of Shaka's generals convinced him of the need to keep the army occupied and he sent his regiments out on a number of expeditions.

The Ngoni diaspora

The sudden rise of the Zulu kingdom led to many peoples being driven from their original homes. Once they had left their crops and their cattle they could only hope to live by plunder and so they tended to move over long distances attacking other peoples as they went and setting them in motion also. After the bloody battle on the Mhlatuse river in 1818, two sections of the defeated Ndwandwe army abandoned their homes and fled northwards into southern Mozambique. They were the Shangane led by Soshangane, and the Ngoni led by Zwangendaba. Both these groups had experienced the value of Zulu fighting tactics at first hand and employed them in conquering other peoples. After a time the leaders clashed with one another. Soshangane was victorious. He remained in Mozambique and brought almost all the peoples of the vast area between the Limpopo and the Zambezi under his control in a Zulu-type kingdom. He forced the Portuguese of Senna and Tete to pay him annual tribute and his forces destroyed some of the other Portuguese forts where the commanders were foolish enough to oppose them.

Zwangendaba travelled westward through the Mwene Mutapa empire wreaking havoc as he went. His warriors hunted down and killed the last Rozvi ruler and brought the ancient kingdom to an end. When he reached the vicinity of modern Bulawayo, he turned northwards, and on 19 November 1835, a day marked by an eclipse of the sun, his regiments crossed the Zambezi. They moved northward by a series of long stages till they reached a place called Ufipa near the southern end of Lake Tanganyika, where Zwangendaba died about 1848. Then his army, swollen with captives from many communities, broke up into a number of sections.

One group, known as the Tuta, cut a path northward into the country of the Nyamwezi people of northern Tanzania. They established their headquarters to the north of modern Tabora and from there they raided as far as the shores of Lake Victoria.

Another section known as the Gwangara travelled east and south as far

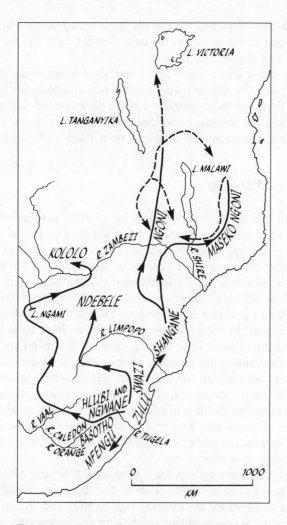

The main movements of people during the Mfecane

as the present Songea region of Tanzania. There they encountered another invading group, the Maseko Ngoni, who had come up from Mozambique by a more easterly route than Zwangendaba's main party. The two groups co-operated at first but then fell to blows. The Maseko were driven south again and finally established themselves in the highlands of the Kirk range near the southern end of Lake Malawi. The Gwangara split into two kingdoms and devastated a vast area. But they found their match in the warlike Hehe people. Several bitter battles were fought and then the two sides agreed to make peace until their children had grown old enough to resume the struggle.

The rest of the Ngoni army split into two main sections, one of which, under Mpezeni, fought many battles with the Bemba and then finally settled near Chipata in modern Zambia. The other under Mbelwa invaded the country of the Kamanga, overthrew the kingdom and forced the Kamanga and neighbouring Tumbuka, Henga and Tonga to enter their age-regiments. All these Ngoni groups absorbed captives into their fighting forces to such an extent that the different groups came in time to speak different languages, although they all remembered their common history and kept the main outlines of the Zulu-type political system they had brought from the south. The Ngoni invasions caused untold suffering and destruction, but they also brought into existence a whole series of powerful states which included persons of many different origins. They encouraged local leaders to arise in self defence and build kingdoms. Undoubtedly they were one of the most important historical developments in East Africa in the nineteenth century before the advent of colonialism.

Other migrations: the Sotho, Mfengu, Kololo and Ndebele

While the Shangane and the Ngoni were carrying Zulu fighting methods to the north, two other chiefdoms, the Hlubi and the Ngwane (a different people from the followers of Sobhuza who later became the Swazi), fled across the Drakensberg on to the central plateau between the Orange and Vaal rivers. They spread destruction amongst the Sotho-speaking peoples of the area and also fought bitterly with one another until the Ngwane finally succeeded in destroying their rivals. The Ngwane recrossed the Drakensberg in 1828 and entered the area near the colonial frontier occupied by the Thembu. They were encountered by the British force which had been sent to protect the peoples of the area against an expected Zulu invasion. The Ngwane were attacked by mistake and the chiefdom broke up. Many remained in the area as homeless refugees called Mfengu. The invasion of the Hlubi and Ngwane drove a powerful Sotho-speaking community to take to a life of plunder. These were the Tlokwa under a warrior queen called Mantatisi and her son Sikonyela. They travelled round much of modern Orange Free State creating havoc until they finally settled on a fortified mountain top in the north of modern Lesotho.

The period of warfare and destruction which suddenly descended on the peaceful Sotho peoples between the Orange and the Vaal rivers had two further important consequences. One group, known originally as the

Fokeng and later as the Kololo, fled across the Vaal and made its way towards modern Kuruman where there was a station of the London Missionary Society. The missionary, Robert Moffat, rode to Griquatown and called on the Griquas for aid and the invaders were defeated. The Kololo moved northwards, spreading destruction amongst the Tswana, until they reached and crossed the Zambezi. They then moved up the river and invaded the Lozi kingdom in Zambia. The kingdom was overthrown and a Kololo empire established which lasted till it was overthrown in turn by a national uprising which re-established the Lozi kings. By this time the Kololo language had gained so firm a hold that it remains the language used by most of the Lozi.

The Kololo kingdom was visited by the missionary explorer David Livingstone who took Kololo porters with him on his journeys of exploration. Some of these remained behind on the banks of the Shire river, which flows from Lake Malawi to the Zambezi. The people of the area were in a pitiful position at the time as a result of Ngoni raids and the activities of slave hunters. The Kololo, with the guns given them by Livingstone and their knowledge of large-scale political organizations, were able to rally the people for their own defence and build up Kololo kingdoms hundreds of kilometres away from the rest of their community.

The second important consequence of the Hlubi and Ngwane invasions was the creation of the Lesotho kingdom by Moshoeshoe. He was the son of an unimportant member of the royal family of a small Sotho chiefdom, but early in life he showed evidence of great foresight and powers of statesmanship. He saw that in difficult times a strong defensive position was of the utmost important and established himself with a few followers on a mountain called Butha Buthe in northern Lesotho. There he beat off a series of attacks from more powerful enemies and increased his following. After experiencing a prolonged siege by the Tlokwa, however, he decided that the mountain was not large enough for his people and moved to the almost impregnable hill of Thaba Bosiu in central Lesotho. There he was able to beat off every attack and gradually gathered the remnants of many Sotho communities around him to form the Basotho people. In 1833 he invited missionaries of the Paris Evangelical Society to come to his kingdom. They proved very helpful in the long struggles with the Boers of the Orange Free State. Unlike many leaders of his time, Moshoeshoe was essentially a man of peace, who preferred to attain his objectives by diplomacy. He was one of the most remarkable statesmen in Southern African history and the independent state of Lesotho is his memorial.

One of the chiefdoms incorporated in the Zulu kingdom was the Kumalo with its energetic young chief Mzilikazi. Contrary to his usual custom Shaka made the young chief a regimental commander, but in 1821 he rebelled and fled with his warriors into the Transvaal. Mzilikazi and his men, who came to be known as the Ndebele, devastated much land in the Transvaal and built up a powerful kingdom there on Zulu lines. In 1837 after being twice attacked, first by the regiments of Dingane and later by the Boers, Mzilikazi fled and ultimately settled in the Matabeleland area of modern Zimbabwe.

As a result of Shaka's campaigns in Natal many refugees poured out of the area and together with the remnants of the Ngwane took refuge with the coastal communities near the colonial frontier. They were known collectively as Mfengu (the colonists called them Fingos).

Developments on the Cape frontier: farmers, servants, missionaries and administrators

Returning to the history of the Cape Colony, we have seen how the settlers had spread, depriving the indigenous inhabitants of their land and employing them as herdsmen on the white farms. At the same time the white settlers had developed strong attitudes towards colour and regarded all non-Europeans as intrinsically inferior and not entitled to the same legal rights as whites. This had created a problem of internal tension in the community between white masters and non-white servants but the problems were to become much more serious when the colonists came in contact with the Bantu-speaking peoples. The San and some of the Khoi had fought fiercely against the white occupation of their lands. Their numbers were too small, however, for their resistance to be effective for very long. When they became reduced to serving as herdsmen on white farms they soon lost their identity and adopted the language and culture of their masters. The Bantu-speaking peoples on the other hand were far more numerous than any other group. They had strong political systems and they were very strongly attached to their culture. They were certainly not prepared to surrender their lands without a fight. So long, however, as the white population of the Colony continued to increase, and farming remained the main occupation of the settlers, young Boers would continue to need new farming land and labour to work on it. The result could only be the addition of severe border conflict to the already existing tensions of the Colony. In this situation any attempt by the central government to ensure fair treatment for non-whites, or to control the expansion of the farmers, would arouse the resentment of the frontier settlers.

This had already happened by 1795, when the attempts of Maynier in the name of the Colony's government to control the farmers' treatment of their Khoi servants had led to rebellion and the declaration of the Republic of Graaf Reinet and Swellendam. The British occupation of the Colony at the end of 1795 did nothing to alter the basic situation. The British Governor forced the republicans to surrender by threatening to cut off their powder supplies. Soon afterwards, however, another rebellion broke out and this time the government sent troops to suppress it.

These troops contained a body of Khoi soldiers and when Khoi servants saw them coming with the British they assumed that a war with their Boer masters was to be fought. They deserted in large numbers, often stealing their masters' guns, and flocked to the British camp. When the commander tried to disarm them, they fled and formed armed bands which began attacking and pillaging the farms of their former masters. In the general confusion the Bantu gained the impression that they were to be attacked and they too joined in. By the end of the first British occupation in 1803 the eastern frontier districts had been severely ravaged and many farmers reduced to destitution.

The British administration marked the beginning of a new influence with the coming of overseas missionaries to South Africa. The pioneer was Dr van der Kemp of the London Missionary Society who arrived in 1802. He took up work amongst the Khoi and began to champion their cause. He argued that the chief cause of tension was the fact that Khoi had no land and were forced to take service with white masters no matter what the conditions. He asked for land to be set aside for Khoi mission stations where they could support themselves and learn skills which would enable them to command higher wages. This idea was supported by the government but before it could be fully carried out the Colony was handed over to the authorities of the Dutch Republic.

The three years of Dutch rule (1803–6) were relatively uneventful. All parties in the frontier area were worn out and anxious for peace. The government continued the policy started by the British of allowing missionaries to establish Khoi settlements, and kept an eye on conditions of service to which Khoi were subjected. In these improved circumstances many Khoi returned to work on white farms, while others settled at the mission stations. Bantu and Boer remained on the Zuurveld and no wars broke out for a time. In 1806 the British recaptured the Cape and this time they kept it.

Under the second British administration the government of the Cape was at first strongly conservative. It tended to favour the farmers rather than their servants. Nevertheless the Evangelical movement was gaining force in Britain and missionaries came out to South Africa in ever-increasing numbers. They began to extend their work even beyond the frontiers of the Colony, and they became increasingly powerful advocates of Khoi rights. In 1809 the Governor issued regulations defining the position of the Khoi. These regulations largely confirmed existing customs and were distinctly favourable to the settlers. Every Khoi was to have a fixed address, which meant an address on a white farm, or he would be liable to imprisonment for vagrancy. If he wished to leave an employer to look for another he must establish a fixed address within 14 days. These regulations made it very difficult for a Khoi to change his employer or take refuge on a mission station. A later regulation made their lot even more difficult; it was laid down that if a Khoi child had been brought up to the age of 8 on a white farm the farmer could keep him as an apprentice for a further ten years. Thus if other means failed the farmer could retain a workman by holding his children as apprentices. Nevertheless, inequitable as they were, the regulations did recognize that the Khoi had rights to fair treatment and payment of wages and that these could be the subject of legal action.

In 1811 missionary protests about the failure of the courts to take an interest in Khoi complaints led to questions being asked in the British Parliament, and the Governor was stung into action. He instructed the Circuit Court to look into every Khoi complaint in the fullest detail and to try all cases on the basis of strict equality before the law. The Circuit Court of 1812 was a new experience for the frontier farmers and became so unpopular that it was called the Black Circuit. Many were summoned to leave their farms to answer charges brought by their coloured employees, a situation they regarded as intolerable and degrading. Many of the complaints proved trival but a good deal of evil was uncovered and two farmers were actually convicted of murder.

So bitter was the feeling against the procedure by which coloured persons could bring their employers to court that another frontier rebellion broke out in 1818. A farmer was summoned to answer a charge brought by his Khoi servant but refused to go. An officer with a party of Khoi soldiers went to arrest him but he fired at them from a cave where he was hiding. They returned the fire and the farmer was shot. His family then vowed vengeance and rode round stirring up the farmers to rise in revolt. The government forces soon rounded up the rebels and they were publicly hanged at Slagters Nek. In future it would seem safer to leave the Colony in protest against the behaviour of government than to start an armed rebellion.

While the affair of the Black Circuit was causing ill-feeling the government was also turning its attention to the frontier. Its idea, like that of its predecessor, was to keep the races apart by drawing a definite line between them, and for this purpose it was decided to make the long-standing Fish river frontier effective. In 1812, 20 000 Xhosa were uprooted from their homes and driven out of the Zuurveld. This did little to resolve the situation, for the arrival of refugees from Zuurveld caused severe overcrowding on the far bank of the Fish.

A prophet named Makana arose who promised supernatural aid to win back the lost territory and in 1818 fighting broke out between his followers and those of Gaika, a Xhosa chief who had always lived outside the frontier and had no quarrel with the Colony. Colonial troops intervened in this affair and the Xhosa then invaded the Colony in force. They were eventually driven back but the only remedy to the situation produced by overcrowding which the government could think of was to take yet another strip of land from the Xhosa to be kept empty of inhabitants as a buffer zone between the two races.

After the 1818 war, the government of the Cape attempted a radical solution to the problems of the Colony. It tried to alter the situation in which the farmers were always demanding more land while their population was too scanty to defend itself adequately. A system of more intensive agriculture on much smaller farms which would not need non-European labour would, it was believed, provide a denser population which could defend itself. It would also give rise to villages and towns and create new avenues of employment so that the Colony need not continue to expand in area but could develop a richer and more varied life. Laws were introduced to encourage Boers to divide their farms amongst their children and it was made more difficult to acquire new land by ending the free distribution of Crown lands and putting them up for auction instead. The main means of bringing this about was by the scheme to settle British families on the Zuurveld on farms of about 40 hectares instead of the normal Boer farm of 2400 hectares. This plan had additional attractions. It would provide a substantial British element in the predominantly Dutch Colony and it might be a way of relieving unemployment in Britain. In 1820 about 1000 British families were settled on the Zuurveld but the experiment failed in its main object. The new settlers did not find it practical to farm on the small farms given them; most drifted away to the towns and the remainder pressed for farms of the Boer type.

In the meantime missionary pressure for an improvement in the lot of the Khoi was growing. John Philip, the energetic general superintendent of the London Missionary Society in South Africa, launched an all-out attack on the laws governing the movements of Khoi, which left them at the mercy of white employers and reduced them to a position of semi-slavery possibly even worse than outright slavery. If Khoi were given equal rights with Europeans, he argued, many would be able to earn better wages and this would create a large market for British goods.

These views, contained in a book called *Researches in South Africa*, created a great stir in Britain and the acting governor at the Cape was asked to draw up regulations freeing the Khoi from their legal disadvantages. In fact he had already done so. After consultation with a philanthropically-minded Dutch official named Andries Stockenstroom he had issued the famous 50th Ordinance. The British Parliament simply decreed that the provisions of the 50th Ordinance should not be altered without reference to the King in Parliament.

The 50th Ordinance freed the Khoi from all their legal disabilities and gave them and all free non-Europeans in the Cape complete legal equality with whites. It was indeed a revolutionary measure for it tried to destroy the whole pattern of racial discrimination which had grown up at the Cape ever since the establishment of the white colony there. It set a pattern of racial equality in the Cape which survived in theory until the unification of South Africa in 1910. But though the 50th Ordinance constituted a legal revolution it did not in practice succeed in destroying the pattern of racial discrimination and the social attitudes which went with it. The Khoi gained their freedom but they were without property or much skill. Most of them remained the poorest members of society and the general pattern continued to be one of white property-owning masters and coloured propertyless servants.

The average white inhabitant of the Colony, and especially the Boers of the frontier areas, objected strongly to the 50th Ordinance. It denied the whole attitude of racial superiority which was the basis of their way of life and it proclaimed an equality between races which they regarded as contrary to the laws of God. It also directly affected their interests, for many Khoi servants took the opportunity to abandon their masters and flock to the towns or mission stations.

This blow to the pride and the pockets of the farmers was followed by another. The campaign against slavery had been gathering force in Britain throughout the early years of the nineteenth century. The abolition of the slave trade in 1809 had caused a steady rise in the price of slaves, and their treatment had been subjected to ever-increasing regulation. In 1833 came the decision to abolish slavery in British possessions altogether. What is more, it was decided that in South Africa the freed slaves, after a period of three years' apprenticeship to their former masters, would fall under the provisions of the 50th Ordinance. That is to say they would have legal equality with their one-time owners. Slave owners were to be compensated for their losses, but the arrangements were mismanaged and many received only a fraction of what was due.

In the meantime tension continued along the eastern frontier, and Boers began to turn away from the fertile lands of the east coast in search of new farms further in the interior. The missonaries also turned their attention to the problem of the expanding frontier. They pleaded for protection for the indigenous peoples and an end to the system of raids to recover supposedly stolen cattle which, they pointed out, caused the innocent to suffer for the guilty and opened the way to many abuses. Governor D'Urban, who came out in 1834 to carry through the emancipation of slaves, also brought with him instructions to reform the frontier system.

The Boer Great Trek

By that time news of the situation in the interior had been reaching the Cape from the British traders and travellers who visited Natal, and from missionaries and travellers on the central plateau. It became general knowledge that there was excellent farming land virtually unoccupied in Natal and also in the areas around the Vaal and Orange rivers. Finding insufficient land in the Colony to provide for their growing families, and furious at the government's attitude to the racial situation in the Colony and to frontier relations with the indigenous Africans, the farmers began to talk openly of migrating into the interior to occupy the empty lands and set up a government of their own in accordance with their cherished principles. In 1834 three spying parties (*commissie trekke*) were sent out to discover if the rumours of good land lying empty were really true. One went to Natal, another to the Transvaal and the third to Namibia. The third gave an adverse report but the other two were enthusiastic and the Trek would probably have started at once if the farmers had not been engaged in another frontier war.

Tension had never ceased on the frontier since the war of 1818 and the decision to take a strip of land from the Xhosa as a neutral zone. This had made the Xhosa even more overcrowded and they naturally looked with envy at the rich herds of the white farmers grazing on land they regarded as rightfully theirs. The situation was made worse by the arrival of thousands of refugees from Natal and the interior, who settled with the Xhosa as Mfengu. Seeing their plight the government had allowed some chiefs to come back to the neutral strip but insisted that this was dependent on good behaviour. Along such an open and unguarded frontier there were inevitably many complaints of cattle theft and as the settlers looked for new farms for their sons they continually pressed for the Xhosa to be driven further back.

When D'Urban arrived he was at first sympathetic to the philanthropic point of view and sent Dr Philip to explain to the chiefs that a new system of regulating the frontier would be put into force which would be more favourable to their people. This produced considerable goodwill and the frontier was quiet for a time, but D'Urban, tied down by paper work concerned with emancipation of slaves, kept delaying his journey to the frontier. In the meantime the military authorities did not co-operate with the new scheme, and continued to send punitive parties into Xhosa territory while the settlers demanded that the Xhosa be driven back. The chiefs became increasingly convinced that Dr Philip's visit had been a plot to lull them into a sense of security while the whites prepared to attack them and take away still more of their desperately needed land. They therefore prepared for war and in 1835 they invaded the Colony in force.

When D'Urban at last reached the frontier he was so horrified at the scenes of desolation that he declared the Xhosa to be 'irredeemable savages' and decreed that they should be driven out of the whole area from the Fish to the Kei rivers for ever. The farmers and the troops succeeded in turning back the invasion of the Colony but the Xhosa fought for their lands with such determination that the military commander admitted that the policy of driving them out altogether was impossible. At the same time the missionaries and the philanthropists in Britain raised a storm of protest against the whole policy of D'Urban. He was told to prepare the public mind for the abandonment of the newly annexed area, which he had called Queen Adelaide Province and the philanthropic Stockenstroom was sent to the Eastern Frontier as Lieutenant Governor.

The farmers had abandoned thoughts of leaving the Colony while they had hopes of gaining new lands in Queen Adelaide Province, but its abandonment was the last straw and during 1836 they poured out of the Colony across the Orange river in ever-increasing numbers. The Great Trek was under way. There were several motives behind it. To some extent it was simply an acceleration of the process of expansion that had brought the settlers from the shadow of Table Mountain to the banks of the Fish river. But the Trek was different from this earlier movement because of its size, and because it was a deliberate attempt to break away from the British government and establish an independent state where there would be no ungodly equality between the races and 'proper relations' would be maintained between masters and servants. From this point of view the Great Trek was a revolt against the philanthropic policies of the British government and the spirit of the 50th Ordinance. Finally the decision to embark on the Great Trek, and the direction in which the trekkers moved, depended on information about empty land in the interior resulting from the devastations of the Mfecane. From this point of view the Great Trek was a response by land-hungry Boers to the opportunities offered by the previous movements of the indigenous Africans.

Turning away from the eastern frontier where the sturdy defence of the Xhosa offered little hope of progress, the trekking parties crossed the Orange river into the plains of the modern Orange Free State. Some

The Boer *laager* — a defensive circle of waggons

lingered on the borders of Moshoeshoe's country but the majority moved on, keeping well clear of the Basotho, towards a meeting place near Thaba Nchu. Then, as they waited for their numbers to increase with new arrivals, some of the first-comers crossed the Vaal to hunt and prospect the land for settlement.

Unfortunately they gave no notice of their coming to Mzilikazi, the Ndebele king, and his regiments mistook them for hostile Griqua marauders. The waggons were attacked and a number of Boers were killed but the rest gathered together under the leadership of Potgieter and beat off the Ndebele attack at the Battle of Vegkop in October 1836. The Ndebele seized their cattle, however, and they were grateful for the help of the Rolong chief, Moroka, who helped them back to their fellows near Thaba Nchu. In the main trekker camp there was much discussion whether to move into Natal or continue the struggle with Mzilikazi. The majority decided to follow Piet Retief into Natal but a few determined to continue on the highveld. In January 1837 they made a daring raid on one of Mzilikazi's military towns and seized a large herd of cattle. Shortly after, Dingane also sent his regiments to attack the Ndebele. Then in November 1837 the Boers launched an all-out attack. Unable to ward off the hail of bullets from the Boer guns or to get near enough to attack the mounted gunmen who used their horses to keep always just out of spear range, the Ndebele were completely defeated. Their military towns were captured one after another in seven days of fighting, and Mzilikazi led his people on' a flight to the north which took them to modern Zimbabwe. The victorious Boers then laid claim to the wide area which had been under Mzilikazi's rule.

In the meantime Retief rode to visit Dingane and ask him for the gift of Natal for his people to settle. But the Zulu king was worried and afraid of this horde of armed white strangers. He had heard from a Xhosa interpreter who had come with the British traders how the white men gradually infiltrated the frontier areas and ended up by overthrowing the chiefs and seizing the land. He wished to avoid this fate for himself and his people but he was afraid to refuse the request outright. According he thought of a plan to buy time. He told Retief that some of his cattle had been stolen by the Tlokwa chief Sikonyela and promised if they were brought back to give Natal to the Boers.

He probably hoped that Retief and his party would be involved in a struggle with the Tlokwa and would leave him alone. But further developments proved even more alarming. Retief tricked Sikonyela into trying on a pair of handcuffs and then locked them on his wrists, making him a prisoner. To regain his freedom he had to surrender the cattle asked for by Dingane. Then the news came that the Boers had defeated Mzilikazi and driven his people from their country. Retief wrote in haughty tones to the Zulu king demanding the fulfilment of his promise and then came riding

A great dance at Mbelebele, a Zulu war settlement. The Zulu used a large number of different dances in connection with many formal occasions in their social life such as marriage, initiation, war and death. (From a contemporary engraving)

to see him. Even before he arrived the Boers began pouring over the passes in the Drakensberg into the fertile land of Natal.

Dingane was desperate and felt that the only way to save himself and his people was to catch the Boers unprepared and destroy them before they could establish themselves firmly. He massed his regiments at his main homestead, Umgungundhlovu, and awaited the arrival of Retief and his men. He received them well and made his mark on the paper they asked for. Then he invited them to a farewell dance and when they were standing unarmed amidst his warriors he suddenly gave the order to kill them. Retief and his party were put to death and the Zulu regiments were sent out at once to attack the Boer waggons unawares. But though the first parties met by the warriors were slaughtered, the firing of guns alarmed the others and the regiments were driven back with heavy loss. Dingane's

Routes followed by the Boers in the Great Trek

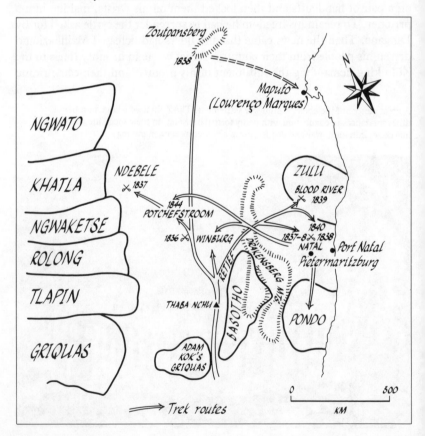

coup had failed. The position of the Boers was not enviable, however, for their numbers were few, they had lost many of their cattle and they dared not disperse to give proper grazing to those that remained. A first Boer counter-attack ended in a retreat from which it got its name, the Vlug Commando (Flight Commando). Many thought of giving up the struggle and returning across the mountains but new reinforcements came from the Cape and some of the Boers on the highveld, and the outstanding leader Andries Pretorius from the Cape, came to the help of their fellows.

A large commando with waggons loaded with ammunition was prepared and advanced towards Umgungundhlovu. On 16 December 1838 the decisive battle of Blood River took place. The superb Zulu discipline proved useless in the face of firearms. They were shot down in large numbers and heavily defeated. The commando advanced to Umgungundhlovu itself, which Dingane had deserted, and found the bodies of Retief and his comrades together with the piece of paper ceding Natal. By this time the government at the Cape was becoming alarmed at the news from the interior and sent a small force to watch developments at Port Natal. It arrived when the Boers were away on the Blood River campaign. When

Boer–Zulu and Boer–Ndebele battlefields

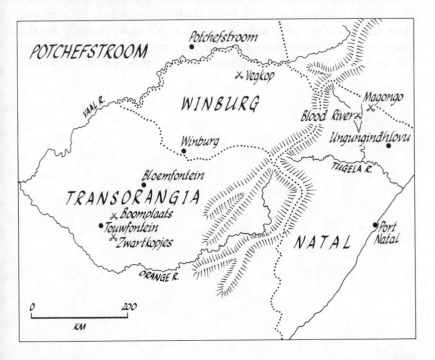

they returned victorious there was little the British force could do except try to arrange terms of peace between the two sides. Both were by this time ready to negotiate. Dingane did not wish to be involved in another encounter, but although defeated he was still strong and the Boers were still not free to disperse and settle down. A meeting was arranged and a peace treaty drawn up. The Boers drove a hard bargain and in a secret clause of the treaty they forced Dingane to give up not only Natal but a strip of territory across the Tugela in Zululand itself. Satisfied that peace had been made but unaware of the full details, the British force then sailed away.

Dingane tried to fulfil his side of the bargain and sent his regiments to clear a way for his retreat by raiding the Swazi. But many of his people grumbled at leaving their land and one of Shaka's surviving brothers, Mpande, seized the opportunity to start a rebellion. He fled with a number of followers across the Tugela and asked for Boer protection. Then as his following continued to grow he proposed to march into Zululand and overthrow Dingane. The Boers were pleased to support him and sent a commando which marched in support of the rebel chief. The two Zulu armies fought a fatal battle at Magongo, and Mpande was victorious. Dingane fled to Swaziland and was captured and killed by a Swazi chief in revenge for his attacks on them. The Boers did not have to fire a shot, but they reaped the fruits of Mpande's victory. They crowned him the new Zulu king and demanded 17 000 head of cattle for their support and as recompense for their past sufferings. At last they were firmly established in Natal and could build up their republic in security.

10 South Africa from the Great Trek to the first Anglo–Boer war

Consequences of the Great Trek

The Great Trek marks the beginning of a new phase in the history of South Africa with important consequences for Southern Africa as a whole. Before the Trek, contact between indigenous Africans and whites had been restricted to the eastern frontier. In that area a situation had developed in which as we have seen the white settlers, impelled by a constantly rising population, were always trying to gain possession of more grazing land. At the same time they were employing more black labour and so turning the indigenous African from a member of an independent society into a subordinate member of a multi-racial society, firmly kept at the bottom by barriers of racial prejudice as well as lack of skills and capital. This situation was only slightly improved by the educational work of the missionaries and by the philanthropic pressures which had caused the government at the Cape to insist on the ending of formal legal discrimination.

Before the Great Trek the number of people affected was comparatively small. As a result of the Boer migrations the problems of racial contact and conflict spread over much greater areas. The white settlers were always trying to advance. The pace of expansion in the new areas of settlement was increased by the fact that as the trekkers gained control of large areas, individuals staked out claims to far more land than they actually occupied. New arrivals thus found no land available for them and pressed for further expansion of the frontiers. At the same time much of the white-owned land remained occupied and farmed by Africans who became tenants of their white landlords and had either to give them a share of their crops or pay a rent in cash or crops. The pressure of the newly established white groups on neighbouring African people was met by brave and determined resistance and in some cases the whites were driven back. White conquest was only completed at the end of the nineteenth century after a long series of bitter wars. The wars increased the sense of insecurity among white

251

settlers and strengthened the determination of the trekkers to preserve the principles of racial distinction.

The Great Trek also presented the British government at the Cape with a difficult problem. The chief value of the Cape to Great Britain, as to the Dutch East India Company, was as a strategic position on the route to India and there was a natural reluctance to spend precious resources on an otherwise poor and unproductive area unless such expenses were directly related to security. On the other hand Britain could not avoid responsibility for the behaviour of her subjects who had trekked into the interior, or for the fate of the indigenous peoples with whom they were in contact. Still more important, a policy of leaving the Boers to themselves, which appeared economical in the short run, might have very expensive consequences in the long run. The direction which the Trek had taken meant that white settlers were established on three sides of a great mass of African societies including the Basotho of Moshoeshoe and the Nguni-speaking peoples along the coastal corridor between the Cape frontier and the southern borders of Natal. As these societies were increasingly short of land and very close to one another, any conflict along one section of the frontier between the races was likely to start a chain of disturbance. Thus if the British left the Boers to themselves in their areas they might find themselves plunged into war on their own eastern frontier at any time. A similar situation also prevailed with regard to the white settlements in Natal and the Transvaal. Both had frontiers with the Zulu kingdom and either might plunge the other into war at any time. Faced with this situation British policy alternated between the two opposite extremes of annexation and withdrawal in accordance with the developing situation in South Africa and shifts of opinion in Britain.

The British annexation of Natal

When the Great Trek took place the influence of the philanthropic movement was at its highest and British admitted responsibility for the conduct of its citizens in the interior by passing the Cape of Good Hope Punishment Act, under which British subjects who committed crimes anywhere in South Africa, south of the 35th line of latitude, were liable for trial at the Cape. The government also refused to entertain a request from the Natal Boers to be considered an independent people but insisted that they were and must remain British subjects. This meant that Britain ought to occupy the areas in which the Boers were settled, as it was useless to declare them subject to the law at the Cape but provide no means of enforcing that law. When it came to taking active steps that would involve expense, however, the Governor at the Cape found that he could not get authorization for even a moderate force to intervene in Natal. The tiny contingent which was sent to Port Natal at the time of the Blood River campaign (1838) was unable to play any major part in influencing events and was withdrawn soon after the Boer victory. The progress of events, however, soon forced the British government to intervene more effectively in Natal.

The jubilant reception given to an adventurer named J.A. Smellekamp who arrived at Natal claiming to be a representative of the king of Holland, as well as the visit of some American ships, created fears lest a foreign power might establish itself on the east coast of South Africa and threaten the route to India. Other reasons for intervention arose from the conduct of the settlers themselves in relation to their black neighbours. The conquest of Natal had given the Boers large areas of excellent farming land, but the heroes of the Zulu war registered so many farms in their names that soon there was no more unallocated land available for newcomers. The cattle paid by the humble Mpande after his victory over Dingane were well in excess of the losses the trekkers had suffered, but their distribution was not controlled firmly enough to prevent the more powerful members of the community from seizing more than their share, so that others did not receive enough to build up a satisfactory herd. When the news of the defeat and death of Dingane became widely known, communities which had fled out of Natal to the south, or been forced to join the Zulu kingdom, began pouring back to settle in their old homes, now the legal property of Boer settlers. The Natal Boers found the utmost difficulty in coping with this ever-growing influx because they only effectively occupied a small proportion of the farms registered in their names.

The government which was called upon to deal with these problems was weak and rickety. When the Boers trekked out of the Cape they regarded themselves as a single body, and this idea was preserved in theory through the life of the Natal Republic. As the main body of settlers had moved into Natal this was the main centre of government. Subordinate governing bodies were established at Winburg in modern Orange Free State and Potchefstroom in the Transvaal. These were represented on the main governing body in Natal and supposed to be subject to it though in fact distance and difficulty of communications meant the local bodies were virtually self-governing. In Natal itself power was divided between an elected legislative body called the Volksraad and the President, who controlled the executive. Both authorities were supposed to be subject to the people and this meant in practice any assembly of settlers.

With such a constitution it was difficult for the Volksraad to prevent policy being decided by the feeling of the moment. Thus even though it

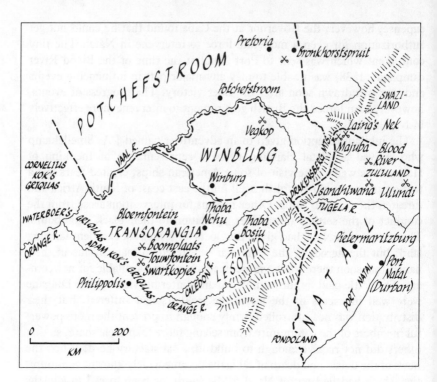

The Trekkers' Republic

was aware of the danger that philanthropic opinion in Britain would exert itself in favour of British annexation of Natal in order to protect the indigenous peoples, the Volksraad was unable to prevent its citizens from an aggressive approach to its non-European neighbours which amply justified the arguments of the humanitarians. Not satisfied with the herds already extorted from the Zulu, the Natal Republic pressed Mpande for still more cattle and proposed to levy a heavy fine on the Swazi, claiming that they had taken Zulu cattle which belonged to the Boers by right of conquest. A still more shocking development was the behaviour of the Boers towards their southern neighbours. The theft of some cattle by San was made the pretext for a raid on the Bhaca, a group made up of communities which had fled from Natal in the time of Shaka and who were living under their chief Ncapayi in the close vicinity of the Pondo. The Boers killed many Bhaca and seized large booty in cattle. At the same time they proposed to take land from the Pondo to provide for the increasing numbers of indigenous African refugees returning to Natal, whom they regarded as a threat to their security. By this time humanita-

254

rian feeling was strongly aroused and the procedures of the Natal government also gave cause for grave alarm from the strategic point of view. If they were allowed to push chiefdoms back from their southern border this must inevitably produce a chain reaction along the closely packed coastal strip, resulting in increased pressure on the frontier of the Cape.

Accordingly, in 1841, a small contingent of British troops was despatched. It halted first at the Pondo and then moved on to Port Natal. When they came in contact with the Boers fighting started and the British government felt too heavily committed to withdraw. In 1845 Natal was formally annexed to the Cape, but already many Boers were leaving the area in disgust to join their fellows on the high veld in modern Orange Free State and Transvaal. Even in the period of the Republic some individuals had begun accumulating numerous claims to farms and building up large speculative landholdings. As the Boers trekked out of the country, recrossing the Drakensberg on to the high veld, Englishmen from the Cape who often had connections with businessmen in London were able to gain title to immense areas of land in the name of land companies. Other land was set aside in substantial blocks as Reserves for the African population. Theophilus Shepstone, who was appointed as diplomatic agent with the African groups and later became Natal's Secretary for Native Affairs, persuaded large numbers to settle in these Reserves but many more stayed on the land of the land companies, on crown land or on land owned by the missionary societies. There they were able to support themselves and to pay their taxes without working for whites. In the 1850s several schemes were adopted for bringing settlers to Natal from Britain. The white population of Natal came to be the most self-consciously British of any part of South Africa. As the British settlers began developing commercial agriculture, especially sugar growing, however, they found it difficult to obtain cheap African labour. They tried to get laws implemented to force Africans off the land but they were checked by the interests of the land companies which wanted to continue to get rent from their African tenants. So in the 1860s it was decided to import cheap Indian labour for the sugar plantations. This was the origin of the South African Indian community which in time spread out of Natal to the Transvaal and the Cape.

The eastern frontier, Moshoeshoe and the Boers

With the annexation of Natal the British government had taken a major step in the direction of bringing the areas inhabited by its runaway subjects under British control. In the meantime events in the area between the Orange and the Vaal rivers were preparing the way for another step in the same direction. When it decided not to allow the annexation of Queen Adelaide Province the British government proposed to adopt a policy suggested by the philanthropic Dutch official Stockenstroom. The idea of this was to persuade the chiefdoms near the colonial frontiers to enter into treaties with the government of the Colony, under which the chiefs would be made responsible for maintaining peace in the frontier areas, catching and returning runaways and deserters from the Colony, and making good any losses of stock stolen by their subjects. This would end the practice of commandos crossing the frontier to recapture stolen cattle which had proved a grave source of injustice and friction in the past. British Residents would be sent to the more important chiefdoms to help the chiefs understand and carry out their obligations and to represent their views to the British government. The policy was to be applied not only to chiefs in the eastern frontier area but also to others further inland.

The plan was never fully tried out. It was very unpopular with the settlers and the military authorities, and the British government was unwilling to spend enough to make it work. In the area between the Orange and Vaal rivers it was faced by especially difficult problems. There the Griquas and Basotho were living alongside a growing white population, made up partly of Boers who had entered the area before the Trek and who regarded themselves as British subjects, and partly by Trek Boers who denied British authority. This white population was greedy for farms and labour and was subject to no single political authority. Both sections were unwilling to be governed by the non-European rulers that the British government recognized as the legal authorities in the area, and possessed weapons which enabled them to defy these rulers. Seeing the situation, Dr Philip urged immediate annexation as the only means of preventing the Boers from seizing the lands of the indigenous peoples and turning them into landless labourers serving on white farms. Nevertheless the British government, anxious to limit expenditure, attempted to apply the treaty system without taking into account the military power of the Boers.

Two Griqua chiefs, Waterboer and Adam Kok, were given treaties in which their authority over their territories was recognized, and they were asked to maintain law and order and return colonial criminals for trial at the Cape in return for small subsidies. A similar treaty was made by Governor Napier with Moshoeshoe, though his request for a Resident to come and live with him was not granted by Napier.

The position of the Basotho ruler was very difficult. He ruled a composite state made up of members of many different chiefdoms. The majority of these had been broken up during the Mfecane and were settled in small groups in his kingdom, under the administration of some members of the

256

paramount's family who had their headquarters in different parts of the kingdom. Others remained substantial chiefdoms governed by their own hereditary rulers under the paramountcy of Moshoeshoe. The majority of the members of this state belonged to the Sotho-speaking group, but there were also considerable numbers who spoke the western Sotho or Tswana tongue. They included the powerful Taung under their brilliant leader Moletsane. Finally there were several groups who spoke Nguni languages and differed considerably in culture from the Sotho-speaking majority. The most important of these were the Phuti or Morosi. On the borders of the kingdom in the north, the Tlokwa of Sikonyela were entrenched in their hilltop position awaiting any sign of weakness to renew their old quarrel, and at Thaba Nchu a powerful group of Tswana refugees – the Rolong under Moroka – refused to accept the authority of the Basotho king, though they had been allowed to settle in what he regarded as his territory.

The Boers, who began to settle on the borders of Moshoeshoe's country at the time of the Great Trek, at first asked for the right to graze their cattle temporarily while they prepared to move further into the interior; but they soon showed signs of settling permanently. They treated the land they occupied as private property which they bought and sold to one another, their numbers increased, and they infiltrated ever deeper into the kingdom. In attempting to preserve the nation he had created, Moshoeshoe had to tread very carefully. He was anxious to avoid an all-out collision with the whites, whose superior armaments must in the end give them the victory. On the other hand he could not afford to offend any of his own followers for, lacking the power which a centralized military system gave to rulers like Shaka or Mzilikazi, he could only hope to rule by consent. A concession made for the sake of peace might, if it sacrificed the interests of some of his people, lead to a breakaway and the disintegration of the state he had created and was trying to preserve.

In his difficult dealings with the whites Moshoeshoe had the support and advice of the French missionaries, and this was invaluable to him. But missionary activity also created problems, for the missionary attack on old and revered customs inevitably had a disturbing effect, and produced divisions between Christian converts and more conservative members of the community. In addition, the fact that the Rolong were served by a different mission, the Wesleyans, was an important factor in preventing them from becoming part of the Basotho nation, and differences of opinion between the French and Wesleyan missionaries made matters even more complicated.

The attempt by the British government to settle the affairs of the area between the Orange and the Vaal, by recognizing the most important chiefs and giving them subsidies, was doomed to failure since it did not give those chiefs any protection against their Boer neighbours. The futility of the arrangement was shown in 1845 when Waterboer attempted to exercise his legal powers under the treaty by arresting a Boer for an alleged crime. The Boers at once flew to arms and threatened to destroy the Griquas once and for all. A hastily assembled colonial force with Griqua support routed the Boers at Swartkopjes, but it was obvious that once it withdrew the problem would arise again. Governor Maitland therefore tried a more realistic plan. The fact was recognized that the Boers occupied, and could not be removed from, much of the area legally belonging to the chiefs. It was also recognized that they would not allow themselves to be governed by the Griqua rulers.

At the same time there was an attempt to protect the chiefs from the loss of any more of their land, and to provide a system of government for the whites and to settle any disputes between whites and non-whites. In arrangements drawn up at Touwfontein in June 1845, it was agreed that each chief should divide his land into two sections, an inalienable section in which no whites could acquire rights and an alienable section in which land might be leased to white settlers. The theoretical ownership of the alienable section would still belong to the chief, but he would delegate his powers in that area to a British Resident, who would be responsible for governing the white settlers and deciding any disputes between them and the indigenous peoples. Any whites living in the inalienable area would have to withdraw and the expense of the Residents would be paid from annual rents on the farms of the white settlers. The plan had much to commend it, but it depended on the Resident being in a strong enough position to prevent the Boers from settling in the inalienable areas, and forcing them to withdraw if they had already done so. This would require a military force that would cost far more than the rents would bring in and the British government was not prepared to pay. Moshoeshoe marked out an area to be classified as alienable, but the Boers who were already pushing deeper into his kingdom rejected it as far too small. A British Resident was appointed but without the power to control the situation.

While tension rose towards a conflict north of the Orange river the situation on the eastern frontier also grew worse. At first the treaty system seemed to work well. The chiefs were anxious to co-operate and the frontier had a short period of unusual calm but magistrates were far too ready to accept farmers' stories about cattle thefts. The chiefs found themselves faced with a lengthening list of demands for the return of stock, some of which had been killed by wild animals or merely allowed to stray out of carelessness. So bitter was the hostility of the settlers to the whole scheme, and to Stockenstroom who was appointed Lieutenant

Governor to carry it out, that he resigned his position in disgust and disillusion. The situation drifted towards yet another war. It was touched off by a minor incident. In 1846 a relative of the Xhosa chief Sandile was arrested for stealing an axe. He was freed by other members of his family, who killed the Khoi policeman escorting the prisoner. Sandile refused to return the murderers and war was declared. It proved to be one of the most bitter and costly in the history of the eastern frontier.

Annexation of British Kaffraria and the Orange River Sovereignty

The War of the Axe was brought to an end just as Sir Harry Smith, a new and energetic governor, arrived in South Africa. He speedily decided that the frontier chiefs were unable to control their own people sufficiently to prevent conflicts with the Colony. He therefore annexed the frontier area from the Fish to the Kei river, declared the people living on it to be British citizens, and proposed to introduce direct rule by British magistrates while recognizing the rights of the indigenous Africans to their land. The newly annexed area came to be a separate little colony called British Kaffraria.

Smith then dashed off to attend to the situation in Natal where the Boers were steadily streaming out of the country. On his way he passed through the area of modern Orange Free State, and concluded that so long

British annexations in Southern Africa up to 1848

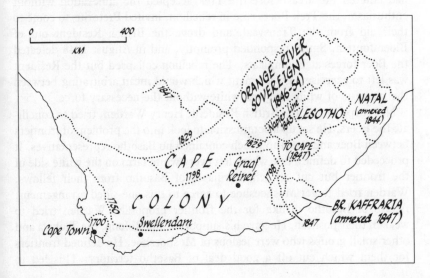

as there was no common, settled and effective government over the different peoples, conflicts would be inevitable which would endanger the peace of the eastern frontier as well. He summoned the chiefs to a short conference and, when he reached Natal, he announced the annexation of the whole area between the Orange and the Vaal as the Orange River Sovereignty (February 1848).

Smith's action was welcomed by Moshoeshoe, who saw in it the only hope for protection against the Boers, but it had been undertaken hastily, without authorization from England and without consideration for the state of opinion there. In Britain, the theory of free trade was gaining increasing strength. According to this theory prosperity could be increased most by trading with every nation freely and without preferences or restrictions. If this were so then colonies were no advantage since one could trade just as well with independent countries. Expenditure on colonial administration was therefore a sheer waste of resources. Britain should restrict her spending on such matters to a minimum, get rid of colonies where possible and at all costs refrain from acquiring new and expensive responsibilities. In this atmosphere the news of the new annexation was far from popular. It was accepted reluctantly and only on the assumption that it would not involve new expense.

Thus Smith's scheme was doomed from the start. Without funds, a force large enough to enable the Sovereignty government to control Boer as well as indigenous African could not be maintained, and the objects of the annexation were unattainable. The first reaction of the Boers in the area was an ill omen for the success of the Sovereignty. While those who had entered the area before the Trek accepted the annexation without enthusiasm, the Trek Boers rose in rebellion, invited Pretorius to come to their aid from the Transvaal, and drove the British Resident out of Bloemfontein. Smith responded promptly, and in August 1848 defeated the Boer forces at Boomplaats. The rebellion collapsed but the Resident was left to exercise a government which would mean arbitrating between the interests of white and non-white without the necessary force.

Not surprisingly, the British Resident, Henry Warden, tried to conciliate the Boers. He set up a commission to look into the problem of frontiers between Boer and Basotho which contained no Basotho representatives. It proceeded to define a line which left every white farm on the white side of the frontier but cut off whole villages of Basotho from their fellows. Warden tried to get Moshoeshoe to agree to this one-sided arrangement. Aware of Basotho dislike for the frontier proposals, Warden tried to weaken their position. He gave his support to the Rolong, the Tlokwa and other small groups who were jealous of Moshoeshoe. He defined frontiers for them which cut off a good deal of Basotho territory. This led to fighting, and to support his frontier arrangements Warden marched against the Basotho ruler in June 1851. He based his hopes for success on the loyal support of the Boers whose interests he had tried to serve, and on the fighting forces of the Rolong and their lesser allies. But the Boers failed to answer the summons with anything like enough men and the strength of the Rolong had been exaggerated. Warden was defeated at Viervoet and had to fall back. The Orange River Sovereignty fell into chaos and was only saved by the restraint of Moshoeshoe, who held his men back from looting the helpless farmers. Warden called for aid from the Colony but by this time Smith's eastern frontier settlement had also broken down. Yet another frontier war was in progress and no troops could be spared. The Governor of Natal sent a force of Zulus to the aid of the Sovereignty, but they were undisciplined and plundered all sides indiscriminately.

The renewed fighting on the eastern frontier, like that in the Sovereignty, arose from the attempt to do too much without the necessary resources, and from a failure to appreciate the need for a law which would respect the customs of the people. After British Kaffraria was annexed it came in theory under the law of the Cape Colony, and although magistrates in practice modified the law in accordance with common sense and local conditions the prohibition of such a sacred institution as the payment of bride-price cattle inevitably provoked violent opposition.

Boer independence in the Transvaal and Orange Free State

The outbreak of war both in the Sovereignty and on the eastern frontier brought opposition to the forward policy of the British government in South Africa to a head. The wars seemed to reveal the uselessness of annexations undertaken to protect the indigenous people. The voice of the philanthropic movement, which had recently suffered a heavy blow in the failure of Buxton's Niger expedition, was almost silenced. The Free Traders criticized colonial expansion as unprofitable. Others, impressed by the inefficiency of government from a distance and the advantage of giving power to local communities, felt that South African affairs should be left to the settlers. Others again, influenced by the theory of evolution, felt that the conquest of black peoples by whites was an inevitable law of history and that it was a waste of time and resources to oppose it.

There was general agreement that the attempt to follow the trekkers into the interior should be abandoned. No further annexations should be made and if possible the Sovereignty should be abandoned. A commission was accordingly sent out to South Africa to look into the matter. Though the war on the eastern frontier was brought to an end in February 1853, and Moshoeshoe still did not take advantage of his victory, the position in the Sovereignty continued to be difficult. The authority of the Resident had broken down, and while some farmers were intriguing with Pretorius in the Transvaal, others were conducting their own negotiations with Moshoeshoe.

The first task of the commissioners was to prevent the Transvaal farmers from taking part in the already complex situation. In view of the changed attitude in Britain they felt able to offer the Transvaalers the legal independence which had always been denied to them in return for a promise not to interfere south of the Vaal river. In 1852 an agreement, known as the Sand River Convention, was drawn up between the commissioners and representatives of the Transvaal Boers. In this convention the British government abandoned its policy of admitting responsibility for the behaviour of its subjects in the interior. The Transvaalers were given complete freedom of action north of the Vaal river, and Britain renounced any right or intention to interfere in that area. Far from attempting to protect the African peoples from the Boers, Britain even sided openly with the white farmers by promising the Transvaalers free access to the gunpowder market at the Cape while not allowing blacks to purchase ammunition there. The Sand River Convention put an end to interference from the Transvaal and a measure of peace and order returned to the Sovereignty, but there seemed no way of establishing effective British government without the expense which Britain was determined to avoid.

Moshoeshoe remained the dominant figure in the area, and Governor Cathcart, who succeeded Sir Harry Smith, felt that no settlement was possible in the Sovereignty until Moshoeshoe had been made to accept the overriding power of British rule. Accordingly, he brought his forces to the borders of Lesotho and demanded payment of a large number of cattle as a fine for the losses caused by Moshoeshoe's men in the recent war. Moshoeshoe begged for time but Cathcart refused to listen, and marched towards Thaba Bosiu. His troops captured a herd of cattle but they got into difficulties with this booty when the Basotho launched their counterattack. Cathcart had to withdraw, to regroup his forces and wait for more men to arrive. Moshoeshoe took advantage of this to bring off a diplomatic coup. He wrote a humble letter to Cathcart saying that as the British had defeated his people and captured many cattle he hoped that they would consider it enough and agree to peace. Cathcart was pleased to be offered an easy way out and agreed. The British forces withdrew leaving Moshoeshoe victorious.

After this there was no longer any question of holding on to the Sovereignty, and in spite of the fact that many of the settlers were reluctant to see the British authority withdrawn, a group was found who were prepared to accept independence, and the Bloemfontein Convention was signed with them in 1854. This document was similar to the Sand River Convention. It denied all British responsibilities in the area north of the Orange river and gave the Boers complete freedom of action. So anxious were the British to be rid of their responsibilities in the area that they failed even to settle the vital problem of the frontier between the Boers and the Basotho. Moshoeshoe claimed that the frontier defined by Warden, to which the Basotho had always objected, had been cancelled by

South Africa after the Sand River and Bloemfontein Conventions

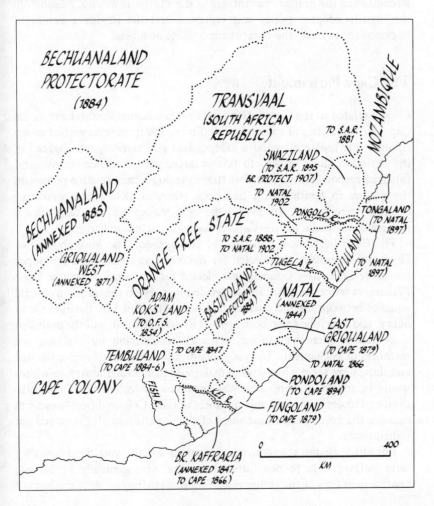

263

war and that he could start negotiations afresh. The Boers maintained that the Warden line stayed the effective frontier. With the departure of the British, the Boers of the Sovereignty area drew up a republican constitution with an elected Volksraad (parliament) and President. Thus the Orange Free State came into existence, but in the circumstances it could not be long before it came into conflict with the Basotho.

The Sand River and Bloemfontein Conventions represented the lowest point of British policy in South Africa. Solemn obligations to the indigenous peoples were cynically given up in the interests of short-term economy. The blacks were left to fight it out with the Boers as best they could, hampered by the gunpowder clauses in the conventions which strengthened the military advantages of the whites. It was not long before this hastily adopted policy was regretted and the British government began to try to undo the consequences of its own acts.

The Cape Parliament

Closely related to the Conventions policy was constitutional reform at the Cape. British critics of colonial expenditure, and those who wished to see colonial rule replaced by more independent government, were agreed in the desire to allow settlers to take a larger part in administrative and financial responsibility. The first step in giving administrative powers to the settlers in South Africa had been taken in 1836 when municipal councils were set up. In 1852-3 the next major step was taken when provision was made for the Cape to have an elected parliament.

The Cape Parliament consisted of two houses. The lower house, or House of Assembly, was elected for five years at a time, and the upper house, or Legislative Council, was elected for ten years. When the Cape Parliament was established it was decided to carry on the tradition of legal equality between the races which had been established by the 50th Ordinance, and which had also been applied in the constitution of the municipal councils. There was to be no racial qualification for the vote for members of parliament. The only qualifications required were economic and these were set at a low level to make sure that at least some non-whites would be entitled to vote. This was known as the 'colour-blind' constitution, and under it considerable numbers of Cape Coloured people came to exercise the vote, and in time some of the Cape blacks also acquired the right to vote.

But although the economic qualifications for the vote were low they were unfavourable to non-Europeans, who were generally by far the poorest members of the community. There was always a large majority of white voters, and when the settlers feared that the situation might change they altered the qualifications to safeguard their majority.

When parliamentary institutions were later established in Natal the principle of the 'colour-blind' system was maintained, but so many difficulties were put in the way of Natal blacks acquiring the vote that they were practically excluded.

The Cape Parliament, whose constitution was decided in 1853, was at first given only legislative powers. Executive power was still in the hands of the Governor and his officials. It was only in 1872 that the Cape acquired a constitution in which the ministers were chosen by Parliament and were responsible to it.

Grey and the eastern frontier

In 1854 Sir George Grey came to govern the Cape. He had been Governor of New Zealand, where he believed that he had successfully solved the problems of relations between the settlers and the Maori. He was therefore confident that he could solve the problems of racial conflict in South Africa. He had also enjoyed considerable freedom in the exercise of power, and he was impatient of control from Britain. One of his plans was to find a permanent solution to the problem of the eastern frontier. His idea was that if white and black were brought into closer contact the blacks would learn the farming practices and general culture of the whites, adopt white civilization and cease to be a threat to security. Accordingly he planned to introduce white settlers into British Kaffraria and in fact settled considerable numbers of German settlers there.

Unfortunately the area was already overcrowded, and by depriving the indigenous African of still more of their farming land his measures reduced them to desperate poverty.

Another war would certainly have broken out if the Xhosa in despair had not looked to supernatural means of salvation. A woman prophet named Nonquase declared that, if all the cattle were slaughtered and the grain destroyed before an appointed day, the sun would rise in the west and the spirits of the ancestors, aided by a mighty wind, would return to help them drive the whites from their land. Under her inspiration the Xhosa destroyed their food supplies, but when the day came no miracle occurred. The disillusioned and starving people were in no condition to fight. Thousands died of starvation, though the British government sent supplies of food. Thousands more took refuge in the colony as workers on white farms. The fighting power of the Xhosa was broken for a time.

Another of Grey's plans was the settlement of Adam Kok's Griquas in a series of valleys at the base of the Drakensberg, between the Basotho and the coastal chiefdoms. Even before the Sovereignty was given up these Griquas, whose territory lay along the Orange river around Philippolis, had been feeling the pressure of land-hungry Boers. After the creation of the Orange Free State the position became steadily worse. Adam Kok and his council made laws forbidding their subjects to lease land to whites but the temptation of immediate gain always proved too much, and once a white farmer was established it was practically impossible to get rid of him again. Though many of the Griquas were comparatively wealthy their territory was steadily shrinking. Adam Kok accordingly decided to look for a new home and Grey proposed that he should settle in the valleys of what was then called Nomansland, where he would act as a buffer between the Basotho and the east coast chiefdoms.

In 1861 Adam Kok sold the Philippolis lands to the Free State and his people undertook their own Great Trek to establish a new state in what is now called Griqualand East. There they built a Griqua republic which flourished for a time, but pressure from the Bantu-speaking peoples and the weakness of the Griquas brought about its ruin. The Griqua progressively mortgaged their property to canteen-keepers from the Cape, in return for loans spent on drink and other commodities. Finally, the Griquas lost almost all their land.

It was with regard to the relations between the Cape and other white settler communities that Grey produced his most ambitious plans. He saw that the peace of the eastern frontier could not be separated from the effects of relations between the Boers and the Basotho and this was particularly impressed upon him by the outbreak of the first Orange Free State–Lesotho war.

The first Orange Free State–Lesotho war, 1858

Though friendly relations between the new white republic and Moshoeshoe in Lesotho were maintained at first, the problem of the frontier inevitably brought them into conflict. In 1858 war broke out and Free State forces advanced towards Thaba Bosiu, but they were not strong enough to storm its precipitous slopes. In the meantime highly mobile groups of Basotho penetrated deep into the Free State. When the farmers camped in front of Thaba Bosiu learnt that their homes were in danger they suddenly broke up the camp and scattered to defend their families. The Free State President found himself in a desperate situation and appealed to Grey for help in making peace. Moshoeshoe, anxious not to earn the hostility of the British, agreed. Under the first Treaty of Aliwal North, the Basotho gained a slight modification of their territory but not enough to satisfy the needs of their population. Moshoeshoe agreed unwillingly to the arrangement. He felt that his people should have been given more after a successful war.

Grey then began to press with increasing determination for a federation of all the white states in South Africa. He argued that so long as the different white groups conducted their relations with their black neighbours without any co-ordination there could be no stable peace in South Africa. What is more, none of the white states was strong enough on its own to maintain law and order by normal means along its frontiers. Incidents were unavoidable, and the only means such weak states possessed for dealing with them was to attack the indigenous Africans in an all-out war, in the hope of striking terror into them. A federal government would adopt a uniform policy to blacks, and would be able to police its frontiers and suppress cattle raids by normal means without recourse to war. It would attract the most enlightened minds from the white population of the sub-continent, and it would be more likely to act impartially and justly than a small local assembly made up of men whose interests were directly involved in the matters they debated. His arguments fell on deaf ears in the British Colonial Office, where it was felt that his schemes would inevitably involve the British government in the affairs of the interior, and thus in all the trouble and expense that it had tried to avoid by accepting the Conventions.

In 1859 Grey received a request from Britain to investigate the possibilities of a federation of the British colonies of the Cape, Natal and British Kaffraria. He took this as an invitation to proceed with his far wider scheme, and without authorization from Britain he caused the idea of a South African federation to be discussed in the Free State Volksraad and introduced for discussion in the Cape Parliament. This was too much for the British government to tolerate and he was immediately recalled. With a change of government in Britain he was sent back the following year (1860) but with clear instructions not to raise the issue of federation again.

The creation of the South African Republic in the Transvaal

Soon after the collapse of the Boer Republic in Natal the trekker community in the Transvaal divided into three main communities. One was in the initial area of settlement around Potchefstroom. This gave rise to offshoots along the line of the Magaliesberg range and in the Marico valley. The second was in the north-east Transvaal near the Pedi kingdom. It was first established at Andries Ohrigstad but the effects of malaria and pressure from the African population led to withdrawal to Lydenburg. The third centre was in the Zoutpansberg mountains. Its prosperity depended largely on the ivory trade, and as elephants were shot out it declined. Under pressure from the Venda people it was eventually abandoned. The three settlements were formally united and a common Volksraad was established in 1849, but in fact they tended to go their own ways and their leaders openly rivalled one another. Andries Pretorius, the hero of Blood river, was the leader of the south-western communities. He took the lead in negotiating the Sand River Convention with the British. He continued, however, to strive to unite all the Transvaal white communities and bring them together with the Boers of the Orange Free State in a single trekker state.

After his death in 1853 his son, Martinus Wessels Pretorius, succeeded to his father's position of leadership and continued to pursue his ideals. In 1856 Pretorius succeeded in persuading the Volksraad to agree to a constitution for the Transvaal which was now to be called the South African Republic. As well as a single Volksraad the constitution provided for an executive president. The Lydenburg community, however, refused to accept the constitution and because of a quarrel over church matters, declared itself a separate and independent republic. Stephanus Schoeman, who had succeeded Andries Potgieter as head of the Zoutpansberg community, also refused to accept Pretorius's position as President. By late 1859, however, unity was restored and all the Transvaal white settlements became parts of the South African Republic under Pretorius's presidency.

At this point, however, the new-found unity was endangered by Pretorius's desire to achieve unity with the Orange Free State. Earlier attempts had been frustrated by resistance from within the Orange Free State and the divisions in the Transvaal. After the Free State defeat by Moshoeshoe, however, the Free Staters looked seriously to the idea of union with the Transvaal. Grey, anxious to unite the Free State with the Cape, stopped this by threatening that such a union would put an end to the Conventions. After Grey's scheme was squashed by the British government, however, Pretorius tried another way of achieving his aims. In 1860 he put himself forward and was elected to the presidency of the Orange Free State, hoping that as President of both Republics he would be able to bring them together. His rivals in the Transvaal, however, forced him to resign his presidency of the South African Republic. His supporters refused to accept this and a civil conflict ensued. In the Orange Free State Pretorius was unable to resolve the problems of relations with the kingdom of Lesotho. In 1864 he resigned and returned to the Transvaal where he was again elected President. The trekker community had been definitely divided into two separate republics.

In the Transvaal as in Natal the trekkers staked out far more farms than they actually occupied. Many were desperately poor and quickly parted with their land claims to more prosperous neighbours or to British traders. The government, moreover, was so hard up that it often had to pay its officials in land claims and to offer large areas of land to foreigners in order to raise loans. Most of the land in the Transvaal thus came into the hands of a class of relatively wealthy landowners who dominated the political life of the country or into those of foreign-based land companies. A growing proportion of the Boers in the Transvaal were landless and lived as tenants (known as *bywoners*) on the land of the wealthier citizens or land companies. Most of this land, however, was actually occupied and cultivated by Africans who in time came to pay a rent whether in labour, or a share of the crop or in cash to their landlords.

The second Orange Free State-Lesotho war, 1865

Although the British government rejected Grey's idea of a South African federation, it soon found itself forced to go back on the Conventions policy and take the road he had suggested. The decisive factor in this was the developing situation between the Basotho and the Boers. The basis of the quarrel between Moshoeshoe and the Free State was simple. As the Boer population increased it needed more and more land, but the Basotho population was also increasing and much of its land had already passed into Boer hands. The Warden line had left many Basotho settlements on the Free State side of the border, and the changes made after the first Free State–Lesotho war did not fundamentally change this situation. The Boers could not tolerate Basotho living in their Republic except as servants on white farms, and as the demand for land became more acute they became increasingly impatient of the continued presence of Basotho villages on their side of the border. Moshoeshoe did not see why the arangement of frontiers should affect the right of those of his own people who were left on the Free State side to continue to live on their land. He had no room to accommodate them in his own overcrowded kingdom and he feared the effects on public opinion of supporting their expulsion. In 1865 the second Free State–Lesotho war broke out.

Jan Hendrik Brand, the new President of the Free State, was both able and forceful. He took advantage of the gunpowder clause in the Bloemfontein Convention. Moshoeshoe on the other hand was very old, he could no

J.H. Brand, President of the Free State

longer keep a firm hold on affairs, and his sons were divided against one another over the question of the succession. The Free State forces were able to overrun most of the fertile areas of the country, and although they failed to capture Thaba Bosiu they were able to reduce the Basotho people to starvation. Moshoeshoe, faced with this state of affairs, decided to buy time, and in April 1866 signed the Treaty of Thaba Bosiu in which he ceded almost all the cultivable area of his kingdom to the Free State. It was only a ruse to enable his people to replenish their food supplies, and as soon as the commandos withdrew the Basotho reoccupied their land and began planting their crops.

British annexation of Lesotho

In the meantime the plight of the Basotho began to attract closer attention from the British government. It was clear that if the terms of the treaty were fulfilled Lesotho would break up. The Free State on the other hand lacked the means to replace the government it was about to destroy. Instead of a relatively peaceful and stable African kingdom there would be chaos which would undoubtedly affect the eastern frontier area, throwing it into turmoil again. Governor Woodhouse, who succeeded Grey in 1862, urged the British government to respond to the repeated requests of Moshoeshoe and annex Lesotho. Pressure in the same direction was exercised by philanthropic opinion, which was further inflamed by the fact that the Boers had expelled the French missionaries from their stations in Lesotho.

The Boers soon realized that the Treaty of Thaba Bosiu was no more than a trick. The first farmers who went to take up land allocated to them in the area ceded under the treaty were immediately murdered by the Basotho. The war then started again, and again the Basotho were reduced to starvation, but Moshoeshoe continued to hold out on his mountain top, addressing ever-more pressing requests for annexation to the Governor. Woodhouse secretly urged him to hold on at all costs till he could get the necessary permission. At last, after Natal had shown an interest in taking over Lesotho, Woodhouse received permission to annex the area provided

Lesotho, showing the territorial effect of repeated attempts to annex the territory

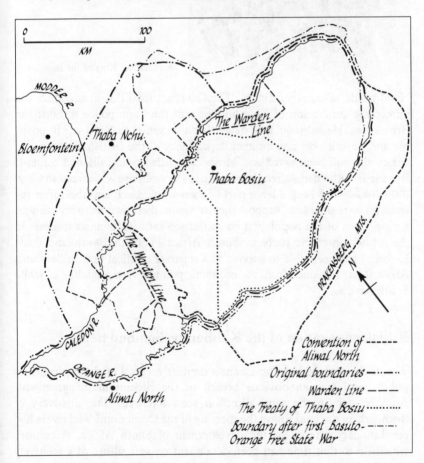

Moshoeshoe, King of the Basotho

Natal would take responsibility. The Governor used this to announce the immediate annexation of Lesotho and sent the Cape police to hoist the British flag. He subsequently stated that annexation to Natal was impossible and Lesotho became a direct dependency of the British crown.

Lesotho had been saved and Moshoeshoe died peacefully and content. But the Basotho had suffered grave losses. Woodhouse was forced to allow the Free State to keep a large part of their fertile land, and thereafter the Basotho were unable to support themselves on their own territory without a proportion of the population going out too earn its living as workers in the white-controlled parts of South Africa. Though Basutoland (now Lesotho) has been able to survive as a separate political unit in Southern Africa it has remained from the economic point of view a satellite of white South Africa.

British annexation of the Kimberley diamond fields

The annexation of Lesotho meant a definite reversal of the Conventions policy, and was an obvious breach of the Bloemfontein agreement. Another step in the same direction soon followed. The discovery of diamonds in the land round the meeting of the Orange and Vaal rivers had revolutionary effects for the development of South Africa. A country which up to that time had been dependent on agriculture of a relatively unprofitable type was suddenly discovered to possess fabulous mineral wealth. Railways would soon be laid across the vast expanse that had previously known only the groaning ox-waggon, and South Africa would be launched on the first step towards becoming the industrial country it is today. Soon after diamonds were first discovered in 1858, near where the Vaal and Harts rivers meet, the rush began and hordes of enthusiastic diggers of many different nationalities arrived in the diamond fields.

Parts of the area in which diamonds were found was claimed by the Orange Free State, and part by the Transvaal. These claims would probably have been accepted by the British government if a lawyer named David Arnot had not seen the possibilities of making a claim to the area in the name of the Griqua chief Waterboer. He managed to get himself appointed by the chief as his agent and then advanced claims in his name, strongly supported by the diggers themselves who rejected the authority of the Republics.

The diamond-yielding areas of South Africa. The political problems described in the text resulting from the bordering of three separate territories on the diamond area are clearly seen

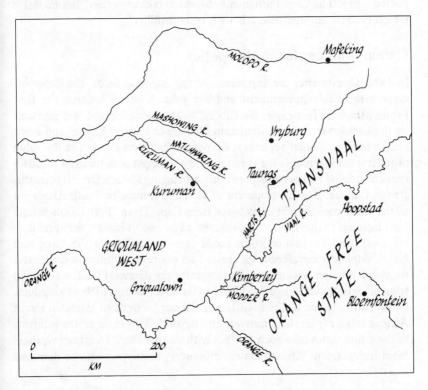

By this time the British government had begun to feel that the only answer to South Africa's problems was a federation along the lines laid down by Grey, in which the Cape would be the senior partner. It was felt that this should be achieved at Cape expense, however, and for this purpose it would be desirable to give the Colony a responsible government. On the other hand if the two Republics became too rich and powerful they might not wish to join a British federation. At the same time philanthropic groups urged British annexation of the diamond fields to save the Griquas from Boer slavery. At the diamond fields the situation became increasingly chaotic, with a turbulent population living under no recognized government. A sailor named Matthew Parker hoisted a flag and declared an independent Diggers' Republic.

The Governor at the Cape, Sir Henry Barkly, was given authority to annex the lands belonging to Waterboer if the Cape Parliament agreed to take them over, but the Cape Parliament did not give a firm assurance and the Governor was anxious to act before the situation became still more difficult. In 1871 he hoisted the British flag. This action was bitterly resented by the Republics, and public opinion in the Cape largely supported them. The Cape Parliament refused to take over the diamond fields which became another direct British responsibility.

Carnarvon's confederation policy

In 1872, shortly after the annexation of the diamond fields, the Cape was given responsible government and Sir John Molteno became the first Prime Minister. In Britain the Liberal government fell and was replaced by the Conservatives with Benjamin Disraeli as Prime Minister and Lord Carnarvon as Colonial Secretary. Carnarvon had a great belief in the value of federal arrangements for creating unity amongst communities of different culture; he had been responsible for bringing about a federal constitution in Canada. The development of diamond mining in South Africa led to the rapid construction of railways from Cape Town, Port Elizabeth and East London to the interior. It also created an export market for agricultural goods and stimulated commercial farming mainly in the Cape and Natal. All these developments created an enormously increased demand for cheap African labour. African labour for the diamond fields was drawn from all over South Africa, and from as far afield as the Ndebele kingdom. Natal similarly, in addition to Indian labour, sought to attract migrant African labour from the Transvaal and beyond. This brought the interests of the white states into open conflict with one another. To attract workers from independent African states, moreover, employers on the diamond fields had to tempt them with the opportunity of buying guns. As African states began to rearm themselves in this way whites became increasingly afraid of the possibility of a general African rising against white authority. The answer to these problems seemed to lie in uniting the white states into a single state and extending its control over the remaining African areas so that Africans could be disarmed and forced by taxation to offer their labour to white employers. Carnarvon believed the way to achieve this was by persuading the white states in South Africa to join together in a federation, and determined to take an active hand in bringing it about. By bringing the Boer states into a federation within the British empire, moreover, Carnarvon hoped to remove any possible threat to the British control of the Cape and to strengthen its security as a bastion of the empire. Another reason for moving in this direction was the feeling that the Free State might have been badly treated over the diamond fields, and federation would be a way for Britain to get rid of its unwanted responsibility for the diamond area.

Carnarvon wanted to go smoothly and therefore wished to be sure of the votes of as many of the white states as possible. He therefore sent Wolseley to try to persuade the settlers in Natal to agree to an increase in the proportion of nominated officials in their legislative council, so that the British government would be in full control. At the same time he sent round a letter to the heads of governments in South Africa suggesting a conference to discuss federation. Finally he sent his friend J.A. Froude, the historian, to South Africa to use his influence in the cause of the scheme.

Carnarvon's plan met with strong opposition from Molteno, the Cape Prime Minister. He saw it as interference in the affairs of a self-governing state. He did not want to share the revenues of the Cape with the poorer Republics at a time when these revenues were already heavily committed to a programme of railway building, and he was afraid that federation might upset the balance of parties at the Cape and bring about the fall of his government. Froude, however, began a public agitation in favour of federation which almost forced Molteno to change his mind. The Orange Free State was not unwilling to consider the matter. In the Transvaal, Pretorius had been deposed for his failure to get better terms from the British over the diamond fields and the more liberal and cosmopolitan T.F. Burgers had been elected President. He was away in Europe trying to raise money for a railway line to be built from Delagoa Bay to the Transvaal but his deputy indicated willingness to consider the proposal. At the crucial moment, however, Carnarvon wrote to suggest shifting the conference to London, and this gave Molteno an excuse for not taking part. As Burgers was also absent and Brand refused to discuss confederation, the London conference was a fiasco.

British annexation of the Transvaal, 1877

Faced with this check Carnarvon looked round for some means of hastening the federation on which he had set his heart, and an opportunity seemed to arise in the Transvaal. In the north-east of the Republic the Leoulu Mountains offered something like the defensive possibilities of the Lesotho mountains, and there the Pedi under Sekhukhuni had built up a paramountcy similar to that of Moshoeshoe. Inevitably, the Pedi and the Boers came into conflict. But the Pedi defended themselves bravely in their mountain strongholds. Horse sickness killed many of the Boer horses. President Burgers was unpopular for his religious views, which were considered too liberal by many settlers. Suddenly the Boers broke up their camp and went home, leaving Sekhukhuni victorious.

The position of the Transvaal Republic was then desperate. The railway scheme had failed and the state was heavily in debt to Cape banks, which refused further credit. There was a danger that the Zulu would take advantage of the situation to invade the Republic. Carnarvon thought that if he could annex the Transvaal it would be easy to bring about federation, as all the white states except the Orange Free State would then be British. He sent an emissary, Shepstone, to see whether the Volksraad could be persuaded to agree. It did not, but several members confessed privately that it was the only way out of a desperate situation, and Shepstone hoisted the British flag in spite of all protests. Carnarvon then felt sure that his plans were bound to succeed and sent Sir Bartle Frere to South Africa as Governor and High Commissioner to achieve the federation.

But instead of federation coming nearer it seemed to become more difficult. The Free State refused to consider it until the Boers of the Transvaal had a representative assembly and were allowed to express their opinions on the annexation. Molteno in the Cape adopted a similar attitude and in the Transvaal the new British government became increasingly unpopular. At first the intention had been to allow the Boers to have a representative council, but Shepstone delayed creating it for fear it might refuse to ratify the annexation. The longer he delayed, the more hostile the Boers became and the greater the volume of protests. Hence the introduction of representative government continued to be postponed. What is more, though the government was generous at first, the British Treasury insisted that the Transvaal must pay for itself, and this meant collecting fairly heavy taxation from a people who were notorious for refusing to pay taxes even to their own government.

In 1878 Sir Bartle Frere seized an opportunity to get rid of one of the main obstacles to federation. In 1877 another war had broken out on the eastern frontier and Molteno asked for the aid of imperial troops. But he refused to allow the Governor to take part in directing the campaign and Frere, aware that the Prime Minister was growing unpopular, dismissed him. A new government at the Cape, under Sir Gordon Sprigg, was favourable to federation, but the problem of the Orange Free State remained. It would never agree to federation until the Transvaalers were given the right to speak their mind, but to allow the Transvaalers to hold a representative assembly while the government was so unpopular would be dangerous.

The 'War of the Guns'

Frere saw the unification of the white states and the extension of their authority over their African neighbours as two inseparable parts of a single policy. After the frontier war of 1877–8 he encouraged Sprigg to extend the Cape's rule over the chiefdoms of the Transkei that were still independent and to disarm those African peoples who were under the Cape's authority. These policies of the Cape soon met a serious setback. A law was passed requiring all guns to be surrendered. This applied also to the Basotho, since administration of Lesotho had been handed over to the Cape in 1871. The measure was bitterly resented by the Basotho, who saw no reason why they should be punished by the confiscation of their weapons and who knew only too well how their military strength had prevented the seizure of their lands in the past. But Sprigg insisted, in spite of the advice of the administrative officers and missionaries in Lesotho and petitions from the chiefs. The result was the outbreak of the 'War of the Guns' in 1880. This prolonged struggle was fought entirely by the Cape forces and ended in victory for the Basotho, for not only did the Cape fail to break their resistance but also had to agree to a settlement under which the Basotho kept their guns. Moreover the government of the Colony relinquished the administration of the kingdom to the imperial authorities. Henceforth it was to remain a separate entity from the rest of South Africa, and on 4 October 1966 became the independent state of Lesotho.

The Zulu war

As his plans for confederation of the white states remained deadlocked,

Frere became convinced that the way to precipitate it lay in the rapid extension of British authority over the African peoples of South Africa. In addition to encouraging the Cape to follow this path, he prepared to use imperial forces to conquer the most powerful of the remaining independent African kingdoms, that of the Zulu.

The Transvaalers had long advanced claims to a strip of land known as the Blood River Territory, which was claimed by the Zulu also. Frere realized that if the Zulu were defeated the Transvaalers could be given the land and could be expected to become more favourably disposed towards federation. The Cape Province too, would be more willing to accept federation if the burden of defending Natal was lightened. Frere therefore came to see the Zulu kingdom as the key to the South African situation and prepared to bring matters to a head. He set up a commission to look into rival claims to the Blood river lands, confident that it would decide in favour of the Boers and that the Zulu king, Cetewayo, would fight rather than give up his territory. Troops were sent to Natal in preparation for the coming struggle. The commission, however, found in favour of the Zulu and declared the Transvaal claims to be valueless.

This left Frere in an awkward situation and he determined to precipitate war with the Zulu by any means. He took advantage of a violation of Natal territory, by warriors pursuing a runaway wife of the king, to send an

Cetewayo, King of the Zulu

ultimatum demanding the break up of the military system on which the Zulu state was based. In 1879 the British troops marched into Zululand for what was expected to be a short and decisive campaign. But almost incredible thoughtlessness and mismanagement led a whole regiment to be trapped by the Zulu at Isandhlwana, with their ammunition in boxes that could not be opened. The Zulu army was able to follow its traditional tactics with success and the regiment was almost completely destroyed. The news of this military disaster produced a great swing of opinion in Britain. Frere was censured for his Zulu policy but not recalled. Instead a lieutenant-governor was sent to Natal who proved incapable of co-operating with Frere. The Zulu war was continued and at the Battle of Ulundi the Zulu armies were finally defeated. Cetewayo was taken a prisoner to Cape Town but British policy in South Africa had lost its momentum. Instead of annexing Zululand the government tried to keep it militarily weak by setting up 13 chieftaincies in place of the old kingdom. In spite of the setback to his leadership Frere made a last attempt to get the confederation policy moving. Sprigg was persuaded to introduce a motion supporting it to the Cape Parliament. Paul Kruger from the Transvaal, however, met Dutch-speaking members of the Cape Assembly and persuaded them to oppose the motion. As a result it had to be withdrawn without a vote.

The first Anglo–Boer war, 1880–1

Noticing the weakening in British policy the Boers of the Transvaal redoubled their protests and even held open-air meetings condemning the annexation of their territory. In Britain an election campaign was under way and Gladstone then in opposition condemned the annexation and the suppression of Boer freedom. The Transvaal was tense with expectation but later, when he came to form his own government, Gladstone discovered the difficulties of the problem. Queen Victoria was strongly opposed to surrendering British territory and the philanthropist wing of his party disliked the idea of leaving the Transvaal blacks at the mercy of the Boers. Gladstone decided to hold on, but the Boers were no longer prepared to wait. They rose in rebellion, besieged the British garrison in Pretoria and routed a relief column at Bronkhorstspruit. Troops were rushed up from Natal but they met a severe check at Laing's Nek. Shaken in his resolution Gladstone decided to negotiate, but before any settlement was reached the final battle was fought at Majuba (1881). The British forces were decisively defeated and the commander killed. Gladstone was then prepared to make peace on any terms less than complete surrender.

The area which the first Boer and Zulu wars were fought over, showing the positions of the major battles. Battles in the Zulu war are underlined

The Pretoria Convention, 1881

By the Pretoria Convention the Transvaal was given self-government under British suzerainty (paramountcy). Foreign policy was to remain under British control and there was to be a British Resident in Pretoria with the right to exercise authority in regard to native policy. In practice the Transvaal had won the war and regained independence in all matters except relations with other European powers. The attempt to produce a British federation in South Africa had ended in failure and a policy of withdrawal which was similar to that of the Sand River and Bloemfontein Conventions.

11 The consolidation of white rule in Southern Africa

The mineral revolution and the scramble for territory

Soon after the rebellion of the Transvaal farmers and the re-establishment of virtual independence for the Transvaal Republic, the history of Southern Africa began to undergo important changes.

The discovery of diamonds had already begun to turn Southern Africa from a poor farming country into a relatively rich industrial one. Within five years of the Pretoria Convention, gold was discovered on the Witwatersrand and the whole economic position of the Transvaal and South Africa was transformed. The old quest for new farming land for white farmers continued but was now linked with the search for minerals, the financial resources of mighty capitalist organizations and international competition for territory in Africa. The racial attitudes of the old farming society were transferred to the new world of mines and industry, the battleground gradually shifting from the country to the towns. The process by which Africans had been brought under white rule was greatly speeded up and extended out of South Africa into modern Zimbabwe, Zambia and Malawi. The Portuguese, after centuries spent holding a few isolated ports, suddenly woke up and established their authority over the vast areas of modern Mozambique. The Germans arrived in Namibia. The struggle between the Boer desire for complete independence in their Republics and the British determination to maintain their paramount position in South Africa led to a major war which was to solve little and leave the deepest problems of South Africa untouched. However, it did prepare for the political unification of the country. By the end of the first decade of the twentieth century, white rule had consolidated itself in Southern Africa.

Immediately following British withdrawal from the Transvaal, the Republic began to expand vigorously. White farmers and adventurers took advantage of disputes between chiefs to grab land and cattle. They supported one side and claimed huge areas in return and in 1882 they were able to set up two small republics on the western border of the Transvaal, Stellaland and Goshen, with the passive support of the Transvaal authorities. The British government was supposed to have overriding authority on questions of native policy in the Transvaal but the British Resident was treated with contempt and would do nothing to prevent the activities of the white adventurers. Similarly, a group of whites helped Dinuzulu defeat contenders for the Zulu throne in return for which he was forced to surrender nearly half the remaining area of Zululand to the east of the Transvaal. A republic, the New Republic, was set up here in 1884.

This affected British interests: Stellaland and Goshen cut across the road to the interior that had been opened by the missionaries, Moffat and Livingstone, thus threatening British traders' access to the far interior. Britain first tried negotiating and in 1883 in London the British agreed to abandon the power of veto on native policy, to reduce the British Resident to Consul and to drop the word 'suzerainty' from the new convention. In return the borders of the new republics were altered so as to leave the road to the north outside them. The British retained control of the Transvaal's foreign policy and the Republic was not to make treaties with any state except the Orange Free State or with any chiefdoms to the east or west without British approval. This 'London Convention' was ratified by the Transvaal Volksraad in 1884.

As long as Britain did nothing to occupy areas supposedly outside the Transvaal, the possibility of their eventually joining that state would still remain. Moreover, a new danger threatened British interests from 1883 when the German flag was hoisted at Angra Pequena Bay in Namibia and the following year Britain was forced to recognize a German protectorate over the territory. It seemed Gemany might try to link this new possession with the Transvaal thus severing the Cape from the interior and threatening the security of the Cape itself. To prevent this, a British expedition under Charles Warren annexed Stellaland and Goshen as British Bechuanaland, and a protectorate was declared over the lands of the chiefs Sechele and Khama and their area became the Bechuanaland Protectorate in 1884.

The eastward expansion of the Transvaal also seemed a danger. The Boers might gain control of a possible port at St Lucia Bay in Zululand and thus make contact with a foreign power, a fear heightened by the fact that the area round the bay was acquired from Dinuzulu on behalf of the Transvaal by a German agent. As a precaution Britain annexed the area by virtue of an old treaty made with the Zulu king, Mpande. The leaders of the New Republic were forced to renounce their authority over the Zulu kingdom and the boundaries of their state were redrawn to keep them well back from the coast. In return Britain recognized the New Republic which later became part of the Transvaal. In 1887 the remains of Zululand were annexed and placed under the Governor of Natal. In 1884 the Cape annexed the lands of the Gcaleka, the Xhosa and the Thembu. In 1886 a show of force ensured the annexation of the Xesibe lands. The Mpondo were still left with internal independence but their coastal area was declared a British Protectorate. (They were finally annexed by the Cape in 1894.)

Thus in the years after the British withdrawal from the Transvaal, European authority over the African peoples of Southern Africa was enormously extended. The Germans established claims to the vast area of South-West Africa (now Namibia). Britain took British Bechuanaland and the huge Bechuanaland Protectorate thus driving a wedge of British territory between the Germans and the Transvaal as far north as the Zambezi river. On the east coast the Zulu kingdom and all the peoples between Natal and the Cape with the exception of the Mpondo were brought under European rule. The only substantial area in South Africa in which African chiefs still ruled in independence was the Swazi kingdom and a short stretch of coast occupied by the Thonga people between Zululand and the borders of Mozambique.

The rise of Cecil Rhodes

Cecil Rhodes was destined to play a major part in the history of Southern Africa. Born in England, the son of a parson, he came to South Africa for health reasons settling first with an elder brother on a farm in Natal and then, as the rush on the diamond fields began, trekking to Griqualand West to seize advantage of the new opportunities.

At first each diamond prospector was allowed to dig in a square patch of ground but as they tunnelled deeper the area became a vast honeycomb. Everyone wanted to dig as much of his claim as possible so the walls between the shafts were very thin and it became increasingly difficult to manoeuvre wheelbarrows laden with diamond-rich soil along them. Earth at the side of the diggings began caving in, often burying miners alive. When the shafts became very deep, water began to seep in and it was difficult and expensive to remove it. Costs thus grew greater and greater. As the mines poured huge volumes of diamonds onto the international diamond market prices slumped and profits consequently dropped. Rhodes realized that if an individual could obtain several patches alongside each other and work this area as a single unit the mining would be more efficient and therefore more profitable. He began buying the claims of bankrupt and disillusioned miners and he was soon making a great deal of money and pressing on with his policy of buying more claims and forming larger units. While studying for a degree at Oxford, he continued his financial business through agents, travelling out to South Africa during each long vacation. As his holdings grew he came to see that to control prices and maintain profits the amalgamation of the entire diamond fields was essential. He had a powerful rival in Barney Barnato, a Jew from London. By 1889 these two men virtually controlled the diamond fields and it remained to be seen which one would absorb the other. Although Barnato held the richer areas, Rhodes, through his friend and business associate, Alfred Beit, obtained powerful capitalist backing from Lord Rothschild. With this support Rhodes was able to force Barnato to amalgamate the two enterprises into one vast company, called De Beers Consolidated. Barnato remained immensely rich and was one of the directors of the new company but the greatest power in the organization was in Rhodes's hands. By 1891 the company controlled most of the remaining mines in South Africa and thus dominated the largest source of diamonds in the world. By this time Rhodes had also acquired a substantial share of the Rand goldfields for his Goldfields of South Africa Company.

Rhodes was never interested in making money merely for its own sake. Money meant power, power to fulfil his own fantastic dreams. He believed fervently in the destiny of the British and other racially related people such

Cecil Rhodes (in the centre of the front row) with officials of De Beers Consolidated Mines. Barney Barnato is sitting to the right of Rhodes

as the Dutch and Germans to dominate the world in the interest of mankind. He envisioned the extension of the British empire throughout Africa, a vast block of British territory linked together by a transcontinental railway and telegraph running from the Cape to Cairo. This block would form part of an imperial federation economically united by a customs union. Britain would ally with the United States and Germany to dominate the world and ensure peace and prosperity. But Rhodes had little confidence in the ability or willingness of the British government to fulfil his dreams.

During his years in South Africa, he had absorbed the attitudes of the white settlers, British and Boer, together with their contempt for Whitehall. Rhodes therefore believed that the extension of British rule throughout Africa should be undertaken from the Cape with assistance of British capital but without direct interference from the British government. The two white South African peoples should be brought together to partake in the venture. His attitude towards the Africans was thoroughly paternalistic. Though at times he mentioned equality, he fundamentally saw Africans as destined to be under white rule for their own good. They would supply the physical labour in combination with European brains and capital. Rhodes considered himself as the central figure in this grand scheme since he alone could provide the leadership and drive to bring about the new world order.

Naturally, the road north must remain open and Rhodes played an active part in the agitation which eventually led to the annexation of British Bechuanaland. And in the constitution for De Beers Consolidated he ensured that a clause was included allowing profits to be used for purposes other than diamond mining. Thus he obtained the essential financial basis for his schemes.

The Transvaal and President Kruger

In 1886 gold was discovered by settlers in the Witwatersrand in the Transvaal and the whole economic and political situation in South Africa was transformed. Until that time a poor farming republic, it had been economically dependent on the Cape and it seemed that the Transvaal might eventually be absorbed by her rich southern neighbour, together with the Orange Free State. It was so poverty-stricken that in 1885 it had been forced to ask the Cape to agree to a customs union but the Cape was too selfish to agree and in the following year the chance had gone, gold deposits had been found and the gold rush was on.

Suddenly, the Transvaal became the richest state in South Africa and soon the other states became dependent on the profits from the supply of goods to their wealthy neighbour. It now looked as if the Transvaal would be in a position to absorb the other white states. Certainly, it had the means to maintain its independence and frustrate Rhodes's ambitions.

The Transvaal was led by President Kruger, a Boer with the characteristic Boer spirit of independence. Though he had little formal education, he was an astute, capable politician with a fierce determination to be rid of British rule. His experiences of British policy up to the Pretoria Convention had given him a deep suspicion of British hypocrisy and deception. He wanted an independent sovereign state with the right to make treaties

Paul Kruger, President of the Transvaal

with foreign powers without interference from Britain.

The British government did not share Rhodes's ideas of a British Africa and continued to regard the acquisition of territory in the continent as an unjustified expense. But powerful factions supported Rhodes, and the government still regarded the possession of the Cape as essential for the protection of the route to India in spite of the rapid increase in traffic via the Suez Canal. Now, alarmed at the Transvaal's wealth and aware of Kruger's determination to escape from British control, the British saw their strategic position in the area threatened and this led to an alliance with Rhodes against Kruger.

Rhodes now prepared for his grand scheme of expansion northward. While he set about consolidating his base in the Cape by attempting to bring about an alliance between the British and the Boers, he sent his agents into the areas of modern Zimbabwe and Zambia to secure treaties to provide a legal justification for his intended occupation of the area. Finally, he sought British government approval for the formation of a chartered company which would undertake the occupation and administer the new areas.

Meanwhile, in South Africa, the successful uprising by the Transvaal farmers against the British government had roused very strong nationalist feelings amongst the Boers. A Boer nationalist organization, the Afrikaner Bond, had been formed dedicated to encourage the use of the Afrikaans language and to protect the interest of the Boer farmers. The society spread rapidly after the rebellion but it died down again in the two Boer Republics, maintaining its strength in the Cape only. Soon the character of the society changed since Afrikaans-speaking whites in the Cape were long accustomed to being part of the British empire. The organization's new leader, 'Onze Jan' Hofmeyr, believed, like Rhodes, in co-operation between the white peoples and a firm alliance grew between the two men which finally resulted in Rhodes becoming Premier of the Cape with the support of the Afrikaner Bond in 1890. Rhodes consolidated his hold over the white electorate by introducing measures to restrict the numbers of African voters.

Rhodes and the conquest of Central Africa

The kingdom of the Ndebele held a key position north of the Zambezi river. Under their first king, Mzilikazi, they had built up a Zulu-type state with a society organized on military lines. Each able-bodied man was a member of one of the various regiments accommodated in a series of military towns.

Even before Mzilikazi died white infiltration had begun. The king had established a close friendship with the white missionary, Robert Moffat, and even after the Ndebele had been driven out of the Transvaal in 1837 Mzilikazi retained his feeling for his white friend. Moffat persuaded him to allow white men into his country so that his capital was crowded with white hunters even before his death in 1868.

The heir to the throne was believed to have been killed on his father's orders but others said that he was still alive somewhere in South Africa. This gave Sir Theophilus Shepstone, an officer of the Natal government, an opportunity to establish his influence over the Ndebele kingdom. He let it be known that one of his servants was Nkulumane, the missing heir, and tried to ensure that he would be chosen as king. The majority, however, were not convinced and supported Lobengula, a rival contender. After a minor civil war, the latter was secure in his position.

But the end of the succession dispute did not end white interference in the area. Europeans clamoured for a written treaty. Lobengula's position was difficult. Aware that his people could not defeat the whites in battle, he needed to re-equip his army with new weapons but this would take time and he had therefore to be careful not to offend the whites too deeply. On the other hand, he knew the whites would take advantage of his ignorance of writing to get him to agree to documents that he did not really understand. He described the position as like a chameleon creeping nearer and nearer the fly: 'He darts his tongue and the fly disappears; England is the chameleon and I am the fly.'

The first treaty to which Lobengula agreed, with the Transvaal, was arranged by Peter Grobler and gave special rights to Transvaal citizens in the Ndebele kingdom. Grobler was appointed consul for the citizens. Britain immediately took counter action and Robert Moffat's son, John Smith Moffat obtained a treaty forbidding the giving away of territory without permission from the British High Commissioner in South Africa. Then Rhodes's three agents, Charles Rudd, Rochfort Maguire and Francis 'Matabele' Thompson, persuaded Lobengula to sign the 'Rudd Concession' which gave Rhodes exclusive prospecting rights in the area. In return, the king was given rifles and ammunition and promised an annual subsidy and a steamboat for use on the Zambezi river.

Soon Lobengula regretted signing this last treaty and sought assurance that Rhodes had the right to dig only for minerals. He even sent envoys to Britain for assurance. His suspicion was justified for Rhodes interpreted his rights to mean that he could occupy the Shona parts of Zimbabwe. He formed a company, the British South Africa Company, to occupy Mashonaland and persuaded the British government to give him a charter giving the company administrative powers in the area.

Lobengula, King of the Ndebele

Rhodes hastened to extend his influence further by encouraging his agents to sign treaties with chiefs far into the interior. He found an able ally in Harry Johnston, another believer in a grand British Africa. Johnston, British Consul in Mozambique, was particularly interested in modern Malawi. This area had been thrown into a state of confusion by the activities of Arab, Yao and Portuguese traders. Small Makololo kingdoms succeeded in holding the Portuguese back from the south of the region. Dr Livingstone's example had attracted many missionaries and this angered the Arab traders who knew that they were determined to end the slave

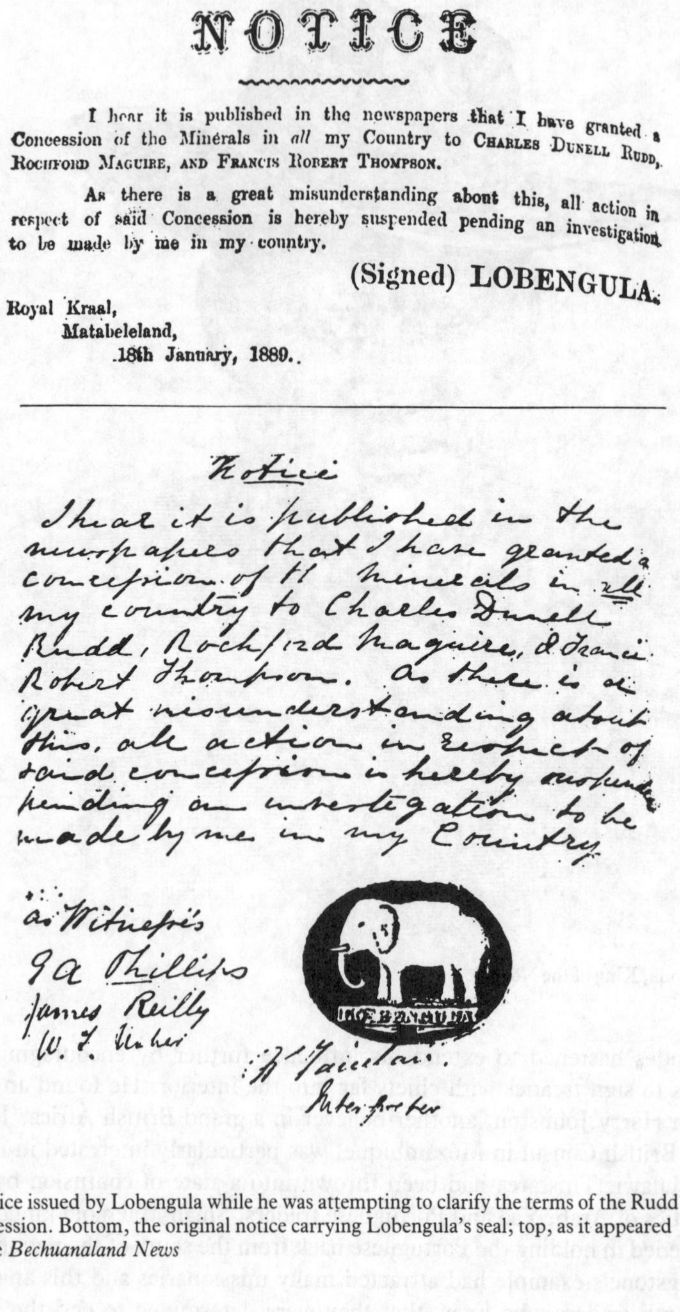

NOTICE

I hear it is published in the newspapers that I have granted a
Concession of the Minerals in *all* my Country to CHARLES DUNELL RUDD,
ROCHFORD MAGUIRE, AND FRANCIS ROBERT THOMPSON.

As there is a great misunderstanding about this, all action in
respect of said Concession is hereby suspended pending an investigation
to be made by me in my country.

(Signed) LOBENGULA.

Royal Kraal,
　　Matabeleland,
　　　18th January, 1889.

Notice

*I hear it is published in the
newspapers that I have granted a
concession of the minerals in all
my country to Charles Dunell
Rudd, Rochford Maguire, & Francis
Robert Thompson. As there is a
great misunderstanding about
this, all action in respect of
said concession is hereby suspended
pending an investigation to be
made by me in my Country*

*as Witness's
G A Phillips
James Reilly
W. F. Usher*

*R Fairbairn.
Interpreter*

A notice issued by Lobengula while he was attempting to clarify the terms of the Rudd
Concession. Bottom, the original notice carrying Lobengula's seal; top, as it appeared
in the *Bechuanaland News*

trade. To help the missions, the African Lakes Company was formed but its resources were too small to be of effective assistance. The Portuguese now realized that they must act quickly to protect their claims in Africa. They planned to seize a wide corridor linking Angola to Mozambique and prepared an expedition to acquire rights in the south of modern Malawi and Zambia. Rhodes retaliated by giving Johnston money and assistance to make treaties with the chiefs in these areas.

Whatever their real worth, these pieces of paper were used to establish the British South Africa Company's rights to Zambia. However, Rhodes's agents were beaten by King Leopold of the Congo in the race to make treaties with the rulers of the Shaba area. Thus the copperbelt was split between two colonial powers.

Rhodes's and Johnston's plans were almost frustrated by the Portuguese when Serpa Pinto began to force his way through the resistance of the Makololo but the British government intervened and the Portuguese plans were abandoned. The area of the modern Malawi came directly under the British government. Rhodes paid Johnston £10 000 annually to establish British rule there and to act as administrator on behalf of the British South Africa Company in Zambia.

Rhodes's quest for official backing in London for his policies faced many difficulties. He wanted the extension of British territory to be undertaken by colonists like himself with minimum interference from Whitehall. London's distrust was increased by Rhodes's association with the Afrikaner Bond and his far-reaching schemes were the dread of more conventional spirits who feared the responsibility and expense. People like the missionaries strongly supported the view that newly acquired areas should be administered from Whitehall in the interests of the indigenous peoples. But in spite of all this opposition, Rhodes had his way with the backing of powerful financial interests.

Rhodes argued that gold in Mashonaland was richer than that of the Transvaal and that a rich, dominant northern region would reverse the economic and political situation brought about by the rise of the Transvaal. The latter could be absorbed into the vastly expanded British sphere without the British government having to pay for it. Rhodes was finally granted a Royal Charter for the British South Africa Company in October 1889. In return, Whitehall insisted on putting powerful, independently minded men on to the Board to watch Rhodes's activities, though Rhodes retained his right to act as sole authority for his company in South Africa. Thus, for all practical purposes he had an almost completely free hand.

Back in South Africa Rhodes prepared his pioneer column to occupy Mashonaland. The majority of recruits were English-speaking but a deliberate effort was made to include Afrikaners. Volunteers were attracted by the promise of prospecting rights and farming land though the Rudd Concession did not give Rhodes's company the right to make such offers. The column set out to the north at the end of June 1890 carrying with it the traditional South African idea of farming with large areas of land worked by labourers and all the prejudices this system produced.

Deeply concerned, Lobengula sent a message to the British High Commissioner at the Cape denying Rhodes's right to enter his kingdom in force but the High Commissioner would do nothing. By September the Union Jack was hoisted at Fort Salisbury (now Harare) and Mashonaland was declared occupied in the name of Queen Victoria.

Rhodes was now a man of gigantic stature: master of the largest diamond mining complex in the world; controller of an important gold mining company in Johannesburg; Premier of the Cape, the largest if not the richest white state; head of the British South Africa Company and therefore the uncrowned king of the newly acquired territories.

Transvaal–British conflict over Swaziland

Meanwhile, in the Transvaal Kruger was seeking to preserve and strengthen the state's independence and the Transvaalers, like the British and Boer settlers at the Cape, saw modern Zimbabwe as a possible area for expansion. The Grobler treaty had been the first step in this direction. But Transvaal's main interest was expansion eastward in the independent Swazi kingdom and a strip of coastline occupied by the Thonga. This strip contained a possible port at Kosi Bay. Swaziland was organized on similar lines to the Zulu and Ndebele kingdoms but was not so highly militarized. Having witnessed the defeat of powerful African peoples by the whites, the Swazi were determined not to be drawn into any quarrel with Europeans. Moreover, Shepstone, the Natal officer responsible for relations with the chiefdoms, had protected them from the Zulu on several occasions. Thus white settlers in the kingdom were well-received. These settlers were of two kinds; Boer farmers in search of new winter grazing land and a host of concession hunters, mainly British, looking for mining rights and other commercial privileges. These two groups naturally opposed each other since prospectors wanted mining rights on land sought for farming by the Boers. The Swazis found this situation very difficult to deal with since the whites despised the tribunals of the chiefs and ignored Swazi custom. The king summoned Shepstone's son to help control the affairs of the European population but the scramble continued. The king was bribed or tricked into signing more and more pieces of paper until he had given away all his land and resources more than once over. Kruger was anxious to take advantage of the situation to win his access to the sea and was even prepared to threaten intervention in the Ndebele kingdom as a bargaining counter with Rhodes. But his intentions were strongly resented by powerful commercial groups in Britain.

A stalemate was reached which lasted for a number of years. In 1890 and again in 1894, Britain and the Transvaal jointly agreed to respect the independence of the Swazi kingdom but as Transvaal pressure increased Britain agreed that the kingdom could be taken over if the Swazi authorities consented. However, the authorities flatly refused and asked for British protection. This was refused and finally in December 1894 the Transvaal was permitted to take over the region whether the people were willing or not. But Kruger's successful occupation of Swaziland was countered by British occupation of the coastal Thonga area and the Transvaal lost its route to the sea. The offer of a railway strip to Kosi Bay was promised but never granted.

Rhodes tries to seize Mozambique

With the successful occupation of Mashonaland, it seemed Rhodes's dreams would be fulfilled. A new powerful British Southern African state seemed about to be born which could eventually absorb the landlocked Boer states further south. But these hopes were not fulfilled. Linked with the occupation of Mashonaland was the intention to seize territory claimed by the Portuguese and thereby obtain a route to the sea. The Transvaal would then be completely surrounded by British territory.

Although the Portuguese claimed wide areas of land, for hundreds of years they had done little more than occupy a few ports along the coast and the Zambezi river. The greater part of Mozambique south of the Zambezi was dominated by the Gaza empire, ruled at this time by Gungunyana who had established friendly relations with the Ndebele; his daughter had married Lobengula. Denying Portuguese claims to his kingdom, Gungunyana sought British protection but this was refused since it was contrary to British treaties with Portugal.

Rhodes believed that if he could obtain concessions from Gungunyana along the lines of the Rudd Concession, he could exploit the region, occupy Mozambique and then squeeze Portugal out of the rest of the area. In 1891 these plans were set in motion and agents were sent to the Gaza capital. But Portugal's position was beginning to undergo a change since trade with the Transvaal was increasing Mozambique's wealth and Lourenço Marques (now Maputo) was steadily growing from a fever-ridden port into a prosperous settlement. Public opinion in Portugal was waking up to the potential value of the colony and imperialist feeling supported the retention and expansion of Portugal's empire. Governmental authority was re-established along the Zambezi and the independence of Portuguese *prazo* (estate) owners destroyed. Rhodes's activities roused Portuguese imperial feelings further and Whitehall realized that if Portugal was humiliated again her present government might fall to a strongly anti-British regime. Rhodes therefore lost backing from Whitehall. His plans to occupy Mozambique were frustrated and Delagoa Bay, which was the key to much subsequent history, remained in Portuguese hands.

Portugal was now determined to establish effective control of the area but, being one of the weakest and poorest European states, she was racked with bitter divisions at home and it took some time before she could summon up the strength to grapple with Gungunyana and the forces of the Gaza empire. Only in 1895 did the Portuguese feel ready to commence hostilities. Gungunyana had long seen that sooner or later Portugal would try to destroy him and he made repeated efforts to obtain British protection. However, all his overtures were rejected and he was left to his fate. At last, the Portuguese found an opportunity for a quarrel and hostilities began. For some time it seemed they might be defeated after all but in the end the bravery of Gungunyana's people was no match for modern European weapons. Gungunyana was captured and exiled and the fabric of his kingdom systematically destroyed.

Rhodes's failure in Mozambique was less disastrous than another disappointment. Far less gold was found in Mashonaland than Rhodes and his backers had hoped. There was a real danger that the Company would go bankrupt and the settlement would collapse. Rhodes therefore turned his attention to lands occupied by Lobengula and the Ndebele. It was rumoured that a ridge of gold-bearing rock ran through Lobengula's capital, Bulawayo, which could rescue the Company's finances and provide for the building up of a prosperous British colony. And even if the gold did not exist, the area contained some of the best grazing land between the Limpopo and the Zambezi.

The destruction of the Ndebele kingdom

Lobengula did all he could to prevent a quarrel with the whites but his fate was also sealed. A party of Ndebele came near to Salisbury in pursuit of royal cattle stolen by the Shona. Rhodes's Company ordered them to withdraw but, since this retreat was not as swift as was demanded, the Company's patrol opened fire and the Ndebele retaliated. The incident was used as a pretext for war. A large section of the Ndebele army was in quarantine for smallpox and, though Lobengula possessed a considerable quantity of firearms, his people were not yet skilled in their use. The whites had the new and deadly Maxim guns and opposition to them was suicidal. Lobengula fled with a small group of devoted followers to make contact with the Ngoro to the north in modern Zambia. He died of fever on the way.

News of the Company's victory restored the investors' confidence and the price of its shares rose to unprecedented heights. But the longed for gold was not found and it soon became apparent that the new settlement would be more of a liability than an asset for many years. The plan to maintain British paramountcy in Southern Africa by creating a richer British state to the north of the Transvaal had failed and inevitably the struggle between Kruger's desire for Boer independence and the British determination to maintain overall control became sharper.

The struggle for the Transvaal

This struggle had many aspects. Transvaal's new-found wealth gave the Republic the need for a greatly expanded and more efficient means of communication with the outside world. It was to Britain's and Rhodes's advantage if the Transvaal could be linked with the railway systems of the Cape as this would entail drawing her into the British orbit. It was also vital to the British and Boer in the Cape who were increasingly dependent on trade with the Transvaal. Natal shared this dependence and the Orange Free State also had a strong interest in trade with the Transvaal. Both the Cape and Natal were anxious to build railway lines to the Transvaal, and the Orange Free State willingly allowed the line to pass through her territory. However, the Transvaal sought an alternative route to the sea and the Portuguese possession of Delagoa Bay provided the opportunity. Even before the British annexation of the Transvaal in 1887, a railway had been planned to the Bay. This had ended in disastrous failure, but now that the Transvaal was so rich the project could begin again.

Kruger resisted the extension of the lines to the south until the Delagoa Bay line was near completion. Rhodes therefore decided that his railway link to the north to Cairo must go through Bechuanaland instead of the Transvaal. Kruger finally allowed the southern lines in return for a loan to enable the Netherlands Railway Company to complete the track from Delagoa Bay; the company was also to control the track from the Orange Free State border to Johannesburg. The Cape line enjoyed a few years' monopoly but the Delagoa Bay line was soon completed and the link with Natal established also. This placed Kruger's state in a stronger position than ever thus threatening British interests in Southern Africa. It could set the Cape against Natal by favouring one against the other and could blackmail the southern states by threatening to close their lines and send all traffic via Delagoa Bay. Nothing would prevent the Transvaal, with independent access to the sea, from establishing relations with foreign powers like Germany and breaking free from British control over her foreign policy.

But Transvaal's wealth gave her grave internal problems. Capitalists and white mineworkers flocked to Johannesburg. The majority were British but they also came from many other parts of the world and Kruger was determined not to allow them the vote. The new settlers' culture and attitudes were very different from the conservative Transvaal Boers. What is more, these Uitlanders (foreigners), had no permanent stake in the country. It was expected that as soon as the gold ran out they would depart leaving deserted mines behind them. Finally, the Uitlanders' vote might bring British influence back to the state and destroy the independence for which the Boers had fought so hard.

On the other hand many of the Uitlanders were discontented with the situation in the Transvaal; they had little in common with government officials, many of whom could speak no English and they resented the lack of English-medium education for their children. Uitlander agitation would have been of little significance, however, if it had not received the backing of some of the most powerful mining magnates. Gold mining on the Johannesburg gold reef (the Rand) involved many difficulties. The layers of gold-bearing material were tilted at an angle of about 20°. They appeared above ground along the ridge of the reef but sank deeper and

Surface (outcrop) mining in South Africa: the Ferreira Gold Mining Company, 1888

deeper further south. Some gold could be mined near the surface (outcrop mines) but to develop mines with a long-tem future it was necessary to strike the gold-bearing layers at deeper levels to the south of the ridge. Mining at these deep levels, however, involved huge expenditure for the construction and maintenance of shafts and underground galleries. The gold, moreover, occurred in small fragments dispersed through masses of rock so that only a few grams of gold could be extracted from each tonne. All this meant that deep-level mines could only hope to make a profit if costs could be kept to the absolute minimum. Kruger's government, however, gave concessions to individuals and companies to carry out a variety of activities in a manner which raised the costs of mining operations. One of the most important of these concessions was the one given to the Netherlands Railway Company for a rail line to bring coal to Johannesburg. This monopoly allowed them to overcharge the mining companies. Another was the dynamite monopoly given to a company to encourage it to manufacture dynamite in the Transvaal. This made one of the most essential mining materials more expensive than it need have been.

The most important need of the mining companies, however, was for abundant supplies of African labour at very cheap rates. The Transvaal farmers, who dominated the government of the Republic were, however, in competition with the mines for available labour and the Republican authorities were not able to enforce pass laws and anti-drink laws efficiently enough to enable the mines to force Africans to work to the absolute limits of their physical endurance for the very low wages the mines felt they could afford to offer. After 1895, when deep-level mining was proved to be practical, therefore, some of the major mining companies decided that the Transvaal government must be replaced by a more modern system that would be more helpful to capitalist profits. One of these major mining concerns was Rhodes's own group of companies. As it became evident that no vast gold deposits were to be found in the British South Africa Company's lands beyond the Limpopo, the profitability of his Goldfields of South Africa Company became a matter of great concern lest his entire, vast economic empire should collapse. Rhodes thus had direct financial as well as political motives to seek to overthrow Kruger's government. He believed that the Uitlanders could easily overthrow the Boer government and that they should be supported lest they establish a republic of their own as anti-British as the former Boer one. Thus an elaborate conspiracy was hatched, involving Joseph Chamberlain, the imperialist-minded Colonial Secretary, Sir Hercules Robinson, British High Commissioner in South Africa, and Flora Shaw (later Lady Lugard), the imperialist-minded colonial editor of *The Times*. Rhodes's plan was to smuggle arms to the Uitlanders who would rise in revolt on a fixed day with the assistance of a column of the British South Africa Company's forces from Bechuanaland. Robinson would announce the annexation of the Transvaal on a pretext of British duty to maintain peace in the area and *The Times* would justify the action of the British public. The attraction of the plan was that it would provide a means of solving Britain's strategic problems in Southern Africa without the direct aid of the British government.

Rhodes began to concentrate his troops in Bechuanaland on a strip of land that had theoretically been given him to protect the railway against the 'ferocious Bechuana' tribes. But as the date for the revolt drew near the Uitlanders began to weaken. Many of the capitalists did not intend to fight but to use the situation to create rumours of war so that the price of gold shares would fall temporarily on the London Stock Exchange. They would make their fortunes when the prices went up again. Rhodes was sent a telegram suggesting that the revolt be postponed. He realized that his scheme was going to collapse but Dr Jameson, his lieutenant in charge of the column in Bechuanaland, had other ideas. He was even more confident than Rhodes that the Boer government would collapse and his successful war against the Ndebele had given him tremendous confidence. He therefore decided to lead his troops into the Transvaal and force the Uitlanders into action. Rhodes was thunderstruck when he heard the news, for he thought it was an unjustified gamble which would have terrible consequences if Jameson's action failed. However, by the time he had sent a telegram to Jameson telling him to stop, the column was already on its way to the Transvaal, the telegraph wires being cut behind it.

The Uitlanders were horrified when they heard that Jameson was coming to rescue them uninvited. A half-hearted uprising took place and if Jameson had reached Johannesburg the plot might have succeeded but the column lost its way. A Boer guide led them into a perfect trap in a shallow bowl with Boers up in the hills surrounding them where the column's Maxim guns were useless. Jameson was forced to surrender and the rebellion collapsed. This was a bitter blow to Rhodes who had to resign as Premier of the Cape and his friendly alliance with the Afrikaner Bond was succeeded by bitterness and mistrust. There was even a danger that Rhodes would lose his control of the British South Africa Company. Kruger, on the other hand, emerged triumphant and in his hour of victory he acted with extraordinary magnanimity. The captive raiders were handed back to the British for punishment and even the Uitlanders were treated leniently.

But the collapse of the Jameson raid could not alter the basic situation; it merely ensured that the conflict must come into the open and be settled by war. It also emphasized the Transvaal's strength and a wave of sympathy swept through the whole of Southern Africa indicating the possibility that the Cape might join the Transvaal in an anti-British federation.

Even the German Emperor sent a congratulatory telegram to Kruger and a German warship was rumoured to have landed marines at Delagoa Bay. War between Britain and Germany seemed possible until the Kaiser offered his apologies to Queen Victoria.

The Shona and Ndebele risings, 1896–7

The Jameson Raid fiasco provided the opportunity for a massive African uprising in Southern Rhodesia (now Zimbabwe). White farmers had introduced a rigid colour discrimination into the lands between the Limpopo and the Zambezi. No sooner was the settlement in Mashonaland established than the Shona lands began to be confiscated to form cattle ranches for the whites, and chiefs were forced to send their men to the mines and the farms. The arrogance of the invaders shocked the African sense of personal dignity and provoked a rapidly growing resentment. After the conquest of the Ndebele kingdom royal cattle were confiscated and the Ndebele were left with the poorest farming lands. Finally, an epidemic of rinderpest decimated their cattle and naturally even this calamity was associated with the whites.

With most of the Company's forces away on the Jameson Raid, an opportunity was offered for striking back. In March 1896 the Ndebele rose in a massive uprising, called *Chimurenga*. Isolated whites were killed on their farms and the forts were besieged. In June, the Shona also rose and succeeded in killing a substantial number of whites in their area. The rising proved long and costly to suppress for the Africans had learnt not to expose themselves to the Maxim guns. In spite of heavy losses, the Ndebele held out in the Matopo mountains. They were in a desperate condition but the Company was also in difficulties. Its debts were mounting without a hope of being able to pay them let alone give its shareholders a dividend. Another costly campaign would be difficult to mount.

At this point Rhodes took the bold step of going into the mountains to negotiate with the Ndebele and in October he persuaded them to surrender in return for concessions and thereby salvaged his personal reputation in white Southern Africa. The Shona resistance continued for a further year but was finally decisively crushed.

The raid was followed by a period of calm in which it looked as if the differences between Britain and the Transvaal might be settled peacefully. But this impression was deceptive. Chamberlain was more than ever determined to maintain British paramountcy and Kruger was confirmed in his worst suspicions of British policy by the raid and what followed. He had expected Rhodes to be tried and publicly disgraced but the Committee of Enquiry was first postponed and then, when it finally met, did everything to hush up the affair. Rhodes, in possession of telegrams implicating Chamberlain, was able to have him make a statement in the British House of Commons that Rhodes had done nothing contrary to his personal honour. Kruger now despaired of reaching any agreement with such a dishonest opponent and the Transvaal entered into a close military alliance with the Orange Free State and both states began to arm themselves with German weapons.

The second Anglo–Boer war, 1899–1902

Chamberlain came increasingly to believe that there was nothing to be done except to force the Transvaal to submit and he was strongly supported by the British High Commissioner in South Africa, Alfred Milner, another dedicated imperialist. As they recovered from the shock of the raid fiasco the mining magnates renewed their efforts to overturn the

South Africa at the time of the second Anglo–Boer War, showing main railway lines

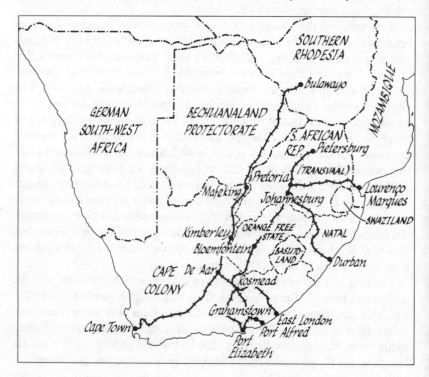

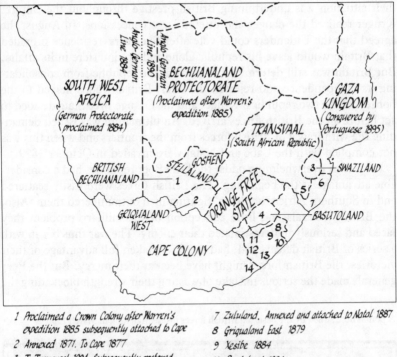

1 Proclaimed a Crown Colony after Warren's expedition 1885 subsequently attached to Cape

2 Annexed 1871. To Cape 1877

3 To Transvaal 1894. Subsequently restored to Imperial Govt

4 Annexed 1858. Joined to Cape 1871. Restored to Imperial Govt 1884

5 New Republic 1884

6 Thonga Land 1895

7 Zululand. Annexed and attached to Natal 1887

8 Griqualand East 1879

9 Xesibe 1884

10 Pondoland 1894

11 Thembu 1884

12 Fingoland 1879

13 Galeka Bomvana 1884

14 British Kaffraria (To Cape 1866)

The consolidation of white rule in South Africa

Kruger government. They backed an imperial pressure group, the South Africa League, which with Rhodes as its chief patron, developed branches in the Cape and Natal as well as in the Transvaal. The League encouraged and organized Uitlanders' agitation in Johannesburg, holding mass meetings, organizing petitions and keeping up a continual stream of propaganda in the Johannesburg *Star* newspaper. The League had a branch in London also where it acted as a powerful pressure group using the British press to rouse public opinion against Kruger and exerting all possible influence to push the British government into open confrontation with the South African Republic. Milner at last prepared to force a showdown. In May 1899 he prepared a despatch comparing the lot of the British in the Transvaal with that of the helots (serfs) in ancient Sparta claiming that their situation was undermining British prestige throughout the empire. Kruger realized the danger and offered large concessions. In August, he agreed that the Uitlanders could vote after five years' residence provided that Britain would leave his republic alone and not interfere in its affairs. But Britain was still determined to prevent the republic from consolidating its independence and rejected the offer, British troops moved to the borders of the two republics. Kruger and the Orange Free State decided to act before all the British forces arrived. An ultimatum was issued demanding the withdrawal of British forces from the frontiers and when this was not complied with the Cape and Natal were invaded in October 1899.

In spite of overwhelming odds, the little Boer republics had a considerable advantage at the beginning. The British forces were vastly scattered and in Southern Africa the Boers' fighting men outnumbered them. Also, the British generals had little conception of the military problem they faced and seriously underestimated their enemy. The war thus began with a series of British defeats and, had the Boers taken full advantage of their victories, the British forces might have been at their mercy. But the Boer generals made the serious mistake of wasting their strength blockading the

A pound note issued by the besieged British forces inside Mafeking in March 1900

ARMY HEADQUARTERS, SOUTH AFRICA.

General Lord Kitchener of Khartoum
            Commanding in Chief

    AND

His Excellency Lord Milner
          High Commissioner

    on behalf of the BRITISH GOVERNMENT

AND

      Messrs S.W.Burger, F.W.Reitz, Louis Botha, J.H.de la Rey,
          L.J.Meyer and J.C.Krogh

acting as the GOVERNMENT of the SOUTH AFRICAN REPUBLIC

AND

    Messrs W.J.C.Brebner, C.R.de Wet, J.B.M.Herzog
        and C.H.Olivier

acting as the GOVERNMENT of the ORANGE FREE STATE

        on behalf of their respective BURGHERS

Desirous to terminate the present hostilities, agree on the
following Articles.

1.   The BURGHER Forces in the Field will forthwith lay down
their Arms, handing over all Guns, Rifles, and Munitions of War,
in their possession or under their control, and desist from any
further resistance to the Authority of HIS MAJESTY KING EDWARD
Vll whom they recognise as their lawful SOVEREIGN.

    The manner and details of this Surrender will be arranged
between Lord Kitchener and Commandant General Botha, Assistant
Commandant General De la Rey, and Chief Commandant De Wet.

2.   Burghers in the field outside the limits of the TRANSVAAL
and ORANGE RIVER COLONY, and all Prisoners of War at present
outside South Africa, who are burghers, will, on duly declaring
their acceptance of the position of subjects of HIS MAJESTY
KING EDWARD Vll, be gradually brought back to their homes as
soon as transport can be provided and their means of subsistence

a period of years with 3 per cent interest. No foreigner or
rebel will be entitled to the benefit of this Clause.

Part of the Treaty of Vereeniging, 1902 (for the rest, and signatures, see next page)

Signed at Pretoria this thirty first day of May in the
Year of Our Lord One Thousand Nine Hundred and Two.

Signatures on the Treaty of Vereeniging

British garrisons at Ladysmith and Mafeking, giving Britain time to reinforce her troops in South Africa. Two first-class generals, Lord Roberts and Lord Kitchener, were sent out to command them and the initiative passed to the British. British troops invaded the Orange Free State, a whole Boer army was captured almost intact and Mafeking was relieved. The news gave rise to wild rejoicing in England. Then the troops marched on Pretoria. During 1900 the annexation of the two states as Crown colonies of Transvaal and the Orange River was announced and Kruger retired down the Delagoa railway line to die in exile. The war seemed over and Milner began to prepare the administration of the new colonies but many Boers refused to surrender. They began a guerrilla struggle which lasted for another year-and-a-half and their commandos even invaded the Cape. But some Boers felt that continued hostilities would destroy the prosperity of the country and joined the British side as a body called the National Scouts. They were naturally regarded as traitors by those who continued the struggle.

Impatient to end the war, Britain was baffled by those Boers who sat quietly at home one day and fired a British troops the next. In retaliation they burned Boer farms in the neighbourhood of guerrilla activity and took women and children into concentration camps. They also began to run barbed wire fences across the country to hem in the Boers but these measures still did not bring about an end to the war. The tough measures increased the bitterness and many women and children died from diseases which spread through the camps. Gradually the Boers' fighting spirit was undermined and they were ready to compromise. The British, too, were ready to make concessions and end the war.

In May 1902 the Boer and British leaders met at Vereeniging where the Boers agreed to surrender their independence in return for vital concessions from the British, the most important of which concerned African political rights. Britain had an opportunity of fulfilling her obligation to the Africans by securing their right to vote, perhaps on the same terms as in the Cape. This might have created a peaceful constitutional advance towards majority rule. But the Boers made it clear that they would rather continue fighting than accept such conditions and Britain capitulated. The question of African voting rights would be set aside until the two ex-republics had returned to responsible government. Britain also agreed to release all prisoners of war, to pardon all those still under arms and to provide massive financial aid to get the Southern African economy back on its feet.

12   States and societies in Middle Africa in the nineteenth century

Middle Africa comprises the tropical part of the continent south of West Africa and the East African Horn, and north of the Benguela Railway and the Ruvuma river in southern Tanzania. This large slice of Africa, lying between northern Africa and southern Africa is divided into the modern western states of Gabon, Congo, Angola and Zaire and the eastern states, Kenya, Tanzania, Uganda, Rwanda and Burundi. In the nineteenth century it was divided into a far greater number of political units, both large and small.

Peoples and rulers

The northern boundary is artificial. There has been regular contact between people on either side. During the nineteenth century whole peoples came down into Middle Africa from the north. This line, however, does roughly represent the northern boundary of the equatorial forest, and beyond it lie the open spaces of the savanna, in which the civilizations of the Sudan had flourished. The Sudanic peoples tended to look northward and eastward across parkland and desert to North Africa, the Nile valley and to Mecca. The equatorial forest was strange to them, the economy and rhythm of life of its peoples was in many ways different from their own. For them, therefore, the forest was a considerable natural obstacle to their southward progress, and the largest movements of Sudanic and Nilotic cattlemen went round its eastern fringes into Uganda and Kenya.

The forest was the natural habitat of the Bantu-speaking peoples who formed the overwhelming majority of the population of Middle Africa. Many Bantu-speakers lived in the forested areas of the Zaire basin and around the Great Lakes. They grew their tubers or bananas in forest clearings, or turned their hands to the savanna cultivation of maize or millet or even to the rearing of cattle. The southern and eastern edges of the forest did not form a sharp dividing line across Middle Africa as did

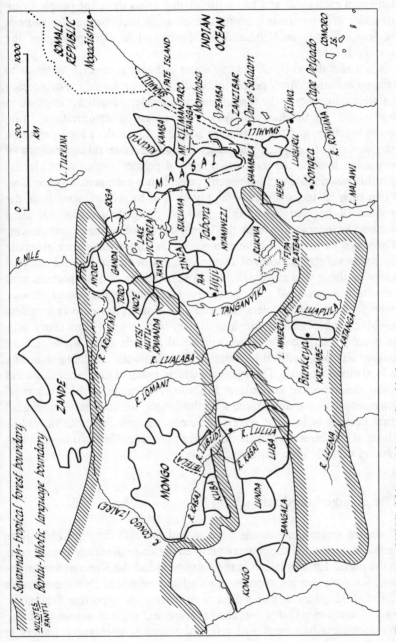

The larger groups of Middle African peoples mentioned in the text

307

the northern forest line. The two different types of environment complemented each other and had a stimulating effect upon the people living just inside or just outside the forest. It was along these fringes that some of the largest states in Middle Africa flourished at the opening of the nineteenth century.

It is a mistake to think of large states as being necessarily superior to stateless societies. Many people in Middle Africa preferred the democracy of stateless societies to the exploitation which rulers sometimes imposed in large states. In the modern world, where easy communications bring people together, and the division of labour and growth of big cities make man dependent on man, the large centralized state ruling millions of people has become the most usual form of political organization. In the past this was neither technologically possible nor economically necessary. When each village was able to supply most of its requirements from the produce of its own fields, there was no compelling reason for large numbers of people to accept the common rule of a single government. Where people agreed to belong to one of the larger states they generally did so because they believed in the strength of the moral and material power of those who ruled and also in their ability to offer protection to subjects who accepted their authority. Once that belief waned or once incompetent or ailing rulers began to lose control, the state or kingdom would crumble and divide into its separate parts – the many self-supporting village communities which had comprised the whole. Unlike today, therefore, political boundaries were constantly changing according to local circumstances. The same was true in much of the rest of the world before the Industrial Revolution. In Europe, for example, the ruling royal dynasties were constantly faced with the danger that their states might fall apart because of internal revolts or foreign defeats. So it was in Middle Africa at the beginning of the nineteenth century. We shall now look at some of these Middle African states.

The Kongo kingdom

During its greatest days in the fifteenth and sixteenth centuries, the Kongo kingdom dominated the country between the Zaire (formerly Congo) river in the north, Luanda Island in the south-west and the Kwango river in the east. Since the coming to power of a Catholic convert in 1506 it had been a Christian kingdom. It had sought to modernize by importing Portuguese traders, craftsmen and priests and in return sent some of its own people to Portugal for educational and religious training. Portuguese traders in Angola through their economic greed, their slave raiding and their assist-

A seventeenth-century impression of Mbanza Kongo (Sao Salvador)

ance to Kongo's enemies, were largely responsible for the kingdom's downfall in 1665. After that time the power of Kongo's kings steadily declined and the kingdom fragmented into small chiefdoms. By the nineteenth century royal authority was not recognized outside the old capital of São Salvador. But literacy and a knowledge of Portuguese survived, as did a centuries-old royal archives until this was destroyed by fire towards the end of the nineteenth century. Although the now power-less Kongo rulers were still crowned by Christian missionaries, for the majority of the Kongo-speaking people Christianity had become absorbed within the local religions.

The Lunda empire and Kazembe

At about the same time that the Kongo kingdom began to disintegrate, another important state to the south-east, the Lunda empire, was rapidly expanding outwards from the upper Kasai basin. By 1800 it stretched from the Kwando river in the west to the Luapula in the east. Its dynasty, whose title Mwata Yamvo (or Mwaant Yaav) survives to the present day, controlled subordinate chiefs who ruled a million people. An efficient system of messengers meant that tribute was regularly paid by subjects from as far as two months' distance from the capital. Such efficiency sometimes meant hardship for the ordinary people, who were forced to work as serfs for the ruling aristocracy. The Lunda developed a great trading empire involving copper, ivory, slaves, cloth, beads and salt. Trading links were established with the Portuguese in Angola and Mozambique, who supplied prestige items for the Lunda aristocracy, while the new crops of cassava and maize gradually replaced millet and bananas. A long period of stability ended in the 1870s, when the empire was successfully challenged by other traders.

In order to extend its control over resources the Lunda often sent out colonists to establish outlying states. One such group moved eastwards into Shaba (formerly Katanga) to exploit the local copper and salt. Its ruler took the title Mwata Kazembe. Kazembe sold ivory and slaves to the Portuguese at Tete on the Zambezi in return for cloth and guns and sent back copper, salt and possibly slaves to the imperial capital. The Kazembe kingdom grew rich on tribute and by the nineteenth century had become almost as powerful as the empire itself. But its wealth attracted rival Swahili and Nyamwezi traders from the east and by the 1870s they had seriously weakened it.

Luba and Kuba

To the east of Lunda lay the Luba empire. This was not a single political unit, but rather a number of different dynastic states drawn together by trade, especially during the heyday of the empire from about 1840 to 1870. The Luba heartland contained rich iron and salt deposits, and as Luba-speakers expanded eastwards across the savanna towards Lake Tanganyika they were also able to exploit ivory, copper palm oil and fish. Political control was exercised through secret societies, known as *bambudye*, which offered hospitality and protection, resolved serious disputes and gathered information. Luba society was noted for its sculpture, its music and its elaborate praise poetry. But it could also be cruel, as when prisoners of war were mutilated and marched in front of Luba armies to terrify and intimidate opponents. From about 1870 the empire began to weaken as ivory supplies diminished and new trading rivals, such as the Nyamwezi and Swahili, arrived with guns. The Luba then began selling their own people as slaves in order to buy guns. This naturally created serious tensions, as a result of which the empire virtually disintegrated in the 1880s.

To the north of Luba and Lunda lay the Kuba state, which reached its peak around 1750. The great seventeenth-century Kuba leader Shyaam is credited with the introduction of maize, cassava, beans and tobacco. Thereafter agricultural output and population expanded rapidly while trading links grew in all directions. Increased specialization led to regular markets and the use of raffia squares, cowries, beads and then copper bars as currencies. The Kuba also developed one of the most complex administrative systems in Middle Africa, including something similar to a modern jury system. But they were best known for their arts, which were strongly encouraged both in ceremonial and in daily life. Their sculpture and their pottery were particularly famous. The Kuba rulers were known as Bushong.

The inter-lacustrine kingdoms

Moving further eastwards across Middle Africa one reached the kingdoms which grew up between the Great Lakes of East Africa. These are sometimes referred to as the inter-lacustrine (between-the-lakes) kingdoms, and they include Buganda, Bunyoro, Toro, Nkore, Haya, Rwanda and Burundi. This is generally an area of good, reliable rainfall and of fertile soils which is able to support a much denser level of population than is normally possible in tropical Africa. Here, too, especially in Buganda, cultivation of the very long-lasting banana plant made permanent settlement possible and desirable. Such factors obviously encouraged the building of states.

These kingdoms resembled each other in their political organization. The king usually possessed strong and often autocratic executive powers in addition to the ritual and symbolic eminence customarily accorded to monarchs in Middle Africa. All state authority was concentrated in the king's hands, though he delegated part of that authority to provincial governors and they in turn to local sub-chiefs. But these provincial governors were normally directly appointed by the king and could therefore be dismissed by him at will. Periods of tutelage at the royal court enabled the ruler to select as officials only those whose loyalty he felt he could trust. In only a few kingdoms, such as Rwanda, did these officials become strong enough to make their posts hereditary. A further safeguard for the monarch lay in the fact that in most kingdoms no clear provision was made for the succession to the throne, and whilst this could sometimes lead to fierce succession disputes on the death of a ruler, it also meant that there was no danger of opposition forming around the person of a chosen heir to the throne.

In virtually all of the kingdoms the ruling dynasties claimed to be foreigners who had come from afar, sometimes through divine intervention. Elaborate royal traditions, emphasizing the superiority and separateness of the ruling classes, were carefully handed down from generation to generation, and these tended to ignore the extent to which local culture had been adopted by the rulers. Often, as in Rwanda, Burundi and Nkore, non-Bantu pastoralists ruled over Bantu agriculturalists, and though clearly pastoralists and farmers needed each other's skills, it was generally true that cattle-keepers were held in high esteem throughout the inter-lacustrine area. Finally, these highly centralized kingdoms were able to extract a great deal of tribute from their subjects, sometimes amounting to as much as one-third of a family's labour time. This enabled the rulers to live in some luxury and enhanced their ability to think of themselves as a superior caste.

Buganda and Bunyoro

The two most powerful of the northerly inter-lacustrine kingdoms were the traditional rivals Buganda and Bunyoro. With the assistance of a secure southern boundary along the shores of Lake Victoria, Buganda increased her size during the eighteenth and nineteenth centuries, largely at Bunyoro's expense. The king, or Kabaka, of Buganda extended his own power greatly and established a permanent army and an efficient navy. In an area of land scarcity – a rare occurrence in Middle Africa – the Kabaka, who was thought to be semi-divine, owned nearly all the land, which he distributed to sub-chiefs, who in turn divided it amongst their followers. Because land was relatively scarce it took on a symbolic value (accorded elsewhere to cattle) and those to whom land was given had to pledge their loyalty to the Kabaka. There was no hereditary aristocracy, no royal clan was allowed to emerge, and close kinsmen of the Kabaka could not become chiefs. With a thriving economy, kept under strict royal control, with excellent internal communications and a population of perhaps half a million, Buganda was in a very strong position to confront and respond to outside influence in the late nineteenth century.

Bunyoro, lying to the south of Lake Albert, was less centralized than Buganda. It tended to suffer more succession disputes and to have greater difficulty holding on to its frontier provinces. Indeed around 1830 one such province broke away to become the independent kingdom of Toro. But a Bunyoro revival later took place under the strong rule of Kabarega. He reconquered Toro in the 1870s and made the kingdom once more a leading military power in the region.

Nkore and Haya

To the south of Buganda and Bunyoro, between Lakes Edward and

Victoria, lay the Nkore kingdom and the Haya states. Nkore, a mixture of ruling Bahima pastoralists and Bairu subjects who were agriculturalists, began to emerge in the eighteenth century and reached its peak in the 1870s, only to decline swiftly as a result of a series of epidemics and attacks from neighbouring Rwanda. While cattle were accorded great prestige in Nkore, there was far more social mobility between rulers and subjects than in most other kingdoms. A very similar social structure existed in the Haya states, which also comprised Bahima rulers and Bairu subjects. These were economically flourishing societies which exported coffee to Buganda, Bunyoro and Nkore in exchange for cattle. They also began to import luxury goods from the east coast.

Rwanda and Burundi

The kingdoms of Rwanda and Burundi were located south of Nkore and the Haya states and to the north of Lake Tanganyika. This is an exceptionally fertile and well-watered mountainous area, capable of supporting extremely dense populations. Here the social and indeed racial division between ruling non-Bantu Tutsi pastoralists (of uncertain origins) and their agricultural subjects, the Bantu-speaking Hutu, was at its most extreme. Intermarriage was expressly forbidden. Highly complex hierar-

A young Mututsi, showing the white robes and traditional hairstyle now rarely worn

chical structures and patron-client relationships were established which rigidly controlled the ownership of cattle. Both kingdoms were militarily strong, with Rwanda the more aggressive during the nineteenth century. They tended to be unresponsive to the new economic opportunities and dangers which were beginning to be felt everywhere in the second half of the century.

Tanzania and Kenya

Moving eastwards from the Great Lakes one comes finally to the lands stretching away to the Indian Ocean, which we know today as Tanzania

Population density in eastern Africa. The map is in two parts as information from the different countries does not in all cases agree

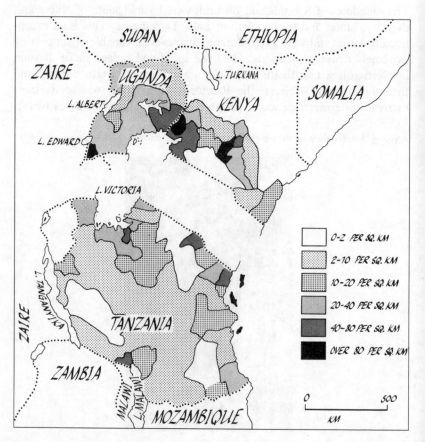

and Kenya. In this area in the nineteenth century there were very few centralized societies (and certainly no great empires) of the type described above. There were very good reasons for this. Over much of the land rainfall is inadequate or uncertain, the soils are poor, agriculture is precarious, and man is engaged in a constant battle with nature. Population densities in the nineteenth century were extremely low, far lower than in the more fertile inter-lacustrine region. Indeed Bantu-speakers were still colonizing the land in Tanzania – one of the last parts of Africa where this was happening. People had concentrated around the more fertile perimeter, leaving large parts of the drier interior virtually unpopulated. In such circumstances there were few incentives towards state formation.

Instead people preferred to live in small groups, able to move on when disputes arose because there was so much land available. Small chieftainships did emerge in Tanzania and societies certainly became more complex during the nineteenth century, but the dominant theme was one of considerable movement and fission. People were constantly colonizing new land, forming new political units, and then breaking off again in search of new land or greater security. Contrary to the beliefs of later European colonialists there were certainly no fixed, unchanging 'tribes' in Tanzania at this time, and such states as did exist tended to be fragile and impermanent. But as people came into greater contact with each other, as they began to occupy the marginal lands of central Tanzania, and as the external pressures increased, so societies began to change more rapidly and to look for new forms of political organization and new rulers with which to meet these challenges.

In Kenya the overall pattern was very similar. Here too there were no great economic pressures for political centralization. Chiefs were few; lineages and age-sets were all important. Even the dreaded and feared Maasai, the Nilotic warrior-pastoralists who dominated the plains of central Kenya and were pushing their way south into northern Tanzania, had neither chiefs nor a centralized form of government. During the nineteenth century the Bantu-speaking peoples of the forests, such as the Kikuyu, began for the first time to hold the Maasai in check. Frustrated and searching desperately for new grazing lands, the Maasai embarked on a series of destructive civil wars. By contrast, Kikuyu farmers, Kamba traders, and Nandi cattle-keepers enjoyed periods of expansion. Though there was undoubtedly fear and mistrust between agriculturalists and pastoralists, there was also trade and some intermarriage. As in Tanzania, a need was felt for new men to assume greater powers in order to offer people greater protection. We shall look at some of these in the next chapter.

A Maasai with traditional hairstyle and clothing at Tabora

Conclusion

Most people in Middle Africa, whether they were subjects of large kingly states like Buganda or inhabitants of small autonomous villages, were not directly involved in high politics. In the kingly states the struggle for office concerned only those classes born to rule or the few adventurous commoners willing to run the considerable risks of attendance at the royal court in the hopes of one day rising to positions of power. Those who lived in small self-regulating communities, such as those of south-eastern Tanzania, tended to be more politically conscious than their counterparts in the kingly states, for a greater proportion of people were involved in dispensing justice and in deciding issues of war and peace. But for most of the people most of the time the dominant concerns were the constant struggles with nature and with disease, the annual planting and harvesting of the crops, the rearing of children who would take their place in the labour force, and the performance of the religious rituals which bound societies together. These societies of Middle Africa were about to be tested by powerful new forces which would ultimately sweep away their autonomy and independence.

13 Crisis, revolution and colonial conquest in Middle Africa, 1840–1900

Introduction

The nineteenth century was a time of crisis and revolution in Middle Africa. It was a century during which outside forces had an ever-increasing impact upon the continent as a whole, culminating in the conquest of Africa by Europe in the 1880s and 1890s. Increasingly Middle Africa was linked to the expanding capitalist economies of western Europe and North America as earlier demands for slaves gave way to demands for commodities such as palm oil, ivory, rubber and wax. These were exported in exchange for the new firearms and the mass-produced cloth of the west, where the Industrial Revolution was now underway, giving Europe a new technological supremacy over the rest of the world.

In the second half of the nineteenth century almost all of Middle Africa witnessed the penetration of traders from the Atlantic and Indian Ocean coasts and the subsequent creation of new kinds of states led by new men who seized power and sought to exploit the new opportunities. Change tended to be more rapid in the savannas than in the forests. The new states with their gangs of mercenaries often resembled mobile armies of occupation. They posed a great threat to the older-established kingly states, which tended to fall easy prey to the new forces. Huge trading caravans shot their way across Middle Africa, those from the west and east coasts eventually meeting and clashing in present-day Zaire. With Europeans and Arabs at the coasts willingly supplying guns and credit, Middle Africa entered a phase of growing violence and insecurity, when strangers were automatically assumed to be hostile. The African imperialism of the Chokwe, Ovimbundu, Nyamwezi and Swahili trading empires almost certainly weakened Middle Africa on the eve of its confrontation with European imperialism. Moreover the rapid commercial revolution associated with ivory and rubber was not accompanied by improvements in agricultural technology and too many scarce resources were plundered and not replenished. The end result was to leave Middle Africa ecologically as well as politically vulnerable at a crucial point in time.

Shipping and commerce

One important external factor which affected Middle Africa during the nineteenth century was the great improvement in naval communications. Up to the close of the Napoleonic wars in Europe in 1815, the seas both west and east of Middle Africa were seldom free of pirates and the ships of warring nations, such as the British, the French, the Portuguese and the Dutch. After that date, mainly beause the British had secured mastery of the seas, there was a period of unprecedented maritime peace which lasted throughout the nineteenth century. Not only were the great naval powers at peace but piracy of all kinds was rigorously stamped out. The seas to the east of Africa particularly benefited from this. While the Atlantic had known a few periods of peace during the eighteenth century, the Indian Ocean had been the scene of continual piracy and warfare for more than three centuries. Now for the first time merchants could load their vessels in the confidence that they would reach their destinations. Obviously this greatly encouraged trade as did the new instruments for navigating at sea and the greatly improved charts of African waters made in the 1820s and 1830s. Ships became larger and faster and were no longer weighed down by guns. Regular postal services were established on the west coast in the 1850s and on the east coast in the 1870s, and these kept businessmen in African ports in touch with markets in other parts of the world. Such developments increased the commercial power of the trading communities on the coasts of Middle Africa.

In addition to this, markets in other countries for certain goods which Middle Africa could produce were steadily expanding. The value of slaves sent to the sugar and coffee plantations of Cuba and Brazil tended to rise in the first half of the century until that traffic was put down. The price of palm oil produced around the mouth of the Zaire river rose rapidly up to the 1860s, the price of ivory which was gathered widely in the heart of Middle Africa rose throughout the century, and in the 1880s there was a boom in rubber which was found in large areas of present Zaire and Angola. At the same time, the price of the goods which Middle Africa imported from the outside world was tending to fall. First Indian and then British and American cheap cotton manufactures came flooding into African ports. The price of haberdashery and metalware was also falling as was the price of those deadly imports – guns. In economists' language, the terms of trade were moving steadily in favour of Middle Africa during much of the nineteenth century. On the one hand this gave a considerable incentive to Africans in all parts of the area to engage in a commerce which year by year yielded increasing profits. On the other hand, the main beneficiaries were the merchants in the coastal towns and those nearest them, who secured the largest share of the rising trade. Throughout the century this was the general tendency: the centres of economic power and initiative moved away from the heart of the continent towards the coasts.

The predominant part played by external commerce in the total trade of Middle Africa, which was so evident at the end of the nineteenth century, was something new in the history of the area. At the beginning of the nineteenth century the people mostly provided themselves with their own cloth and manufactured their own tools and weapons. Foreign trade was a fringe affair which affected the lives of only a few in such states as Lunda or Kazembe. The main trade routes ran north and south rather than east and west, and the bulk of the commerce was carried on between the populous states of the inter-lacustrine area and the Zaire basin. Much of the trade was on a fairly local basis, such as the manufacture and distribution of hoes and other farming implements by specialist blacksmiths, or the trade in raffia work and bark cloth. Nevertheless, some of the markets for these commodities were to be found hundreds of kilometres from the place of manufacture, and this was even more strikingly the case with the copper products of Katanga (now Shaba), which were traded as far west as the Luba kingdom on the Kasai and as far east as Nyamwezi country in modern Tanzania.

New firearms and diseases

With the increase in foreign trade came a vast increase in the number of firearms imported into Middle Africa. Their impact generally was to make warfare far bloodier than it had been before, thus offering new opportunities to rulers but bringing greater misery to people who were raided. During the eighteenth century and for the first half of the nineteenth century, the standard infantry weapon was the flintlock musket. It was not very effective. It was heavy, it took up to a minute to reload and was very inaccurate when aimed at distances of more than 50 metres. Even in the open country of much of Europe, soldiers who used it also carried a bayonet which enabled them to convert the musket into a stabbing spear. In the close warfare of the forests and tall grasses of Middle Africa it was noisy, but scarcely more effective than the spear or the poisoned arrow. The late nineteenth-century rifle, however, was an entirely different gun.

Weapons used in Middle Africa: *right*, an eighteenth-century musket with fixed bayonet. *Left*, a nineteenth-century officer of an indigenous East African army armed with a repeater rifle

It was lighter and easier to handle, it was far quicker to load, and it could kill someone 300 metres away. From around 1850 western firearms technology advanced rapidly, guns quickly became out of date and each time inventors designed new improved models they were bought by the armies of Europe and America, and the old models were sold off cheaply. A growing number of these cheap but increasingly effective firearms found their way into Middle Africa after 1860, and they greatly facilitated the acquisition of slaves, war captives and ivory. Only in the 1890s, when the Europeans were trying to conquer Middle Africa, did they attempt to restrict the sale of arms.

The ships, which called ever more frequently at African ports bringing firearms and other western goods, also introduced deadly new diseases, such as smallpox, cholera, jiggers and rinderpest. The combined impact of new firearms and new diseases was devastating. In the later nineteenth century large parts of Middle Africa presented an almost apocalyptic picture of people fleeing from their homesteads in the plains to seek the safety of stockaded villages on hilltops or the less comfortable security of marshes. Many became refugees when their homes were plundered and destroyed by marauding bands of mercenaries. Cattle keepers, their herds destroyed by disease or captured by raiders, wandered in search of new means of livelihood. Whole areas were abandoned because of war, disease or famine and that enemy of man, the tsetse fly, moved in to occupy many of the vacant lands.

These hard times threw up a number of outstanding leaders who, by harnessing and controlling the dynamic forces of the period, were able to offer security and prosperity to their followers, though generally at the expense of less fortunate neighbours. Some were traditional rulers but a greater number were self-made men with trading and military skills. We shall be looking at the careers of some of these men in this chapter.

Sayyid Said and Zanzibar commerce

The trading communities of the east coast of Africa had remained where they were for several centuries, without making any significant attempt to move inland or make contact with the densely populated areas around the Great Lakes. They were mostly of mixed African and Arab blood, representing several waves of immigrants who, over a long period of years, had settled in such places as Kilwa, Mombasa and Zanzibar, intermarried and made their homes there. They were known as Swahili. In the early nineteenth century, especially after 1820, things began to stir in the coastal towns. The community of Indian traders, already well established when the century began, swelled in numbers and became more active. Many of them were agents of firms established in the large commercial and manufacturing cities of north-western India. These firms were well-organized and enterprising, and many were linked indirectly with the growing economic power of Britain. They had money to invest and as the Indian Ocean became safe for business they were encouraged to take a closer interest in East Africa. Then there were the Arabs of the Persian Gulf, warlike men who were being squeezed out of their own waters by British and Indian pressure. Omani Arabs had a long history of shipping and trading contact with East Africa, but in the nineteenth century they came in larger numbers and with more warlike intent than before.

The influx of these new elements into the coastal towns was presided over and controlled by Sayyid Said, Sultan of Oman in Arabia. Omani dynasties had held important possessions on the East African coast since the seventeenth century. In the early years of his reign, between 1806 and 1820, Sayyid Said tended to neglect his East African dominions. But after 1820, when his efforts to enlarge his empire in the Persian Gulf were visibly failing, he switched his attention from his Arabian homeland. His visits to Zanzibar became more frequent and in 1840 he established his capital there permanently. By that time he had consolidated his control over most of the ports between Mogadishu and Cape Delgado. He had

Sayyid Said, Sultan of Zanzibar

also, by his diplomacy, cemented an alliance between the enterprising Indian businessmen and the Arab soldiers and sailors, and directed the energies of both toward the economic exploitation of the interior. Extensive clove plantations were established on the islands of Zanzibar and Pemba, most of them owned and run by Arabs and backed by Indian capitalists who provided the money to buy African slaves to work on them.

The inland trade was also developed by the same combination of Arabs and Indians. Indians provided goods on credit which enabled caravans to set off from the East African ports laden with articles to exchange with the peoples of the interior. Indians also provided the money to stock trading depots, such as that at Tabora in central Tanzania. The leadership of these expeditions to the interior was mostly in the hands of immigrant Arabs and Swahili families established at Zanzibar. By 1825 men from the coasts were trading near Tabora, and by 1850 they had reached the Kabaka's court in Buganda, and were established at Ujiji on the eastern shores of Lake Tanganyika, from where they traded with the people of the Zaire basin further west. Two Arabs even crossed the continent to the west coast. The Arab caravans sought principally slaves and ivory. Slaves were needed to provide labour for the Zanzibar clove plantations, and for export to Arabia, Somaliland and islands in the Indian Ocean. Ivory found a ready market in Europe and America, and it was shipped off with the cloves by the American, French, German and British Indian vessels which

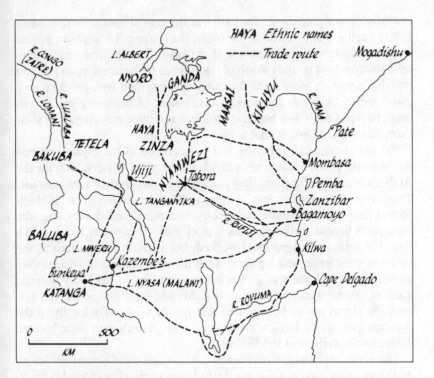

Trade routes in Middle Africa

called in increasing numbers at the port of Zanzibar from the 1830s
onwards.

Nyamwezi and Arab traders

The spectacular extension of Zanzibari trading activity between 1820 and
1850 was by no means a purely Indo-Arab affair. Men from the coast may
have led the caravans, but the guides and the men who actually carried the
goods came mostly from Nyamwezi country in western Tanzania. Indeed
many of the trade routes which the Arabs are credited with discovering
were in fact those which the Nyamwezi, and other African traders such as
the Kamba and the Yao, had long been using. The Nyamwezi were one of
the greatest trading peoples of Middle Africa. They had already developed
trading routes north to Buganda, south to Katanga (Shaba) and east to the
coast. Indeed Zanzibar's first contact with the far interior had been
through their agency. They had come down with the produce of their own

323

and neighbouring countries for barter in the coastal towns. But, as more Indian capital was invested in the trade, the commercial initiative passed from the Nyamwezi to the people of the coast. The Indians were able to send thousands of pounds worth of trade goods to the interior, and sit and wait for a year or more until their caravans returned with produce they could sell to European shippers. Thus, instead of beginning in Unyamwezi, business deals now began at Zanzibar and those entrusted with their execution were people of that town.

Yet the commercial expertise and co-operation of the Nyamwezi was still essential to the trade. They provided most of the porters, both for the Arab caravans and for those they continued to run on their own account. They were also more or less in command of the trade routes. In 1839 Sayyid Said signed a commercial treaty with them, and shortly after the Nyamwezi agreed to the passage, free of tolls, of caravans flying Said's flag. For a time the agreement worked, but it came under strain as the caravans grew larger and ate up more of the food supplies of villages they passed through. Food was always hard to come by in the badly watered areas of central Tanzania, where droughts and local famines were common. So it was not to be expected that people would take kindly to the constant passage of hungry caravaners, and quarrels over tolls became exceptionally serious in the 1850s.

The result was trouble between the Arabs and their Nyamwezi hosts, and to maintain their position the Arabs began to interfere in local politics, backing one clan of the fragmented Nyamwezi against another and involving themselves in chieftaincy disputes. The Arab depot at Tabora became a stronghold rather than a group of warehouses, and by 1860 it was fighting a regular war with Mnwa Sele, a leading Nyamwezi chief. Mnwa Sele was defeated and beheaded in 1865, and the Arabs thus secured control of the central point of communications in this area. But they were not to remain undisturbed for long, for while they were quarrelling with their former allies the Nyamwezi, the whole of western Tanzania was being torn apart by new forces advancing from the south.

The Ngoni impact

The effects of the great Mfecane, already discussed in connection with the history of Southern Africa, were not confined to that part of the continent alone. Zwangendaba's Ngoni warriors moved northward as far as the Fipa plateau between Lakes Tanganyika and Rukwa, and when that leader died, around 1848, his followers set off on a typical Ngoni career of conquest across the grasslands to the north and east. They brought a new ruthless professionalism which was to revolutionize the art of warfare. They struck northward towards Ujiji, which they devastated in the 1850s. From there they moved north again but failed to make any headway against the solidly organized Ha people and the kingdom of Rwanda. Instead they struck eastward, laid waste Uzinza and western Sukumaland, and then made off south-westward again to the neighbourhood of Ujiji, where they were active in the late 1880s. While this was going on in the north, another large body of Ngoni had pushed across the Ruvuma river in the 1850s and begun to terrorize vast areas of southern Tanzania and northern Mozambique.

Most of these Ngoni were Ngoni in name only and not by descent. They had been prisoners of war taken during the long migrations, and then brought up within the Ngoni military system as full-time soldiers. Wherever they went they disrupted the societies with which they came in contact. Some communities were scattered, some were absorbed within the Ngoni armies, while others reorganized themselves along Ngoni lines in a desperate effort to survive. When a community did this it in turn became a threat to its neighbours, and so the torch which the Ngoni lit was carried further afield by others until much of western Tanzania was ablaze.

Among the imitators of the Ngoni was Munyigumba, who ruled the Hehe people to the north-east of Lake Rukwa between about 1855 and 1879. A brief description of the methods by which Munyigumba built up the nucleus of a unified state will give some impression of how a Ngoni imitator worked and what sort of revolution the Ngoni brought about. Munyigumba's conquest of a Hehe chiefdom, of which about thirty were eventually absorbed into his state, may be divided into three phases. Phase one – the 'break in' – was achieved by force of arms. Munyigumba's soldiers would attack a neighbouring chiefdom, carry off its cattle and force its leaders to accept his rule. During phase two the traditional rulers would either be driven out and replaced by younger brothers or, if their loyalty could be relied upon, they would be confirmed in their positions and made sub-chiefs under Munyigumba's control. At the same time members of Munyigumba's large 'school' of 12-to-20-year old followers, trained in the ideology of the new state, would be sent out as military colonists among the chiefdom to spread the idea of loyalty to Munyigumba. By the end of the second phase the people would be completely absorbed. In the third phase, they would be called on to provide warriors for the central army and some of their young men would be selected for training in the royal school. They would render obedience to Munyigumba, who controlled the collection of ivory and distributed coastal trade goods to each according to his rank. He also monopolized the function of rain-making, and his ancestors were made the object of special ritual offering by the whole state.

A striking feature of Munyigumba's work was its amazing permanence. Altough it was a very recent creation, the Hehe state, under his son Mkwawa, stood solidly together against the Germans when they arrived in the 1890s, and some thirty years of direct rule thereafter failed to make the people forget the idea of unity and loyalty to the dynasty.

The Hehe state has been described at some length because, although it was comparatively small it contained significant features common both to Ngoni groups and to their many imitators to the south, west and east of Uhehe. In many cases those who wished to follow Munyigumba's example had no need to 'break in' to the territories of their neighbours. The breaking had already been done for them by the ravages of the Ngoni. During the period between 1850 and 1880 thousands of villages were destroyed and burnt by raiding forces, and young men wandered off in search of new ways of making a living. Some became *dagga* (cannabis)-smoking hooligans, 'ruga-ruga' as they were often called, who formed small gangs and sallied forth with spears and guns to rustle cattle and terrorize peaceful villages, like their contemporaries in the American West after the Civil War. Others joined one or other of the emerging states or the trading caravans. They were essentially mercenaries. Even in peaceful villages in Unyamwezi there was a growing urge among adventurous youths to take to the road in search of a quick fortune. Men of this type combined with others from the shattered west to form the backbone of the great trading empires established by two outstanding Nyamwezi leaders, Mirambo and Msiri.

Mirambo and Msiri

Mirambo was born around 1840. He spent his youth as a caravan porter and succeeded to the chiefdom of a small district north-west of Tabora in about 1858. With the assistance of the Ngoni and ruga-ruga warriors he gradually gained control of the surrounding chiefdoms, obtaining regular tribute in the form of ivory and young men for his armies. He also plundered many guns from passing caravans. By 1871 he controlled the vital Tabora–Ujiji trade route and demanded tolls from the caravans. This provoked a war with the Arabs, who were defeated and eventually agreed to pay tolls. Mirambo used the tolls to extend his influence over a wide area of north-western Tanzania. He was certainly aware of the dangers facing nineteenth-century African rulers and he pursued an ambitious foreign policy, seeking alliances with Buganda, with Msiri and Tippu Tip in eastern Zaire, and with the British at Zanzibar. He sought European missionaries and traders to act as a counterbalance against the Arabs. His was essentially an empire of the trade routes, far-flung but also loose-knit and vulnerable. It was not sufficiently well established in the minds of the people to survive Mirambo's death in 1884.

Mirambo's work was more spectacular but less lasting than Munyigumba's. But while he lived Mirambo's name was feared along all the approaches to the inter-lacustrine kingdoms from the east, and his activities contributed to the revolution in people's ideas and their ways of life which was taking place in much of Middle Africa at this time.

There are striking similarities between Mirambo's career and that of his fellow Nyamwezi, Msiri. Msiri was born around 1830 and was the son of a trader whose main business lay in the region of Katanga (now Shaba). Msiri too became a porter and caravan leader, and about 1858 he established himself in the country to the west of Lake Mweru, which was rich in copper and ivory. His own people, called Yeke by the local inhabitants, were already trading there in considerable numbers. But it was Msiri who conceived the idea of turning from trade to politics. He brought in guns from the east coast and a flood of uprooted young men from western Tanzania. With these tough warriors at his back, he interfered in the quarrels of local chiefs, forced the settlement of disputes and imposed his own rule on the successful parties. By 1869 he was powerful enough to break away from Kazembe's overlordship and declare himself king (*mwami*) of the area he controlled. He established his capital at Bunkeya, which became one of the largest towns in Middle Africa, he stopped and pushed back the Luba who had been advancing from the north, and he cut communications between Kazembe and the main Lunda empire to the west. In the 1870s he married the daughters of a Portuguese trader from Angola and an Arab trader from the east coast, and soon caravans were leaving Bunkeya on the journeys of over 1500 kilometres to the Atlantic port of Benguela and the Indian Ocean port of Bagamoyo, opposite Zanzibar. The caravans carried goods such as ivory, slaves, copper, rubber and wax.

His empire, which he called Garenganze, was located between the upper Lualaba and Luapula rivers and was one of the most successful conquest states of Middle Africa. Whereas Mirambo had concentrated on controlling the trade routes, Msiri sought to control the sources of production, especially of copper and ivory. His provincial governors were primarily concerned with the collection of ivory. But the subject people were beginning to revolt in the late 1880s, and when Msiri was killed by an agent of the Congo Free State in 1891, the empire quickly collapsed.

Tippu Tip and the Arabs

While Msiri was building up his kingdom in Katanga, Arab traders were moving into the country to the north from their base at Ujiji. They came initially in small numbers to trade, but by the 1860s they had turned to raiding for ivory and slaves, and had established fortified strongholds. The bulk of the Arabs' supporters were in fact Nyamwezi and other Africans from western Tanzania with, in addition, new recruits raised from the remnants of the many broken villages in what is now eastern Zaire. Many of these were Tetela people, who adopted a form of Islam and the Swahili language. They were responsible for spreading Arab/Swahili culture throughout a large area of eastern Zaire, where Swahili became widely spoken. But in their search for ivory and slaves they destroyed the power of local rulers and spread much terror and anarchy, as well as Swahili.

Some degree of political order was then established by Tippu Tip. He was an Afro-Arab, born in Zanzibar around 1830. He worked on his father's Tabora plantations and then in the caravan trade. In the 1870s when he decided to move into the ivory-rich Tetela territory of eastern Zaire, he had the wisdom to construct for himself a genealogy which made him the alleged descendant of a Tetela princess. The Tetela were at this time coming under heavy pressure from their Luba neighbours, and to

Tippu Tip

328

make himself more acceptable to his prospective subjects, Tippu Tip defeated a Luba force. On arrival among the Tetela he delivered to them some of their captured sons whom he had released from Luba captivity. According to Tippu Tip's (no doubt idealized) own account, the chief immediately resigned in his favour. Tippu Tip thus became a Tetela ruler and so was able to obtain ivory as tribute instead of having to pay for it. He made his capital at Kasongo on the Lualaba river, established roads and plantations, and stopped raiding within his own domains. He had to allow his followers to raid elsewhere, for slaves for the plantations and for ivory which was sent to Zanzibar, helped by an agreement with Mirambo giving his caravans safe passage. In the 1880s he became involved in a violent struggle for control of the resources of eastern Zaire with agents of what was to become the Congo Free State. Though initially successful he was forced to admit defeat by 1890, when he retired to Zanzibar a rich man. There he died in 1905, the last of the great but ruthless caravan traders.

Arab traders in Kenya and Uganda

North of a line from Mount Kilimanjaro westward to the southern shores of Lake Victoria, people were not affected by the same destructive combination of Ngoni raids and Arab penetration as those further south. It is true that Arabs traded in these parts; they first reached Buganda from their base at Tabora in 1844. Then in the 1860s they began to take over the trade routes leading from the east coast opposite Pemba island to western Kenya – routes which had up to that time been monopolized by Kamba traders. But the quality of the Arab impact was different. They met with very strong African resistance, especially from the Maasai who constantly raided and sometimes captured well-protected Arab caravans. Moreover the Kikuyu and Nandi refused to let them through and so the caravans were forced to bypass them. The Arabs could only establish small depots, not major centres as they did further south and west. There was little slaving along this route; the Arabs sought ivory in return for cloth and other items from the coast.

To the west of Lake Victoria lay the inter-lacustrine kingdoms, most of them too powerful to be dominated by even the strongest Arab caravans. Immediately to the south of Lake Victoria the Ngoni had managed to create havoc in the Zinza kingdoms by interfering in succession disputes. But that was as far north as they were able to reach. Immediately to the north the Arabs also interfered in a succession dispute, in the Haya state of Karagwe. But beyond that they were within the sphere of influence of the powerful kingdom of Buganda. There they traded successfully, but they did so only on terms laid down by the ruling Kabaka. These included no trading with rivals like Bunyoro or outside the capital of Buganda. The Arabs were barred from entering Buganda during the years 1852 to 1862, but they were then allowed back by Kabaka Mutesa, who needed their guns in the face of a threat from Egypt on his northern border. Instead of playing the role of itinerant caravan leaders, most Arabs settled down to commerce pure and simple, spiced with a certain amount of political intrigue. They also made more conversions to Islam than elsewhere, and the establishment of a Muslim faction in Ganda society was to be an important factor in the religious civil wars which shook Buganda later in the century.

Bark cloth had always been much in demand in Buganda. When the Arabs came, their cotton cloth replaced it as the fashionable wear for men about the court. The new textiles were much sought after as were the guns which the Arabs also brought. But Buganda had little ivory to offer in return. Instead it began to raid its neighbours for the ivory and slaves needed to pay for its imports. It is thought that during Kabaka Mutesa's reign from 1856 to 1884, Buganda made no fewer than sixty raids on its neighbours. This activity brought it into direct conflict with its rival

Mutesa, Kabaka of Buganda

Bunyoro, which was undergoing a revival under its ruler Kabarega (1869–97). In both kingdoms in fact the power of the rulers was tending to increase as a result of the growing importance of firearms, most of which passed into the hands of the kings. Buganda got most of its guns from the Zanzibari Arabs, Bunyoro from Arabs from the north, from Khartoum. For the inter-lacustrine kingdoms were situated at the edge of the commercial empire which the Egyptians built up between 1841 and 1884 on the upper Nile. From the late 1850s indeed, 'Khartoumers' began slave raiding in Acholi and Lango country in present-day northern Uganda. But the Egyptians were never able to acquire the same sort of influence as the Zanzibaris in either Buganda or Bunyoro. The Zanzibaris were for the most part regarded as friendly traders, while the Egyptians were representatives of an expansionist state close enough to pose a serious threat. While Bunyoro carefully sought to avoid hostilities with them, Buganda tried to secure their alliance against Bunyoro. In fact, although Egyptian officials claimed to have annexed both states formally in the 1870s, and although Egyptian posts were established in northern Bunyoro, the two kingdoms were just too powerful and too far south to be dominated by Egypt. Instead they were soon to fall under British control.

Angola, western Zaire and the Atlantic trade

Over in the western half of Middle Africa, many of the same influences were making themselves felt as in the east. There was a continuing demand from the Atlantic ports for ivory and slaves, and later for palm oil, rubber and beeswax, while more and more western goods and firearms found their way into the interior. As a result, the old kingly states such as Lunda, Luba and Kazembe found themselves increasingly challenged by new trading empires built on modern guns and the thousands of displaced refugees prepared to join anyone who promised them booty. Violence was inseparable from the search for slaves, ivory and rubber. The violence penetrated well into the equatorial forests and few areas of Middle Africa escaped it. By the 1870s the Atlantic trading zone pushing eastwards met the westward-expanding Indian Ocean trading zone in the middle of the continent, in the present Zaire.

The Chokwe provide an excellent example of a hitherto relatively insignificant people rising to prominence through long-distance trade. They began the nineteenth century as small-scale producers of beeswax and hunters of ivory in their eastern Angolan homeland. They sold these commodities to the Ovimbundu, the traditional long-distance traders of western Middle Africa. With the profits the Chokwe bought guns and women and began their long period of expansion northwards and eastwards into Zaire. This expansion took place partly because the Chokwe had killed all the elephants in their homeland, and partly because they switched from being producers to being traders. They moved into slaves and rubber and organized huge caravans, supported by highly efficient armies. In the 1870s they got involved in succession disputes in the Lunda empire, and they captured the Lunda capital in 1886. By this time they had become masters of large parts of northern and eastern Angola and western Zaire. The Chokwe expansion was a destructive process however; not just the violence associated with Chokwe trading, but the wholesale slaughter of elephants and destruction of rubber trees, with no attempt to replenish them.

A similar pattern of destruction was to be found in southern Angola. Here the Ovambo and Nkhumbi people, impressed by modern Portuguese firearms following a series of clashes around 1860, began to buy guns from the proceeds of their trade in ivory and hides. But they too had shot out all their elephants by 1880, and thereafter they annually raided the Ovimbundu and others for cattle in a desperate attempt to keep their army up to date. Violence in this area escalated right up to the time of effective colonial occupation.

The position of the Portuguese on the Angolan coast tended to decline during much of the nineteenth century and their energy at the end of the century was largely a response to the increasing imperialism of other European powers, notably France and Britain. In Luanda, the capital, the white population of 2000 were mostly deported criminals while the military garrison comprised local African convicts. Luanda was heavily dependent upon the slave trade, the importance of which steadily declined. Further south a serious attempt was made at white colonization around the fishing town of Mossamedes. Trades in ivory, cattle, slaves and beeswax was established, but the area suffered from increasingly severe Ovimbundu raids. A new element was introduced in the 1880s with the arrival of Afrikaners from what was to become South Africa.

The colonial invaders and the Berlin Conference

Five European powers – Portugal, France, Britain, Germany and King Leopold of Belgium – took part in the invasion and conquest of Middle Africa which occurred in the last two decades of the nineteenth century. The underlying causes of what Europeans referred to as the 'Scramble for Africa' – but which in fact was the conquest and subjugation of the continent — are discussed in the Conclusion to this Volume. Here we shall be concerned solely with events relating directly to Middle Africa.

Portugal had maintained possessions on the coast of Angola since the sixteenth century. During the seventeenth and eighteenth centuries these had prospered from the slave trade but had then declined and during most of the nineteenth century were poor settlements struggling to change from the slave trade to a trade in palm oil, beeswax and ivory. The Portuguese garrisons were small and poorly paid and seldom ventured beyond the ports. The few Portuguese traders in the hinterland were dependent upon the goodwill of African trading societies, such as the Ovimbundu, to conduct their business. Although deriving little profit from Angola or from their settlements in Mozambique, in south-east Africa, the Portuguese were very jealous of these possessions because, together with their imperial possessions in China and India, they represented Portugal's main claim to distinction and importance among its larger and economically stronger European neighbours. Portugal was anxious to retain and, if possible, extend them. In 1884 an opportunity to do this came when Britain offered to recognize Portugal's claim to the mouth of the Congo (now Zaire) river. Up to that time the British had been hostile towards any extension of Portuguese claims to the coastline because Portugal imposed heavy taxes on trade and this antagonized British merchants. But in 1882 the British government had become worried that the French, who were exploring the area of the Ogowe river to the north, might themselves claim the mouth of the Congo and then close the basin of that river to British trade. The British and Portuguese governments thus negotiated an agreement by which Britain would have recognized Portugal's claims to the mouth of the Congo in return for trade concessions. However, before the agreement could be ratified, France and Germany protested and the whole matter was referred to a conference of the European powers and the United States which met in Berlin in October 1884.

The main business of the Berlin West Africa Conference was to decide the fate of the Congo basin. The Conference itself did not deal with claims to territory, but mainly with the facilities which occupying powers should offer to traders and missionaries of other nations. While the Conference was going on, the various European governments negotiated their territorial claims in Middle Africa. King Leopold of the Belgians put forward the claims of the International African Association, a private organization working under his presidency, which had already sent a number of expeditions to the Congo area. When first formed in 1877 it may have had no territorial ambitions, but when Portugal, Britain and France began to quarrel about claims to the mouth of the Congo, Leopold suggested that it be given to his organization, so that the river would be neutral. He promised that he would impose low duties on exports from the area and thus satisfy the traders of all nations. The United States and Germany supported this idea and, with assurances that Leopold would protect their interests, France and Britain also agreed. Thus by the end of the Berlin Conference in February 1885, Leopold's Congo Free State had emerged as a new government recognized by the European powers with a claim to most of the Congo basin, together with agreed boundaries near the coast separating its territory from the French colony of Middle Congo to the north of the river and from Portuguese Angola to the south.

Germany also acquired a colony in Middle Africa. In February 1885 the German government gave a charter to the German Colonization Society, permitting it to hold territory on Germany's behalf in East Africa. The British government gave a similar charter to the Imperial British East Africa Company. Neither government intended at first to remove the control which the Sultan of Zanzibar exercised over the coastline. The two companies were supposed to operate beyond a 16-kilometre coastal strip belonging to the Sultan. However, there was constant friction between the Germans and the Sultan's men and in 1890 Germany and Britain combined to force the Sultan to renounce his claim to the Tanganyikan coastline. The Sultan still had a claim to the coastline of Kenya further north, and the British East Africa Company continued to act as the Sultan's agent until the Company handed over to the British government in 1895. In fact the administration of the Kenya coastline had effectively slipped from the Sultan's hands by 1890.

By about 1885 the various colonial powers were preparing to move in and conquer those parts of Middle Africa which they had so arrogantly assigned to each other in Berlin and elsewhere. The Portuguese were anxious to advance from their positions along the coast of Angola. King Leopold sent off more expeditions to push out along the lower Congo river up to Stanley (now Malebo) Pool. The Imperial British East Africa Company was examining the resources of the domain it had acquired. But claims on paper (or on maps) were very different from realities on the ground. Before 1890 the agents of European colonialism made little impact on the life of Middle Africa and were able to secure a position of command in only a few places. The period of exploration continued but Europeans did not penetrate far beyond the main routes. The caravans of European missionaries, traders and political agents were scarcely distinguishable from African, Arab or Swahili trading caravans. Europeans seldom ventured beyond the trade routes or the capitals of the major states. It was there that they first began to intrigue and manoeuvre towards positions of real power.

The establishment of European power on the coast

On the east coast the Germans and British first pushed themselves into a commanding position in areas directly under the Sultan of Zanzibar's control. The Sultan's rule was itself of very recent origin. Sayyid Barghash had begun, from the middle of the 1870s, to establish a regular administration over the peoples of the coastal districts where his predecessors had exercised only very informal influence. Barghash appointed *fumbes*, or

Sayyid Barghash, Sultan of Zanzibar

chiefs, to rule over groups of villages and they were supported by a small disciplined army. His administration was still pushing inland along the trade routes when the German and British companies arrived. The Sultan's capital on the island of Zanzibar lay open to blockade or the threat of bombardment by European fleets, and both methods were used to extract concessions from Sayyid Barghash and his successor. His administration in the coastal areas also depended on European goodwill. An English officer commanded his army and British advice and support had helped him establish his administration. But after conflicts between the Sultan's officials and agents of the German Colonization Society, the German government insisted on limiting and finally removing his jurisdiction. Although Britain would have preferred that the Sultan retain nominal control over the coastline, she was not prepared to challenge Germany on this issue. But while the Sultan was obliged to make diplomatic concessions, his subjects and followers were less conciliatory. They resented the high-handed actions of European officers, and when the Sultan conceded to the Germans the right to raise their flag and collect customs taxes in August 1888, they rose in revolt. The 'Abushiri rising', which affected the coastal districts under British as well as those under German rule, caused the German government to assume direct control as the German Colonization Society was unable to cope with the belligerent situation that developed.

During 1889 the German and British governments blockaded the coast to prevent the import of modern arms, and in May a German government officer arrived with a thousand well-equipped soldiers recruited in other parts of Africa. By the end of 1889 Abushiri bin Salim, the principal leader of the revolt, had been executed and German forces were imposing their rule on the coastal districts until by the end of 1891 they were in control of the entire coast of German East Africa (later called Tanganyika). To the north the British, operating from Mombasa, also suppressed opposition to their rule. They were not however firmly in control until 1895, with the formal declaration of British rule in the East Africa Protectorate (later called Kenya).

On the west coast the major starting points for the routes into the interior were already in European hands by 1885. The Portuguese had garrisons in the ports of Angola. King Leopold's agent, H.M. Stanley, had pushed his way along the lower reaches of the Congo and established stations that secured access to the navigable stretches of the river. By about 1890 the Europeans were ready to begin their assault on the interior. Before doing this they made agreements amongst themselves at the Brussels Conference of 1890 to ensure that modern weapons, especially machine guns, did not fall into the hands of African rulers. They were able to enforce this agreement by virtue of their naval supremacy and their control over the coastline of Middle Africa.

The establishment of European power in the interior

Between 1885 and 1890 the various European expeditions which travelled through Middle Africa generally negotiated their safe passage with the African or Arab authorities who still held power. But during the 1890s the situation changed rapidly. In 1890 the Portuguese at last moved inland, defeated Ndunduma, one of the most important Ovimbundu leaders, and won a commanding position on the Bihe Plateau at the centre of the largest trading system in the interior of Angola. In 1891 Leopold's Katanga Company sent a force to Msiri's capital, Bunkeya. Msiri refused to surrender his authority to the Belgians and was shot. His empire quickly disintegrated. Other columns broke the power of Chokwe caravans operating in Lunda territory. The uneasy alliance between Tippu Tip and the Congo Free State broke down by 1890 and the Belgians proceeded to drive most of the Arabs and Swahili out of the Congo between 1892 and 1895, making themselves military masters of the eastern Congo basin.

Meanwhile in East Africa the Germans had suffered two defeats; one at the hands of the Hehe led by Mkwawa in August 1891, the second by the Chagga at Moshi in June 1892. But then the tide began to turn in the Germans' favour. In January 1893 they defeated Isike, the Nyamwezi leader at Tabora, and gained control of the central caravan routes. In August 1893 they won a decisive battle against the Chagga and secured control of the Kilimanjaro region. In October 1894 they stormed the Hehe capital, and although Mkwawa carried on a guerrilla campaign until 1898, the Germans were free of the threat of serious Hehe attacks after 1894. Further north, in what was to become Kenya, the British made an agreement with the Maasai which guaranteed them free passage over most of the territory's principal trade routes. The neighbouring Nandi were not so easily won over however, and when the British attacked them in 1895 the result was inconclusive. They continued to attack British caravans and railway builders until they were finally subdued in 1906.

To the west in what became Uganda, the British advance was greatly facilitated by an alliance made by missionaries with a faction at the Kabaka of Buganda's court. The agents of the British East Africa Company came as allies of Buganda. The British victories were the victories also of Ganda soldiers who provided the main body of the armies which marched against Bunyoro in 1891 and 1893. Individual Ganda also helped in the establishment of British rule in Busoga, Nkore and northern Uganda. In the early

A LITTLE PARTY IN EAST AFRICA ONLY GOING TO COLLECT A FEW
BUTTERFLIES AND FLOWERS FOR THE DEAR KAISER, THAT IS ALL!!

"We came very near to having Kilima-Njaro attached to the British Empire, only the
German Emperor said he would very much like it, because he was so fond of the *flora* and
fauna of the place . . . Would the English have expected to get any territory on account
of their great interest in the *flora* and *fauna* here."—*Stanley speaking at Chamber of
Commerce, May 21.*

A cartoon depicting a German 'scientific' expedition in East Africa

stages the establishment of British rule in Uganda was hardly more than an
extension of the Ganda political system over the neighbouring peoples.
Meanwhile, through skilful diplomacy and by exploiting the rivalries of
the different factions at the Kabaka's court, the British gradually altered
their position from being allies to becoming the arbiters of politics in
Buganda. The years 1897 to 1900 were crucial. Kabaka Mwanga was
deposed, his party defeated, the faction favoured by the British installed in
power, and the 1900 Uganda Agreement signed. As a result the principal
Ganda leaders recognized British sovereignty over Buganda and the rest of
the area included within the Uganda Protectorate.

Disease and famine

While the European colonial powers were pushing their way inland from the coasts, Middle Africa was shaken by a series of unparalleled natural disasters which gravely weakened people's ability to resist the invaders. In 1889 the first recorded outbreak of rinderpest in Africa outside Egypt was noted in Somalia. Within a year it had spread to Kenya, then crossed East Africa and reached Lake Malawi by 1892. Thereafter it swept back and forth across the whole of Middle Africa – and Southern Africa too – attacking the herds of most cattle-keeping peoples. When the plague struck severely it could kill every animal a community possessed. Pastoralists such as the Maasai or the Bahima, who knew no other life but herding, were absolutely devastated by the rinderpest. Many people starved to death – perhaps half the Maasai of German East Africa – while survivors fought over the few remaining cows. Others who kept cattle as a store of wealth found their riches obliterated overnight. Less dramatic but more prolonged and debilitating was the spread of new diseases against which people had no immunity. Jiggers appeared in Angola in the 1870s and had reached the east coast by the 1890s. Outbreaks of smallpox occurred in the Congo basin and elsewhere in the wake of the European invasion. Sleeping sickness around the turn of the century killed perhaps half the population of Buganda and the lower Congo region. Venereal diseases also became more virulent during and after the period of invasion. The last two diseases not only killed the living but also caused a dramatic fall in the birth rate. On top of all this there were also particularly severe famines. One of the worst occurred in Kenya where, together with disease, it severely reduced the Kikuyu and Kamba populations, leaving wide areas of formerly inhabited land vacant – and soon to be seized by white settlers. There was famine also at a crucial moment in Katanga, just when the troops of the Congo Free State arrived in 1891. It continued after Msiri's death, killing large numbers of the population. It is little wonder that the societies of Middle Africa were unable strongly to resist the coming of the Europeans.

Conclusion

14 The European conquest of Africa

Africa before colonial conquest

For a great part of recorded history Africa has been in contact with peoples living outside the continent in Europe and in Asia. This contact was closest in the case of the peoples living north of the Sahara desert. North Africans, Egyptians and, to a lesser extent, Ethiopians discussed religion and trade and disputed power with neighbours beyond Africa's shores in southern Europe and the Middle East. As for the rest of the continent, contacts with non-Africans were mainly confined to the coasts and their immediate hinterland. Above all Africa was seldom successfully attacked by forces from outside. While conquering hordes and powerful states from time to time swept across the Eurasian land mass between China and India and the shores of the Atlantic and while every substantial state in that area had to calculate the strength or weakness of its neighbours, Africa south of the Sahara was very much a closed world of its own which made its own adjustments between rising and falling African empires without reference to the state of things in Europe or Asia.

Apart from the Portuguese incursions into Angola in the seventeenth century, the Europeans, Arabs and Indians who traded on Africa's coasts did not venture far beyond their trading ships or forts at any time before the nineteenth century. The foreign traders on the coast could to some extent influence the politics of the hinterland especially by their encouragement of the slave trade. But the impact of the slave trade has often been exaggerated by historians as have been the estimates of the number of slaves carried across the Atlantic. The political influence of foreign traders did not reach far inland and the traders themselves seldom secured more than a local dominance while many carried on their businesses by leave of the African rulers. The peoples of North Africa who were involved in power struggles with non-African states were, from the time of the seventh-century Arab invasions onward, more or less able to hold their own. Between the eighth and tenth centuries they extended their empires to Spain and Syria. In the sixteenth century all North Africa up to Morocco fell under Ottoman rule but the local governments maintained a large measure of autonomy within the Ottoman system. Egypt in particular remained an important centre of power within the Ottoman empire and from time to time parts of western Arabia fell under the control of Cairo.

It is easy to confuse Europe's subjection of people of African descent in the Americas with European dominance over Africa itself. Such a confusion existed in the minds of many people in Europe from the late eighteenth century onward. The fact that African rulers and traders sold prisoners of war, convicted criminals and others into European slavery did not of itself diminish the political independence of those who made such sales. The slaves once sold became a subject people but Africa remained as free as ever. The European trading posts on the African coasts were, until the nineteenth century, like flies on the back of an elephant. Africa went its own way, settling its own problems without having to take account of the pressure of invading forces from outside.

This situation began to change during the nineteenth century, as the chapters in this volume have shown, and by 1900 most of Africa had been invaded by outsiders for the first time in its history and had fallen into the possession of a number of European states. Egypt, which, despite invasion in 1798, had driven off a British attacking force as late as 1807, was occupied by Britain in 1882. Morocco, which had once ruled Spain, was partitioned between Spain and France in 1912. Everywhere throughout the continent the Europeans in the small trading forts along the coast had pushed out over the land, and soldiers and administrators from European countries had imposed their rule upon the people of the continent. Why did all this come about? Why did Africa so suddenly fall, for the first time, and, as it turned out, for a very brief period in its history, under foreign rule? These are the questions we shall be seeking to answer in this conclusion.

Many historians and others have tried to find answers to these questions. Much thought has been given to the question of why Europe *decided* to occupy Africa in the late nineteenth century. Somewhat less attention has been paid to the related question of why Europe *was able* to do so. It is easy to take it for granted that whenever Europe decided to occupy Africa it could do so and that therefore one only looks for European motives. We need not agree that Europe could have taken Africa whenever it liked. First, however, let us investigate the former question which has concerned so many historians, 'why did Europe decide to occupy Africa in the late nineteenth century?'

The Industrial Revolution and the search for markets

In the hundred years before the 1880s Europe had been steadily drawing ahead of the rest of the world in the fields of economic organization and application of science and technology to production. The Industrial Revolution began in England in the eighteenth century as large cities grew and the numbers of those working in industry began to exceed those engaged in agriculture. From England, large-scale industry spread in the early nineteenth century across the Channel to Belgium, north-east France and western Germany. Thence it extended further, reaching the Hapsburg empire and northern Italy by the end of the century. Europe during the nineteenth century became the workshop of the world with an insatiable appetite for the raw materials to feed her industries and an ever-vigilant eye on the growth of markets for her manufactures. By the late nineteenth century this concern about sources of raw materials and markets had become more serious in the different European countries than at any time hitherto. European industry in the 1890s was still producing more or less the same things – iron and steel goods and textiles – as it had at the start of the Industrial Revolution. But the numbers of firms producing these goods had steadily multiplied, and they were competing vigorously with one another. Improved methods of production usually favoured larger firms with larger financial resources and so the smaller, weaker businesses were being increasingly driven into bankruptcy or eaten up by the larger. All were engaged in a race for survival. The smaller firms were trying desperately to maintain their positions, the larger were seeking to extend themselves to avoid being overtaken by their rivals. All were subject to the effects of periodic trade depressions when it became particularly difficult to sell goods, so that factories and men stood idle. At the height of the 'Scramble', 1884–5, European industry was in a depressed condition and industrialists were especially anxious at that time to protect themselves. They asked their government to help them by imposing high tariff barriers to keep out foreign goods. In 1880 Germany went over to a high tariff policy. Within twelve years, France, the United States and many European countries (except Britain) had followed suit. This ended the free-trade period of the mid-nineteenth century. There followed a period when the idea that governments should protect their industries became one of the strongest economic ideas in Europe.

It was but a short step from the idea of protecting a market for industry at home to the idea of creating a new, protected market for industry by seizing colonies abroad. This was especially so in the late nineteenth century because the idea of what 'colonies' were was changing. In the early nineteenth century, 'colonies' had been thought of mainly as places where

Europeans could go and settle – like Canada, Australia, New Zealand or Algeria. The setting up of this sort of 'colony' did not particularly interest industrialists. It was also the sort of 'colony' that men like Otto von Bismarck, the Chancellor of Germany, did not want. But at the very time that Bismarck was saying that he did not want 'colonies', some writers were changing the meaning of the word 'colony'. They spoke of 'colonies of exploitation' where Europeans would not settle but where European money could be used to increase production and create new markets and sources of raw materials. This sort of colony *did* interest industrialists. The idea of such colonies also became popular among people generally, apart from those directly connected with industry. As enthusiasm for such colonies grew, people began to press governments to establish them and create new markets for national industry which would, they expected, be protected from the competition of goods produced in other countries by high tariffs. Britain still stuck to free trade. But as other powers, anxious to challenge Britain's position as the leading industrial power, became interested in establishing colonies with high tariff barriers, British industrialists became alarmed and called on the British government to set up colonies where British goods would not be kept out. Moreover the late nineteenth century was a period of increasing political tension and national rivalry in Europe, following the unification of Italy and Germany by 1870. The emergence of a powerful united Germany under Bismarck upset the traditional 'balance of power' between Britain, the leading naval power, and France, the dominant land power. In particular, France's humiliating defeat at the hands of Germany in 1870, involving the loss of Alsace and Lorraine, left her seeking revenge and compensation elsewhere. After 1870 Europe rapidly became an armed camp, and European rivalries were exported to Africa, Asia and the Pacific, with colonies increasingly being seen as symbols of national prestige.

The development of protectionist ideas and the background of industrial and political rivalry which gave rise to them in Europe produced a general disposition favourable to the acquisition of colonies. It strengthened the already prevailing belief that governments had a duty to use national power overseas to support national economic enterprise. But this general disposition favourable to the acquisition of colonies should not be confused with specific pressures placed upon government actually to seize territory in Africa. These broad ideas may have altered the level of national aggressiveness but they were not necessarily followed through in detail in all circumstances. For example, despite what was said of the necessity to secure exclusive markets, the goods and trade of other European countries were not in fact excluded from the great majority of colonial territories seized by particular European states in Africa. Furthermore, Africa was not regarded as an area in which huge commercial profits could be made. The existing trade between Europe and Africa was small in the 1880s by comparison with European trade with other parts of the world. In particular, industrialists in Britain, which was to acquire such a large number of African colonies, had a low opinion of Africa's commercial potential. Germany's trade with Africa was rising at the time of the 'Scramble' but so was Germany's trade elsewhere and the African proportion of Germany's total foreign trade was extremely small. The competitive search for markets and sources of raw materials that was growing in Europe only affected European attitudes to Africa in a very general way. Few of the great producers of goods in Europe put direct pressure on their governments to occupy territory in Africa.

European pressure groups in Africa

Direct pressure came rather from those in Europe who were already directly involved economically in Africa at the time the 'Scramble' began. It came from those who had invested money in trading establishments on the African coasts, those who had lent money or secured concessions of land in Egypt and North Africa, and those who were making money from South African diamond and gold mines and who hoped to make more by extending their operations northward. All of these groups had behind them the financial power of industrial Europe. To a greater or lesser extent they could draw upon the capital resources of the European money market which during the nineteenth century had become incomparably larger, better organized and wider spread than any money market the world had hitherto known. During the nineteenth century the European banker or moneylender could lend money more cheaply and in larger quantities than anyone else. The European trader who could more easily borrow from these sources could wait longer than his rivals for repayment for the goods he sold. The result of this was that wherever legal arrangements were favourable, European merchants, moneylenders and their local agents had penetrated African society and secured control of a large part of the economic life of particular countries.

This was most outstandingly the case in Egypt and North Africa where the system of 'capitulations' which placed Europeans and their protegés under a special legal statute operated to their advantage. The 'capitulations' were only meant to provide the sort of special arrangements that predominantly agricultural societies all over the world had frequently accorded to the small communities of foreign or cosmopolitan traders. But the amount of credit available in North Africa and Europe was not equal and the 'capitulations' opened the door to large European investment in trade and other branches of North African economic life. Not only this but North African governments who wanted loans to extend their activities had to turn to Europe which alone could provide finance on the scale required. Elsewhere in Africa there was not the same scope for the penetration of the economy by European finance. Along most of the West African coast, the inland movement of European economic enterprise was blocked by so-called 'middlemen' – these were states or groups of individuals who combined the control of politics and economics in the areas close to the coast and who would not permit the establishment of direct contact between European firms and those in the hinterland. The 'middlemen' themselves absorbed substantial amounts of credit from European sources but they made their own commercial links with neighbouring peoples, thereby hindering the free flow of credit. In East Africa European merchants were active and, in addition, the Indian merchants used the capital concentrated in the money markets of western India to finance trade along the routes from Zanzibar to the Great Lakes. In South Africa English law prevailed although its form was modified in the case of the Boer Republics. Generally speaking, European capital could move in freely and it did so in the form of investment in diamond mines and railways and, after 1886, in the important gold mines of the Transvaal. Those who had invested money in Africa were apt to turn from time to time to seek the assistance of European governments in protecting their investments or furthering their trade.

Before the late nineteenth century European merchants in West Africa were not very enthusiastic about getting European governments to interfere in Africa. When they were doing good business, as they had been at the middle of the century, government interference could sometimes be more of a hindrance than a help. Certainly they were happy to have government warships come and help them collect debts. But the actions of the government could often cause them inconvenience. For example, in the middle of the nineteenth century, the interference of the British government in the Niger delta made it easier for new European and even African traders to start business in competition with the old-established European merchants on the coast. The traders in Senegal quickly tired of the political interference and consequent wars of the colonial government during the 1850s because the wars were too often paid for by taxes on their trade. But in the 1880s business for European traders in West Africa was bad. Trade was stagnant and the prices in Europe of palm oil and groundnuts – needed to lubricate the new factory machines and cleanse the industrial workforce – were not rising as they had been thirty years before. The European merchants therefore had either to find new ways of employing their capital, or else they had to force Africans with whom they were trading to accept lower prices. If they failed, their profit margins diminished. A number of them sank into bankruptcy as a result. The rest anxiously sought ways out of their difficulties either by combining to force down producer prices or by forcing their way past the middlemen to employ their capital in organizing the purchase of cash crops nearer the source. The twists and turns they made to achieve these ends brought them into conflict with African traders and rulers who were under similar pressure, and as relations deteriorated the European traders turned to European governments for political and military assistance.

But which governments were to interfere? This question frequently produced divisions among the traders because each tended to fear that the government of some country other than their own would tend to discriminate against them. So, in most cases, each set of merchants appealed to its own government to interfere first before the other governments had a chance to act. And when it came to the question of breaking through to the interior markets, which interested merchants so much in the 1880s, another reason for international rivalry came up. The traders in each port feared that the land behind the port would be taken by a European colonial power which owned another port nearby. For example the French at Cotonou might take Abeokuta and divert all the trade of Egbaland away from Lagos. The Lagos merchants would thereby lose many of their customers and the valuable shops and warehouses they had built would become worth much less. The Germans in Douala similarly feared a British movement round Cameroon mountain, and the French in Ivory Coast feared the British moving across from the Gold Coast. Merchants in all the ports of West Africa were very anxious that as a much as possible of the country behind the ports should be brought under the same government as the port itself. So they petitioned their governments in Europe to take land in the interior.

Such petitions from European merchants in West Africa carried less weight than the clamour of those who had money invested in Egypt and North Africa, either privately or in Egyptian or Tunisian government bonds. The Egyptian public debt amounted to 96 million Egyptian pounds in 1884, most of which was held in Europe. Much of the debt had been incurred during the middle 1860s when Egypt was exporting cotton heavily at attractive prices. When the American Civil War ended and American cotton began once more to compete, Egypt's economic boom came to an end. The Khedive was not able to find the money to repay debts he had contracted and to cover other commitments, and so he had to borrow more at ruinous rates of interest. Egypt had scarcely the resources available to continue paying the interest on the debt but the European bondholders were determined to have their 'pound of flesh'. The bondholders were numerous and vociferous especially in France. They included more men of importance in European political society than the West African merchants could muster. The bondholders did not actually tell the governments of Europe to occupy Egypt but they insisted that the interest on their loans be repaid and it soon became clear that no Egyptian government which depended on the consent of the Egyptian people could afford to do that. Their demand for repayment therefore amounted to a demand that Egypt be brought under European control.

Traders in West Africa and bondholders in Egypt were trying to get governments to protect investments which had gone sour. Investors in South Africa sought government sanction for new optimistic enterprises beyond the frontiers of Cape Colony in present-day Zimbabwe and Zambia. The British South Africa Company had less difficulty in raising capital than any of the European chartered companies that operated in Africa in the 1880s. British investment in South Africa amounted to £34 million in 1884 and increased tenfold over the next 27 years. The South African economy was booming in the 1880s as Transvaal gold was added to Kimberley diamonds. The imperialist entrepreneur Cecil Rhodes hoped to find new goldfields to the north and so did other groups and individuals who scrambled across the Limpopo river. When Rhodes asked the British government for a charter for his British South Africa Company and permission to bring new territories under the British flag, he was asking that the government sanction a self-financing force which would thrust as far northward as it could in search of new mineral resources. The British South Africa Company was hoping to make substantial profits; elsewhere in Africa European investors and traders during the 1880s were mostly asking governments to shoulder a political burden in order to save them from losses.

Merchants and investors, however, were not the only people who were pressing European governments to invade Africa. There were also adventurers and visionaries of various types who hoped to cut a figure for themselves and boost their own prestige by acquiring territory. There was King Leopold of the Belgians who hoped to give his country an empire in Central Africa if nowhere else. There was Carl Peters who hoped to do likewise on behalf of Germany in East Africa. There was the ambitious Francesco Crispi who hoped to divert attention from his government's failure to solve Italy's internal problems by securing an empire in Ethiopia. French army officers – after the defeat by Germany – sought to win promotion and glory by successful campaigns in Senegal and Mali. And then there were the missionaries who had become politically involved in such areas as the Lagos hinterland, Uganda and Lake Malawi, and who had come to regard the intervention of European governments to protect them and their growing Christian communities as essential to the extension of Christianity.

With all these groups at various times demanding government intervention one might assume that the cause of Africa's invasion has been identified. But governments did not always respond to such pressures. In the first place although the various investors and merchants interested in Africa carried weight in the politics of European countries, they were not as influential as some similar groups interested in trade and investment elsewhere. Europe's trade and investment in Africa was small by comparison with her trade and investment in other continents such as North and South America and Australasia. So long as what those urging government action in Africa asked for did not conflict with what others wanted the government to do – for example reduce taxation or provide protection for trade elsewhere – the comparative weakness of the pressure groups interested in Africa would not matter. But if it did, and the government had to make a choice between conciliating them or others, the fact that they so often represented a minority even among the small class of influential capitalists would tell against them.

The response of European governments to the pressure of the traders and investors was regulated by the state of the relations between the various European powers themselves. Each watched the other before moving. If a European government felt it would weaken itself in relation to others by grabbing African territory, it would hold back. If it felt that it could do so with impunity because others were doing likewise it would be encouraged to go ahead. In the early 1880s European governments were hesitant on this score; as time went on they became less so because they were able to make agreements with each other as to who should have what in Africa.

Obstacles to conquest

There was however one other important factor which all European governments had to take into account and which, unlike the diplomatic factor just mentioned, always stood against the political intervention by European governments in Africa. This of course was the armed force of the peoples and governments of Africa itself. The peoples and governments of Africa were the major obstacle to the European invasion of Africa. The European governments had to take the strength of African opposition into account because although the various groups in Europe, already mentioned, were telling governments to occupy, no government wanted to fight costly and diplomatically compromising wars in order to do so. It was extremely difficult to get European parliaments to provide men and money for wars in Africa. Governments feared to approach parliaments on such matters as they knew that they would be asked embarrassing and unpleasant questions and perhaps fail to secure the necessary money in the end. This was the case during the 1880s whether the country was Britain, France or Germany. The government could count on the support of those who had an interest in securing African territory in any particular instance but they had to contend with the opposition of the mass of members of parliaments who did not want higher taxation. If the occupation of Africa meant costly wars and therefore higher taxes, most members of parliament would have been strongly against any such idea. Apart from a minority who worried about international morality, the peoples of Europe were generally prepared to welcome an extension of their national territory. But they did not want to pay for it. They would certainly have objected strongly if the governments had asked them to pay a very high price.

This was why European governments at least in the early stages of the invasion sought for ways of occupying Africa without asking their parliaments to pay anything. For this reason the British government allowed the Royal Niger Company, the Imperial British East Africa Company, and the British South Africa Company to occupy various parts of the continent. This was why the German government persuaded the German East Africa Company to occupy East Africa and the merchant Adolph Lüderitz to occupy South-West Africa. It had hoped to do the same in the Cameroons and Bismarck was much annoyed when he had to do it himself. King Leopold occupied the Congo through his own organization, quite independent of the Belgian government and parliament. Another method used by governments to occupy Africa without recourse to parliament was to make the few existing colonies pay for expansion out of their own revenues. But this was difficult in the 1880s because most African colonies were short of revenue. Much use was made during the 1880s of naval vessels which could be despatched without consulting parliament, but they could only work on the coasts or in areas adjacent to navigable rivers. The British government employed contingents of Indian soldiers – an old method of avoiding parliamentary scrutiny. King Leopold got the Belgian army to transfer fully paid officers to the Congo. Various other means were used to find resources for small wars in Africa. Perhaps the worst case was the 1897 Benin expedition which was paid for by selling the looted art treasures of Benin to museums in Europe and the United States.

This brings us again to the question 'why was Europe *able* to occupy Africa in the late nineteenth century?' European powers had seized colonies in Africa before the 1880s and had fought wars there but the colonies they held were small and close to the coast. Only in Algeria and what became South Africa had European powers occupied territory any distance inland. In both these cases, the wars resulting from moving inland had involved European governments in considerable expense. At the peak of its campaign to occupy Algeria in 1847, France had 100 000 soldiers in that country, the largest European army to stand on African soil before the end of the nineteenth century. The frontier wars fought by the British in South Africa were costly too. About one-tenth of the British army had to be maintained there even in peacetime. These examples were enough to discourage European powers from attempting to move inland in other parts of Africa during most of the nineteenth century. Interference by European warships on the coast was common enough but European governments feared moving away from the sea. They feared defeat by African armies. In many instances even victory would have been so costly as to be worthless.

Early European military campaigns, 1867–85

European powers received some clear reminders of the dangers of meddling in African politics in the twenty years before the Berlin West Africa Conference of 1884–5. In 1863 the British and French consuls in Ethiopia had both been imprisoned by Emperor Tewodros for disrespectful behaviour. The British government anxiously tried to get their man released, but failed. In 1867, after four years of unsuccessful negotiations the British government decided, after much hesitation, to send an expeditionary force to free the consul. Since it was feared that Tewodros, whose empire was already crumbling, might still be strong enough to defeat any force sent, it was announced, to avoid angering the whole of the Ethiopian people, that there was no intention of occupying the country. The expendition was to go in, release the prisoners, and leave as fast as possible. To do this limited work the commander of the British army in India was told he could spend as much as he pleased to ensure victory. The force sent was the largest the British believed could be transported across the Ethiopian mountains. It succeeded: but at a cost of £9 million – at that time a very large sum. The government was severely criticized for spending so much of the taxpayers' money. After this Britain stopped meddling in Ethiopian affairs for some considerable time.

In 1874 another British expedition was sent to the interior of Africa, again after much hesitation, this time against the Asante of Ghana. The Asante of Ghana had already defeated one British army and killed its commander in 1826. In 1863 they had marched to the coast through

British protected territory while the British watched powerless from their forts. The first episode had led ultimately to the British government's abandonment of the Gold Coast forts; the second brought about a general reappraisal of British West African policy in favour of caution. Fear of the Asante persuaded the British in 1863 not to strike back. In 1874, however, ambitious military men who had reorganized and re-equipped the British army with new weapons persuaded the government that they were strong enough to beat the Asante. Two thousand picked troops were sent and with the help of thousands of Fante allies the Asante were defeated and their capital, Kumasi, taken. The British commander maintained that he had proved at last that British soldiers could fight successfully in West Africa. But again the object was limited. After Kumasi had been taken and burned the British troops hurried back to the sea. The expedition was costly and the commander admitted that were it not for his superior weapons, the Asante would probably have won. The British government remained as impressed as before by the fighting qualities of the Asante and were anxious to avoid another war with them.

In 1878 Britain fought another African power – the Zulu under Cetewayo. The British commander was overconfident. His army had superior weapons but the Zulu impis moved too swiftly. The result was a decisive victory – and what was left of the British army struggled back to Natal after the battle at Isandhlwana. The British sent out reinforcements, raised men from throughout South Africa and the Zulu were finally defeated, but their courage became a legend in Britain and the war was regarded as a mistake. It had cost £4 million and the ministers responsible were violently attacked. These events in South Africa were one of the main reasons for the government's defeat at the subsequent election.

The next major battle between Britain and an African power came in 1882 when a British force of 40 000 men met at Egyptian army of much the same size and strength. The British won after a surprise attack on the main Egyptian fortress at Tel-el-Kebir. The British disembarked on the Suez Canal after a clever surprise manoeuvre and the final battle was fought along the short line of railway between the Canal and Cairo. Two years later a British force was sent to relieve General Gordon who was besieged in Khartoum deep in the Sudan. The force never reached its objective and suffered severely at the hands of the Mahdi's army. This failure so impressed the British that they were prepared to risk leaving the Sudan a threat to Egypt rather than try to defeat these Sudanese forces. A new expedition was not sent until 1896 and then it advanced to victory while taking the most careful precautions.

The French had similar difficult experiences which made them reluctant to engage in military adventures. The French Assembly approved the establishment of a Protectorate in Tunisia in April 1881 but turned round and violently attacked the government in October when it had to gather together 50 000 soldiers to suppress the subsequent rising. The French Chamber also withdrew its support from the project for building a railway from the Senegal to the Niger in 1885, when four years of campaigns showed that military costs had absorbed the greater part of the funds voted for construction. At the time of the Berlin Conference of 1884–5 therefore, the European powers were hesitant about moving inland in force because they still had not found the means of fighting wars in the interior at an acceptable cost. They concerned themselves mainly with claims to the coast and the main navigable rivers.

The deadly new weapons

From the 1860s onward important improvements were made in the manufacture of weapons in Europe. In time these were greatly to facilitate the conquest of Africa, Asia and the Pacific. Hand firearms were produced with rifled barrels making them more accurate than the smooth bore 'dane gun' type. The rate of fire was improved with the introduction of rifles which could be loaded at the breech instead of at the muzzle. Further improvements in this system in the 1870s made it possible to increase once again the accuracy of the shot, its range and killing power. In the 1870s the magazine or repeater rifle was invented. This most effective weapon came into general use in the middle 1880s. In the late 1860s the first machine guns were invented – the French *mitrailleuse* and the American Gatling gun. These fired shots rapidly from revolving barrels but they were heavy, difficult to handle and often broke down. In 1889 a far more effective machine gun was invented by H.S. Maxim. Its performance was not basically different from modern machine guns. It had only one barrel but the recoil from each shot mechanically reloaded the gun so that it could fire an almost continuous stream of bullets. This gun, one of the most deadly weapons man has ever invented, ultimately forced armies to change radically their methods of fighting.

Before the late nineteenth century most European weapons could not be used properly in Africa. Powerful cannon had been used for a long time on the battlefields of Europe but until the second half of the nineteenth century few cannon were seen in the interior of Africa. Poor, narrow roads made it difficult to wheel these guns inland and often there were no horses or mules to pull such heavy weapons. Ships at sea and on the rivers could carry them – many coastal African states were well equipped with cannon. But inland, especially in thick bush, heavy cast-iron or cast-bronze cannon were usually more trouble than they were worth. Even the early models of the Gatling gun were too heavy and cumbersome to use there. But the Maxim machine gun was not. And in the second half of the nineteenth century, better and lighter steel cannon were devised until it ultimately became possible for one of these guns of substantial calibre to be carried by two men. Between 1860 and 1890 one after another of these revolutionary weapons came out of the arms factories of Europe. After 1870 nearly every large expedition that went to Africa from Europe carried with it yet another new and more terrible weapon of war. When the French Assembly was becoming disgusted with the cost of wars in the Western Sudan in 1885, new magazine rifles were on their way to the French forces there which enabled them to win battles even with the restricted funds available.

Most European commanders insisted on having the latest and best weapons the arms factories could give them for expeditions to Africa. In fact some expeditions were used to try out the most modern systems of fighting. The British expedition against the Asante in 1874 was of this sort and the men carried the newest rifle just issued to the British army. They also had the new light cannon and Gatling guns. The deadly Maxim gun was first tried on a large scale against the Ndebele of Zimbabwe in 1893, though one had been used in Uganda in 1891. In 1896 it was still a very new weapon and the inventor Maxim himself helped to prepare the six machine guns for the Royal Niger Company's expedition against Bida in that year.

Most invading armies used these newest guns in as large numbers as possible. The West African Frontier Force, for example, which the British government raised in 1897, was deliberately equipped with an abnormally large number of machine guns and cannon. No army unit in Europe at the time or for the next fifteen years had so large a proportion of machine guns to fighting men. The Royal Niger Company force which marched against Bida in 1896 was little more than an escort for its four small and one large cannon. It marched on Bida as a small square with the large 12-pounder steel gun in the centre. And it was the 12-pounder gun that defeated Bida by bombarding the city while machine guns and rifles kept the Nupe army at a distance. The European commanders had no intention of fighting it out man to man with the African armies if they could avoid it. They deliberately set modern European technology against African men. In fact the European armies that invaded Africa were predominantly African in composition. Almost all the soldiers were African; in the French armies some of the officers were Africans too. But the European-controlled armies, although much smaller than the defending African armies, were incomparably better armed.

As the power of the weapons increased so the cost to Europe of fighting wars in Africa fell. As victories became easier and cheaper for Europe, so European military men in Africa became anxious for further victories and higher promotion for themselves. The power of their weapons also boosted the morale of the invading armies and they became bolder and more daring. Although such boldness sometimes brought disaster it more frequently resulted in victories for the small powerful army over the much larger opposing forces. The boldness of the invading armies and the terrible effects of the new weapons contributed to widespread demoralization among African states. Stories of the awful destructiveness of the white man's cannon and machine guns spread throughout the continent. One might say that some African armies were beaten in spirit before they ever reached the battlefield and resistance to invasion was thereby greatly weakened.

Advances in medical knowledge, which drastically reduced the death rate of Europeans in West Africa, also made conquest less costly than it would have been earlier. In general by 1880 Africans found themselves in a rapidly shrinking world of iron ships, telegraphs and machine guns which enabled European armies to arrive quickly, to keep in touch with their home bases, to call reinforcements from thousands of miles away – as in the case of the South African War in 1899 – and to massacre the traditional massed armies of Africa. It is true that on the ground European armies were by no means always in a position of overwhelming superiority, but the power of their ultimate ability to retaliate was very soon appreciated. Buttressing their military power was a racist ideology which persuaded most Europeans to believe quite genuinely that they were doing great benefit to the world by conquering it.

Divisions in African society

The severe divisions that existed in African society at this time made things much easier for the foreign powers. The nineteenth century had seen a whole series of political, religious and military revolutions in Africa south of the Sahara which had produced sudden and severe changes in the political systems. The campaigns of Usman dan Fodio, Samori Ture and others in the Western Sudan had brought widespread and continuing political change throughout the valley of the Niger and beyond. In the eastern Sudan, the military incursions of Muhammad Ali Pasha and his successors followed by the Mahdist movement and the activity of such men as Zubair and Rabih produced vast changes in that area also. From the southern confines of the continent the effects of the Mfecane and the growth of new military empires spread northward almost reaching the area of jihadist turbulence in the north. Also, from the middle of the nineteenth century, an increasing flood of European firearms poured in from ports all round the continent, usually confirming, but also on occasion undermining what the African revolutions had achieved. The number of new states multiplied at the expense of self-governing independent farming communities.

By the late nineteenth century a number of these 'new states' which had been set up earlier in the century had achieved a measure of internal stability. The emirates in the north of present Nigeria, Ibadan in the west of Nigeria, al Hajj Umar's Tukulor empire, the Hehe and other similar states in East Africa were fairly stable internally. But most of these states were so dynamic socially and politically that they were almost compelled to expand. Most of them were empires which did not recognize any clear limits to their growth since so many were based on a revolutionary challenge to the existing social and political order. Those which followed a policy of jihad were usually able to adjust their relations with each other within each caliphate. The Sokoto caliphate system was on the whole more successful in solving disputes among the constituent emirates than the 'Concert of Europe' was in maintaining peace among the governments of Europe. But the jihadist states did not properly recognize independent non-Muslim communities. Thus although some states were internally strong and stable, the international system as a whole was weak and vulnerable. The new states often created wide areas of conflict around them and were feared and hated by neighbouring communities which believed they would be the next to be attacked.

The European invaders were able to exploit these divisions in African society especially during the diplomatic phase of the invasion which preceded military conquest. The agents of the European governments were very short of money at this time but they had the advantage of having powerful guns to sell. Arms-selling was a profitable business because, as European armies changed to new rifles, they sold their old guns cheaply and in large quantities. Therefore the European explorers and trading companies had a good supply of cheap weapons which African rulers and communities in most parts of the continent were anxious to buy. African rulers who fought from time to time against European colonial powers were often ready to make agreements with their European enemies in order to acquire guns for defence or attack. Indeed governments all over the world were trying to buy modern military equipment from Europe and were prepared to run the risk of falling under European control by asking for loans in order to do so. While the European powers were scrambling for other peoples' territory, African rulers were scrambling for European guns, railways and other items of military value. This was because the new technological discoveries had changed the basis of military power. Modern rifles and cannon produced a revolution just as the discovery of iron, of war chariots and effective cavalry equipment had fundamentally altered the basis of military power in past periods of human history.

The new weapons, by reducing military and other costs and weakening the effectiveness of African resistance, provided European governments with increasingly tempting opportunities. They produced a context in which the invasion of Africa became increasingly possible and likely. But each power still had to consider the reactions of its European neighbours before undertaking schemes of African conquest. Changes in the diplomatic situation in Europe were of crucial importance in determining whether, when and how Africa would be invaded. In this respect, the British occupation of Egypt in 1882 represented an especially important turning point because it produced a set of diplomatic circumstances which favoured, and in the view of some European statesmen, required a forward movement by particular European powers in Africa.

The Egyptian crisis and its consequences

The British occupation of Egypt resulted from the breakdown of the system of informal control that Britain and France had been trying to exercise over Egypt with varying success since the beginning of the nineteenth century. Both powers had important interests in that country. France had created strong commercial, financial and cultural links with Egypt and was concerned also about the distant threat it could possibly pose to French Algeria. Britain was interested in Egypt as one of several routes across the Middle East by which European forces might advance towards Britain's important colony of India and her commercial interests in the Far East. Egypt was part of the Ottoman empire and while France had tried to secure influence there by supporting Egyptian attempts to break free of the Empire, Britain until the 1870s sought to control Egypt as well as the other Middle East routes by supporting the Ottoman sultan's claim to suzerainty. During the 1870s Britain's policy altered. The Ottoman sultan appeared to be too weak to defend the routes to the East effectively, his finances were in a bad state, his government seemed unprogressive, his European provinces were in revolt and his new pan-Islamic policy of claiming the allegiance of all Muslims threatened the British position in Muslim countries, including India. Furthermore, the completion of the Suez Canal in 1869 had made the Egyptian route to India more vital than ever because now a European navy as well as an army could travel to India by that route. British eyes were focused more closely on Egypt and the purchase of the Suez Canal shares in 1875 from the Khedive gave Britain a financial lever to strengthen her influence there. Britain therefore swung towards the policy of supporting the Egyptian Khedive against his Turkish master, and this made possible a deal with France which was pursuing a similar policy, and which had also been upset about the possible disturbing effect of the Sultan's pan-Islamic ideas in Algeria. The two governments agreed to share influence in Egypt.

The Khedive's bankruptcy in 1876 helped the French and British governments to exercise a joint control over the Egyptian government. Their determination to make Egypt pay the interest on its £96 million debt was politically motivated. It enabled them to force on the Khedive two of their nationals as controllers to supervise the Egyptian government's finances. But as Egypt was squeezed dry to satisfy its creditors, political disadvantages began to appear. The economies and severe taxes imposed alienated various sections of the Egyptian people – the overtaxed peasants, the landowners, the sacked army officers and civil servants. Traditionalists and modern nationalists rallied the people against the hated regime and the movement of protest found a leader in Arabi Pasha. The British and French governments were too suspicious of each other to adjust to this situation. They backed the Khedive against the nationalist movement and refused financial concessions. The result was a conflict between the two European governments and the nationalists, and when Arabi Pasha threatened to seize the Suez Canal the British government sent a force which defeated the Egyptian army in September 1882 and occupied Cairo.

The British government hoped that having removed Arabi Pasha from power they would be able to withdraw. But they soon found that the state of nationalist sentiment was such that they could not establish a government which would at the same time co-operate with Britain and be sufficiently popular to maintain itself without the backing of British arms. It appeared that the British troops would have to stay and Britain in effect became responsible for Egyptian affairs. Being placed in this position, the British government felt that it would have to have a free hand in trying to organize the Egyptian government. So it told France, which had refused at the last minute to participate in the occupation, that the Anglo-French dual control in Egypt was at an end. This enraged French opinion and from then on France tried to upset the British position in Egypt and also began aggressively to acquire positions elsewhere in Africa in retaliation whenever opportunities offered. Britain had become responsible for a country which was burdened with debt and with a complicated machinery of international financial control which could not be got rid of. France was still represented on the International Debt Commission which controlled

60 per cent of Egyptian revenue. So was Germany. With France hostile, Britain was dependent on German support and Bismarck was determined to secure the maximum benefit from this situation.

Various people in Germany were pressing Bismarck to allow them to establish colonies in Africa. Adolph Lüderitz wanted to collect guano in South-West Africa. German merchants in West Africa wanted political support for their commercial ventures. Carl Peters hoped to build a great empire in East Africa. Bismarck himself may not have been very interested in seizing colonies, but for various reasons of domestic and international politics it became rather advantageous for him to do so in 1884 and 1885. At the wave of his 'Egyptian stick' – the threat to vote against Britain in Egypt – Britain gave him what he wanted in Africa. The British government told the colonial government at the Cape to give up its claim to keep others out of South-West Africa and to let Lüderitz in. The British consul in Zanzibar was told to use his influence over the sultan to allow Peters to make 'treaties of protection' with African chiefs, who feared any extension of the sultan's power into the interior. The British attempt to prevent the mouth of the Congo (Zaire) from falling under French control by recognizing inactive Portuguese rule over that area was stopped largely owing to Bismarck's intervention, and the way was open for Leopold to embark on his Congo schemes. The large inroads made into areas where Britain had hitherto exercised informal control made it clear that the old system of informal control was no longer effective and Britain herself entered the race to claim the coastline. These changes in the diplomatic situation made it expedient for governments to pay more heed to the urgings of interested merchants and investors who had been asking them to seize African territory.

In addition to this, the financial weakness of Egypt and the rising of the Mahdi in the Sudan in 1884 led Britain to force the Egyptian government to cut its losses by abandoning control of the whole African coastline from the confines of Egypt to the borders of present-day Kenya. This evacuation of Khedive Ismail's African empire in order to avoid financial and diplomatic complications exposed another large part of the African coastline to European encroachment. The Italians moved into Eritrea and the French and British (and later, the Italians) established themselves in Somalia. The British occupation of Egypt had even wider-spreading repercussions because within seven years it became clear that the White Nile was vital to Egypt's irrigation. The headwaters of that river became the object of a race primarily between Britain and France but in which Leopold and Peters also participated. The prize was the control of a vital area which could closely affect the still unstable British position in Egypt. Investors and merchants did not need to encourage the British government to take an interest in or occupy the area of present-day Kenya and Uganda; it decided that for strategic reasons the route to the Upper Nile had to be secured.

On the eve of the conquest

By 1885 the inland rush had still not begun and for five years the Europeans advanced gradually from their positions on the coasts and navigable rivers, selling their guns, gathering information and making treaties. Sometimes they allied with the powerful new African states and sold guns to them; sometimes they sold guns to the older and smaller communities which the new states were trying to absorb or destroy; sometimes they allied with one new state against another. The French in Senegal for example, allied at different times with almost all the different states and groups – with the Tukulor empire, with their Bambara enemies, with Samori Ture and with his enemies at Sikasso. The British at Lagos sought good relations with all the contending parties in Yorubaland at different times. The Royal Niger Company supplied arms both to the emirates of northern Nigeria and to those who fought them. King Leopold's agents in the Congo sometimes allied with Arab state builders like Tippu Tip and sometimes they supplied arms to their opponents. The Imperial British East Africa Company and Lugard allied with Buganda against Bunyoro, with Christian Ganda chiefs against Muslim Ganda chiefs, and with the Protestant Ganda faction against the Catholic faction in Buganda. And thus during this diplomatic phase of the invasion the European agents twisted and turned in several parts of Africa allying now with this, now with that African power, but always strengthening their own position and proving to their governments that the occupation of Africa was perhaps not so difficult as it had seemed.

There was, however, a limit to what diplomacy could achieve and by the end of the 1880s that limit was being reached in several parts of the continent. African rulers were becoming increasingly suspicious of European intentions. Some began to launch serious attacks on European establishments and expeditions. There was a violent flare-up of opposition in the coastal areas of East Africa, 'the Abushiri rising', in 1888 and news of this spread quickly along the trade routes of Middle Africa. On the other hand diplomatic successes were making the European agents bolder. They became impatient, wanting to rule and control rather than ally with the African states.

At about this time Europeans began to speak of their 'civilizing mission' – an idea which suggested that Europe had not only a right but a duty to conquer Africa. The troubles and many wars being waged in Africa in the late nineteenth century were taken in Europe as evidence that Africa was unable to rule itself. Also, the reports from European agents in various parts of Africa of how they were winning battles with their modern weapons helped the idea to develop that Europe could easily conquer Africa and impose its rule. The fear created by the military skill and courage of such people as the Asante was now forgotten as confidence in the overwhelming superiority of modern European arms grew, or rather confidence simply in European superiority over Africans. People in Europe easily confused the superiority of the weapons with the superiority of the men who handled them. Since the middle of the nineteenth century European writers, when speaking of 'race', gave the impression that man was imprisoned by the customs of his society, that the ideas of each 'racial' society were fixed in time and that there could be no flow of ideas between societies of different race. They also maintained that the 'races' of the world could be arranged in order of superiority, and of course they put themselves at the top. As these ideas spread Europeans became increasingly arrogant in their dealings with other peoples. When these ideas were first put forward Britain was involved in quarrels with Abeokuta, with the King of Asante and with Tewodros of Ethiopia and, consequently, British people were inclined to believe that the fewer dealings they had with Africa the better. Moreover, the racialist writers suggested that because of racial differences peaceful co-operation between Europe and Africa was impossible. But in the late nineteenth century, when Europe had the weapons to win wars in Africa, the idea of racial superiority spread fast and was given a new meaning. The supposed 'scientific' proof of European racial superiority was used to suggest that Europeans had some sort of natural right to conquer and rule Africans. The idea of racial difference which had earlier been used as an argument for leaving Africa to itself was now used as an argument for excluding Africans from the government of their own countries.

The European governments were pleased at the change in public opinion towards invading Africa because they too were favouring occupation of the interior. African resistance to European encroachment was growing and was threatening even the first European settlements on the coasts and rivers. The 'Abushiri rising' of 1888–9 had made things difficult for the Germans and the British. The Arabized states in the Congo had begun to oppose King Leopold's agents. Samori Ture blocked the path of the French on the Upper Niger and various African rulers were opposing British agents around Lake Malawi. Most of the African powers concerned were 'new states' which possessed some fairly modern weapons purchased from British, German, Belgian, Portuguese or French sources.

The European invaders began to realize that by competing with one another they were enabling Africans to buy modern guns with which they could keep out all European forces. For example, in East Africa, those involved in the 'Abushiri rising' bought guns from the British to repel the Germans and guns from the Germans to push back the British.

The anti-slave trade campaign provided the governments with a means of halting this situation in a comprehensive fashion. In 1889–90 the European powers held a conference at Brussels on the slave trade and agreed on an arms blockade of Africa, particularly of modern arms. The import of the old dane guns, which were ineffective against well-armed European forces, was permitted. Modern weapons were restricted to European colonial powers who were only permitted to allow guns to pass through their territories if they were required by another colonial power. The blockade, although never fully effective, was gradually extended from East Africa to other parts of the continent and it spelt the doom of large-scale African resistance. Two major African countries, however, avoided its effect. In particular, Ethiopia, through the skilful diplomacy of Emperor Menelik, was still able to buy modern arms since his country was excluded from the effect of the Brussels agreement. Huge quantities of the latest rifles were purchased by the Emperor from French and Italian traders and with them the Ethiopian army was able to defeat a large Italian army at Adowa in 1896. Morocco was also unaffected since the sultan continued to exploit European rivalries until the European powers combined against him at the Algeciras Conference of 1906. Morocco was by then well-armed and when the French began to occupy the country in 1908 they had to send one of the largest armies ever sent to Africa in order to occupy just one section of the country. At that stage Germany was still opposed to the French invasion and modern arms from Germany enabled to Moroccans to put up a powerful resistance. But Germany was bought off by France in 1911 by a gift of land in the Cameroons and in 1912 a French Protectorate over Morocco was proclaimed. The Moroccans were still heavily armed and France was far from occupying the whole country when the First World War broke out in 1914. Elsewhere in Africa the European arms blockade was more effective and Africans were thus deprived of the means of successful resistance.

As the European governments prepared to attack the new states in Africa they found they needed more money for their campaigns. The small groups with direct interests – merchants, investors and so on – pressed the governments to act but the public, the taxpayers, had to be persuaded to provide the money. The anti-slave trade campaign, widely publicized among sections of the public who had hardly even heard of Africa before, offered a means of doing this. People were told that the comparatively small sums needed to invade Africa were to be used to put down the slave trade and alleviate human misery. This helped to convince the German parliament to provide money in 1890 to take over modern Tanzania from the German East Africa Company and raise forces for conquest there. This was largely how the British parliament was persuaded to provide money for, building the Uganda Railway and for the occupation of Kenya and Uganda after 1893. King Leopold used the same argument to persuade the governments of Europe to allow the Congo Free State government to collect large taxes on European trade in the Congo with which he could finance his military campaigns.

The conquest of the powerful African states

By about 1890 the colonial powers were united in their determination to conquer a then divided Africa. They agreed which parts of the continent each should have and promised to help each other against African resisters. The African states mostly stood alone, except for some attempts at co-operation between Muslim rulers in the Western Sudan and in East Africa. One after another the powerful African states were defeated in battle or forced into submission. In 1890 after a brief campaign, Segu, the principal city in the Tukulor empire, fell to the French. Between 1891 and 1898 Samori Ture was driven back, skilfully fighting rearguard actions and seeking to maintain his supply of the precious modern arms and ammunition from European traders on the coast. In 1896 the European arms blockade became fully effective against him and two years later Samori was forced to surrender. The Mossi empire of Ouagadougou was overthrown by the French in 1896 and a powerful British force occupied Asante in the same year. Btween 1892 and 1894 the kingdom of Dahomey was occupied after strong resistance. In 1892 the power of the Ijebu kingdom was broken by the British. After the terrible effects of its new weapons had been shown, the British colonial government at Lagos was able to penetrate the whole of Yorubaland. In 1896 the Royal Niger Company defeated the Nupe army and entered the city of Ilorin. In 1897 the kingdom of Benin fell. Between 1901 and 1903 a series of major battles around Kontagora, Yola, Kano and Sokoto left the great emirates of northern Nigeria under the control of the British. With the increased firepower of the new weapons this Nigerian campaign cost the British about one-tenth of what they had spent on the war against the Zulu people twenty-five years earlier when they had no Maxim machine guns.

The assault in the east and south

While the states of the Western Sudan were thus collapsing, the British after careful preparation, sent a large Anglo-Egyptian force into the Sudan and broke the Khalifa's power at the battle of Omdurman in 1898. Two years later, Rabih ibn Fadlallah, who had recently established his power in Borno using rifles imported across the Sahara, was killed by the French. The new Arab states in the eastern Congo basin were destroyed between 1892 and 1895. From 1891 the British manoeuvred themselves into a dominant position in the inter-lacustrine kingdoms and imposed their sovereignty over their main ally, Buganda, in 1900. On the East African coast the leaders who had risen with Abushiri were defeated during 1889 and 1890. In 1893 Isike the Nyamwezi leader and Meli the Chagga leader were beaten by the Germans. Mkwakwa, the Hehe ruler, was hunted down in 1898 after bitter fighting. Further south the Ndebele suffered a heavy and bloody defeat in 1893 and in 1898 the Ngoni west of Lake Malawi were broken. In 1895 Gungunhana, the powerful leader in central Mozambique, whose predecessors had kept the Portuguese garrisons in the coastal ports in a state of terror, was overthrown by a small Portuguese forced armed with magazine rifles and modern cannon.

Europe seizes the commanding heights in Africa

It was the 1890s then that finally saw the rapid destruction of almost all the most powerful states in Africa. But the small European forces were not immediately capable of effectively occupying all parts of Africa and they were slow to enter the more remote areas and the territory of small self-governing communities whose complex social and political organizations often baffled them. Once paralyzing blows had been struck to the major African states colonial officials went out with small escorts over a large part of the continent ordering chiefs great and small to arrest opponents of the new regime, to provide labour, collect taxes, change laws, or abolish tolls; to permit European mining or settlement, to admit missionaries, grow certain crops, give land for railways, or protect telegraph lines. In short, to become agents of colonialism. The conquest was over. The business of actually imposing their authority throughout Africa would take the new colonial rulers much longer.

Index

271; and Carnarvon's confederation policy, 275; 1st Anglo–Boer War, 279–80, *280;* Afrikaner Bond, 287, 291; Swaziland, 292–3; 2nd Anglo–Boer War, 300–5

Bonny, 55, 56, 116

Boomplaats, battle of (1848), 260

Borgu, 98, 121, 126

Borno (Bornu), 17, 65, 72–3, 77, 86, 87, 89, 92, 121, 128, 363

Botswana (formerly Bechuanaland), 15, 282, 283, 285, 298; *see also* Tswana

Brand, Jan Hendrik, 269, *270,* 275

Brazil, Brazilians, 29, 30, 51, 55, 103, 115, 318

Britain, British, 38, 43, 184, 349; in West Africa, 46, 62, 63–9, 70, 72–3, 93, 100, 102, 104–5, 115–17, 118–28, 345, 350–1, 359, 362; Industrial Revolution, 48, 62, 308, 317, 342; and abolition of slavery, 49–59, 62–3, 103, 108; founding of Sierra Leone, 56–9; and the Sudan, 63, 65–6, 67, 68–9, 125, 126, 157, 351, 363; missionaries, 73–7; Asante wars, 106, 108–13, *114,* 350–1, 353; and Egypt, 133–4, 141–2, 145–7, 148–9, 157, 162–3, 183, 341, 351, 356–8; and Ethiopia, 161, 167, *168,* 174–5, 350; Fashoda Incident, 163–4; and Libya, 182, 183, 204, 207; and Morocco, 194, 195, 196; and Tunisia, 198, 199, 201; in South Africa, 228, 240–5, 249–50, 252–80, 282–7, 295–9, 347, 350, 351; and Boer Wars, 279, *280,* 300–5, 354; and consolidation in Southern Africa, 287–305 *passim;* in Middle Africa, 327, 332, 333–3, 335–6, 337–8, 363; in Kenya and Uganda, 336, 337–8, 353, 358–9, 362

British Kaffraria, 259, 261, 265, 267

British South Africa Company, 146, 288, 291–2, 294, 297, 298, 299, 347, 349

Brussels Conference (1890), 336, 361

Buganda, 21, 311, 312, 313, 324, 326, 329, 330–1, 337–8, 359, 363; Kabaka of, 312, 322, 330, *330,* 338

Bugeaud, General, 188, 189, 191

Bunyoro, 21, 311–13, 330, 331, 337, 359

Burundi, 21, 306, 311, 312, 313–14

Bushmen *see* San

Busoga, 21, 337

Buxton, Thomas Fowell, 69

Caillié, René, 70

Cairo, 63, 66, 89, 130, 149, 357

Calabar, 55, 74, 128

Cameroon(s), 3, 4, 55, 117, 121, 125, 126, 346, 349, 361

Cape Colony, 30, 221–8, 229, 239–44, 253, 256, 261, 267, 274, 276, 283, 287, 295, 296, 298, 301; white settlement, *221,* 221–4; Khoisan resistance, 224–6; Commando system, 225; Cape Coloured and Griqua peoples, 226–7; Xhosa resistance wars, 228; frontier society 239–44; British administration, 240–5, 252–3, 255, 275; Great Trek from, 244, 245–50; and Natal, 252–5; Parliament, 264–5, 267, 274, 279; administration of Sotho by, 277; 'War of the Guns' (1880), 277; and 2nd Anglo–Boer War, 302

Carnarvon, Lord, 274–5, 276

Cathcart, Governor, 262

Cetewayo, King of the Zulus, *278,* 278–9, 351

Chad, 95

Chagga, 337, 363

Chamberlain, Joseph, 114, 297, 299–300

Chewa, 21

Chokwe, 317, 331–2, 337

Christianity, Christians, 6, 8, 9 10, 11, 12, 15, 19, 21, 28, 31, 37, 204, 308, 309, 359; Coptic Christians, 27, 129, 139; in West Africa, 33–4, 38, 43, 44, 56, 73–7, 78–9; and abolition of slave trade, 49, 50, 59–60, 69; in Egypt, 27, 129, 132, 133, 139; in Sudan, 150–1; in Ethiopia, 150, 161, 164, 165; in South Africa, 224; *see also* missionaries

Church Missionary Society (CMS), 73, 74, 75, 76, 77, 105

Clapperton, Hugh, 66, 67, 72–3

Clarkson, Thomas, 49

Congo (formerly French), 19, 162, 291, 306, 308–9, 333–4, 337, 349, 358, 359, 363

Congo Free State, 327, 329, 334, 337, 339, 362

cotton production/trade, 48, 70, 116, 137–8, 153, 330, 346

Courts of Mixed Commission, 51, 53, 58

Cromer, Lord, 144, 148, 157

Crowther, Bishop Samuel Ajayi, 128

Cyrenaica, 204, 206, 207, 208, 209

Dahomey, 18, 41, 42, 47, 54, 74, 75, 98, 108, 128, 362; invasions of Yorubaland by, 102–5; French conquest of, 118, 121, 127; *see also* Benin

Danish, 38, *47,* 115, 116, 117, 182

Darfur, 17, 153, 155, 157, 161

De Beers Consolidated, 284, *284,* 285

128; in South Africa, 240–1, 242–4, 257, 271, 282, 288
Mkwawa, Hehe chief, 337, 363
Moffat, Robert, 227, 238, 288
Moletsane, 257
Mollien, G., 70
Molteno, Sir John, 274, 275, 276, 277
Morocco, 1, 11, 12–13, 176–80, 182, 190, 193–7, 205, 206, 341; the monarchy and *baraka*, 176–8; Berbers, 178–80; European pressure on, 193–5; Hassan III, 196–7; Abdel Aziz, 197; partitioning of, 341, 361
Moroka, Rolong chief, 246, 257
Moshoeshoe, King of the Sotho, 238, 246, 252, 256, 257, 258, 260–1, 262, 263–4, 266–7, 268, 269–70, 271–2, 272
Mossi, 127, 362
Mozambique, 19, 21, 29, 32, 215, 216, 218, 235, 236, 325; Portuguese in, 218–20, 235, 281, 291, 293–4, 310, 333, 363
Mpande (Zulu king), 250, 253, 254, 282
Mpondo, 283
Msiri, Nyamwezi leader, 326, 327, 328, 337, 339
Mthethwa, 230, 231, 233
Muhammad the Prophet, 24, 81, 157, 158, 177, 192
Muhammad Ahmad, the Mahdi, *156*, 156–61, 205, 207, 208
Muhammad Ali Pasha, *wali* of Egypt, 134–43, 144, 145, 185, 186, 194, 206, 354; destruction of Mamluks, 135–6; military reforms, 136; economic reforms, 137–9; foreign policy, 140–2; conquest of Sudan by, 140, 152–3, 154
Muhammad al-Kanemi, Shaikh of Borno, 65, 72–3, 87, 89, 128
Muhammad Bello, Sultan of Sokoto, 65, 72–3, 89, 93, 128
Muhammad es Sadek, Bey of Tunis, 197, 198–201, 203
Munyigumba, 325–6, 327
Mustapha Khazinda, 200
Mutesa, Kabaka of Buganda, 330, *330*
Mwata Yamvo, King of Lunda, 19, 21, 219, 310
Mwene Mutapa, 23, 29, 218, 220, 235
Mzilikazi, 238–9, 246–7, 257, 287–8

Namibia (South-West Africa), 15, *212*, 214, 215, 227, 244; Germans in, 281, 282, 283, 349, 358
Nandi, 315, 329, 337
Napier, Sir Robert, expedition to Ethiopia

(1867), 167, *168*, 172, 350
Napoleon I Bonaparte, 182; conquest of Egypt by, 131–4, 182
Natal, 229, 233, 234, 239, 259, 265, 267, 271–2, 274, 275, 278, 279, 283, 295, 296, 301; Boer Great Trek, 244–50; British annexation of, 252–5; and 2nd Anglo–Boer War, 302
Navarino, battle of (1827), 140
Ndebele, 239, 246, *249*, 274, 287–8, *289*, *290*, 293, 294–5, 298, 353, 363; *Chimurenga* uprising, 299
Ndwandwe, 230, 231, 233, 235
Nelson, Admiral Lord, 133–4
Ngoni, 235–7, 238, 324–6, 329, 363
Nguni, 215, 216, 224, 228, 229, 252, 257
Ngwane, 237, 238, 239
Niger, (formerly French), 127
Nigeria, 3, 16, 17–18, 38, 42, 49, 77, 78, 79, 355; Islam in, 28, 91, 93; trade and slave trade, 40, 43, 54, 55; British in, 93, 115, 120–1, 125, 127, 128, 359, 362; Northern, 121, 126, 127
Nilotes, 14, 21, 215
Nkhumbi, 332
Nkore, 21, 311, 312, 313, 337
Nubians, 7, 8, 15
Nupe, 18, 65, 87, 120, 362
Nyamwezi, 235, 310, 317, 319, 323–4, 326–7, 328, 337, 363

Oil Rivers, 47, 62, 67, 69, 72; Protectorate proclaimed (1885), 121
Omdurman, 161, 162; battle of (1898), 164, 363
Orange Free State, 214, 237, 238, 245, 253, 255, 259–60, 266, 267, 268, 273, 274, 275, 276, 277, 285, 295; Boer independence in, 263–4; Sotho wars, 266–7, 269–70, 271; 2nd Anglo–Boer War, 302, 304–5
Orange River Sovereignty, 260–3, 266
Orlam communities, 226–7
Oromo (Galla), 10, 165, 169, 170
Osei Bonsu, Asantehene, 106
Osei Kwame, Asantehene, 106
Oshogbo, battle of (1840), 100
Ottoman Empire (Turkey), 6, 12, 13, 26, 65; Egypt under, 130–1, 132, 133, 134, 135, 140–2, 145, 341, 356–7; and the Sudan, 152–7; and Ethiopia, 169, 174; Maghreb, 176, 180–2, 185, 196, 198, 200–1, 204, 341; Libya under, 204–5, 207, 208–10
Ovambo, 332
Ovimbundu, 317, 331, 332, 333, 337

369